IMPERIALISM
AND POPULAR
CULTURE

IMPERIALISM AND POPULAR CULTURE

edited by
JOHN M. MACKENZIE

MANCHESTER UNIVERSITY PRESS

Copyright © Manchester University Press 1986

While copyright in this volume is vested in Manchester University Press, copyright in the individual chapters belongs to their respective authors and no chapter may be reproduced whole or in part without the express permission in writing of both author and publisher.

Published by Manchester University Press
Oxford Road, Manchester M13 9PL, UK
and 51 Washington Street, Dover
New Hampshire 03820, USA

British Library cataloguing in publication data

Imperialism and popular culture.
    1. Imperialism—Public opinion   2. Public
opinion—Great Britain   3. Great Britain—
Intellectual life—19th century   4. Great
Britain—Intellectual life—20th century
    I. MacKenzie, John M.
    325′.32   JN276

Library of Congress cataloging in publication data

Imperialism and popular culture.
        Includes index.
        1. Great Britain—Popular culture—History—19th
century—Addresses, essays, lectures.   2. Great
Britain—Popular culture—History—20th century—
Addresses, essays, lectures.   3. Great Britain—
Territorial expansion—Addresses, essays, lectures.
4. Great Britain—Colonies—History——Addresses, essays,
lectures.   I. MacKenzie, John M.
    DA533.I46   1985   941.082   85–13657

ISBN 0 7190 1770 4 *cased*

Photoset by Wilmaset, Birkenhead, Wirral
Printed in Great Britain
by Bell and Bain Ltd., Glasgow

CONTENTS

LIST OF ILLUSTRATIONS

LIST OF CONTRIBUTORS

John MacKenzie is Senior Lecturer in History at the University of Lancaster and author of *Propaganda and Empire*.

Penny Summerfield is Lecturer in the Social History of Education at the University of Lancaster and author of *Women Workers in the Second World War*.

John Springhall is a Lecturer in History in the Faculty of Humanities of the University of Ulster at Coleraine and is the author of *Youth, Empire, and Society* and editor of *Sure and Stedfast: a History of the Boys' Brigade*.

Jacqueline Bratton is Reader in Theatre and Cultural Studies, Royal Holloway and Bedford New College, University of London, whose publications include *The Victorian Popular Ballad* and *The Impact of Victorian Children's Fiction*.

Ben Shephard read History at Oxford and has worked in British television since 1970, mainly on historical documentaries such as *The World at War* and several films on African themes for the BBC. He currently works for Channel 4.

J. A. Mangan, Head of the Department of Education in Jordanhill College of Education, Glasgow, is the author of *Athleticism in the Victorian and Edwardian Public School*, and *The Games Ethic and Imperialism*, co-founder of the British Society for Sports History, and senior editor of the *British Journal of Sports History*.

Jeffrey Richards is Senior Lecturer in History at the University of Lancaster, whose publications include *Visions of Yesterday* and *The Age of the Dream Palace*.

Stephen Constantine is Lecturer in History at the University of Lancaster and author of *Unemployment in Britain between the Wars* and *The Making of British Colonial Development Policy*.

Allen Warren is Provost of Vanbrugh College in the University of York; he is working on a study of Anglo-Irish relations and on the history of Scouting and Guiding.

CHAPTER 1

INTRODUCTION

John M. MacKenzie

Restraint and understatement have long been prized as characteristics of the British (or, more accurately, English) stereotype. Perhaps this explains why British historians have seldom felt comfortable with historical theories based on popular excitements. While few have denied the existence of popular imperialism in the late nineteenth century, strenuous efforts have been made to discount its significance. Its time scale has been compressed almost out of existence. David Fieldhouse suggested that it could be dated only from 1894,[1] while several scholars have seen the famous al fresco rejoicings of 'mafficking' as its concluding climax. Stephen Koss argued that the divisions of the Boer War destroyed the imperial urges of Methodism.[2] For Bernard Porter, the excitements of the last years of the nineteenth century were stilled by Edwardian apprehension, an age of stocktaking and anxiety.[3] Others have attempted to limit its class appeal. Richard Price, in his efforts to accuse and acquit specific social classes, absolved the working class and pinned the popular outbursts of the imperial war on the lower middle class.[4] And most historians have agreed that any residual popular imperialism was killed by the First World War.

It seems to be the fate of contemporary explanations of historical events that they undergo swift revision by succeeding generations. Contemporaries noted the popular excitements generated by (or generating?) imperial expansion, but J. A. Hobson destroyed any respectability a theory of imperialism rooted in them might have had by linking them with his press and Rand magnates' conspiracy in his pungent book, *The Psychology of Jingoism* of 1901.[5] Less than twenty years later, Joseph Schumpeter, eager to portray imperialism as a late nineteenth-century aberration which capitalism was better without, described its effect on the British masses as being that of a 'toy', 'a political arabesque',[6] which was acceptable so long as no politician tried it in earnest. Such a view was convenient to historians of both left and right in succeeding decades. Henry Pelling argued that imperial concerns, with only one or two mild exceptions, seldom played any part in British elections.[7] A. J. P. Taylor created a school of 'Little Englander' historians which saw imperialism as essentially an irrelevance to domestic British history, a view which continues to be reflected in the writings of many historians today. Max Beloff noted that 'the British were not an imperially minded people; they lacked both a theory of empire and the will to engender and implement one'.[8] The proponents of these views were men whose intellectually formative years coincided with the thirties and the Second World War. They were either concerned to demonstrate that the British working class were interested in more hard-headed domestic affairs or to distinguish the British from the aggressive and imperially minded Germans. Others, again from both left and right, noted the influence of imperialism on British patriotism in order to decry it. Both George Orwell and Esmé Wingfield-Stratford argued at the outbreak of the Second World War that a new and necessary British patriotism could only be constructed when it was divorced from the imperialism of the previous fifty years.[9] While British nationalism was imperial in the late nineteenth century, a nationalist historiography in the twentieth century sought to divest itself from the taint of imperialism. Meanwhile, the historians who have written about imperialism have been principally concerned with its political, strategic and economic dimensions, with the official mind rather than the popular psychology. Thus the centrifugal effects of imperialism have come in for much more attention than the centripetal, and a vacuum has been left in consideration of its role in British social history.

Yet there have been contrary eddies in this prevailing historiographical wind. In an important article Freda Harcourt has relocated the beginnings of Disraeli's imperialism to the Abyssinian campaign of 1867, and has linked his espousal of foreign adventurism directly to his perceptions of the dangers of social disorder and the problems presented by the Second Reform Bill.[10] Thus Disraeli's 'Leap in the Dark' was performed at least with the safety net of foreign diversion. In adopting this tactic, he must have been well aware of the public interest and excitement that had already been created by the Crimean War and the Indian Mutiny, and must have recognised that it could be a double-edged weapon. But it was a risk worth taking in the light of the Christian militarism, the hero-worshipping cults, and public school athleticism and militarism which had grown out of those mid-century events. It is certainly from 1867 that the historian can identify outbursts of public interest in foreign and imperial matters.

Bouts of popular excitement and agitation accompanied a succession of events from the early seventies, the disappearance and death of David Livingstone; the Ashanti campaign of 1874; the purchase of the Suez Canal shares; the Russo-Turkish war of 1878,[11] with its famous jingoistic outburst; the Afghanistan and Zulu disasters of 1879; the Egyptian and Sudanese crises of 1882, 1884–5, and 1896–8; the Emin Pasha relief expedition of 1887–9;[12] the Portuguese treaty of 1890; the anxieties surrounding the possible imperial retreat of Gladstone's fourth ministry in 1892; the Jameson Raid; and the Boer War, among others.

It would be a mistake, however, to concentrate too much on these imperial climacterics, popular reactions to specific events, dramatic displays of chauvinistic emotion. These were merely the surface ripples, occasionally whipped up into storms, of a much deeper intellectual and social current which had been set up by the second half of the nineteenth century. Eric Hobsbawn has identified a Europe-wide retreat from classical liberalism in the last decades of the century.[13] In the emergence of the new nationalisms 'state, nation, and society converged', and the elite which promoted this convergence created new rituals, a whole range of invented traditions and cults through which it could be communicated to the public. Architecture, statuary, public ceremonies, parades, displays and all manner of publications were bent to these ends.

If the wedding of European nationalism to the New Imperialism was a response to what seemed to them to be the outrageous and unmerited scale of British power, so in Britain the nationalist convergence took a distinctively imperial form in the defence of real and imagined colonial interests. The attacks on *laissez-faire* by such dominant figures as Carlyle, Dickens, Kingsley and Ruskin fed into the nationalist historical and philosophical teachings of the universities in the later nineteenth century. The national and imperial history of Froude and Seeley had its counterpart in the neo-Hegelian philosophy of Green and Bradley. Significantly, this was a period of considerable intellectual exchange between Germany and Britain.

The new traditions of Christian militarism,[14] militarist athleticism in the public schools,[15] and a recreated and perverted 'medieval' chivalry[16] contributed readily to the national rituals and political progresses which were part of the British imperial cult. The Queen was swiftly transformed from petulant widow to imperial matriarch. Through the Cardwell reforms and the success of the Volunteer Movement,[17] the army lost its old unpopularity and became a central element in national life. Cults of heroes from both the distant and more recent past were assiduously promoted through children's literature, a powerful iconography, and the new education. By the 1890s, the 'external' form of Social Darwinism postulated by Benjamin Kidd and Karl Pearson was providing an ideological justification for colonial war and conquest which swiftly found its way into popular literature and school textbooks. Theatrical historians have pointed to the remarkable topicality of the nineteenth-century stage and the excitements of the music hall,[18] while the historians of the working-men's clubs have noted the manner in which the clubs transformed themselves into arenas of patriotic entertainment by the end of the century.[19] By that time intellectual and popular tastes had converged to an extent seldom encountered before or since. Thus nationalist composers like Elgar and writers and poets like Kipling and Newbolt could achieve that rare combination of critical acclaim and a popular following. In many respects this remarkable cultural combination had its most profound expression in the youth movements commencing in the foundation of the Boy's Brigade in 1883 and culminating in Baden-Powell's Boy Scouts in 1908.[20] It was expressed too in the nationalist and militarist movements of Edwardian times, which are often characterised as right wing, but which in fact drew support from across the political spectrum.[21]

This capacity of an imperial nationalism to create some semblance of unity across class and party lines becomes more easily comprehensible when set in its wider cultural context. Disraeli had placed imperialism in a prominent place on the agenda of British politics, a place it retained under the influence of Lord Randolph Churchill and Joseph Chamberlain, and for the same reason, the maintenance of the working-class Tory vote. That Gladstone's fourth ministry in 1892 did not inaugurate the expected retreat from territories like Egypt and Uganda was a measure of their success. If the Liberal Unionists had confirmed their apostasy by going over to the Conservatives, they left behind them Liberal Imperialists whose views on many imperial questions were eventually to be close to those of their nominal Tory opponents. The aged Gladstone sold the pass on imperial retreat by sending Rosebery, who was later to write of the need to associate Liberalism with the 'new sentiment of Empire which occupies the nation', to the Foreign Office. Uganda and Egypt were indeed retained, and Grey made his celebrated 'declaration' on a future forward policy in the Sudan. By 1906 the Liberal imperialists held the most important offices in the Cabinet after the prime ministership itself. Imperialism had, in fact, broken the mould of nineteenth-century politics. It repeatedly became the rallying ground for the proponents of a third and national party, from the Unionist splits of 1886, through Rosebery's espousal of National Efficiency to such inter-party alliances as the Coefficients and the Social Imperialists.[22] Fabians, some national socialists, Liberals and Unionists could all find common cause here.[23]

Colin Matthew has argued that the Liberal Imperialists took up imperial issues because 'such affairs were prominent, not because they were inherently interesting'.[24] Rosebery's imperial rhetoric was designed for electoral consumption rather than practical politics. At the very least this concedes the imperial pressures on politicians in the period and admits the electoral dangers which were perceived as lurking in 'unpatriotic' anti-imperial policies. But any attempt to absolve Liberal Imperialists of their imperialism, or at least suggest their ineffectiveness in this area, misses the profound significance of imperial ideology in their thinking. Even if they disagreed about extensions of Empire, they were fundamentally concerned with policies appropriate to the possession and retention of existing Empire. Like most of their contemporaries, they were, perhaps, imperial rather than imperialist. Nonetheless, the idea that the politician ignored imperialism only at his peril seemed to be confirmed by the two notably imperialist elections of 1895 and 1900. In the former, an Indian, Sir M. M. Bhownagree, was able to defeat a working-class sitting member in Bethnal Green North-East by espousing fashionable Unionist and imperialist views.[25] Fine distinctions in imperialism were lost on Cecil Rhodes too. He remarked in his usual direct manner in 1899: 'They are tumbling over each other, Liberals and Conservatives, to show which side are the greatest and most enthusiastic Imperialists'.[26]

Rhodes was speaking, of course, at the outbreak of the Boer War which seemed to constitute the final bout of popular imperial fervour. The war over, although the last acts of the partition of North Africa were yet to come, from the British point of view the spoils had already been divided. It is perhaps not surprising that the British should have moved on to an apprehensively defensive imperialism in this period. But that surely need not suggest that popular imperialism had come to an end. It is likely that the manifold imperial influences of the late nineteenth century had penetrated all the more successfully to the educational, entertainment and propaganda media of the age. Even those who had been pro-Boers were capable of conventional imperial rhetoric by 1914, and Labour had embarked on its equivocal approach to Empire. Empire had not only become bound up with social reform, but had developed some of the vision of economic idealism which was to come front of propaganda stage after the First World War. Schumpeter's definition of imperialism as 'the objectless disposition on the part of the state to unlimited forcible expansion' is surely too narrow.[27] Any definition must also embrace the control and exploitation of existing Empire and the communication of the justifications for that to the populace of the imperial state.

There is a good deal of evidence from working-class autobiographies, other memoirs and oral evidence on the power of imperialism not only in the late nineteenth century but also in Edwardian times. Indeed the most significant working-class testimony comes from the latter period. Anyone who expressed 'unpatriotic' socialist tendencies in Alfred Williams's railway factory was mocked.[28] Fred Willis recounted the imperial and racial content of geography lessons in his late-Victorian schooling.[29] Robert Roberts, more powerfully than any other, described the pervasive nature of imperial and patriotic ideas, and the pageantry, publications, advertising and ephemera through which they were expressed, in his Edwardian Salford slum.[30] H. M. Hyndman, founder of the Social Democratic Federation, noted the extraordinarily jingoistic behaviour of the lower end of the London poor in his *Reminiscences*.[31] Stephen Humphries, in his valuable collection of oral evidence from the more rebellious elements of the working class, has reported on the power of imperialism among them:

> However, interviews reveal that working-class children were generally much more responsive to lessons and activities that were inspired by imperialism . . . Many children clearly welcomed games lessons, colourful stories of heroism and national glory and imperial celebrations as a relief from the monotony of school routine. Most important, however, the ideology of imperialism made a direct appeal to working-class youth because it reflected and reinforced a number of its cultural traditions, in particular the street gangs' concerned with territorial rivalry, and the assertion of masculinity.[32]

There are some echoes of Hobson's Psychology of Jingoism in this.

Further up the social scale, any amount of evidence can be adduced. When Earl Attlee, the retired Labour Prime Minister, was asked to give the Chichele lectures at Oxford in 1960, he chose the subject 'Empire and Commonwealth'. In his first lecture, he described the excitements of youthful imperialism. When the news of the Jameson Raid broke, his father, a Gladstonian liberal, was shocked, 'but to us Dr Jim was a hero . . . On the wall at school hung a great map with large portions of it coloured red. It was an intoxicating vision for a small boy . . . We believed in our great imperial mission.'[33] Esmé Wingfield-Stratford commented on the 'rumbustious and stentorian' patriotism of the 1890s.

> I can dimly remember the first Jubilee, and the second very clearly indeed; my favourite literature as a schoolboy consisted in accounts of future wars from which, after an agreeably awful slaughter, the British Empire would emerge vaster and more imperial than ever. Even the South African War, which was just a year old when I went up to Cambridge, was a series of magnificent thrills, in which everything – thanks to dear old Bobs and iron-hearted K. of K. – was bound to come right in the end, though it certainly did trail off into boredom and disillusionment unspeakable before the end. But about patriotism in those empire conscious days there was no doubt or room for doubt. It meant an honest-to-God or Satan – love for your country, right or wrong – not that she ever was wrong, to signify – and loving your country meant shouting, and going all out, and, at need, dying, for that empire on which, as we were constantly reminded, the sun never set. To doubt this, or oppose it in any way, was treason.[34]

He goes on to say that such patriotism did not outlive the Boer War, but that seems very much like the intellectual's *ex post facto* judgment. Robert Roberts describes a form of it, still very much alive, in Salford ten years later. And George Orwell remembered patriotic excitements of his childhood too: 'The earliest political slogan I can remember is "We want eight (eight dreadnoughts) and we won't wait". At seven years old I was a member of the Navy League and wore a sailor suit with H.M.S. *Invincible* on my cap.'[35] That agitation, it will be recalled, was in 1909. All of this surely gives point to Freda Harcourt's suggestion that imperial historians should look less to the 'official mind' and more to the complicated interplay between government and society.[36] What was true of 1867 surely derived even more point during the ensuing fifty years. It may even be the case that a truly popular imperialism, interest in the defence of an existing Empire rather than in its acquisition was stronger *after* the imperial climacterics of the late nineteenth century had ceased. It has been objected that the public did not resist the speedy devolution of responsible government to South Africa,[37] but in all social and economic terms British war aims had been achieved, and no one doubted for many more years that South Africa was 'British'.

Those commentators who have been primarily concerned with imperialism as an intellectual phase, the concerns of an elite, have always seen the Great War as the crucial turning point. Revulsion from the nationalist militarism which had produced the war led to the rejection of the imperialism with which it seemed inseparably connected. The multifarious societies which saw the war as their great opportunity found themselves, in Porter's telling phrase, as 'officers in search of troops'.[38] The imperial elite had developed specific ambitions, notably Imperial Federation, which failed. That atmosphere of failure seemed to be confirmed in the twenties, by British economic decline, Dominion nationalism, and the growth of nationalist agitation in India and the dependent territories. The literary, and to a certain extent, the academic, world had moved on. Imperialism as an intellectual construct had failed, and the critics of Empire had secured the ascendancy.

Intellectual culture, and the satirists who contributed to the gaiety of the 'long weekend' of the inter-war years, depicted the effort to reinvigorate popular imperialism at the Wembley Exhibition of 1924–5 as a failure. The Exhibition was derided by intellectuals, who formed the WGTW, Won't Go to Wembley, Society, and treated, it was suggested, as no more than a funfair by the populace. It was an easy butt for Noel Coward ('I've brought you to see the wonders of the Empire and all you want to do is go on the dodgems') and P. G. Wodehouse ('I mean to say, millions of people, no doubt, are so constituted that they scream with joy and excitement at the spectacle of a stuffed porcupine fish or a glass jar of seeds from Western Australia – but not Bertram . . . everything pointed to my executing a quiet sneak in the direction of that rather jolly Planters' Bar in the West Indies section'). H. G. Wells remarked that nineteen out of twenty Englishmen knew as much about their Empire as they did about the Italian Renaissance or the Argentine Republic. (He might have chosen a different example after 1982.) This atmosphere of ignorance and indifference was apparently confirmed by the Colonial Office surveys of 1948 and 1951.[39] Fifty-nine per cent of those interviewed in 1951 could not name a single British colony. One man suggested Lincolnshire. Three per cent thought that the United States was still a part of the Empire. And no one, perhaps not surprisingly, could distinguish the difference between a dominion and a colony.

Yet there is ample evidence to suggest that the role of Britain as a world power deriving from its unique imperial status continued to be projected to the British public after the First World War. Victory in war had confirmed rather than diminished that status, however much the economic indicators pointed the other way. On the contrary, in the economic storms of the inter-war years it was possible again, as in the late nineteenth century, to depict the Empire as a saviour from decline. Children's literature, educational texts, and national rituals directed towards these ends were joined by the powerful new media of the cinema and broadcasting. Even if the idea of official propaganda had, to a certain extent, been discredited by the war, these were years when the business of public relations, propaganda, advertising and censorship came of age.

More significant than any of the intellectual and satirical strictures on Wembley is the fact that it was featured, admiringly, in almost every children's annual for 1924 and in the weekly comics. Billy Bunter and his chums went and their excited reactions to the imperial pavilions were faithfully reported by Frank Richards in *Magnet*.[40] The new school history and geography of the late nineteenth century survived the First World War and can be found in a whole range of texts published in the period.[41] Racial concepts deriving from climatic determinism are particularly prominent. Commercial packaging, which Schumpeter had identified as an important vehicle for the imperial idea,[42] continued to highlight the old themes, as did the continuing boom in ephemera and 'free gifts'. A. H. Halsey remembered that his village classroom of the 1920s 'was steeped in officially sanctioned nationalism. The world map was red for the Empire and dull brown for the rest, with Australia and Canada vastly exaggerated in size by Mercator's projection. The Greenwich meridian placed London at the centre of the world. Empire Day and 11 November ritualised an established national supremacy.'[43] And John Julius Norwich described the pervasive imperial imagery of his boyhood in the thirties: 'Empire was all around us, celebrated on our biscuit tins, chronicled on our cigarette cards, part of the fabric of our lives. We were all imperialists then.'[44]

There can be little doubt that, however active the propagandists were, the British public never came to grips with the principles or practice of imperial rule. They knew little or nothing of specific territories or of their administrative, 'native' or economic affairs. Moreover, the elections of both 1906 and 1923 showed that the cry of the 'dear loaf' was always likely to be more potent than any amount of imperial sentiment linked to tariff reform when those options were put before the British electorate. But the rejection of tariff reform was not, surely, coterminous with the rejection of Empire any more than ignorance of Empire represented uninterest in it. If party and faction – and their supporters – fell apart over specific policies, it was still possible for the British to retain a world view embracing unique imperial status, cultural and racial superiority, and a common ground of national conceit on which most could agree.

It should be made clear that it is this generalised imperial vision rather than any sophisticated concept of Empire which is implied in the title of this book. It was a world view which rendered the principal elements of British patriotism distinctively imperial in this period. So much would be accepted by all the contributors to this collection. Only the extent of its social penetration and its 'shelf-life' are in question. So far as the 'popular culture' of our title is concerned, there are perhaps some who would argue that the media we examine are not 'popular cultural' at all. The culture of the people is usually located in the pub, the club, the football ground, the dog track, and other areas of popular sports and pastimes. But not even all of these can be described as a culture made by and for the people. One of the characteristics of the later nineteenth century was the manner in which many aspects of working-class culture came to be controlled, aimed at rather than created by the people.[45] The 'popular culture' of this book, embracing as it does everything from music hall to children's literature, was certainly beamed at the people, but that there was an insatiable demand for patriotic music hall, cinema, broadcasting, and other forms of entertainment and leisure activity cannot be gainsaid. It might indeed be argued that the truly popular culture is one which crosses class lines, as many of the cultural elements examined here did. Whether that cross-class interest was engineered from above or demanded from below is, of course, another matter. By the 1920s it can be said that the literary culture of at least some parts of the intelligentsia had begun seriously to diverge from the common causes of the period before the First World War, but the ideas and attitudes of the 1890s and the Edwardian era continued in many respects to be promoted in immensely popular media like the cinema.

If historians are to arrive at a clearer understanding of the manner in which this world view was communicated to the British public – or, remembering Harcourt's complex interaction between government and society, the reactions of the politicians to its existence in both the elite and popular mind – then there must be more studies of popular cultural forms and of the educational and propagandist processes. The historians of imperialism and of popular culture have invariably worked in isolation, while the students of propaganda have generally concentrated on external rather than domestic propagandist activities. This volume is offered as a preliminary attempt to create this conjuncture. It may be, however, that it is too early to answer convincingly the fundamental questions that lie behind its contributions. These are: to what extent were popular cultural elements suffused with the ideology of imperialism in the period under review? How successful were popular cultural vehicles in conveying an imperial world view to the British public? Were popular ideas merely a reflection of, or were they instrumental in, imperial policy? Can these activities and ideas be seen as surviving the First World War?

This volume seeks to escape the conventional concentration on the pre-First World War period by surveying the influence of imperialism on a variety of media and leisure activities between the late nineteenth century and the Second World War. Thus the contributions are equally divided between the pre-1914 period and the inter-war years. It makes no pretence to ideological purity and readers will detect within it contrasting views on the power of imperial ideas and propaganda.

The music hall was of course identified as the prime medium of popular imperialism by J. A. Hobson, and as a result it has always received its fair share of attention. Penny Summerfield has revealed how much more remains to be done in this field, and here she examines in particular both the class base of the music-hall clientele and the variations in the ideology presented through the songs and scenes performed in it. On the other hand, there have been almost no studies at all of imperial iconography. Well-known examples are familiar to us all, and were clearly significant in Victorian hero cults and in the creation of myths which influenced future action – the Gordon myth is the classic case.[46] John Springhall examines the most notable of the war artists, particularly Melton Prior and Caton Woodville, and demonstrates the manner in which the engraving process tended to romanticise the more realistic sketches actually made at the front. Lady Elizabeth Butler's work, which was of course not based on direct experience of battle, enjoyed a quite extraordinary vogue which is quantified in the royalties she secured on the sale of prints. This imperial and militarist iconography, reproduced and pirated in prints, magazines, posters and postcards, surely constituted the prime visual stimuli for popular imperial attitudes.

A great deal of children's fiction in the late nineteenth and early twentieth centuries was devoted specifically to Empire, but Jacqueline Bratton argues that the imperial ethos can equally be found in much Victorian children's literature which was not overtly imperial in setting. Historical romances bore a message from a modern imperial race and the images of England and of English patriotism were part of the 'energising myth of Empire'. Thus Englishness was presented as a complex of historical, moral and heroic values which justified the possession of Empire. By so clearly delineating the attributes of the British 'race', the writers of juvenile fiction placed other races firmly beyond the pale. Thus, marriage across racial lines, as in the case of 'Prince' Peter Lobengula, offended every canon of distinctiveness.

The case of Peter Lobengula is in fact a fascinating example of the manner in which imperial powers tend to create shows out of the peoples they dominate, subjecting them to all the isolation of spectacle. There was a considerable tradition of this in the nineteenth century. The 'native village' became a central part of imperial exhibitions and, at times, a familiar sight in seaside entertainment. Colonial wars were swiftly represented on the theatrical stage or in the circus ring, and the sting of black opponents was drawn by their appearance at shows acting out the resistance which had so recently been bitterly fought out in reality. Ben Shephard sees the case of Peter Lobengula as a focus for racial attributes in late Victorian and Edwardian times, and he suggests that the press would repay further examination for imperial and racial content.

J. A. Mangan offers a bridge between the pre-1914 period and the inter-war years and between the public school and state school systems. He sees the public schools as disseminators of a crudely militarist imperialism and notes that their headmasters played a part in the national debate about citizen training and in the invention of traditions and rituals which would bond the different class-based sectors. In this he identifies a connection between the public-school ethos, with its anti-intellectual athleticism, its propagandist magazines, its concern with 'character' and discipline through cadet corps, and the various movements associated with the Earl of Meath. It was through these associations, concerned with patriotism, duty, discipline and imperialism that public school ideas reached the state school system. As Dr Mangan has pointed out elsewhere, there were other routes too, through the games ethic and through the concern of HM inspectors that the state schools should be primarily concerned with character training, conforming with the norms laid down in the public schools.[47]

The public schools had a remarkable influence upon juvenile literature and other aspects of popular culture. Writers without a public-school education wrote of them lovingly, and, as Robert Roberts suggested, working-class boys identified with them.[48] Even so brash and modern a medium as the cinema attempted to recreate the public-school world, and John Reith and others were anxious to introduce its values into broadcasting. All social observation of the inter-war years indicates the great importance of both the cinema, undergoing tremendous growth and technical change in this period, and the exciting new medium of broadcasting. Jeffrey Richards argues for the central role of the imperial adventure tradition in a significant and popular area of the feature film output of both the British and Hollywood cinema industries, and also illuminates the nuances of the imperial visions presented in them. My own contribution is a preliminary exploration of the domestic propaganda of the BBC, a topic largely unexplored. It is significant that, as Stephen Constantine indicates in the case of the Empire Marketing Board, the legitimacy of imperial propaganda was frequently taken as read. There might be controversies about the nature of that propaganda, but few were prepared to deny the centrality of the Empire in British public life. Thus, a BBC programme-maker anxious about 'imperialistic' programmes hedged his criticisms with the remark that he did not suggest for a moment that the imperial idea was dead, just that it was reclothing itself, while many BBC executives, including Gladstone Murray, in charge of public relations from 1924 to 1935, considered that identification with Empire sentiments was politically important to the Corporation, and won it public support.[49]

Stephen Constantine demonstrates the manner in which the imperial economic vision lay ready to hand for the publicists and public relations men who saw the Empire Marketing Board as one of the great opportunities in the inter-war years to develop their craft. The EMB exploited the full range of media available, the cinema, posters, ephemera, broadcasting and also outlets through education and youth organisations. It therefore constituted one of the most important means by which British propaganda developed its techniques. Given the great difficulties in assessing the full scope of the EMB's public impact, Dr Constantine is, however, wary about seeing it as successfully contributing to a 'dominant ideology'. On the other hand, the EMB represented a rare attempt at 'formal', government-inspired, propaganda. It may be that its most important influence was not in reaching the public directly, though remarkable and extensive efforts were made to do so, but in maintaining the elite's concern with imperial values in education, public ritual, broadcasting, and film making.

Allen Warren argues that whereas the Scout movement was created in the atmosphere of defensive Empire in the Edwardian period, Scouting ideology underwent a significant change in the post-war years. In any case, however much the thinking of Baden-Powell and other Scout leaders changed in this period, the Scouts themselves entered the movement primarily for the opportunities it afforded for recreation, particularly the open-air activities of the camp. This is a salutary reminder of a very real problem in attempts to assess the influence of imperial rituals and ideologies. Would not the Empire Day half-holiday loom larger in children's minds than the imperial vision it was intended to convey? How far did schools' broadcasting, children's literature, and the cinema make any impact on the child's simple delight at a few hours free from school? Jeffrey Richards argues that it was the pervasive nature of the imperial ethos in all media – and even the Scouts, he suggests, must be approached in this context – which made the imperial world view too difficult to avoid. Allen Warren also makes interesting remarks about the Girl Guides, which should remind us that the role of girls and women in youth organisations and imperial ideologies, with some notable exceptions,[50] has been too little studied.

Reflection or instrument? Supply- or demand-led? Elite manipulation or popular psychology? National delusion or merely elite self-delusion? These are some of the questions posed by imperialism in the continuing debate on the problematic relationship between culture and ideology. This debate has been extended and deepened in recent years. Marc Ferro has exposed the power of images and stereotypes transmitted by school textbooks and the educational process generally.[51] Donald Horne has examined the re-presentation of history through museums and monuments, finding in them confirmation of the notion that 'reality is a social construction'.[52] Some of the contributions in *The Invention of Tradition*, edited by Ranger and Hobsbawm, have pointed to the distinctiveness of the late nineteenth century as a period when rituals and 'traditions' were made to conform to the new nationalist patterns.[53] My own *Propaganda and Empire* set out to demonstrate the pervasiveness of imperialism as an ideological cluster in this process, and the extraordinary staying-power of some of the components of that cluster in the twentieth century.[54]

No doubt some of this material will feed back into the lively discussions of sociologists and students of the media on the nature of popular culture, the role of the media in connecting ideology to it, the existence or otherwise of dominant ideologies, and the class dimensions of cultural interactions.[55] Tony Bennett has argued that popular culture should be seen neither as imposed hegemonically from above nor welling up from below, but as an 'area of exchange' between classes.[56] This collection of essays should illustrate afresh the distinctive character of such an interaction, if it was such, in the late nineteenth and early twentieth centuries. Imperialism, or at least imperialist nationalism, surely produced a striking and unique convergence which added a touch of the febrile to that 'interaction', producing a rare coherence of Establishment, intellectual and popular interests. In the post-First World War period, intellectual culture diverged, throwing out 'patriotism', as George Orwell never tired of pointing out, as it did so. But the evidence of such central entertainment forms as cinema and broadcasting suggests that the congruence, natural or engineered, between the nationalist concerns of the Establishment and the masses continued in force. With these media at least the *action* of censorship and of Establishment control seems the more important component of the 'exchange' or interaction, even if viewers and listeners filtered out what they wanted and made of it what they willed.[57] If the formal propaganda and public relations work of the Empire Marketing Board had limited appeal, maybe the inherited influences of juvenile literature, an immensely popular iconography, imperial and patriotic theatre and ethnic shows, the connections between education, pressure groups, and youth organisations all set up currents in the popular memory so powerful that it took more than one war to turn them aside. In the BBC we can find intellectual dissidence,

Establishment desires, and mass demand sometimes at variance, while in the Scouts it may be that there was an attempt to accommodate the old Establishment concerns to a new intellectual climate. At any rate the central role of imperialism must now be noted in all debates about culture, media, and society in the period between the 1870s and the 1940s.

Acknowledgements

My thoughts on popular imperialism have been developed in (often unrestrained) discussions with Donald Simpson, Terry Ranger, Shula Marks, Freda Harcourt, Andrew Roberts, Peter Blight, Nigel Dalziel, the contributors to this volume, and my students at the University of Lancaster. I am grateful to them all. I remain, of course, solely responsible for the views expressed in this introduction.

Notes

1   D. K. Fieldhouse, *Economics and Empire*, London 1976, 75–6.
2   Stephen Koss, 'Wesleyanism and Empire', *Historical Journal*, XVIII, 1975, 105–18.
3   B. Porter. 'The Edwardians and their Empire', in D. Read (ed.), *Edwardian England*, London 1982.
4   Richard Price, *An Imperial War and the British Working Class*, London 1972.
5   J. A. Hobson, *The Psychology of Jingoism*, London 1901.
6   Joseph Schumpeter, *Imperialism and Social Classes*, New York 1955 (first published 1919), 14.
7   H. Pelling, *Popular Politics and Society in Late Victorian Britain*, London 1979.
8   Max Beloff, *Imperial Sunset*, I, London 1969, 19.
9   George Orwell, *The Lion and the Unicorn*, London 1941. Esmé Wingfield-Stratford, *The Foundations of British Patriotism*, London 1940.
10 Freda Harcourt, 'Disraeli's imperialism, a question of timing, 1866–68', *Historical Journal*, XXIII, 1980, 87–109.
11 Hugh Cunningham, 'Jingoism in 1877–78', *Victorian Studies*, XIV, 1971, 429–53. See also Hugh Cunningham, 'The language of patriotism', *History Workshop*, XII, 1981, 8–83.
12 Iain R. Smith, *The Emin Pasha Relief Expedition, 1886–1890*, Oxford 1972.
13 E. J. Hobsbawm, 'Mass-producing traditions: Europe, 1870–1914' in E. J. Hobsbawm and T. O. Ranger (eds), *The Invention of Tradition*, Cambridge 1983.
14 Olive Anderson 'The growth of Christian militarism in mid-Victorian Britain', *English Historical Review*, LXXXVI, 1971, 46–72.
15 Geoffrey Best, 'Militarism and the Victorian public school' in Brian Simon and Ian Bradley (eds), *The Victorian Public School*, London 1975, 129–46. J. A. Mangan, *Athleticism in the Victorian and Edwardian Public School*, Cambridge 1981.
16 Mark Girouard, *The Return to Camelot*, New Haven, 1981. For the working

out of chivalric ideas in the Primrose League, see J. H. Robb, *The Primrose League, 1883–1906*, New York 1942.

17 Hugh Cunningham, *The Volunteer Movement*, London 1975.

18 Michael Booth, *English Melodrama*, London 1965. Michael Booth, *Victorian Spectacular Theatre*, London 1981. J. S. Bratton, 'The theatre of war' in David Bradby *et al.* (eds), *Performance and Politics in Popular Drama*, Cambridge 1980. Lawrence Senelick, 'Politics as entertainment, Victorian music-hall songs', *Victorian Studies*, XIX, 1975, 149–80. Peter Bailey, 'Custom, capital, and culture in the Victorian music hall' in Robert D. Storch (ed.), *Popular Culture and Custom in Nineteenth Century England*, London 1982. Penelope Summerfield, 'The Effingham Arms and the Empire' in Eileen and Stephen Yeo (eds), *Popular Culture and Class Conflict*, Sussex 1981.

19 John Taylor, 'From self-help to glamour, the working-men's club 1860–1972', History Workshop pamphlet no. 7, 1972. T. G. Ashplant, 'London working-men's clubs, 1875–1914' in E. and S. Yeo, *Popular Culture*.

20 J. O. Springhall, *Youth, Empire, and Society: British Youth Movement, 1883–1940* London 1977. J. O. Springhall (ed.), Brian Fraser, and Michael Hoare, *Sure and Stedfast, a History of the Boy's Brigade 1883 to 1983*, Glasgow 1983. Paul Wilkinson, 'English youth movements, 1908–30', *Journal of Contemporary History*, IV, 1969, 3–23.

21 Anne Summers, 'Militarism in Britain before the Great War', *History Workshop*, II, 1976, 104–23. Anne Summers, 'The character of Edwardian nationalism, three popular leagues' in Paul Kennedy (ed.), *Nationalist and Racialist Movements in Britain and Germany before 1914*, London 1981.

22 Geoffrey Searle, *The Quest for National Efficiency*, Berkeley 1971. See also Walter Nimocks, *Milner's Young Men*, London 1970, and Terence H. O'Brien, *Milner*, London 1979.

23 Bernard Semmel, *Imperialism and Social Reform*, London 1960. Partha Sarathi Gupta, *Imperialism and the British Labour Movement 1914–64*, London 1975.

24 H. C. G. Matthew, *The Liberal Imperialists*, Oxford 1973, 151. See also Keith Robbins, 'Sir Edward Grey and the British Empire', *Journal of Imperial and Commonwealth History*, I, 1972–3, 3–21.

25 Barry A. Kosmin, 'London's Asian M.P.s', unpublished paper delivered to the conference on the History of Black People in London, November 1984.

26 Quoted in Semmel, *Imperialism*, 53.

27 Schumpeter, *Imperialism*, 6.

28 Alfred Williams, *Life in a Railway Factory*, London 1915.

29 Fred Willis, *101 Jubilee Road*, London 1948.

30 Robert Roberts, *The Classic Slum*, Manchester 1971.

31 H. M. Hyndman, *Further Reminiscences*, London 1912.

32 Stephen Humphries, *Hooligans or Rebels?*, Oxford 1981, 41.

33 Clement Attlee, *Empire into Commonwealth*, London 1961, 5–6.

34 Wingfield-Stratford, *Foundations*, x.

35 Orwell, *The Lion and the Unicorn*, 63.

36 Harcourt, 'Disraeli's imperialism', 109.

37 Vernon Bogdanor, 'Food for Jingoes', *Times Literary Supplement*, 21 December 1984, 1464.

38 Bernard Porter, *The Lion's Share*, London 1975, 285.

39 David Goldsworthy, *Colonial Issues in British Politics, 1945–61*, Oxford 1971, 399.

40 *The Magnet*, 11 October 1924.

41   John M. MacKenzie, *Propaganda and Empire*, Manchester 1984, 188–9. See also F. Glendenning, 'School history textbooks and racial attitudes, 1804–1911', *Journal of Educational Administration and History*, V (2), 1973, 33–43, and 'British and French colonialism in school books', *Educational History*, 3 (2), 1974, 57–72. There is an excellent chapter on education in M. D. Blanch, 'Nation, Empire, and the Birmingham working class', University of Birmingham PhD thesis, 1975.

42   Schumpeter, *Imperialism*, 11. See also W. Hamish Fraser, *The Coming of the Mass Market, 1850–1914*, London 1981.

43   *The Listener*, 6 January 1983, 10.

44   *3, The Radio Three Magazine*, November 1982, 42.

45   Peter Bailey, *Leisure and Class in Victorian England: Rational Recreation and the Contest for Control, 183–85*, London 1978.

46   Douglas H. Johnson, 'The death of Gordon, a Victorian myth', *Journal of Imperial and Commonwealth History*, X, 1982, 285–310. See also C. I. Hamilton, 'Naval hagiography and the Victorian hero', *Historical Journal*, XXIII, 1980, 381–98.

47   J. A. Mangan, 'Imitating their betters and disassociating from their inferiors: grammar schools and the games ethic in the late nineteenth and early twentieth centuries', *Proceedings of the Annual Conference, History of Education Society of Great Britain*, December 1982, 1–45, and J. A. Mangan, 'Grammar schools and the games ethic in the Victorian and Edwardian eras', *Albion*, XV, 1983, 313–35. See also Blanch, 'Nation, Empire', 47–8.

48   Roberts, *Classic Slum*, 127–8.

49   BBC, Written Archives Centre, Caversham, file R34/213/1.

50   Brian Harrison, 'For Church, Queen, and family: the Girls' Friendly Society, 1874–1920', *Past and Present*, LXI, 1973, 107–38. Anna Davin, 'Imperialism and motherhood', *History Workshop*, V, 1978, 9–65.

51   Marc Ferro, *The Use and Abuse of History or How the Past is Taught*, London 1984.

52   Donald Horne, *The Great Museum, The Re-presentation of History*, London 1984.

53   Hobsbawm and Ranger (eds), *Invention*. See particularly the contributions of Cannadine, Hobsbawm, Cohn and Ranger.

54   MacKenzie, *Propaganda*.

55   N. Abercrombie, S. Hill and Bryan A. Turner, *The Dominant Ideology Thesis*, London 1980. James Curran, Michael Gurevitch and Janet Woollacott (eds), *Mass Communication and Society*, London 1977. Michael Gurevitch (ed.), *Culture, Society, and the Media*, London 1982. Bernard Waites, Tony Bennett and Graham Martin (eds), *Popular Culture: Past and Present*, London 1982.

56   Tony Bennett, 'Popular culture: defining our terms' in Block 1 of the Open University course U 203 book, *Popular Culture: Themes and Issues*, 1, Milton Keynes 1981, 86. See also Block 2 *The Historical Development of Popular Culture in Britain* of the same course.

57   Jeffrey Richards, *The Age of the Dream Palace, Cinema and Society in Britain 1930–1939*, London 1984, part 2, chapters 5–8.

CHAPTER 2

PATRIOTISM AND EMPIRE
MUSIC-HALL ENTERTAINMENT
1870–1914

Penny Summerfield

Nineteenth-century music hall was known as the 'fount of patriotism'. While some observers praised this development,[1] others such as J. A. Hobson condemned the music hall for manipulating working-class opinion in favour of exploitative imperialist policies. Hobson was convinced, by the absence of mass opposition to the Boer War and by the working-class celebrations of victories such as the relief of Mafeking, that the working class was infected with jingoism. To him this meant an 'inverted patriotism whereby the love of one's own nation is transformed into the hatred of another nation, and the fierce craving to destroy the individual members of that other nation'. He saw music hall as a 'potent educator' transmitting this 'mob passion' throughout the country by way of the artist who 'conveys by song or recitation crude notions upon morals and politics, appealing by coarse humour or exaggerated pathos to the animal lusts of an audience stimulated by alcohol into appreciative hilarity'.[2]

Hobson has been taken to task by several historians in the last two decades for being, in the words of R. N. Price, 'duped by the seeming mass excitement caused by the war into believing that . . . something was very rotten in British society'.[3] Price has argued that the true jingo crowd was not that which celebrated war victories, but the much smaller type of group which broke up peace meetings for politically Conservative reasons. Price suggests that this crowd was not working-class, but middle-class, or more specifically lower-middle-class, composed principally of shopkeepers and clerks suffering from 'status-anxiety'.[4] The working class did participate in patriotic celebrations such as those on Mafeking night, 19 May 1900, but Price sees these as 'harmless saturnalia'.[5] His conclusion after investigating five areas in which members of the working class might have been expected to express feelings about imperialism is that the dominant attitude was one of indifference, except when imperialism 'directly related to their own

"BRITANNIA."

An entirely New and Original Entertainment, Written and Produced by

PAUL VALENTINE.

Music by WILLIAM CORRI.

Scenery by E. BANKS. Dresses by

Mrs. MAY.

The Vocal parts Sung by

MISS JOAN RIVERS.

Supported by

MISS NELLY AUDUS, THE BELL QUARTETTE,

AND CHORUS.

The various Dances, National, Characteristique and Fancy, are performed in the following order.—

ENGLAND	- -	BY THE EDEN TROUPE.
IRELAND	- - -	- BY THE BELLS.
AUSTRALIA	- Misses SMITH, WHITEFOOT,	
		HENRY, and WESTFIELD.

PAS SEUL, Miss PAULINE RIVERS.

WELSH - Misses ADA MALVERN and CARLOTTA GRIMANI,

INDIA - - Misses WALL and AUDUS.

PAS SEUL, Miss KATE FLORETTA.

CANADA - - BY THE EDEN TROUPE.

SCOTCH - Misses M. HENRY, L. WESTFIELD and MADLE.

SWORD DANCE, Miss ANCELL.

experience',[6] as in the case of volunteering to serve in the army during periods of high unemployment.

There does however, seem to be a major flaw in Price's argument. His depiction of jingoism and patriotism as separate sets of ideas and feelings is artificial when they had in common the celebration of Empire in Victorian and Edwardian Britain, albeit with different degrees of political focus and aggression. And patriotic 'saturnalia', however 'harmless', can hardly be regarded as signs of indifference to the nation and its Empire. J. A. Hobson's anxiety was based on the fear of an elision of patriotism (wholesome love of country) and jingoism (unhealthy xenophobia) during the Boer War, for which he held the music hall particularly responsible. However, neither Price nor other critics of Hobson's thesis, such as Hugh Cunningham and Henry Pelling, make a serious investigation of the charges which Hobson laid at the door of music hall. Cunningham and Pelling look briefly at the issue, both concluding that, in Cunningham's words 'the apparent jingoism of the music halls was less significant than it has usually seemed to be'.[7] However neither author quotes more than one or two songs, and both leave aside issues such as the composition of audiences, their degree of control over the content of songs, and the significance of the varieties of patriotism that were expressed in the halls.

In contrast another historian, Laurence Senelick, concludes his study of the political content of music-hall songs by agreeing with Hobson about the manipulative Conservatism of music hall entertainment, though Senelick's conclusions on the success of this manipulation are ambiguous. At one point he suggests that music-hall politics grew into a 'creed' which explains 'why the downtrodden British working-class was so submissive and never rebelled'. At another he argues that music hall's political influence declined because 'it increasingly contributed to the formation of public opinion without drawing on the authentic attitudes of the public itself'.[8] Referring to the nineteenth century, Senelick states that the growth of the 'creed' occurred 'over the course of decades' and that the decline of music hall's political influence happened 'as the century wore on'.[9] But since the two opposite tendencies could not have occurred simultaneously, the argument only makes sense if Senelick is taken to mean that manipulation was successful in an earlier period and failed thereafter. This raises questions which Senelick does not address, concerning the feasibility of periodising music hall's influence and the possible causes of change.

The purpose of this essay is to advance the debate about the influence of music hall on attitudes towards imperialism in the period 1870–1914,

---

Britannia, 'An entirely New and Original Entertainment': programme from the Oxford Music Hall, 24 October 1885. By courtesy of the Guildhall Library.

firstly by discussing the development of music hall, in particular the social composition of audiences and the determinants of the content of the songs and acts they watched, and secondly by offering an interpretation of the various meanings given to patriotism in music hall and related entertainment. The objective is to identify and explain changes in music-hall patriotism over time, and by so doing to throw some light on the complex issue of popular attitudes towards the Empire in this period.

The term 'music hall' covers a number of different types of institution, and also genres of entertainment. Its development was shaped by the interaction of both economic and political factors. The desire to increase the sale of drink by providing entertainment stimulated the tavern free-and-easies of the late eighteenth century and the song saloons established alongside pubs from the 1820s, and the urge to make a profit from the sale of entertainment encouraged publicans to turn saloons into separate music halls, just as it motivated those who set up penny gaffs, popular theatres and later theatres of variety. Politically, the process was shaped by the licensing laws, a complex set of pieces of legislation intended to control both the sale of alcohol and the presentation of entertainment.[10]

By 1870 there were two different kinds of entertainment licence. Each had a bearing on the right of a proprietor to obtain an excise licence for the sale of drink, though the licences were quite separate. The origin of the stage play licence lay in legislation passed in 1660 and re-affirmed in 1737, which endeavoured to restrict the production of stage plays to theatres holding the Royal Patent. Inevitably minor theatres grew up challenging the monopoly. In 1843 a new Theatres Act made it possible for theatre proprietors to produce stage plays legitimately, if they made successful application to the Lord Chamberlain or the Justices (depending on the area), for a stage play licence. They had to submit their plays to the same authorities for censorship, and they were not permitted to sell intoxicants or to allow eating or smoking in the auditorium.[11] Under the legislation, a matter of continuing dispute was precisely what constituted a 'stage play' and therefore required the licence. 'Penny gaffs', small street theatres, often set up in ramshackle structures, showing short plays interspersed with singing, tried to dodge the licensing procedure.[12] Some melodrama theatres, many of which were in barely more permanent accommodation, did the same, sometimes avoiding dialogue or using song instead of speech in order to claim that they were not showing stage plays.[13]

The other entertainment licence was known as the music and dancing licence. Under the Disorderly Houses Act of 1751 all places of 'public entertainment', (i.e. those offering 'music and dancing') had to obtain a licence from the magistrates each Michaelmas quarter-sessions. This licence could be held jointly with the excise licence for the sale of drink, and in the years between 1790 and 1860 those running taverns and public houses became increasingly keen to offer their customers drink and food coupled with entertainment. At first the common form was the 'free-and-easy', a concert held in the pub itself. Later saloons and music halls were set up, separate from pubs, with the objective of enlarging the entertainment side of the business, while still combining it with alcoholic and other types of refreshment. Applications for music and dancing licences in the County of Middlesex rose from sixteen in 1828 to 148 in 1849, and a Middlesex magistrate estimated that at least twice as many were in fact open for public entertainment, in that year.[14]

The objective of the licences was to enable the state to patrol popular haunts, long suspected as cradles of crime and vice. This involved both monitoring the behaviour of those who frequented theatres and pubs, and controlling the content of the entertainment presented. Licences were withheld on suspicion of disorder, crime or indecency or entertainment considered conducive to any of these. In London increasing vigilance after 1860 led to a decrease in the number of pubs licensed; and the creation of the London County Council in 1888, with a majority committed to temperance reform, led to a purge on the licensing of both pubs and saloons for public entertainment.[15]

It is possible that pubs denied music and dancing licences managed to offer clandestine musical entertainment, just as penny gaffs dodged the stage play law. But where the investment in a purpose-built place of entertainment was large, as in the case of many music halls, proprietors could not afford to lose their licences, and they were sensitive to their vulnerability at the hands of the licensing authorities. During the 1880s and 1890s there was a series of occasions on which music hall proprietors put forward their case, which amounted to the claim that they could guarantee the respectability and good order of music hall entertainment without sacrificing its essential features. These were drink, food, a mobile audience and an intimate relationship between artist and audience, characteristics which in the eyes of the authorities contributed to intemperance, prostitution and impropriety. Managers of music halls said such undesirable features had disappeared from 'legitimate' halls by for example the use of stewards who removed unruly or undesirable members of the audience and by controls over the performers, who had to abide by house rules which required them to submit material for performance beforehand, and not to deviate from it in patter or impromptu act, on penalty of loss of salary.[16]

After 1890, however, proprietors increasingly deferred to the preferences of the authorities for fixed seating and the removal of food and drink from the auditorium. Simultaneously they encouraged the development of sketches and, in the 1900s, 'revue', a compromise between the individual turns of a succession of performers and a full stage play. As well as its benefits for the performer, who typically 'starred' against the background of a company of singing and dancing girls, revue had the benefit for the proprietor of being a set piece, scripted and approved or censored in advance. Such performances, interspersed with shorter acts, became the staple of 'variety'. The new-style halls, many of which originated in provincial towns and spread across the country in heavily capitalised 'chains', run by individuals such as Moss, Stoll, Thornton and McNaughton, were called theatres of variety.[17] Eventually the overlap between variety and theatrical performances was accepted, and from 1912 it was possible for a theatre of variety to obtain both the music and dancing and the stage play licence. Though the advent of film, which originated as a 'turn' within music hall, provided an increasingly popular rival to variety, even in 1951 Rowntree and Lavers judged variety 'the most widely supported form of theatrical production in England and Wales, especially in the provinces'.[18]

Thus pub free-and-easies, saloons, music halls, theatres of variety and melodrama theatres all coexisted in the late nineteenth century, though by a process of selection the smaller, less heavily capitalised places were ceasing to lead a legal existence by the 1890s, and the theatre of variety was becoming the dominant 'legitimate' form.

The social composition of audiences varied as between the different institutions, according to type, size and level of capitalisation, though less according to location. Information is more readily available for London than elsewhere, but it is probably generally true that the variation was basically between places attracting a homogeneous audience from a single social segment, and those attracting a socially mixed audience, in which category many music halls, some popular theatres and all theatres of variety, belonged.

One may assume that most free-and-easies, saloons and penny gaffs drew their audiences from the immediate neighbourhood, and that their small size and low prices beckoned the youthful and uniformly poor crowds described in many nineteenth-century reports, such as one newspaper article on a gaff in Poplar which spoke of an audience of 'ragged boys, each one with his pipe, potatoe and (we must add it) his prostitute'. Youthful prostitution was often suspected in these places, and was given as a reason for refusing a licence to many saloons and small music halls in the 1860s. There are suggestions that for some young women it was one of the few ways in which they could obtain admission money.[19]

Melodrama theatres like the Bower Music Hall, Southwark, which charged 1*d* and 3*d* admission in the 1870s and music halls like Collins', Islington, the New Gaiety Palace of Varieties, Preston, and Sebright's, Hackney, which charged 2*d* or 3*d* to 1*s*, in 1880, 1884 and 1885 respectively, probably also anticipated an essentially local audience.[20] The better off and more respectable would occupy the higher priced stalls, while the pit and the gallery would still be filled by working-class youngsters including girls and women some of whom brought babies and young children with them.[21]

However, in developing such places of entertainment proprietors endeavoured to attract an audience from further afield and also a more respectable 'family' audience. Charles Morton, who turned the Canterbury Arms, Upper Marsh, Lambeth into the New Canterbury Music Hall in 1854, is a case in point. He deliberately tried to combine the kind of food, drink and song which was provided for upper-class men at song and supper rooms, with operetta and acrobatics of the kind that appealed to middle-class frequenters of tea gardens, and with the melodrama and comic acts which were the staple of the working-class free-and-easy. He priced his seats appropriately. In 1870 the Canterbury, which now accommodated 1,500, charged from 6d to 2 gns, depending on whether one chose the upper gallery, the hall, a 'numbered fauteil' or a box.[22] Other similar enterprises included the Islington Empire which charged 1s to 1 gn in 1872, and the Bedford, Camden Town from 1861, the Royal Cambridge, Shoreditch from 1864, and Lusby's, once the Eagle Tavern, in the Mile End Road, which all charged 6d to 1 gn in 1878. These are examples of halls situated in working-class areas, whose proprietors adopted a deliberate policy of attracting an audience from beyond the immediate neighbourhood and from more than one socio-economic group. For example, Frederick Charrington, keeping watch on 'vice' outside Lusby's Music Hall in the East End of London in the early 1880s, observed groups of 'young and inexperienced clerks' and the 'West End type of customer' amongst the crowds of local tradesmen, labourers and sailors coming and going from the hall.[23] The development of socially mixed halls in such areas is often overlooked. They and the entertainment taking place within them are dubbed 'working-class' in contrast to the apparently middle-class halls growing up simultaneously in provincial city centres and the West End of London. In fact the pricing policies of these halls indicate that they also aimed to be socially heterogeneous. For instance the Alhambra, Leicester Square, the London Hippodrome in the Strand, and the London Pavilion, Piccadilly, all charged 1s to 1 guinea in the 1880s or '90s, and the Oxford, Oxford Street, and the Middlesex, Drury Lane, charged 6d to 2 gns.[24] The creation of the theatre-of-variety chains referred to earlier, after 1890, reinforced the trend towards 'mass' audiences. As well as penetrating city centres, chains colonised the new suburbs of the late Victorian and Edwardian era, where prices of entry had a lower 'ceiling' than those of the earlier established mixed halls, aiming mainly at lower middle-class and upper working-class members of suburban society.[25]

As Clive Barker shows in his careful research on the audiences of the Britannia, Hoxton, a theatre showing mainly melodrama, the proprietor's policy *vis à vis* audiences was often one thing, and actual attendance another. Thus the Britannia management apparently failed to attract suburban multitudes from every train and bus route passing its door. Barker believes that it recruited mainly ex-Hoxtonians who had moved northwards as they moved up in the world, but who returned to their old haunts for entertainment, prepared to mix with the tradesmen and women who had not moved, as well as with less well off 'immigrants' to Hoxton from inner London areas.[26] A similar special link may have existed for the 'more respectable class of man' observed by J. E. Ritchie in the higher priced seats of the Canterbury in 1869, in contrast to the predominantly artisan audience he had observed twelve years before.[27] Increasing emphasis was placed on attracting a 'family' audience, which meant, in effect, that women accompanied by husbands were officially more welcome than women on their own, who were suspected of offering themselves for hire, but many observers testify to the distinctively masculine atmosphere of the music halls of the 1870s to the 1890s. From the proprietor's point of view the challenge involved in entertaining a 'mass' audience drawn from different walks of life and grades of income, was that there must be something to appeal to everyone and no section of the audience must be alienated.

Barker's research indicates the difficulties of assessing the social composition of the audiences at nineteenth century places of entertainment. Further complications are raised by Douglas Reid's work on Birmingham where, he argues, theatre audiences were drawn from different social segments on different nights of the week. Nevertheless, the evidence sustains a division of music halls into at least two categories, those with local, working-class audiences and those with a mixed clientele, often from a wider area than the immediate neighbourhood. The second category can be further divided into halls like those in the West End of London which attracted audiences from widely diverse backgrounds, and those in suburbia with more limited expectations of heterogeneity.[28] As has already been pointed out, by the 1890s in London and probably elsewhere, the operation of the licensing laws and economic competition favoured the socially mixed institutions, at the expense of the others.

There was some overlap in the types of entertainment presented in the different institutions. Most obviously song was presented on the stage of the melodrama theatre and melodrama was included as a 'turn' in music halls. In the late nineteenth and early twentieth centuries almost all these different types of entertainment had a patriotic content, and patriotism, as J. M. Robertson noted in 1899, by now inevitably embraced some celebration of Empire.[29] But as I shall go on to argue, the precise nature of the patriotic entertainment offered varied according to the social tone of the institution concerned, and as certain types of institution were supplanted over time their distinctive treatments disappeared with them, leading inevitably to standard presentations of imperial themes. It is now time to look at this patriotic entertainment, embracing in our enquiry melodramas, sketches and revues, as well as the songs which are the more obvious component of Victorian and Edwardian music hall.

It was the songs of the 1870s which earned music hall its reputation as the 'fount of patriotism'. The most famous, widely quoted by historians, was 'By Jingo' written by G. W. Hunt in 1877 and performed by G. H. Macdermott during the crisis of 1877–8, when the Russians threatened to take Constantinople, the Turkish port guarding both the entrance to the Black Sea and the route through the Mediterranean. The British stake in the issue was to keep the route East to India, the principal British colony, free from interference by any of the European Great Powers. The irony was that before the 1870s, Turkey, whose defence was now advocated as a moral imperative, had been regarded in less than sympathetic terms as a despotic 'heathen' power endangering the independence of the Balkan states.[30] However, it was precisely such subtleties that music hall jingoism ignored. Its appeal depended upon the presentation of complex issues of international politics in black and white, with Britain's cause always just and inevitably victorious. 'By Jingo', also known as 'We don't want to fight' and 'The Dogs of War', went as follows:

> The 'Dogs of War' are loose and the rugged Russian Bear,
> Full bent on blood and robbery, has crawled out of his lair,
> It seems a thrashing now and then, will never help to tame,
> The brute, and so he's bent upon the 'same old game'.
> The Lion did his best to find him some excuse,
> To crawl back to his den again, all efforts were no use,
> He hunger'd for his victim, he's pleased when blood is shed,
> But let us hope his crimes may all recoil on his own head.
> *Chorus*: We don't want to fight, but by jingo if we do,
> We've got the ships, we've got the men, we've got the money too.
> We've fought the Bear before, and while we're Britons true,
> The Russians shall not have Constantinople.[31]

The song is supposed to have been written in a few hours by G. W. Hunt after reading a statement in the morning paper, and was bought with full copyright by Macdermott for £5 (rather over the market price of 10*s* 6*d*).[32] Macdermott, originally a bricklayer's labourer and subsequently an actor in melodrama, was by 1878 well established as a 'lion comique', that is a singer of 'swell' songs celebrating the life of an upper-class rake. His fee was in the highest bracket, around £60 a week in the 1870s,[33] and it is unlikely that any but the halls whose income was enlarged by the range of prices charged to a socially-mixed audience could have afforded to hire him. The demand for 'By Jingo' in the big socially-mixed halls is indicated by J. B. Booth's record of Macdermott's performances on one evening in London in 1878. 'He was timed for 4.15 p.m. and 8.15 p.m. at the Royal Aquarium, 9.10 p.m. at the Metropolitan, 10 p.m. at the London Pavilion and 10.50 p.m. at Collins'.[34] In addition there is evidence that he was a regular performer at the Royal Cambridge, Shoreditch from April to June 1878 and toured the larger provincial halls in 1878 and periodically thereafter, until he turned from performance to management in the 1890s.[35]

Macdermott's performances of 'By Jingo' were undoubtedly popular in the halls where he was hired. Contemporary descriptions emphasise the artist's complete commitment to his message. He would abandon the frivolous 'yellow wig, hat and dust coat' of the 'lion comique', and reappear in evening dress for 'By Jingo', his 'square jaw, magnificent enunciation and stentorian voice' resembling for some that symbol of British grit, a bulldog.[36] Allegations that Conservatives subsidised him to sing 'By Jingo' and his other patriotic songs are probably far-fetched, though one can accept rumours that Conservative MPs invaded the London Pavilion to learn the words, which were quoted in Parliament and *The Times*.[37]

'By Jingo' is said to have averted war with Russia, and to have put a new word into the English language.[38] It certainly contributed to the legitimation of a more bellicose foreign policy, and it gave 'by jingo', earlier simply an expression of surprise, its special connotation of the aggressive assertion of British power. The phrase was rapidly picked up by other song writers. For example Clement Scott, author of many patriotic songs, as well as dramatic critic of the *Daily Telegraph*, incorporated it in 'True Blues, Stand to Your Guns', performed by Macdermott as part of a 'New Patriotic Entertainment entitled Albion's Nationality', performed at the Oxford in July 1878:

> We have suffered in silence the impudent banter
> Of cowards that swore that foul war was our cry.
> Come pledge our false friends in a merry decanter
> They shot behind hedges – we never said die!
> We can laugh – we have won – though they dragged the old island
> To a verge of a precipice loyalty shuns.
> But in spite of deserters – an ocean and dry land,
> By Jingo! Old England has stood to her guns.[39]

The 'jingo' songs of 1878 were not however a new departure, but part of a spate of songs and spectacles on the theme of the righteousness of British predominance, performed at the larger socially mixed halls from early in the 1870s. The 'Bear' had already become the villain of such halls.

For instance, in February 1871 the Oxford offered a programme of national war songs, in which 'Sailor Williams' sang 'We've Swept the Seas Before Boys'. The last verse and chorus ran:

> The Russians threaten war, boys,
> And gather a proud host:
> And think the task quite easy
> To land on Turkey's coast:
> But let them try it on, lads,
> They'll find who rules the main:
> We've thrashed them well before, boys,
> And so we can again.[40]

A similar show was put on at the Alhambra a year later in February 1872.[41] M. Julien's 'British Army Quadrille', followed by 'War Songs of the Day', were performed as a 'Promenade Concert' in the last hour of the evening, and concluded with an assertive rendering of 'Rule Britannia'.[42] The 'Quadrille' involved 350 performers, including the Reed Band of Scots Fusilier Guards. A nautical version, 'Trafalgar', was shown at the Canterbury several times between 1871 and 1880.[43] References were made to the Russian threat in all sorts of songs, such as Arthur Roberts' whistling song, 'It's all explained in this', published in 1882. The keynote was that the Tsar of Russia was unfit to rule, and the song's disdain for accuracy was typical: 'Old England's name is honoured still wherever waves her flag / We always give our foes the best, and never bounce or brag'.[44] Charles Godfrey was still recalling the theme in the 1890s, with his sketch 'The Seventh Royal Fusiliers, A Story of Inkerman' written in 1892: 'Through deadly Russian shot and Cossack spears / We carved our way to Glory! Oh! Glory!'.[45] The jingoism of such songs accords well with Hobson's definition.

A different element entered jingoist entertainment in 1879, and was increasingly stressed during the 1880s. The theme was that for years Britain had been resting peacefully, unaware of the threats to the Empire coming from jealous foreigners. Ultimately aroused, loyal colonial subjects came to Britain's aid and the threat was quashed amidst the celebration of British might. For example G. W. Hunt put a 'New Patriotic Song' into the 'Indianationality' spectacle shown at the Oxford in 1879. It combined the threatening defensiveness of 'By Jingo', expressed through animal characterisations of nations, with an image of the Empire as a unity of colonies whose inhabitants were loyal to the Imperial Crown out of gratitude for the 'freedom' and 'justice' its hegemony was supposed to have brought. The last two verses ran:

> The Afghan Wolf may friendship make
> With cunning Russian Bear,
> But the Indian Tiger's wide awake

And bids them both beware!
The prowling foe on plunder bent
By this should surely know
The British Lion's not *asleep*
As in the years ago.

The dusky sons of Hindostan
Will by our banner stand.
Australia, aye, and Canada,
Both love the dear old land!
No foe we fear — we fight for right!
No day we e'er shall rue,
If England, dear old England,
To herself be only true.[46]

During the 1880s the isolation of England (it was usual for the nation to be thus narrowly defined), and her resulting dependence on the colonies, was a growing preoccupation within the larger, socially mixed music halls. The context was not now the Russian threat to the security of Britain's imperial trade, but the rival claims of Belgium, France, Germany and Portugal to parts of Africa, which blew up into the crisis known as the 'scramble for Africa' in 1884–5.

'Britannia', shown at the Oxford under the auspices of J. H. Jennings in October 1885, sums up the concern. The spectacle opened with Britannia enjoying a 'well earned rest' after years of empire building. The drowsy idyll was shattered by a messenger announcing that as a result of 'greedy love of gain' among other nations, war loomed, threatening England's welfare. Britannia, awaking, silenced all fears:

There will come from the East, there will come from the West,
Willing hands, loyal hearts, the noblest and the best,
To help old England's sons, when danger hovers near,
For love of mother country their fathers held so dear.
There's little fear for England,
With brave Colonial sons,
Ready at the hour of need,
With money men and guns.
Above all price such service
Forgotten ne'er will be,
Long may their love continue
That all the world may see.

Although it turned out that 'War's dark cloud has passed away' Britannia would not allow her 'colonial sons' to be sent away, but announced:

Britannia's not so poor but she can ask
A few from every clime that owns her sway
As guests but once a year a loving task
To share the pleasures of a festive day.[47]

There was no specific reference to the Imperial Federation League, founded the year before, in 1884, nor are any contacts known between J. H. Jennings and supporters of the League. But even without such contacts, 'Britannia' clearly propagated the imperialist thought nurtured within the League and expressed by Lord Salisbury at the first Colonial Conference in 1887. The immediate need, he said, was not the *Zollverein*, or customs union, but 'the Kriegsverein . . . the Union for purposes of mutual defence'.[48] The League also suggested that the self-governing colonies should send their prime ministers to London regularly, to consult with the heads of the home government, after their first visit on the occasion of the Golden Jubilee in 1887, an idea which 'Britannia' presaged.

A sketch like 'Britannia' was an elaborate and expensive type of performance. It would not be shown once only, but repeatedly, and might well be taken on tour of those halls which could afford it.[49] This method of presenting a highly topical imperial theme was developed in other halls, such as the Alhambra, which showed a 'Grand Military Spectacle: Le Bivouac' in March 1886, 'Our Army and Navy' in July 1889 and 'Victoria and Merrie England' for the Diamond Jubilee in 1897.[50] The Empire, also in Leicester Square, London, staged similar performances, especially during the 1890s and 1900s.[51] Examples include 'The Girl I Left Behind Me' depicting soldiers and sailors on imperial service, performed in February and May 1894, 'Round the Town', whose '5th Tableau', entitled 'Our Empire', consisted of the dances of the British Empire, which was performed during both 1895 and 1899, and 'Our Crown', a 'spectacular divertissement' to celebrate the Coronation in 1902. The programme notes indicate how, in the sixth to twelfth tableaux, colonial unity was asserted:

Announced by the Clarions of Fame, a Messenger of Peace appears to summon the various colonies to contribute their resources to fashion the new imperial crown for King Edward VII . . . The Spirits of Commerce attend the revolution of the Globe revealing in turn . . . The Gold of Australia . . . The Rubies of Burmah . . . The Sapphires of India . . . The Pearls of Ceylon . . . The Diamonds of Cape Colony . . . The Ermine of Canada.[52]

In these 'patriotic extravaganzas' the colonies were presented as willingly subservient. The desire for independence growing within many of them was completely ignored. Unity was advocated in terms of the racial superiority of Anglo Saxons wherever they might be found. The most blatant expression of this was Charles Godfrey's song, 'It's the England Speaking Race against the World'.[53]

We're brothers of the self-same race
Speakers of the self-same tongue,
With the same brave hearts that feel no fears
From fighting sires of a thousand years;

Folks say, 'What will Britain do?
Will she rest with banners furled?'
No! No!! No!!!
When we go to meet the foe,
It's the English-speaking race against the world.

The inhabitants of the Indian subcontinent, characterised as 'the dusky
sons of Hindostan', were, like the Chinese, depicted as coolies, the willing
serfs of the Empire.[54] The Indian Mutiny of 1857, the power relations
within India's complex society, and the tensions on India's borders, could
not of course be acknowledged in the music-hall version of imperial unity.

The same was true of the desire of Dutch South Africans for independence. In the 1880s and 1890s the Boers had to be presented, like others
resistant to British authority in Africa, as traitors or savages.[55] The
extension of British power abroad could only be right. There was no room
for questioning.

After 1902 there were repeated references to imperial grandeur and
British power in sketches and also in 'revue', which was an extension of
the sketch, linking together different turns with a single theme.[56] But
though 'political' in the sense of offering unquestioning support to the
established order of Crown and Empire, these acts tended to be less
directly topical, in the sense of delivering judgments on current events,
than the jingo songs of the 1870s and patriotic spectacles of the 1880s.
The 'political' song was under attack. For example, in 1892 Collins' music
hall included in its house rules the following clause:

No offensive allusions to be made to any member of the Royal Family; Members
of Parliament, German Princes, police authorities, or any member thereof, the
London County Council, or any member of that body; no allusion whatever to
religion, or any religious sect; no allusion to the administration of the law of the
country.[57]

How such a clause might be acted upon is illustrated by Percy Honri's
experience at the London Palladium in 1918. He introduced into one of
his songs some couplets about the 'khaki election' of that year, in which
Asquith lost his seat at East Fife, but was sternly told not to repeat them
by the proprietor: 'A music hall audience is an all-party audience – and
your couplets probably offended at least fifty per cent of the patrons'.[58] It
was safer in view both of the mass audience and the attitudes of the
licensing authority to make generalised statements of political loyalty.

The evidence of playbills and programmes is that jingo songs and
spectacles were favoured by the proprietors of large halls endeavouring to
attract a 'mass' audience in the 1870s and '80s. Of course, songs that
became popular on their stages may have been repeated over the years in a
wider social setting. However, artists other than the copyright holder were
not supposed to perform them publicly, a legal requirement which the

Performing Rights Society was active in enforcing from 1875. Thus one may locate the sentiments of jingoism with some justice in the category of heavily capitalised halls catering for a socially mixed clientele. The social mix, it should be remembered, was predominantly male, and the songs were performed in the main by men. If the late Victorian music hall had a strongly masculine gender identity, then so too did the aggressive nationalism which pervaded so many of its performances.

A quite different brand of patriotism co-existed in specifically working-class places of entertainment, such as penny gaffs, popular theatres and smaller music halls, in the 1870s and 1880s, which found its fullest expression in melodrama.

Melodrama of course depended upon the polarisation of good and evil, a dichotomy into which 'British' and 'foreign' could easily be slotted. But on the whole national superiority was seen to derive from the good qualities of the redcoats and bluejackets themselves, rather than from anything as abstract as 'Albion', and hostility was rarely directed at an enemy with a distinct national identity, but usually at 'evil' in general.

This tradition in melodrama had long roots. The theatre historian Willson Disher believes that 'Jolly Jack Tar' first appeared as a character in the late eighteenth century. As both the personification of 'virtue triumphant' and an expression of the love of freedom, Jack Tar was written into numerous scripts which otherwise made no reference to seafaring life.[59] He was also the principal subject of many 'blood and thunder' melodramas whose main characteristics are summed up by another historian of popular theatre, Michael Booth:

Cannon roared and smoke rolled; flames swept the stage; ships sank and forts blew up; the Union Jack waved exaltedly over all, and the Great Commander and the Great Common Man alike declaimed patriotically, fought heroically, behaved magnanimously to the vanquished foe, treated their womenfolk tenderly, and to the rest of the world displayed the finest sentiment and the noblest conduct.[60]

There is abundant evidence of the resilience of this genre in the second half of the nineteenth century. Typical titles shown at the Bower Music Hall, Southwark, in the 1870s were, 'The Sailor's Grave or the Perils of the Dark Blue Waters' featuring Jack Junk and Harry Helm 'true British sailors', performed in February 1870, 'The Pirate King, or the Rover of the Sea and the Perils of the Ocean Wave' featuring Joe Jolly 'one who proved a True Blue to the Last', shown repeatedly during 1872, 'The Sailor's Progress' shown in July and 'Sinbad the Sailor, the Demon of the Sea' shown in December 1872. During 1873 'Perils of the Ocean Wave, or the Lass that loves a Sailor' was shown in March, 'Sons of Britannia or Death and Glory' in June, 'The Sea King's Vow, or the Struggle for Liberty' in July, 'Blackbeard the Smuggler, or the British Bulldogs and the Privateer', in October and 'True Blue or Sharks Alongshore' in December. Nautical melodramas continued to be strongly represented in the Bower programmes for 1874 and 1875.[61]

Documentation for the Bower is particularly full, but similar shows appear to have been put on at other East London halls, such as the Pavilion, Stepney, the East London Theatre, Whitechapel, and the Surrey, Lambeth as well as at numerous impermanent penny gaffs, 'geggies' (in Glasgow) and 'dives' (in Liverpool).[62] Indeed 'blood and thunder' appears to have become more firmly entrenched in melodrama theatres as changing technology made more spectacular illusions possible. The same play was frequently pirated and presented under different titles. For example, a pencilled note on a Bower playbill states that 'Sons of Britannia or Death and Glory' (June 1873) was actually 'My Poll and Partner Joe' a melodrama originally written in 1835. Since melodrama was necessarily stereotyped, such semi-concealed repetition probably did not matter much. The script of 'My Poll and Partner Joe' is available,[63] and as it is likely that it was frequently plagiarised, it can be used for the purpose of illustration of the genre.

The characters Poll and Joe are in fact largely irrelevant to the plot. The main focus is the virtuous Battersea waterman, Harry Hallyard, and an evil debt collector, Black Brandon, whose press-gang abduct Harry on the eve of his wedding to Poll. Despite these unpromising beginnings, Harry is instinctively a 'True Blue' and distinguishes himself at sea for three years on board HMS *Polyphemus*. Then Black Brandon's ship is sighted. A boarding party led by Harry overcomes Brandon's men. Harry is saved from being stabbed in the back by a shot killing Brandon, his assailant, from a comic tailor hiding in a barrel. Brandon's badly treated slaves are freed, to the accompaniment of a declaration of the 'freedom' and 'justice' believed to be embodied in the Empire, by Hallyard: 'Dance, you black angels, no more captivity; the British flag flies over your head, and the very rustling of its folds knocks every fetter from the limbs of the poor slave'.[64] Following the release of the slaves, Harry takes on an apparently impregnable pirate fortress, single handed, and hoists the Union Jack as it blows up. He returns to Battersea with a fat legacy left him by an admiring officer. Poll and Joe now make their appearance. During Harry's long absence Poll has married Harry's waterman partner, Joe, but Harry and Poll barely have time to get upset before Joe is carried in fatally injured. He gives the rightful union his blessing, and expires.

The romance and excitement of 'Poll' is infectious. Its appeal in waterside communities such as Southwark and Whitechapel in London, and on the dockside in Liverpool and Glasgow, rested on an exaggeration of the role an individual waterside worker or sailor could play in imperial adventures. The tradition reached back to the heroism of Elizabethan sea-dogs such as Drake or Ralegh, rather than forward to the power and responsibility derived from empire-building, which was being celebrated in the sketches and spectacles of the halls catering for a social cross-section. Jack Tar's magnanimity towards the enemy contrasts sharply with the aggression of jingoist entertainment. It was embodied in such recurrent melodrama lines as 'to insult even a foe labouring under misfortune is unworthy the character of an Englishman'.[65] Most importantly, the idea that British rule symbolised freedom is treated quite differently in the two genres. Nautical melodrama had emerged from a 'drama of oppression' which gloried in bringing liberty to the slave in whatever guise or corner of the earth he or she might be found. Patriotism in such drama was embodied in the claim that such liberation was a particularly British mission.[66] Some jingo songs also spoke of the justice and freedom to be found beneath the British flag, but, as we have seen, it was coupled with an assertion of the duty which 'free' colonial populations owed to their Empress in return for the benefits of British rule. There was a major difference in emphasis. In working-class halls the soldiers and sailors whose freedom liberated others were celebrated. In the socially mixed halls the power bestowed on the nation, its Queen and its statesmen, by colonies subjugated through battle, was lauded and justified.

The two different treatments were presented in coexisting halls serving different sections of the population in the 1870s and '80s. But it was claimed by some proprietors that halls presenting melodrama were under attack from several sources in these decades, including their rivals the straight theatres,[67] the licensing authorities, and the local councils whose requirements concerning structural alterations mounted after a Building Regulations Act of 1878. The economics of running a place of entertainment for a single social segment were spelt out at a meeting held by the London County Council in 1889, by Morris Abrahams, manager of the New East London Theatre.[68] Because proprietors like himself had to charge a low admission fee (sixpence at the most) to attract their clientele, and because they opened only two or three times a week, they could not afford the improvements in accommodation insisted on by the authorities and provided by the larger halls. Abrahams' own hall closed in 1897. The Bower Music Hall was shut down earlier, in 1877. City of London Theatre, Bishopsgate closed in 1887, and Astley's, Lambeth, 1893. Few melodrama theatres continued far into the twentieth century. The Britannia, Hoxton closed in 1923, the Surrey, Lambeth in 1921, the Metropole, Glasgow and the Gaiety, Ayr in 1925. They lasted this long by widening their audiences and range of admission prices, as well as by surviving the particular theatrical ecology in which they had to operate.[69]

Nautical and military melodrama was included in the programme of such halls, and also in that of some late nineteenth-century music halls particularly those serving the suburbs. But its character changed. 'Cheer Boys Cheer', written in 1895, is representative. Its heroes and heroines are not ordinary folk, but titled ladies and gentlemen; the lowest rank referred to is that of sergeant, and he plays a minor part. The plot is as follows. The heroine and her party stumble upon a Matabele uprising in South Africa whereupon their Boer guides 'slink off'. Lady Hilyard announces 'We are Englishwomen, sir, and do not fear any danger they would skulk from' and boldly undertakes a night ride to warn the cavalry of the impending danger to a small group of soldiers including the hero. This brave band is attacked in a scene called 'The Last Stand' during which the ammunition runs out, at which point all including the wounded rise to sing 'God Save the Queen'. The Matabele respectfully cease firing as they sing, but in spite of the respite the two rivals for the heroine are the only survivors when the cavalry arrive. The right man lives. The other gallantly expires.[70]

Military spectacle and patriotic expression are infused in 'Cheer Boys Cheer' with a more belligerent nationalism than Harry Hallyard's freeing of black slaves by waving the Union Jack over them. Black 'natives' are now enemies to be coerced under the authority of the 'Great White Mother' and even white men in the far-flung Empire cannot always be trusted, viz. the 'skulking' Boer guides. The image is of Britain beleaguered and defensive.

It could be that events had overtaken the liberating melodramas played in the 1870s. The prolonged Sudan War (1882–98) and the restlessness of the Boers suggested that both black and white inhabitants of some parts of the Empire were not in fact experiencing freedom under the British flag. The contradiction between the ideal of British liberty and the reality of coercion in the maintenance of an empire which undoubtedly brought benefits to British workers in the form of trade and employment, weighed heavily on the minds of some working-class leaders, notably Robert Blatchford, editor of the *Clarion* in the 1900s.[71] But even if the particular interpretation of imperialism embodied in the Jack Tar melodramas was politically outflanked, it is undeniable that it was also eclipsed by the disappearance after 1890 of the majority of the specific halls in which it had been performed.

At the same time that the scripts of the black inhabitants of Empire were being rewritten in melodrama, the role of the blacked-up minstrel on the music-hall stage was changing. Ragged and weird, Jim Crow, originating in the 1840s, was linked with slave life and liberation from it, and lived on in the negro minstrels and slave melodramas performed to working-class audiences in the 1870s.[72] But they were supplanted by another interpretation of the same theme fostered in the socially mixed halls. The beautifully dressed 'coon' personified by G. H. Chirgwin 'The White-eyed Kaffir',

Eugene Stratton, and G. H. Elliott 'The Chocolate-Coloured Coon', became fashionable in the 1880s. He lived in an already liberated land of which he sang in idylls, peopled by smiling coal-black mammies, piccaninnies and faithful Lilies of Laguna, against a background of silv'ry moons, buttermilk and little wooden huts.[73] While in part the image derived from the ending of American slavery by the victory of the North in the American Civil War in 1864, Stratton, Chirgwin, Elliot and others did not pretend to be anything but British. Possibly they represented an idealised future for the British male emigrant to the colonies, be he artisan or administrator.

The numerous nostalgic and romantic songs about emigration may have appealed across classes to an experience common within families in the second half of the nineteenth century, for example Leo Dryden's 'The Miner's Dream of Home', Tom Costello's 'I've made up my mind to sail away' and Fred Barnes' 'Black Sheep of the Family'. The patriotism of these songs was not bombastic or coercive like that of the jingo songs previously quoted, but was above all personal, epitomised by the longing to return 'to my own native land, To my friends and the old folks at home' of 'The Miner's Dream of Home'.[74]

The representation of the ordinary soldier or sailor on the music hall stage, after the disappearance of Jack Tar, marked an elision of this personal patriotism with jingoism. Songs celebrating the heroism of individual soldiers and sailors had traditionally been popular, particularly at times of intensive recruitment of volunteers. For example, while Macdermott roared out 'We've got the men' to mixed audiences in the spring of 1878, 'the men' themselves were singing 'Let me like a Soldier Fall', 'The Soldier's Chorus', 'The Dying Soldier', 'Think of me Darling', 'The Soldier Tired', 'Saved from the Storm' and 'The Tar's Farewell', in class-specific places of entertainment, such as working-men's clubs.[75] But in the 1890s a trio of rather different war songs became popular. In 'Soldiers of the Queen', 'Sons of the Sea' and 'The Absent Minded Beggar', the celebration of the ordinary soldier and sailor was wedded to bombastic indignation that other nations should dare to challenge the time-honoured 'Queen of the Sea'.

'Soldiers of the Queen' was written in 1881 by Leslie Stuart for Albert Christian to sing in the West End halls. Its theme of a sleeping nation awoken by the impudent and dishonourable threats of others echoes spectacles like 'Britannia':

> War clouds gather over every land
> Our treaties threaten'd East and West.
> Nations we've shaken by the hand
> Our honoured pledges try to test.
> They may have thought us sleeping

> Thought us unprepared
> Because we have our party wars
> But Britons all unite
> When they're called to fight
> The battle for old England's common cause.

The chorus then departs from earlier jingo songs in asserting that the common soldier is the maker of the fabric of the Empire:

> So when we say that England's master,
> Remember who has made her so . . .
> It's the soldiers of the Queen, my lads,
> Who've been, my lads, who've seen, my lads,
> In the fight for England's glory, lads,
> Of its world wide glory let us sing.
> And when we say we've always won,
> And when they ask us how it's done
> We'll proudly point to ev'ryone
> Of England's soldiers of the Queen.[76]

In the specific context of the Boer War the song became more widely known. It was sung in and out of music halls and by soldiers in action.[77]

A second song, 'Sons of the Sea', written for Arthur Reece to sing at the Diamond Jubilee in 1897, contains a similar jingoistic contempt for foreign competitors and assertion of national superiority coupled with the celebration of the ordinary sailor:

> Have you heard the talk of foreign pow'rs
> Building ships increasingly?
> Do you know they watch this isle of ours?
> Watch their chance unceasingly?
> Have you heard the millions they will spend
> Strengthening their fleets and why?
> They imagine they can break or bend
> The nation that has often made them fly.
> But one thing we possess, they forget, they forget
> The lads in blue they've met, often met, often met.
> Sons of the Sea! All British born!
> Sailing in ev'ry ocean. Laughing foes to scorn.
> They may build their ships, my lads,
> And they think they know the game,
> But they can't build boys of the bulldog breed
> Who made old England's name.[78]

Thirdly, Rudyard Kipling contributed his own song on the theme of the ordinary man's contribution to imperial defence, 'The Absent Minded Beggar'. Whereas the others quoted were politically generalised, this was specifically located in the issue of the Boer War, and was intended as a fund-raiser for the troops and their families. The stereotype it tried to create was one of the young idealistic Tommy who had dropped everything (including young wives, or possibly girlfriends, with families on the way) to go out and 'hammer Paul' while the rest of the country merely talked about Kruger. It was deliberately populist in the sense of trying to weld together different sections of the population. But like the other two songs, it emphasised the soldier's position as a worker in the Empire. The chorus of the second verse went:

> Cook's son – Duke's son – son of a belted Earl –
> Son of a Lambeth publican – it's all the same today!
> Each of 'em doing his country's work
>   (and who's to look after the girl?)
>   Pass the hat for your credit's sake,
>   and pay-pay-pay.[79]

'Doing his country's work' meant, of course, uncritical participation in a coercive imperial policy. It is not surprising that on hearing such songs in the places of popular entertainment that had become dominant by the time of the Boer War, J. A. Hobson became convinced of the 'inversion' and corruption of working-class patriotism.

Tommy Atkins, who was to the common soldier after 1815 what Jack Tar had been to the sailor since the eighteenth century, became the subject of numerous songs. His first appearance on the popular stage seems to have been in 'A Gaiety Girl', a musical comedy of 1894, performed under George Edwardes' auspices at the Prince of Wales Theatre. The song conjured up a picture of Tommy loyally fighting for the Empire wherever he might be sent:

> And whether he's on India's coral strand,
> Or pouring out his blood in the Soudan,
> To keep our flag aflying, he's a doing and a dying,
> Ev'ry inch of him a soldier and a man.[80]

In the period 1900–18 he was romanticised and, usually, depoliticised. For example, the earlier of two songs entitled 'Tommy Atkins you're all right' (published in 1890) continued the earlier association of the military uniform with virility and sex appeal.

> Tommy Tommy with your heart so big and warm
> Don't he look a picture in his dandy uniform,
> Tommy Atkins all the girls are on your track,
> Tommy, Tommy you're the pride of Union Jack.[81]

The other, written during the First World War, in 1916, sentimentalised Tommy's inevitable separation from his sweetheart, whose parting words were:

> Goodbye Tommy Atkins you can fight on land or sea
> Goodbye Tommy Atkins just send a kiss to me

When you reach old Berlin city give a cheer with all your might.
You are all true blue and we're proud of you.
Tommy Atkins you're all right.[82]

The celebration of the soldier and sailor in these songs was wholly masculine, and if women were visible at all, they were in passive roles, as objects of attraction or as dependants left behind, needing support or waiting for news. The same was true of two other widely-sung sentimental war songs of the time, 'Break the News to Mother' (1898) and 'Goodbye Dolly Gray' (1900).[83] Women had been given a more active role in melodrama. They were frequently depicted as adventurers themselves, prepared to don male disguises in order to accompany their loved ones in the rigours of 'life on the ocean wave',[84] a tradition not forgotten, as we have seen, in Lady Hilyard's heroism in the melodrama 'Cheer Boys Cheer'.

The spirited young woman patriot did make an appearance on the music-hall stage, though now she put on men's clothing not as a disguise that was part of the act, but as an impersonation. The earliest was probably Bessie Bonehill, who sang 'Here Stands a Post' by the patriotic songwriter, Clement Scott, and 'The Old Tattered Flag', dressed as a sailor boy and with a war-scarred Union Jack as her main prop.[85] Bonehill, who performed in the 1870s and '80s belonged in the 'principal boy' pantomime tradition of women being better equipped to play boys than boys themselves. In the 1900s a trio of women presented full grown men 'in miniature', and two in particular, Vesta Tilley and Hetty King, chose military or naval dress as their favourite style. The preoccupation of their best known songs, 'Jolly good Luck to the Girl Who Loves a Soldier' first sung by Tilley in 1907, and 'All the Nice Girls Love a Sailor' sung by King in 1909, was not with the objectives of military or naval power, whether liberation or domination, but with the life and physical attractions of the soldier or sailor as such.[86] In these songs patriotism was completely personal, wholly invested in the individual represented, and it was thereby free of jingoism, if not of racism (e.g. 'And you can trust a sailor, He's a white man all the while').[87] It was said to be their close observation and careful portrayal of the uniform and mannerisms of servicemen of different ranks and regiments, coupled with the romance and curiously inverted sex appeal with which they imbued the role, which earned the male impersonators their popularity.[88] More significantly, perhaps, such performances allowed these women to step across the sexual divide of Edwardian society into the male preserve of militarism, now such a vital facet of imperialism. Their unusual genre (*female* impersonators have been much more common in popular entertainment) serves to underline the masculine identity of late Victorian and Edwardian popular imperialism.

Throughout the period 1870–1914 there was also a strand of comic patriotism in music hall songs, which in some cases bordered on satire, though always of a light-hearted kind. For example, in 1878 Henry Pettitt guyed Hunt's 'By Jingo' in the following song, sung by Herbert Campbell.

> Newspapers talk of Russian hate
> Of its ambition tell,
> Of course they want a war because
> It makes the papers sell.
> Let all the politicians
> Who desire to help the Turk
> Put on the uniform themselves
> And go and do the work.
> I don't want to fight
> I'll be slaughtered if I do,
> I'll change my togs, I'll sell my kit,
> I'll pop my rifle too,
> I don't like the war, I ain't a Briton true
> And I'll let the Russians have Constantinople.[89]

Campbell performed at some of the same halls as Macdermott. One can only speculate about how audiences responded to Campbell's apparent rejection of jingoism. It was, of course, part of music-hall tradition to unite opposites in a single bill, by for example including the toff songs of a 'lion comique' with songs celebrating the misfortunes of working-class life, like Marie Lloyd's 'My Old Man said Follow the Van', and it is possible that, aware that Macdermott's song was strongly partisan, proprietors may have included Campbell's song to appease those in the mixed audience who did not care for 'By Jingo'. In any case, Campbell made a speciality of 'take offs' of successful songs.[90] Further, audiences may have understood and appreciated the professional rivalry which had prompted Pettitt's parody. He had written one of Macdermott's earlier successes, 'If Ever there was a Damned Scamp', but thereafter received no commissions.[91] Lastly, while Pettitt's song is anti- jingo, it laughs as much at the character who is going to pawn his rifle because he does not want to be slaughtered, as at the newspapers and politicians who are keen on creating war. It does not strike a blow at imperialism, and it is a send-up rather than a critique of militarism.

In comparison, the satire of broadside ballads published earlier in the century was more incisive, a point which Laurence Senelick's research supports. For example, the songs 'Ben Battle' and 'Thirteen Pence a Day', both published as broadside ballads, were sung at working-class free-and-easies and saloons between 1800 and 1860. 'Thirteen Pence a Day' was an ironic exhortation to young men to enlist:

> Come and be a soldier lads, march, march, away.
> Don't you hear the fife and drum, march, march, away.

Come to the battlefield make the enemy to yield,
Come and lose your eyes and limbs, for thirteen pence a day.

In the song the audience is told that the real meaning of 'honour' and 'glory' is that you must shoot 'men you never knew, who never did you harm', that you will have no alternative but to forget your wives and children 'when you're dead and rotten', and that it is the height of foolishness 'to fight for kings and queens'.[92] In contrast, Alfred Lester's 'Conscientious Objector's Lament' and Wilkie Bard's 'When the Bugle Calls', written between 1870 and 1900 do not contain any critique of power and its consequences, but merely send up natural cowardice. For example Bard's chorus goes:

When the bugle calls we shall march to war
And there's not a man will fear it.
I don't care how soon the bugle calls
So long as – I don't hear it.

In similar vein Lester's song contains the verse:

Call out the Boys of the Old Brigade,
Who made old England free.
Call out my mother, my sister and my brother
But for God's sake don't send me.[93]

Another parody, written by Major H. Corbyn during the Boer War and apparently popular with the troops, develops the same theme:

Riding in the ammunition van,
Amidst the shot and shell I've been.
While my comrades fought,
(As comrades ought)
I was nowhere to be seen.
I was covered over with the Flag,
Listening to the din and strife
When the fight was o'er, out once more,
And that's how I saved my life.[94]

In this, as in the others, the keynote is that England's power is justified and war is right (comrades 'ought' to fight), but that there is humour in the understandable desire to avoid it. Many of the songs popular with the troops both in outposts of Empire and also in Flanders in the First World War, celebrated and consoled ordinary soldiers and sailors in a not dissimilar way, treating patriotism with humour rather than with the serious sentiment characteristic of jingo songs. 'It's a long way to Tipperary' is one of the best known.[95] First sung in 1912 as the tale of an Irishman's visit to London, it was revived on the music-hall stage by Florrie Ford as a marching song in 1914. As Christopher Pulling points out, it was the line 'Good-bye, Piccadilly; Farewell, Leicester Square' which appealed to the

troops, 'the majority of whom cared little how far it was to Tipperary'.[96]
'Pack Up Your Troubles' sung by Florrie Ford and published in 1918, is one
of the most obviously consoling, concerning the diminutive Private Perks
'with his smile – his funny smile', whose role in Flanders and at home is to
urge his fellows to:

> Pack up your troubles in your old kit bag, and smile, smile, smile, –
> While you've a lucifer to light your fag,
> Smile, boys, that's the style, –
> What's the use of worrying?
> It never was worth while, So
> Pack up your troubles in your old kit bag, and smile, smile, smile.[97]

Underlying the comforting good cheer is a message counselling political
apathy.

The jingoist content of a song about Tommy Atkins written in 1917 is
relatively unusual. 'Tommy Atkins saved his Empire from the Hun'
celebrates the individual Tommy, 'the man behind the bay'net and the gun',
who will defend the Empire 'till his numbers fall to "nil" ', and also asserts
imperial unity: Australia and Canada are depicted as coming forward
willingly to help.[98] This song harks back, through 'Sons of the Sea' and
'Soldiers of the Queen' to the jingo spectacles of the 1880s, while admitting
more than they do the grimness and carnage involved in defending the
Empire. It is possible that this song was more popular with those
experiencing war vicariously at home, than with servicemen themselves,
during the First World War.[99] Several authors suggest that there was a
growing dislike of any form of patriotic entertainment among the troops.
Peter Honri writes:

'Tommy-on-leave' wanted above all else to see glamour – light and colour and girls.
'If you were the only girl in the world', as sung by George Robey and Violet Loraine,
provided for those who were on a few hours' leave from the horrors of the trenches
the escapism they sought'.[100]

In this context the commercial success of pre-war developments like the
revue and the bioscope was assured.

What can one conclude from this discussion of the versions of
imperialism presented in places of popular entertainment in the late
nineteenth and early twentieth centuries? One is confronted not with a
linear development, but with interaction between different genres embodied
in changing institutions. However, some periodisation is possible. The
nautical, military and slave melodramas played to working-class audiences
largely disappeared with the institutions in which they had been performed,
after 1890. All the same, some elements of melodrama carried on, through
the 'coons', and the soldiers and sailors of music hall and theatre of variety.
What was lost was the message that the goal of British power was freedom.

Instead the virtuous British serviceman was either a jingo shouldering the responsibilities of Empire in sketches and revues of the 1880s and 1890s or he was a humorous hero in comic patriotic songs of the 1900s and the First World War. There was no anti-imperialism. Criticism was muted; parodies were self mocking.

What can one say about the audiences which watched these types of entertainment? The development towards a 'mass' audience, in the sense of a socially mixed rather than homogeneous one was extremely important.[101] With it went fewer opportunities for audiences to participate in, and actually shape, the performances played to them. Accommodated in fixed seating at graded prices they were expected to watch, applaud, and at the most to join in the occasional chorus, a tendency reinforced by the advent of the sketch, the revue and, ultimately, film. Of course proprietors had to take into account as a matter of commercial reality what those paying to go to music halls or theatres of variety indicated they liked. But this was not a simple issue, since proprietors were investing in entertainment which had to appeal to the different elements comprising mixed audiences, and in addition they had to take into account the preference of the licensing authorities for the avoidance of political debate after 1890. Uncritical support for the monarch, the Empire and the government of the day was not, however, considered 'political'. Choice of such themes was reinforced by the fact that proprietors of large halls, such as those represented by the Music Hall Proprietors' Protection Society, were themselves inclined towards conservatism, a political position reinforced by their opposition both to temperance, a liberal cause, and more specifically to Liberal or Radical local authorities whose attempts to curb music halls represented a threat to their investments.

The prohibition on political debate on the music hall stage, in addition to the need to strike a compromise with the mixed audience, may help to explain why, by the time of the First World War, the focus of the patriotic songs of the music-hall and theatre-of-variety stage had shifted away from power as an abstract concept. It may inadvertently have muted jingoism, as well as stifling criticism. It was more acceptable all round to focus on the everyday life and virility of servicemen, than to celebrate them as pillars of the Empire. However the commercial success of the patriotic themes which proprietors, song writers and artists selected from the strands of tradition here described during the period 1870–1914, does not support Senelick's view that there was a decline in music hall's political influence, nor does it betoken the 'indifference' towards Empire which Price attributed to the working class during the Boer War. On the contrary it suggests that patriotism and Empire continued to be highly marketable products in the world of popular entertainment, for all that the packaging changed over time.

Notes

1 The source of the quote is W. J. MacQueen-Pope, *The Melodies Linger On: The Story of Music Hall*, London 1950, 185. Rudyard Kipling was, of course, one of these who approved of music-hall patriotism. See *Something of Myself for my friends known and unknown*, London 1937.

2 J. A. Hobson, *The Psychology of Jingoism*, London, 1901, 1, 3, 9, 3.

3 Richard Price, *An Imperial War and the British Working Class: Working-class Attitudes and Reactions to the Boer War 1899–1902*, London 1972, 176.

4 Price, *An Imperial War*, and Richard N. Price, 'Society, status and jingoism: the social roots of lower middle class patriotism, 1870–1900', in G. Crossick (ed.), *The Lower Middle Class in Britain 1870–1914*, London 1977.

5 Price, *An Imperial War*, 175, n. 150; Price, 'Society, status and jingoism', 95.

6 Price, *An Imperial War*, 238–9.

7 Hugh St Claire Cunningham, 'British public opinion and the eastern question 1877–1878; University of Sussex DPhil, 1969, 245; see also Henry Pelling, *Popular Politics and Society in Late Victorian Britain*, London 1968, 87–8.

8 Laurence Senelick, 'Politics as entertainment: Victorian music hall songs', *Victorian Studies*, XIX, No. 2, December 1975, 156 and 180.

9 Senelick, 'Politics as entertainment', 155 and 180.

10 For a more detailed discussion of the development of music hall, see Penelope Summerfield, 'The Effingham Arms and the Empire: deliberate selection in the evolution of music hall in London', in Eileen and Stephen Yeo (eds), *Popular Culture and Class Conflict 1590–1914*, Sussex 1981.

11 *Halsbury's Statutes of England*, ed. Burrows, 2nd edn., London 1951, XXV, 14–17.

12 Paul Sheridan, *Penny Theatres of Victorian London*, London 1981, 3, 12.

13 Maurice Willson Disher, *Blood and Thunder: Mid-Victorian Melodrama and its Origins*, London 1949, 59.

14 John Adams, *Letter to the Justices of the Peace in the County of Middlesex on the subject of licences for Public Music and Dancing*, 25 Geo ii c 36, London 1850, 17–19.

15 See Summerfield, 'The Effingham Arms', 214–18.

16 See for example 'Report of a Conference between the Theatres and Music Halls Committee of the London County Council and a deputation of Managers of Theatres and Music Halls held . . . 20 November 1889' in LCC Theatre and Music Halls Committee, 'Minutes', II, Oct. 1889–June 1890, Greater London Council Archive; House of Commons Select Committee on Theatres and Places of Entertainment, *Report*, 1892.

17 J. G. Mellor, *The Northern Music Hall*, Newcastle upon Tyne 1970; Felix Barker, *The House that Stoll Built: The story of the Coliseum Theatre*, London 1957. *The Encore*, 23 October 1902, 6, noted that Manchester justices tended to refuse licences to 'halls other than legitimate variety halls'.

18 B. S. Rowntree and G. R. Lavers, *English Life and Leisure: a social study* London 1951, 259.

19 Sheridan, *Penny Theatres*, 54, 50–2; Summerfield, 'The Effingham Arms', 214–16.

20 Sources for prices of entry here and *infra* are playbills of the halls in question unless otherwise stated. New Gaiety, Preston, see Peter Honri, *Working the Halls*, Saxon House, Hants 1973, 28–33. Two reference books, Diana Howard, *London Theatres and Music Halls 1850–1950*, Library Association,

London 1970 and L. Senelick, D. F. Cheshire and U. Schneider, *British Music Hall 1840–1923*, Conn. 1981, provide information on the location of collections of playbills.

21 Clive Barker 'The audiences of the Britannia Theatre, Hoxton', *Theatre Quarterly*, IX, summer 1979, 31, 34.

22 Harold Scott, *The Early Doors*, London 1946, Chap. VIII; Canterbury playbills.

23 F. N. Charrington, *The Battle of the Music Halls*, London 1885.

24 See, for example, F. Anstey, 'London music halls', *Harpers Monthly Magazine*, XXI, 1891, quoted by Senelick, 'Politics as Entertainment', 154. For evidence which supports the idea of multi-class audiences at halls with a wide range of admission prices see J. E. Ritchie, *The Night Side of London*, London 1858, 69–70 and 218; Dion Clayton Calthrop, *Music Hall Nights* London 1925, 2–3.

25 Typically prices reached down to 6*d* or 3*d*, but went no higher than 10*s* 6*d*. See, for example, prices of entry quoted on the playbills of Woolwich Hippodrome 1899, Kilburn Empire 1912, Holloway Empire 1901 and the Empress, Brixton 1900. Evidence on the composition of audiences at such halls can be found in Charles Booth, *Life and Labour of the People in London*, London 1902, final volume, 54, and *The Sketch*, 14 August 1907. See also Peter Bailey, *Leisure and Class in Victorian England: Rational Recreation and the contest for control 1830–1885*, London 1978, 154–6.

26 Barker, 'The audiences of the Britannia', 36, 38–9.

27 J. E. Ritchie, *The Night Side of London*, London 1858, 70 and new edition, revised and enlarged, London 1869, 232.

28 In an earlier piece of research on London music halls, 'The imperial idea and the music hall', University of Sussex BA dissertation, 1973, I referred to halls attracting a social cross-section as 'Category A', later suburban developments with a more limited mix as 'Category B', and exclusively working-class places of entertainment as 'Category C'. I have chosen here not to represent the three categories in this way, which I now regard as clumsy, but simply to describe the type of hall I am discussing. Douglas Reid's work can be found in David Bradby *et al.* (eds), *Performance and Politics in Popular Drama*, Cambridge 1980.

29 John M. Robertson, *Patriotism and Empire*, London 1899, e.g. 138: 'Patriotism, conventionally defined as love of country, now turns out rather more obviously to stand for love of more country'.

30 See L. C. B. Seaman, *Victorian England: Aspects of English and Imperial History 1837–1901*, London 1973, 210–19.

31 G. W. Hunt, *Macdermott's War Song*, London *c*. 1875. The real motive behind threatening Russia with war is unblushingly declared in verse two: 'Of carnage and of trickery they'll have sufficient feast, / Ere they dare to think of coming near our Road unto the East'.

32 MacQueen-Pope, *The Melodies Linger On*, 416. (H. Chance Newton, *Idols of the 'Halls': Being My Music Hall Memories*, Wakefield 1975, 81, claims Macdermott paid only one guinea for the song.)

33 MacQueen-Pope, *The Melodies Linger On*, 318–19.

34 J. B. Booth, *The Days we Knew*, London 1943, 36.

35 *East London Observer*, April 20–June 1, 1878; Mellor, *The Northern music Hall*, 49, 58–9; MacQueen-Pope, *The Melodies Linger On*, 319.

36 Booth, *The Days We Knew*, 36; Scott, *The Early Doors*, 170; MacQueen-Pope, *The Melodies Linger On*, 319.

37 Christopher Pulling, *They Were Singing And What They sang about*, London 1952, 185; Booth, *The Days We Knew*, 36.

38 MacQueen-Pope, *The Melodies Linger On*, 185.

39 Oxford Playbill, July 1878; Clement Scott, 'True Blues, Stand to Your Guns', quoted by Peter Davison, 'A Briton True? A short account of patriotic songs and verse as popular entertainment', *Alta, The University of Birmingham Review*, II, spring 1970, 214.

40 *The Oxford, A Weekly Musical and Dramatic Record*, 27 February 1871.

41 Alhambra Programme, February 1872.

42 On Victorian renderings of 'Rule Britannia' see Davison, 'A Briton True?', 216. He argues that slight changes in the punctuation and wording of the song during 'Victorian times' made the song 'assertive' rather than 'hortative'.

43 Canterbury programmes, 1871–80.

44 H. Clendon and H. Nicholls, 'It's all explained in this', London 1882.

45 George Le Brunn and Wal Pink, 'The Seventh Royal Fusiliers, A Story of Inkerman', London 1892.

46 G. W. Hunt, 'If England to Herself be True', *The Oxford*, January 1879.

47 'Britannia, an entirely new and original entertainment, written and produced by Paul Valentine, music by William Corri', Oxford Programme, 24 October 1885.

48 British Sessional Papers, House of Commons, *Minutes of Proceedings of the Colonial Conference*, 1887, 5. Address by the Marquis of Salisbury, Prime Minister.

49 Honri, *Working the Halls*, 67, explains the investment in this type of sketch.

50 Alhambra Programmes, 1880–1900.

51 Empire Programmes, 1890–1902.

52 Empire Programme, 3 November 1902.

53 Quoted by Booth, *The Days We Knew*, 39. I have been unable to trace this song in the British Library Music Catalogue, and therefore cannot give the date of publication.

54 A song in 'Indianationality', entitled 'Boy's Coker Nut Song', contained the following verse:

> When Sahib beat Bengalee man, Ohey, Ohey O!
> He catch it warm from cane rattan, Ohey, Ohey O!
> When Sahib give Bengalee pice,
> He fill him full of curry and rice.
> And then he go to sleep so nice.
> When the moon shines down.

The Oxford, January 1879.

55 See, for example, G. W. Hunt, 'The Time is Coming', London 1885; G. Le Brunn and F. C. Smale, 'Kruger's Dinner Party; or we'll be there' London 1899.

56 Honri, *Working the Halls*, 154 for an explanation of 'revue'.

57 House of Commons Select Committee on Theatres and Places of Entertainment, *Report*, 1892, Appendix 3.

58 Honri, *Working the Halls*, 187.

59 Maurice Willson Disher, *Blood and Thunder: Mid-Victorian Melodrama and its Origins*, London 1949, 53–4.

60 Michael R. Booth, *English Melodrama*, London, 1965, 93.

61 Bower Music Hall Playbills 1870–77.

62 Pavilion Playbills, 1878: *East London Observer*, weekly advertisements 1870,

1878; Sheridan, *Penny Theatres*, 90, Daniel Farson, *Marie Lloyd and Music Hall*, London 1972, 31.

63   Michael Booth (ed.), *Hiss the Villain: Six English and American Melodramas*, London 1964, 87–144.

64   Booth, *Hiss the Villain*, 122.

65   Booth, *English Melodrama*, 100.

66   Willson Disher, *Blood and Thunder*, 109 and 155. Davison, 'A Briton True?', 213–14, quotes some early nineteenth-century street ballads which contain the same ethos, e.g. 'Albion's Isle' (1826): 'The poor wretched slave is unshackled and free / The moment he touches our land'. Senelick, 'Politics as entertainment', 152 suggests that street ballads were overtaken commercially by collections of songs printed cheaply for use in saloons, and by the subsequent tendency for songwriters to sell their songs to specific artists.

67   See for example Clifford Musgrave, *Life in Brighton From Earliest Times to the Present*, London, 1970, 305–11, on the struggle between Ginnet's Hippodrome, Brighton, and the Theatre Royal.

68   LCC Theatre and Music Halls Committee, 'Minutes', II, Report of a Conference . . ., 20 November 1889, 17.

69   For dates of closure of London theatres see Howard, *London Threatres and Music Halls*. On Glasgow see Mellor, *The Northern Music Hall*, 50 and 55.

70   Booth, *English Melodrama*, 174.

71   Laurence Thompson, *Robert Blatchford, Portrait of an Englishman*, London 1951, 210. Blatchford wrote, in 1908: '. . . imperialism without militarism is impossible. Without arms you cannot hold the dominant place in an armed world. You cannot rob other people and hold the loot by means of sermons on brotherhood and prayers for peace . . . I am a Little Englander . . . But I recognise that to lose the Empire, to be attacked and defeated, would be a bloody, a ruinous and horrible business.'

72   Willson Disher, *Blood and Thunder*, 106–9, 153–5, 244–53.

73   See Pulling, *They were Singing*, 203–4.

74   Will J. Godwin, 'The Miner's Dream of Home', London 1891; Bennett Scott, 'I've Made Up My Mind to Sail Away', Francis and Day's Musical Bon-Bons, No. 24, 1902; Fred Davis, 'Black Sheep of the Family', quoted by Colin MacInnes, *Sweet Saturday Night: Pop Song 1840–1920*, London 1969, 61. This contained the words 'I'll go out to the colonies, / And there I'll rise or fall . . . / And when I come back, / The sheep that was black / Will perhaps be the whitest sheep of all'.

75   *East London Observer*, notices on 9 February 1878, 5 January 1878, 2 March 1878 referring to 7th Tower Hamlets Rifle Volunteers' Entertainment, Bow and Bromley Institute and Hackney Club and Institute.

76   Leslie Stuart, 'Soldiers of the Queen', London 1896. This is the earliest edition held in the British Library. Pulling, *They Were Singing*, 79, says Stuart wrote it in 1881.

77   Pulling, *They Were Singing*, 79. It was later included in Noel Coward's 'Cavalcade', London 1931, which perpetuated its fame; Lewis Winstock, *Songs and Music of the Redcoats, A History of War Music of the British Army 1642–1902*, London 1970, 252, attests to the popularity of the song among the troops.

78   Felix MacGlennon, 'Sons of the Sea', London 1897.

79   Arthur Sullivan, 'The Absent Minded Beggar', words by Rudyard Kipling, facsimile edition, London 1899.

80   Sidney Jones, 'Private Tommy Atkins' in 'A Gaiety Girl', libretto and lyrics by

Harry Greenbank; London 1894. Rudyard Kipling's poem 'Tommy' preceded this by two years. 'O' it's 'Tommy this an' Tommy that, an' Tommy, go away'; / But it's 'Thank you, Mister Atkins', when the band begins to play'. The use of the phrase dates from 1815 when 'Thomas Atkins was the name used in the specimen form, accompanying the official manual issued to all army recruits, supplied to show them how their own form requiring details of name, age, date of enlistment, etc., should be filled in'. See *Brewer's Dictionary of Phrase and Fable* London 1981, 1124.

81 George M. Cohan, 'Tommy Atkins You're All Right', New York 1908. Another similar song is J. R. Hall, 'Tommy Atkins', London 1918.

82 Dick Coleman, 'Tommy Atkins You're All Right', 1916. See also George S. Hyde and Miriam K. Flynn, 'Tommy Atkins Good-bye', Framington, Mass. 1915, which is on the same theme but has even fewer references to Tommy Atkins' actual political circumstances.

83 Charles K. Harris, 'Break the News to Mother', Toronto 1898; Paul Barnes, 'Good-bye Dolly Gray', words by W. D. Cobb, Toronto 1900–1: 'I have come to say goodbye, Dolly Gray. / It's no use to ask me why, Dolly Gray. / There's a murmur in the air / you can hear it ev'ry where, / It is time to do and dare, Dolly Gray.'

84 Willson Disher, *Blood and Thunder*, 59–60.

85 W. C. Levey, 'Here Stands a Post', words by Clement Scott, London 1878; J. MacNicoll and J. Harrington Young, 'The Old Tattered Flag', London 1887.

86 Kenneth Lyle, 'Jolly Good Luck to the Girl who loves a Soldier!', words by Fred W. Leigh, London 1907. MacQueen Pope, *The Melodies Linger On*, 202 and Pulling, *They Were Singing*, 80, confusingly attribute the song to Tilley's husband, Walter de Frece. Tilley glamorised the soldier in an even more pressing way in Leslie Stuart's song 'I want to be a Military Man', London 1914. 'Oh the man that's dressed as usual / Is out of it today / For a regular dandy man / No single woman cares / She won't look upon your suit, or you, / I've heard the worldly say / Till you've donned the garb that Tommy Atkins wears . . . *Refrain*: I want to join the military-tary / I've got no chance with Jane or Flo or Mary; / I want to hear the martial rat-a-plan / I want to be a military man'. Bennett Scott, 'Ship Ahoy' (All the Nice Girls Love a Sailor) words by A. J. Mills, London 1909.

87 Scott, 'Ship Ahoy'.

88 Farson, *Marie Lloyd*, 139–43.

89 Henry Pettitt, 'I ain't a Briton True', quoted by Davison, 'A Briton True?', 216. He dates it 1878.

90 For example, Campbell's version of 'The Miner's Dream of Home' tells how 'pa was boozing nightly and his mother was shifting the gin, / while the lodger was taking the old gal out and the old man in'. Quoted by MacQueen-Pope, *The Melodies Linger On*, 320.

91 See MacQueen-Pope, *The Melodies Linger On*, 318–19 and Davison, 'A Briton True?', 216. W. H. Hunt later wrote a song for Campbell with a title that was possibly intentionally ironic: 'Serve Him Right! or a Good Job Too', London 1882.

92 Charles Chilton, *Victorian Folk Songs*, London 1965, 86–7. For 'Ben Battle' see 92–3. Unfortunately Chilton edited the songs and does not state the original sources.

93 Both these songs are quoted by Pulling, *They Were Singing*, 80 and 81.

94 Major H. Corbyn, 'Riding in the Ammunition Van', quoted by Winstock, *Songs and Music of the British Redcoats*, 242.

95 Jack Judge and Harry Williams, 'It's a Long, Long Way to Tipperary', London 1912.

96 Pulling, *They Were Singing*, 81.

97 Felix Powell, 'Pack Up Your Troubles in Your Old Kit Bag', words by G. Asaf, New York 1918.

98 Charles Barnard, 'Tommy Atkins saved his Empire from the Hun', London 1917.

99 The same must surely be true of 'Tommy's Army' by A. W. Marchant, Philadelphia 1915, about one hundred 'little lead soldiers, gallant and true': 'I'd like to be a soldier / And wear the red and blue, / I suppose the shots don't hurt as much / As people say they do'.

100 Honri, *Working the Halls*, 154. See also Pulling, *They Were Singing*, 82.

101 All the same, the extent of social mixing may have varied greatly, as between theatres of variety in the heart of large cities like London, Liverpool, Manchester and Glasgow, and those in their suburbs, in spite of the consistency of the policy developed by the proprietors of theatre chains. This is obviously an area needing more research.

CHAPTER 3

'UP GUARDS AND AT THEM!' BRITISH IMPERIALISM AND POPULAR ART, 1880–1914

John Springhall

Historians who attempt to interpret the incredible expansion of Europe overseas in the late nineteenth century and after have concentrated largely on unromantic political and economic factors. The fundamental causes of the new imperialism have been located in the demand for raw materials, the availability of surplus capital for overseas investment or in the stirrings of an emergent nationalism. Among such weighty historical factors, little attention has been paid until recently to those forces which John Hobson believed were responsible for imperialism's successful hold on the public imagination: 'hero-worship and sensational glory, adventure and the sporting spirit: current history falsified in coarse flaring colours, for the direct stimulation of the combative instincts'. If the idea of Empire was to be sold to the great British public, in other words, then the propaganda appeal of lonely exploration along African rivers, of missionaries converting the heathen or, more importantly, of heroic military exploits, was obviously far greater than that of shareholders investing capital in chartered companies or of politicians haggling with rival powers over treaty boundaries. It was no accident that the 'little wars' of Empire, which took place in almost every year of Queen Victoria's reign after 1870, provided the most readily available source for magazine and newspaper editors of romantic adventure and heroism set in an exotic and alien environment. For these small-scale military campaigns remind us that imperialism was not merely a matter of trade and diplomacy but also meant the recurrent forcible and bloody suppression of largely ineffectual native resistance. 'Imperial powers used force more often than they have been prepared to admit', as D. A. Low remarked twenty years ago.[1]

These decades saw a succession of brilliant and not so brilliant imperial campaigns, against Zulus, Ashanti, Afghans, Boers, Burmese and Sudanese, which made popular heroes of generals such as Wolseley, Buller and

Roberts, and immortalised Tommy Atkins. The prestige of the British Army was probably higher than at any time before or since and military values became mandatory for all young Englishmen. 'The belief in war as a test of national power and a proof of national superiority added a scientific base to the cult of patriotism', argues Zara Steiner in discussing the origins of the First World War. 'In Britain a real effort was made to teach boys that success in war depended upon the patriotism and military spirit of the nation and that preparation for war would strengthen "manly virtue" and "patriotic ardour".' It was the cultural and intellectual world of the 1880s and 1890s, the golden age of the war correspondent and war artist, which, subsequently popularised, formed the outlook of the pre-1914 generation of schoolteachers, army officers and Scoutmasters. Thus the large-scale paintings of colonial warfare, associated with Lady Elizabeth Butler and Richard Caton Woodville, and the sketches of the 'specials' or war artists, such as Melton Prior and Frederic Villiers, will be discussed here as representative types of a British popular art which gave cultural expression to and reflected imperialism in politics. Lack of space unfortunately prohibits the analysis of other popular art forms, such as commercial advertising, school text book illustrations, postcards, cigarette cards, cheap reproductions and other ephemera which appropriated and mediated the work of the artists mentioned above. It is essential to the argument of this essay that the popular art of the period needs to be placed in the context of a heroic and romantic vision of Empire which helped to widen the appeal of British imperialism and which newspaper and magazine editors, often contrary to the wishes of the artists themselves, insisted on communicating to the new mass reading public.[2]

'You're sent out when a war begins, to minister to the blind, brutal, British public's bestial thirst for blood', the war artist Dick Heldar accuses the Nilghai, a famous war correspondent modelled on Archibald Forbes, in Rudyard Kipling's first novel, *The Light That Failed*, written in 1890: 'they have no arenas now but they must have special correspondents.' Removed from later editions of the novel, these sentences convey the youthful Kipling's cynicism about the relationship between war reporting and the demands of the public at home, avid for news of the latest campaign in some remote but colourful corner of the Empire. Yet, if the expansion of Empire provided steady employment for the war artist, the tradition of war reporting had become firmly established in the British press since the Crimean War days of William Howard Russell and George Alfred Henty. In the decades that followed the British newspaper reading public viewed the mass of 'little wars' that pepper the history of British imperial expansion, and hence most of what little they knew about the struggles and meaning of Empire, almost entirely through the eyes of war correspondents and the war artists who accompanied them. Their importance in popularising the Army and its imperial role cannot be denied. 'Newspapers were quick to appreciate the value of reporting "small wars" to a semi-literate reading public likely to be interested in sensational fare, and these campaigns were sufficiently remote for the public to be able to view them almost as a form of entertainment', suggests a recent commentator. War was a highly profitable experience for the popular artists employed by the illustrated weeklies and they eagerly purveyed romance and adventure to the public serving, as the author-correspondent Vincent Sheean put it, 'as professional observers at the peep show of misery'. Since the misery they were observing was usually that of natives or foreigners at the wrong end of the Maxim gun, it did not really matter all that much to the readers at home.[3]

Between 1882–8 and again in 1898, Egypt and the Sudan, on which the attention of this essay will be focused, drew scores of correspondents and war artists, providing a stream of incidents for the chroniclers and portrayers of patriotic adventure, including a list of exotic sounding battles: Tel-el-Kebir, Abu Klea, Tamai, Abu Kru, El Teb and, much later, Omdurman. When the British Army arrived in Egypt in the early summer of 1882 to put down the nationalist revolt of Arabi Pasha that threatened British domination of the Suez Canal, Frederic Villiers (1852–1922) was thirty, a special artist for the *Graphic* who had gained his apprenticeship as a war reporter and artist in the Balkans, where the renowned and irascible correspondent Archibald Forbes (1838–1900) was his mentor. Between the Serbo-Turkish War in 1876 and the first Balkan War in 1912, Villiers served in no less than fifteen conflicts, most of them the 'little wars' of Empire. He drew most frequently for the *Graphic*, which from 1869 challenged the famous *Illustrated London News* (ILN), the original (1842) British illustrated paper. Both papers were too costly at sixpence a week to be bought by the working class but were widely read by a large middle-class reading public. Villiers was stocky and self-confident, with waxed moustaches, a neatly trimmed beard and the permanent air of a ruffled angry bantam. His personality was distinctly theatrical, a terrible poseur who did much to perpetuate his own legend, he delighted in lecturing on his exploits as a war artist in full campaign uniform and medals. *The Times* thought him an artist of only moderate ability and his figure drawing was certainly weak but 'he was one of the most prolific and ubiquitous of the old school of war

---

Overleaf – (*a*) Melton Prior's eye-witness sketch 'Storming the trenches of Tel-el-Kebir', which appeared in the *Illustrated London News* on 14 October 1882, a month after the battle, as a 'facsimile of a sketch by our special artist'. (*b*) Richard Caton Woodville's worked-up drawing of Prior's original, engraved as a woodblock entitled 'Battle of Tel-el-Kebir: the charge at the bayonet's point', from the *Illustrated London News* of 7 October 1882. By courtesy of the Illustrated London News Picture Library.

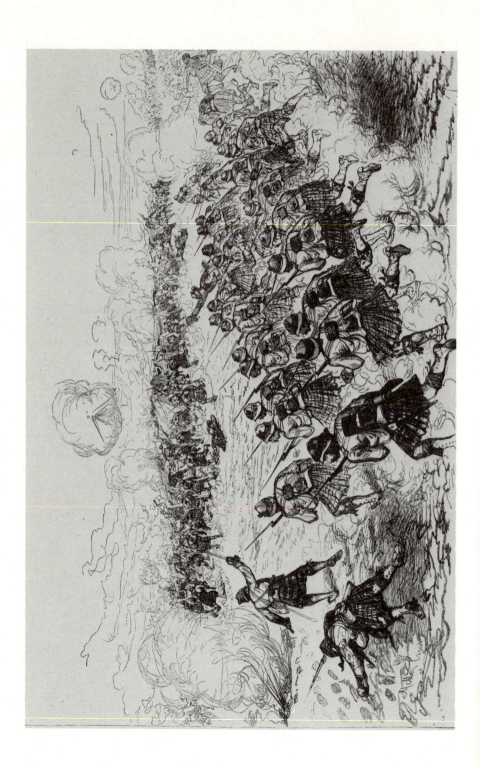

correspôndents and he always carried with him into the lecture room that air of the swashbuckler which was at one time considered the correct comportment for the soldier of the pen'. Villiers lived long enough to see the First World War, trying vainly to function as an artist on the Western Front until his spirit was broken by War Office restrictions and censorship.[4]

Villiers' most redoubtable and experienced rival in Egypt was the thirty-seven year-old Melton Prior (1845–1910), representing the *ILN*, the leading special artist in the great age of war illustrators, who eventually covered at least a dozen colonial campaigns all over the world. Prior, the son of a landscape painter and illustrator, was short, tubby, energetic and businesslike, with side whiskers and spectacles that gave him an avuncular appearance belied by his ruthless pursuit of a story and success as a quick-fire artist. His speech never lost a certain roughness, presumably picked up from following the army, and his shrill laugh and bald head won him the nickname of the 'screeching billiard ball'. Prior began working for the *ILN* in 1868 and five years later was sent to cover the Ashanti war in West Africa where he first started sketching under fire. He followed all the campaigns in Egypt and the Sudan, except Omdurman, and was besieged in Ladysmith during the Boer War, ending his career at the Russo-Japanese War of 1904–5. During his adventurous career, he spent only the whole of one year (1883) at home. His last overseas assignment in Tokyo deeply depressed him because of the Japanese refusal to allow access to the fighting front. 'I fear that I must own that at last I am sick and sick of this campaign, just as all the other correspondents are,' he confided to his diary on 20 August 1904. Prior returned to England from Japan full of gloom about the future of his calling and died, aged sixty-five, in 1910. He had a keen eye for the dramatic situation and his pencil drawings are remarkably detailed and convincing. The 'specials' like Prior developed their own brand of adventure story disguised as news, with themselves often cast as the heroes in the events they portrayed or, on occasion, wrote about. During the Boer War, Prior became – after the leading generals and popular heroes like Baden-Powell – the most portrayed character of the war in the pages of the *ILN*. Villiers and Prior were certainly among the last of the great figures among the ranks of the special artists who, from the 1870s to the 1900s, helped both to reflect and shape the popular vision of the Empire at war.[5]

In Egypt, Villiers was a freelance who worked initially for the *Graphic*, whereas Prior remained loyal to the *ILN* throughout his long career. It has been suggested that the sands of the Nile became a 'cockpit' for an intense rivalry between them but, while there is little evidence to support this interpretation, they frequently sketched and fought side by side during the North African campaigns, sharing the dangers of Dervish spears and capsised steam launches along the Nile. Prior and Villiers probably felt for each other the comradeship that bound together members of their profession, a feeling boyishly evoked in Kipling's first novel. However, such was the competition between correspondents and artists that probably each tried constantly to outsmart the other in being first at the scene of the action or in getting their sketches home by the swiftest possible means of transport in the desert. As neither makes much mention of the other in his memoirs, Peter Johnson, author of the excellent survey *Front Line Artists* (1978), is of the opinion that their professional rivalry extended, to some degree, to personal competitiveness. Villiers, in any case, excelled himself in reporting the naval bombardment of Alexandria in 1882, the subject of his sketches in the *Graphic*, and one of the rare instances when a nineteenth-century special artist was employed in depicting shipborne action. Prior, meanwhile, was also on hand to send sketches of the British action to the *ILN*, while Villiers increasingly played the role of the war correspondent as well as artist. When the latter arrived to throw in his lot with the Highland Brigade on the eve of the battle of Tel-el-Kebir, he found his arch-rival Prior already waiting for battle to commence. Tel-el-Kebir, whose aftermath was to be painted by Lady Butler, closed one chapter of the Nile story and Villiers signed off by sketching Arabi Pasha in his prison cell in Cairo.[6]

Events now moved further south, where the Mahdi was raising the Sudanese tribes or Dervishes in a holy war against the unpopular Khedive of Egypt which could damage the British presence in the Sudan. Gladstone only gave the Khedive nominal support but this included the appointment of Hicks Pasha to command a rabble of Egyptian gendarmerie massacred at El Obeid in November 1883, where war correspondent Edmund O'Donovan and special artist Frank Vizetelly lost their lives. In February 1884 the Liberal government, as a further lukewarm gesture, sent a former Governor-General of the Sudan, Charles 'Chinese' Gordon, to Khartoum to report on the situation and to organise the evacuation of Egyptian garrisons hard pressed by the Mahdi's revolt. Gordon arrived in Khartoum shortly after an Egyptian force under General Valentine Baker had been destroyed in the Eastern Sudan at the wells of El Teb, just south of Suakin on the Red Sea coast, by the Hadendowah tribe under their Mahdist leader Osman Digna, a former slave trader. Two British brigades of infantry and one of cavalry were sent to Suakin to avenge the defeat of Baker's forces but Villiers complained that his paper vacillated about sending him to the Sudan until the British troops were actually moving on the enemy. 'The result was that I nearly missed the first fight of the campaign', he recalled with some regret. On March 1884, a month after Baker's defeat at the hands of the fanatical Dervishes, the British under General Sir Gerald Graham met Osman Digna in battle on almost the same ground. In the midst of the fighting were those inseparable rivals Frederic Villiers and Melton Prior. Both mention in their memoirs the Sir Henry Curtis-like figure of Colonel Frederick Burnaby, with shirt sleeves tucked up above the elbow, picking off the enemy with a double-barrelled shotgun filled with buckshot, as if he was killing big game. Villiers had a narrow escape after the battle, while sketching a supposedly dead pile of Arab bodies, when one of the 'dead', no more than a boy, sprang into the air and rushed after him with a short corkscrew knife – he was killed with a single shot from a nearby soldier who had heard Villiers' cries for assistance.[7]

The fanaticism of the 'fuzzy-wuzzies' and their feigning of death, as illustrated by the previous incident, made the Black Watch and the Royal Welch Fusiliers at El Teb less fastidious than they might have been about respecting the wounded. A facsimile of a sketch made by Melton Prior during the battle, published in the *ILN* of 22 March 1884, fuelled a blaze of protest from anti-government forces about the apparent brutality which it showed the British exercising towards the Dervish wounded. Prior had written incautiously on his sketch, as a direction to the engravers back in London, 'shooting wounded Rebels in the trenches', and copies of the *ILN* were subsequently waved in Parliament as alleged evidence of British atrocities. Prior, supported by Villiers, later argued that in the face of such fanatical native resistance, the British troops had no alternative but to bayonet and shoot the wounded Dervishes. As Prior had written on his original sketch: 'They dug small ditches with room for 2 or 3 of the Enemy and then as we advanced jumped up and attacked us with their spears. The long trench was a nasty one to take, and after we *had taken it* the trench was 2 deep full of the Rebels.' When the campaign was over, Gladstone, who had defended the Army's behaviour in the Commons, assured Prior that his sketches had been as valuable to him in the soldiers' defence as they had been to the opposition in attacking the government. Prior added, in a comment notable for suggesting the influential circulation of the *ILN*, that:

I felt exceedingly proud, for he (Gladstone) said that he had always taken a great interest in the sketches which I had sent home to my paper, and he had no reason to doubt the truthfulness of the drawing in question or the necessity for the troops to act as I had represented.[8]

The media image of an expeditionary force led by General Sir Garnet Wolseley marching to the rescue of a besieged Gordon in a Khartoum surrounded by a sea of heathens, lent the 1884–5 campaign in the Sudan an almost crusade-like appearance to the British press and public one hundred years ago. 'It was above all things necessary that England at breakfast should be amused and thrilled and interested, whether Gordon lived or died, or half the British Army went to pieces in the sand,' as Kipling put it. Hence on 13 September 1884 the *ILN* informed its readers with a fanfare that its star special artist, Melton Prior, was already on his way to the front, only a few months after returning to London from the earlier campaign. In fact, Prior was in the famous Shepheard's Hotel in Cairo, organising his transport, crates of whisky and invaluable tinned Irish stew, when he received a telegram telling him that he was about to be joined by Walter Ingram, the twenty-eight-year-old brother of William Ingram, the *ILN*'s proprietor. Walter brought with him his own steam launch which considerably improved Prior's means of transport for himself and his servant. Frederick Villiers, with Charles E. Fripp representing the *Graphic*, kept up with his rival but lacking Ingram's launch had to rely on the patronage of Wolseley's official party – it always paid to be on good terms with the military. Both Prior and Villiers came to grief along the Nile cataracts when the boats they were travelling in overturned but they put the experience to good use by sending back sketches of their misfortunes which were converted into engravings by their respective papers.[9]

The Gordon relief expedition faced its severest test on 17 January 1885 at the battle of Abu Klea: when the war artists on the spot saw the enemy break into the British square, the Gatling seize up and – in the murderous hand-to-hand fighting which ensued – the spearing to death of Colonel Frederick Burnaby:

> The sand of the desert is sodden red, –
> Red with the wreck of a square that broke; –
> The Gatling's jammed and the Colonel dead,
> And the regiment blind with dust and smoke.
> The river of death has brimmed his banks,
> And England's far, and Honour a name,
> But the voice of a schoolboy rallies the ranks:
> 'Play up! play up! and play the game!'

In the subsequent running fight to reach the Nile with its precious water supply, known collectively as the battle of Abu Kru, bullets were flying so thickly that every member of the press contingent save one was struck and John Cameron of the *Standard* and St Leger Herbert of the *Morning Post* were killed outright. Twenty newspapermen had been sent by their editors to North Africa to follow the British Army's progress in the Sudan and of these seven did not return. (There is a memorial plaque to them in the crypt of St Paul's Cathedral.) Eventually, Sir Charles Wilson's column came within sight of Khartoum only to learn that two days earlier the Mahdi had stormed the place and put Gordon to death. The Wolseley campaign had at least supplied romantic adventure, amusement, thrills and excitement for the newly literate masses back home, despite the failure to rescue Gordon and the cost in lives from bullets, spears and disease. In Rudyard Kipling's ironic prose:

The Sudan campaign was a picturesque one, and lent itself to vivid word painting. Now and again a 'special' managed to get slain – which was not altogether a disadvantage to the paper that employed him – and more often the hand-to-hand nature of the fighting allowed of miraculous escapes which were worth telegraphing

C

home at eighteenpence the word. There were many correspondents with many corps and columns, – from the veterans who had followed on the heels of the cavalry that occupied Cairo in '82, what time Arabi Pasha called himself King, who had seen the first miserable work round Suakin when the sentries were cut up nightly and the scrub swarmed with spears, to youngsters jerked into the business at the end of a telegraph-wire to take the place of their betters killed or invalided.[10]

In the late 1890s the Sudan once more provided the newspapers with an exciting 'arena' for war reporting, but the methodical conquest of the Dervish by Major-General Sir Horatio Herbert Kitchener – who had been a major with the Gordon relief expedition – was not destined to provide the same glamorous or tragic spectacle as the earlier campaign in the desert. The host of war correspondents and artists who swarmed out to be in at the death of Mahdism found comparatively little to enliven their narratives because of the determined machine-like precision with which the campaign was organised. The battle of Omudurman on 2 September 1898, although few realised it at the time, was to mark the beginning of the end of the golden era for the special artist. For this bloody campaign provided not only an early example of a concerted attempt to impose efficient military censorship, it also introduced into a British colonial war the agency that was to render the artist virtually obsolete – the moving picture camera. It was Frederic Villiers himself, representing both the *ILN* and the *Globe*, who had brought a movie camera (and a bicycle) along with him to the desert which he had last seen thirteen years earlier. Villiers afterwards claimed that he used the cinematograph camera for the first time in the history of campaigning during the 1897 Greco-Turkish War but this has proved difficult to verify.[11]

There is, however, corroboration of Villiers' account of his attempt to film during the 1898 Sudan campaign. He claims to have found himself in mid-stream when the battle of Omdurman opened, having taken advantage of a gunboat's dark hold to load film into the unwieldy camera because of the brilliant moonlight of the night before. Villiers was eager to try out the new equipment but fate, alas, was against him:

The dervishes were now streaming towards us in great force – about ten thousand spearmen – just as I wanted them, in the face of the early sun and in the face of my camera. I had just commenced to grind the 'coffee pot' when our fore battery opened fire. The effect on my apparatus was instantaneous and astounding. The gunboat had arrived on the Nile in sections and had evidently been fixed up for fighting in a hurry, for with the blast of her guns the deck planks opened up and snapped together, and down went my tripod. The door of the camera flew open and my films were exposed. However, I had no time to weep over spilt milk, for the fighting had commenced. I pulled out my sketchbook, and my only comfort was that from my vantage point I saw many things I should have missed ashore and that no camera of my kind could have registered.

Even if we accept the veracity of this account – it might seem suspicious that the camera should overturn so conveniently – Villiers' claim to exclusivity has been challenged by evidence that he was not the only correspondent with a cine-camera at the battle. Meanwhile, the British artillery fire from the gunboats moored on the Nile and the Army's Lee-Metford rifles and deadly Maxim machine-guns relentlessly mowed down the oncoming Dervishes. There is something ultimately rather chilling about the stern Kitchener's extermination of Arab resistance to the British invasion of the Sudan which resulted in 11,000 killed at Omdurman for a small British loss. The *Daily Mail*'s George W. Steevens, one of the new breed of war correspondents, broke away from the patriotic bombast that typified so much of the period's war reporting in his account of the battle: 'it was a most appalling slaughter. The dervish army was killed out as hardly an army has been killed out in the history of war.'[12]

To what extent was a more heroic and romantic element introduced into sketches from the front by those in control of the medium of representation? For before the war artist's drawings, often rough and hasty, could be printed in the illustrated papers, they had to be revised, finished or even redrawn by the home engravers. Villiers and Prior were, above all, consummate technicians and for the most part they drew accurately what they saw; yet their choice of subject matter, dictated by the need to make dramatic impact, naturally favoured action and heroism, a bias strengthened by the engraving process back in London. By concentrating on these twin themes, a certain emphasis crept in, character was sacrificed, carnage rare, looting by the British seldom recorded. There were even cases where editorial requirements or military censorship reinforced a bias that would otherwise have been largely unconscious. This is hinted at, for example, in Kipling's *The Light That Failed*, where the war-artist hero is asked by his art manager to redraw a 'brutal and coarse and violent' soldier for reproduction in a weekly, since the subscribers would prefer a 'glossy hero' in a lovely red coat. A more empirical method of testing the validity of such accusations is by contrasting the special's original sketches with the eventual published engravings in the pages of an illustrated newspaper. Thus the National Army Museum in London has in its possession seventy-eight papyrotype reproductions of what are probably most of the sketches made by Melton Prior during the 1884–5 Gordon relief expedition and these can be compared with the finished engravings preserved in the *ILN* picture library. There is space here only to mention a Melton Prior drawing of the battle of Tel-el-Kebir in 1882 and the difference between his original sketch and its engraving by Richard Caton Woodville. But first, what was the actual process whereby a sketch sent by the artist from the field of battle in time reached the reader over the breakfast table?[13]

Once the special's sketch had reached his newspaper by camel, steamer and boat from the Sudan, the main outlines were redrawn, or traced, in reverse on to boxwood that was divided into separate blocks, each measuring about $3\frac{1}{2}''$

by 2″. A double page spread might need as many as forty of these blocks and several artists working simultaneously on them, one specialising in architectural detail, another in topographical, another in figures and so on – a form of art by committee. When the drawing was finished, the blocks were bolted together with much care being taken to ensure that there was the closest fit where the pieces of wood met. Then the work was sent to the engravers who cut away all except the lines. A wax impression of the wood engraving was made from which a metal printing block carrying the reversed image of the original could be electrotyped ready for the printing press. Even if little or no alterations were made to the original sketch outline, it is clear that the wood engraving process meant that the work of the intermediate artists, however good, all too often obliterated the individual style given to his drawings by the man at the front. With this process in mind, some artists at the front preferred to work on flimsy paper which could be reversed and from which the home-based artists traced the salient lines directly onto the wood. This could account for the relatively few original sketches still in existence today compared with the huge volume of material despatched from the field by the specials to their papers. Colonel Sir Frederick Maurice (1841–1912), a member of the 'Wolseley Ring' among staff officers present at the Egyptian and Sudan campaigns from 1882–5, complained of the public being content to take the dreams and fancies of London wood engravers, men who knew little of life outside of a four-mile radius from Charing Cross, as substitutes for the realities of war. The sketches of the war artists drawn at the scene of the fighting were, he wrote indignantly, overlooked by editors for, 'productions drawn from the fancy of their excellent wood engravers, which have less relation to anything that ever happened than Mr Tenniel's cartoons have to actual scenes in Parliament or elsewhere'. Illustrations composed in the backrooms of Fleet Street or the Strand often appeared, Maurice alleged, long before it would have been possible for the most zealous war artist to have sent home from Africa or Asia the slightest sketch of an imperial war. It was especially provoking to a soldier like Maurice, who had looked over the war artist's shoulder as he sketched in West Africa or the Sudan, to see the travesties that replaced such work or even those that anticipated its arrival by several weeks.[14]

Thus on 7 October 1882 the *ILN* published a 'worked up' drawing by Richard Caton Woodville of a Melton Prior original sketch, engraved as a woodblock and entitled: 'Battle of Tel-el-Kebir: the Charge at the Bayonet's Point', sub-captioned: 'From a Sketch by Our Special Artist'. On 14 October 1882, a month after the battle, *ILN* readers were able to judge the difference between the original and the engraving when Prior's signed sketch of the Highlanders' attack was published above the caption: 'Storming the Trenches of Tel-el-Kebir', with the sub-caption: 'Facsimile of a Sketch by Our Special Artist'. Woodville had changed the scene considerably from Prior's original drawing, adopting a different viewpoint, dramatising the stance of key figures, and changing the position of several. It is clear that he had given a romantic and heroic gloss to what was a fairly straightforward original of kilts flying as the Highlanders charge on trenches which do not even feature in the engraved version. (See Figures 1 and 2) Prior's original drawing was able to appear in the *ILN* because by 1882 printing techniques had improved to such an extent that it was now possible to reproduce original line work by photographic means: 'This sketch, together with many others, was only received on Tuesday last, and was reproduced by the Direct Photo-Engraving Process in ten hours!' (*ILN*, 23 February 1884). These new methods of photographic reproduction make Sir Frederick Maurice's complaint appear rather academic but until original line drawings could be transferred onto a block by photography and published as 'facsimile sketches', the system placed the special at the mercy of the home engravers. The new printing methods, which meant that readers now had the opportunity to see the scenes exactly as the specials drew them under fire, did not, however, mean that the home-based artist was to find himself made redundant. The two kinds of illustrations were to continue in tandem for some time to come.[15]

Richard Caton Woodville (1856–1927), who depicted a score or more wars in 'death or glory' style for the *ILN* and other publications, was brought up in St Petersburg, studied art in Düsseldorf and ended his life as a retired Captain in the Royal North Devon Hussars. He came to London in 1877 at the time when the Russo-Turkish War was in progress, 'and when the British public was taking one of its periodic fits of interest in battle paintings and drawings'. Five years later, while in Cairo helping to design uniforms for the Egyptian Army, he was commissioned by Queen Victoria to paint in oils 'The Guards at Tel-el-Kebir', which he prepared for by taking photographs and making sketches on the site of the actual battlefield. Despite some biographical entries to the contrary, there is no evidence that he was ever actually present as a war artist during a battle. In 1891 he went to America during the Sioux uprising where he made the acquaintance of the 'Western' artist Frederic Remington. Woodville was famous as the painter of numerous action-filled watercolours and large-scale oil paintings exhibited annually at the Royal Academy, with titles such as 'Up Guards and At Them!', 'Saving the Guns at Maiwand' and 'All That Was Left of Them!', widely reproduced as photogravure supplements to the weeklies. In addition, he was responsible for engraved illustrations which appeared as pull-out enclosures in the *ILN*, purportedly based on the original sketch of a special. Woodville possessed an immense knowledge of military detail and rapidly produced a prodigious output of war illustrations, drawn from the imagination in his well-equipped London studio, whose high gloss and glamour earned him comparison with Meissonnier and enabled him to stamp his histrionic vision of imperial warfare on the popular consciousness. Frederic Villiers was an admirer of this artist's work, saying that although Woodville had 'never witnessed a shot fired in anger nor seen anything of campaigning, yet in his pictures there is all the real dash and movement of war'. Ironically, it is the home-based artist like Woodville who is best remembered as a nineteenth-century war illustrator, not the man at the front like Villiers or Prior. That the latter generally believed in and shared the same imperialist outlook as the home-based artists like Woodville cannot be denied, although their sketches from the front appear muted in comparison with the patriotic style of the engravings based upon their originals. Woodville's paintings show war in terms of individual heroism and offer rather stilted military poses which to the modern eye are more selfconsciously 'Victorian' than the work of those in the field. The studio-based artist must, therefore, bear more responsibility than the man on the spot for encouraging the romantic and heroic elements in the image of war conveyed to the readers of the illustrated weeklies. Hence their work was always good propaganda for the imperial cause, representing British actions in the best possible light, 'an artist's victory over many a British defeat'.[16]

During the attempt to rescue Gordon in 1884–5, command of the boats navigating the Nile cataracts was given by General Wolseley to Lieutenant-General William Francis Butler (1838–1910) who, as a young lieutenant, had taken part a decade earlier in the famous Red River expedition in Canada. This experience led Butler to recommend that a special civilian corps of Canadian boatmen be recruited by the British to take a flotilla of river boats up the Nile to Khartoum. An impassioned Irish nationalist, Butler was in his mid-forties when he followed Wolseley to fight in, 'the very first war in the Victorian era in which the object was entirely worthy and noble'. He is of interest to us because in 1877 he had married Elizabeth Thompson (1850–1933), the Victorian military painter who was to do for the soldier in art what Rudyard Kipling was to do for him in literature. The nature of the relationship between Butler, 'an intuitive sympathiser with rebel nationalists all over the Empire', and his wife Elizabeth, whose art reflected the military heroism endemic in contemporary popular culture, is one which will be explored here by looking at the paradoxical nature of their joint careers.[17]

A suitable starting point might be William Butler's presence as a staff officer in September 1882 when Wolseley's forces crushed the uprising of Arabi Pasha at the battle of Tel-el-Kebir. Not long after this celebrated British victory his wife, Lady Elizabeth Butler, started making preparations for a large oil painting which was to represent Wolseley and his staff reaching a bridge over the Sweetwater canal at the end of the battle.

Curiously, her husband – despite his own appearance in the painting – was not at all enthusiastic about the subject matter, believing that the Egyptians had fought with great determination against overwhelming odds:

To beat those poor fellaheen soldiers was not a matter for exultation he said; and he told me that the capture of Arabi's earthworks had been like 'going through brown paper'. He thought the theme unworthy, and hoped that I would drop the idea. But I wouldn't; and seeing me bent on it, he did all he could to help me to realise the scene I had chosen.

Lord Wolseley himself agreed to give the strong-willed artist a rather fidgety sitting at his home in London, 'his wife trying to keep him quiet on her knee like a good boy'. The completed oil painting, *After the Battle*, although not one of her best, was nonetheless exhibited at the Royal Academy of 1885 and later engraved for popular reproduction. The success or otherwise of this work is now difficult to gauge, except from the engravings, for the simple reason that it no longer exists in its original form. After General Butler's death in 1910, his wife had the original canvas cut to pieces, as if to appease her departed husband's angry shade.[18]

William Francis Butler was born into a large family, at Ballyslateen, Suirville, County Tipperary, on 31 October 1838, the son of a small-scale Irish Catholic landowner. In 1858, on the recommendation of a distant kinsman, General Sir Richard Doherty, he had been nominated to a direct commission without purchase; although for an Irish Catholic the British Army would seem to offer little hope of normal promotion. Yet by the time of his marriage in 1877 Butler had risen to Major, having hitched his wagon to General Wolseley's rising star, serving with his Chief in Canada, the Ashanti War and in Natal. Both men expressed nothing but admiration for one another in public but they were poles apart in temperament and political attitudes. Butler, for example, dismissed most colonial campaigns with contempt as 'sutler's wars', fought to humble the deserving and line the pockets of the unworthy – not a viewpoint Wolseley could be expected to share. Butler also believed the 1882 British intervention in Egypt came about as a result of the financiers controlling the politicians, 'and letting loose the dogs of war'; a view influenced at the time he came to write his autobiography by a reading of Wilfred Scawen Blunt's anti-imperialist *Secret History of the English Occupation of Egypt* (1907). Butler was not just a remarkable professional soldier, he had also published several books, including a history of his regiment, two books on his adventurous journeys in the Canadian Northwest and an account of his experiences in the 1873 Ashanti campaign. After his marriage he followed this up with a successful juvenile novel, *Red Cloud* (1882), an anonymous prophetic novel, *The Invasion of England* (1882), a stirring account of the Gordon relief expedition, *The Campaign of the Cataracts* (1887), serviceable popular biographies of Generals Gordon, Napier and Colley, and a posthumous autobiography which is one of the most readable written by a nineteenth-century soldier.[19]

In 1898–9 General Butler's glittering career was tarnished by a serious conflict with Sir Alfred Milner, High Commissioner of South Africa, when he was unexpectedly appointed Commander-in-Chief of the British forces in South Africa and, in Milner's absence, acting High Commissioner. As a staunch Home Ruler, it might have been predicted by the War Office that Butler would find himself sympathetic to the Boer predicament and hostile to the crafty manoeuvres of the Uitlander business element, led by Cecil Rhodes in Johannesburg, which received the powerful backing of Milner and the Colonial Secretary, Joseph Chamberlain. At the end of the Bloemfontein Conference on 14 June 1899, Milner made his opinion of Butler's unsuitability plain to Chamberlain:

The General. He is too awful. He has, I believe, made his military preparations all right, but I cannot get him to make the least move or take the slightest interest. There are a hundred things outside his absolute duty which he ought to be thinking of, especially the rapid raising of volunteers . . . in case of emergency. He simply declines to go into it. He will just wait for his W[ar] O[ffice] orders, but till he has his commands to mobilise, he will not budge an inch or take the slightest interest. *His sympathy is wholly with the other side.* At the same time there is nothing to lay hold of. He never interferes with my business and is perfectly polite. But he is absolutely no use, unless indeed we mean to knuckle down, in which case he had better be made High Commissioner. [my italics]

Butler was eventually compelled to resign by the High Commissioner ('Butler or I will have to go') on 4 July 1899, throwing away his last chance of leading an independent command in the field of battle. General Butler's career never recovered from the unjustified slur that he had left the army unprepared for the subsequently engineered conflict between British and Boer and he died an embittered man, convinced of the moral rectitude of his critical stand on the 'forward policy' in South Africa.[20]

Elizabeth Thompson was born in Lausanne in 1850 and had nothing military or imperialist in her immediate family background. Together with her younger sister Alice, who became better known as the poet Alice Meynell, she had a bohemian childhood unusual for a future general's wife and was educated abroad by her dilettante father. Thomas James Thompson lived on inherited income from property and, after several unsuccessful attempts to enter Parliament as a Free Trade candidate, decided to devote his leisure to the education of his daughters – 'loving literature he never lifted a pen except to write a letter'. Elizabeth's childhood was consequently spent in a succession of temporary homes, particularly on the Italian Riviera above Genoa, where she studied painting with a tutor, and then at the South Kensington School of Art. Her adolescent sketchbooks of the 1860s, held in the National Army Museum, exhibit a bewildering variety of colourful and dramatic vignettes, showing Italian peasants, tradesmen, boatmen, priests, carnival groups, carabinieri and Garibaldians, as well as the military sketches of cavalry and soldiers with which she was later to be prominently associated in the public mind.[21]

Elizabeth exhibited watercolours and had paintings rejected by the Royal Academy, until in 1872 she had what she described as her first introduction to the British Army at autumn manoeuvres near Southampton. Her painting *Missing*, an imaginary scene of the aftermath of a battle in the Franco-Prussian War, was accepted by the Academy in 1873 but hung so high ('skied') as to be virtually lost to the public view. It did, however, lead to a commission by Charles Galloway, a rich Manchester industrialist, and the result was her famous *Calling the Roll Call after an Engagement, Crimea*, popularly known as *The Roll Call* – a sombre memorial to the soldiers of the Grenadier Guards. This painting was an instant sensation on exhibition at the Royal Academy in May 1874 and made her a success overnight. So great were the crowds that flocked to see it that a policeman had to be stationed beside it to move people on. 'One stands and waits one's turn for the 'Calling of the Roll' [*sic*], the chorus of 'Wonderful!' rising all day around this work', wrote F. T. Palgrave in the *Academy*. Elizabeth wrote to her father of the events of 'this most memorable day', the private view of 1 May: 'I don't suppose I ever can have another such day, because, however great my future successes may be, they can never partake of the character of this one. It is my first great success. I have suddenly burst into fame, and this *first time* can never come again.'[22]

Why was Elizabeth Thompson's first major canvas the painting of the year and one of the handful of the most successful Academy pictures of the century? The Crimean subject matter was still a highly charged and emotional public memory, although twenty years past, and the sober, almost photographic realism of the treatment – showing the sufferings of the soldiers after the battle – rendered the violence and heroism of the actual fighting the more potent by being implicit. That such a brilliantly realised scene of warfare should have been painted by a woman at all, let alone such a young one, was too much for most commentators. Thus the *Times* wrote of *The Roll Call* as: 'a picture from the battle-field, neither ridiculous, nor offensive, nor improbable, nor exaggerated, in which there is neither swagger nor sentimentalism, but plain, manly, pathetic, heroic truth, and all this the work of a young woman'. Over a quarter of a million copies of Elizabeth Thompson's photograph were sold within a few weeks of her Academy success, evidence that the patriotism manifested in her painting had made her into a national heroine with a fame surpassed only by that of the Crimean 'Lady with a Lamp', Florence Nightingale. When her next painting, *Quatre Bras*, was exhibited in the following year, John Ruskin, in a much-quoted passage from his 1875 Academy notes – his first for fifteen years – wrote of it:

I never approached a picture with a more iniquitous prejudice against it than I did Miss Thompson's, partly because I had always said that no woman could paint; and secondly, I thought that what the public made such a fuss about *must* be good for nothing. But it is Amazon's work this, no doubt about it; and the first fine pre-Raphaelite picture of battle we have had; profoundly interesting and showing all manner of illustrative and realistic faculty . . . [It exhibits] gradations of shade and colour of which I have not seen the like since Turner's death.[23]

One of the admirers of *The Roll Call* at the Royal Academy had been Major William Butler, an officer-patient at Netley Hospital recovering from a fever caught while serving in West Africa. Elizabeth Thompson did not meet the Major until 23 April 1876, an event mentioned in her diary, which chronicles the 'society' circles her fame had gained her entrance into: 'Went to lunch at Mrs Mitchell's, who invited me at the Private View [of *Balaclava*], next door to Lady Raglan's, her great friend. Two distinguished officers were there to greet me, and we had a pleasant chat . . .' One of the two was Major W. F. Butler, author of *The Great Lone Land*. The couple were married in June 1877 by Cardinal Henry Manning at the Church of the Servite Fathers in London, their guests including Wolseley and his staff who had all been together in West Africa. Elizabeth had been converted to Rome in 1873 and expressed a longing, soon realised, to see the Host carried through English fields. 'By her marriage the painter of heroes became the wife of a soldier of experience in every quarter of the earth', as her brother-in-law Wilfrid Meynell exclaimed.[24]

Lady Butler's life now followed the expediencies of her husband's military career. A tranquil, dignified woman, she accompanied him to Egypt and South Africa, lived in Ireland and in various English military residencies. Despite the disruption of routine this involved, in successive years she painted large and meticulous canvases of battle scenes and military exercises which were exhibited annually at the Royal Academy: *The Remnants of An Army* (1879); *The Defence of Rorke's Drift* (1880); *Scotland Forever* (1881); *The Dawn of Waterloo* (1895); *Steady the Drums and Fife* (1897). Several of her most famous paintings, including *The Roll Call*, can be seen in the appropriate surroundings of the Officers' Mess of the Military Staff College at Camberley, Surrey, and they all reveal her detailed attention to military uniforms and accuracy in the portrayal of horses – skills which go far to explain her popularity with the military. 'Thank God', she once said, 'I never painted for the glory of war, but to portray its pathos and heroism. If I had seen even a corner of a real battle-field, I could never have painted another picture.' Lady Butler's cult of the heroic, and the public-school ethos underlying it, is most eloquently summed up in her painting *Floreat Etona!* (1882), which delivers the imagery that fed an insatiable public appetite for national glory. It depicts a bathetic incident that supposedly took place at Laing's Nek during the South African campaign of 1881, when Lieutenants Elwes and Monck, fellow Old Etonians, led an attack by the 58th Regiment against the Boers. The young Adjutant, Monck, is shown in the painting at the moment when his horse is shot from under him, while Elwes encourages him on by shouting: 'Come along, Monck, "Floreat Etona!", we must be in the first rank', but is himself shot dead as he speaks. Wilfrid Meynell, ever the faithful interpreter of his sister-in-law's work, confirmed that by the 1890s the terminology of sport had become the vocabulary of war, when he wrote of this painting:

The cry which was the last uttered by the young soldier eager for glory, is significant of the spirit of enterprise with which the English man and boy alike enter upon war – which is, in part, the spirit of sport . . . Sport and battle have each a share in the aspiration, gravity, and happiness of a worthy fight, as an Englishman understands it.[25]

Some estimation of the immense popularity of Lady Butler's work can be derived from the archives of the Fine Art Society in New Bond Street, who were responsible for the publication of a large number of engravings from her paintings. The Society estimates that the sales of the cheaper prints ran into the tens of thousands, and their Minute Books reveal that the Society paid the immense sum of £13,500 to the *Roll Call* copyright subscription list in 1876, £3,000 to Lady Butler alone for the copyright to the *Return from Inkerman* in 1877, £2,500 for *The Scots Greys at Waterloo* and £1,500 for *The Remnants of an Army* in 1879. In addition, the engraver, F. Stacpoole, received an average of £200 plus bonuses for his work. In paying such stiff prices, the Society obviously expected to recoup their money from sales of the prints to the general public who had seen the paintings in the Royal Academy, and in addition they held an exhibition of their own of the artist's work in April 1877. The agreement signed with Miss Thompson's father, when the *Return from Inkerman* was purchased, had her agree not to paint any battle piece above a certain size in 1878 and to offer to the Society any religious subject that she might paint – the latter a guaranteed best seller in the 1870s. The above figures relate to only one period of her output and to one outlet through which representations of her paintings reached the public.[26]

The Butlers had six children and Lady Butler survived her husband by twenty three years; he had retired to Bansha Castle, County Tipperary, in 1905 and died five years later. Two of her sons took part in the First World War, one of them as a Roman Catholic chaplain and the other was seriously wounded at the first battle of Ypres. This war has been seen by some commentators as a great watershed both for imperialism and for representational art. For it was not the increasingly anachronistic and rhetorical paintings of Lady Butler which captured the public imagination during this conflict (*The Canadian Bombers on Vimy Ridge*; *The Charge of the Dorset Yeomanry at Agagia, Egypt*) but the modernist work of the official war artists like C. R. W. Nevinson, the sole English Futurist, and Paul Nash – work which expressed the horrors of war whatever its propaganda utility. In 1924 the painting which Lady Butler submitted to the Royal Academy, exactly fifty years after *The Roll Call*, was rejected by the hanging committee. Changing public taste in pictures and the greater use of photography in newspapers and magazines had reduced the demand for old-style military paintings. 'Photography had liberated art forms from the necessity of representation', as Nevinson put it. 'It is true that Lady Butler was still alive and painting', wrote Mary Clive, Lady Pakenham, of her childhood in the 1920s, 'but she was a relic of another age, and the engraving we had of her famous "Roll Call" was hung in that place of banishment, the wing.' On her death in 1933 at the age of eighty-two, Lady Butler was remembered as a once famous painter whose work was really without modern significance except as a reflection of the age of imperialism through which she had passed. Today few of her paintings are to be found on public display in England but her present obscurity, as Germaine Greer once pointed out, lies as much in the downfall of her subject matter as in any aspect of her handling of it.[27]

The popular and critical acclaim Lady Butler received in the heyday of Empire, followed by her virtual eclipse even before the First World War, suggests that her art can only be fully understood if it is placed within the context of a clearly defined historical frame of reference. In the Victorian era of 'little wars', important events were expected to be commemorated in the form of paintings and engravings. Thus each Royal Academy summer exhibition provided a kind of 'visual journalism' with its selection of battle scenes and military processions. Alongside the engravings based upon Melton Prior's sketches in the *ILN* or Frederic Villiers' work in the *Graphic*, Lady Butler's paintings supplied the British public on a regular basis with the visual imagery for the great imperial events of their times. Popular art was thus instrumental in defining the public image of warfare to Victorian Britain. Reproductions of Lady Butler's work were to be found not only in the mess rooms of the British Army but in 'Kipling-haunted little clubs', in sitting-rooms, schools and institutes across Britain and the colonies. Her work, in the form of coloured prints on classroom walls and derivative illustrations in school history textbooks, assisted in the formation of patriotic values in the younger generation. Until the vogue for large mounted pictures declined, engravings of her most famous paintings decorated many middle- and upper-class homes, reflecting their self-confidence and unrestrained patriotism. It is, of course, a long way from the tracing of cultural influences to the formulation of government policy or even to the creation of favourable public attitudes towards the British Empire. Equally, it remains difficult to measure what effect the reporting of the 'little wars' of Empire had on the conduct of foreign policy in the age of imperialism. However, in 1901 Prime Minister Lord Salisbury complained that 'the diplomacy of nations is now conducted quite as much in the letters of special correspondents, as in the dispatches of the Foreign Office'.[28]

Cause and effect in the popular culture of imperialism may be difficult for the historian to disentangle but it is quite possible to speculate that popular art was just as important as war reporting or popular fiction in helping to provide confirmation and support for the imperialist policies of statesmen like Milner and Chamberlain. Certainly, the war artists and painters discussed here must bear some of the responsibility for the almost sacrosanct status which the British Army enjoyed in the public mind until the disasters of 'Black Week' in the second South African or Boer War ultimately shook public confidence in the military. Through popularised reproductions of their work, these artists helped to sustain popular support for the 'little wars' of the late Victorian Army and supplied the second-hand adventure and romance which was an integral part of the imperialist mood that gripped the British public and their rulers towards the end of the nineteenth century. In their work can be found all the qualities – hero worship, sensational glory, adventure and the sporting spirit – which John Hobson identified as responsible for imperialism's successful appeal to the imagination of the late Victorian mass reading public. Yet now the work of the 'specials' and the home-based military artists, which was once regarded as presenting an accurate and valid image of colonial warfare, is much more eloquent of how the age of imperialism saw itself. To end with the words of Sir Roy Strong, Director of the Victoria and Albert Museum, on the Victorian painter and the iconography of his favourite historical theme – the Elizabethan age of British history:

These scenes from our national history have long lost their potency for us. It has been eroded by two world wars, by the collapse and dissolution of Empire, by demands for devolution, by a revolution in the teaching of history both in universities and, even more, in schools. These pictures now remain as monuments to the lost era which strove so boldly to relive its own past. They speak to us of optimism and heroism, of pride in the past and tranquility within the present in that second greatest of all our ages, the reign of Queen Victoria.[29]

Notes

1   J. A. Hobson, *Imperialism: A Study*, London 1938 edn., 222; Byron Farwell, *Queen Victoria's Little Wars*, London 1973; D. A. Low, *Lion Rampant: Essays in the Study of British Imperialism*, London 1973, 22.

2   Zara S. Steiner, *Britain and the Origins of the First World War*, London 1977, 155, 157. Work needs to be done, for example, on the life and career of Harry Payne who specialised in military subjects for postcard companies like Tuck's and produced a series on the uniforms of British and colonial regiments in a highly romanticised form, as well as large composites used in whisky advertisements and for the frontispieces of boys' annuals.

3 Rudyard Kipling, *The Light That Failed*, Harmondsworth, Penguin edn., 1970, 51; Edward M. Spiers, *The Army and Society, 1815–1914*, London 1980, 213; Edward B. Orme, 'Victorian small wars' *Book and Magazine Collector*, No. 1, March 1984, 29; Philip Knightley, *The First Casualty*, New York 1975, 44.

4 Obituary, *The Times*, 6 April 1922; Peter Johnson, *Front Line Artists*, London 1978, 169; Frederic Villiers, *Villiers: His Five Decades of Adventure*, 2 vols., New York 1920.

5 Obituary, *The Times*, 3 November 1910; Harry Furniss, *My Bohemian Days*, London 1920, 128; Pat Hodgson, *The War Illustrators*, London 1977, 22–6; Simon Houfe, *The Dictionary of British Book Illustrators and Caricaturists, 1800–1914*, London 1978. There is a memorial to Prior in the crypt of St Paul's Cathedral.

6 Johnson, *Front Line Artists*, 114–15; Rupert Wilkinson-Latham, *From Our Special Correspondent: Victorian War Correspondents and their Campaigns*, London 1979, Chap. v.

7 Villiers, *Villiers: His Five Decades of Adventure*, I, 292, 303–4; Melton Prior, *Campaigns of a War Correspondent*, London 1912, 187. Sir Henry Curtis is a character in Rider Haggard's *King Solomon's Mines* (1885).

8 Facsimile in *The Illustrated London News*, 22 March 1884; Prior, *Campaigns of a War Correspondent*, 189.

9 Kipling, *The Light That Failed*, 21; Julian Symons, *England's Pride: The Story of the Gordon Relief Expedition*, London 1965; Johnson, *Front Line Artists*, 133–351.

10 Henry Newbolt, *Collected Poems, 1897–1907*, London n.d., 132; Kipling, *The Light That Failed*, 21. Prior thought Kipling, whom he met during the Boer War, 'a charming man and absolutely without an atom of "side" . . . it was interesting to compare his natural manliness with the offensive style of some of the other men one met out there.' Prior, *Campaigns*, 234.

11 Steve Bottomore, 'Frederic Villiers: war correspondent', *Sight and Sound*, XLIX, No. 4, autumn 1980, 250–5; Wilkinson-Latham, *From Our Special Correspondent*, 229–46.

12 Villiers, *Villiers: His Five Decades of Adventure*, II, 264; George W. Steevens, *With Kitchener to Khartoum*, London 1898, 284–5.

13 John Springhall, 'Eyewitnesses to Empire: the men who recorded imperial events', *The British Empire*, No. 53, 1973, 1471; Kipling, *The Light That Failed*, 43–5.

14 Paul Hogarth, *The Artist as Reporter*, London 1967, 26–7; Johnson, *Front Line Artists*, 12–13; Lt. Col. F. Maurice (ed.), *Sir Frederick Maurice: A Record of His Work and Opinions*, London 1913, 210–13.

15 Johnson, *Front Line Artists*, 123; *Illustrated London News*, 7 and 14 October 1882. In March 1883, when Melton Prior lectured on the campaign to the Prince of Wales and guests at the Savage Club, 'with battle scenes thrown by the limelight on to the screen', it is evident from the illustration in the *ILN* that he used a blow-up of his own sketch of the trench assault at Tel-el-Kebir.

16 R. Caton Woodville, *Random Recollections*, London 1914, 12; Hodgson, *The War Illustrators*, 160; Johnson, *Front Line Artists*, 15–16; Frederic Villiers, *Peaceful Personalities and Warriors Bold*, London 1907, 24.

17 Edward McCourt, *Remember Butler: The Story of Sir William Butler*, London 1968, 168; James Morris, *Pax Britannica: The Climax of an Empire*, London 1968, 336.

18 Elizabeth Butler, *An Autobiography*, London 1922, 194; Joseph H. Lehmann, *All Sir Garnet: A life of Field Marshal Lord Wolseley*, London 1964, 331.

When, in response to popular demand, Lady Butler painted *The Defence of Rorke's Drift* (1880), her husband had exclaimed: 'One more painting like this and you will drive me mad!'

19 McCourt, *Remember Butler*, 8, 118, 168; Lt. Gen. Sir W. F. Butler, *Autobiography*, London, 1911, 218–19; a 'sutler' is one who sells liquor or provisions to soldiers in camp or garrison.

20 Butler, *Autobiography*, 385–450; Cecil Headlam (ed.), *The Milner Papers: South Africa, 1897–1899*, London 1931, 425–6, 509–10.

21 Wilfrid Meynell, 'The life and works of Lady Butler', *The Art Annual for 1898*, London 1898, 1–31; Alice Meynell, *Prose and Poetry*, London 1947, 227; Krzystof Z. Cieszkowski, 'The Pallas of Pall Mall: The life and paintings of Lady Butler', *History Today*, XXXIII, February 1982, 30–5.

22 F. T. Palgrave cited: Rosemary Treble, *Great Victorian Painters: Their Paths to Fame*, Arts Council Exhibition, 1978, 79; Butler, *An Autobiography*, 108.

23 Treble, *Great Victorian Painters*, 79–81; *Times*, 5 May 1874; Meynell, 'Life and works', 8.

24 Butler, *An Autobiography*, 152; McCourt, *Remember Butler*, 130.

25 'An appreciation', *The Times*, 4 October 1933; Meynell, 'Life and times', 14.

26 Directors' Private Minute Books, 1876–9, Fine Art Society, New Bond Street, London.

27 Michael Lee, 'A centenary of military painting: the life and work of Lady Butler', *The Army Quarterly and Defence Journal*, LXXXV, No. 1, October 1967, 89–95; Merion and Susan Harries, *The War Artists: British Official War Art of the Twentieth Century*, London 1983, Chaps. ix and xi; Mary Clive, *The Day of Reckoning*, London 1964, 99; Germaine Greer, *The Obstacle Race: the Fortunes of Women Painters and their Work*, London 1979, 84.

28 Cieszkowski, 'The Pallas of Pall Mall', 30–1; Salisbury cited: Winifred Baumgart, *Imperialism: The Idea and Reality of British and French Colonial Expansion, 1880–1914*, Oxford 1982, 53; Zara Steiner, *The Foreign Office and Foreign Policy, 1898–1914*, Cambridge 1969, 186–92.

29 Roy Strong, *And When Did You Last See Your Father? The Victorian Painter and British History*, London 1978, 154.

Appendix

Engravings after paintings by Lady Butler, from *An alphabetical list of engravings declared at the office of the Printsellers' Association, London* (Printsellers' Association, 1892 & 1912).*

After the battle (Tel-el-Kebir), mezzotint by Richard Josey, $39\frac{1}{2} \times 19\frac{1}{8}''$, publ. by H. Graves & Co, declared 28 June 1888: 200 artist's proofs (15 gns), 25 presentation copies, 25 proofs before letters (10 gns), 100 lettered proofs (5 gns).

Balaclava, mixed-medium engraving by F. Stacpoole, $37\frac{3}{4} \times 20\frac{5}{8}''$, publ. by The Fine Art Society, declared 20 Apr. 1876: 525 artist's proofs (15 gns), 25 presentation copies, 250 proofs before letters (10 gns), 350 lettered proofs (7 gns).

Balaclava (reduced size), mixed-medium engraving by Richard Josey, $30 \times 16\frac{1}{4}''$, publ. by The Fine Art Society, declared 29 Oct. 1890: 50 artist's proofs (4 gns), 25 presentation copies, & undeclared number of prints (1 gn).

Floreat Etona (Battle of Laing's Neck), mixed-media engraving by J. Cother Webb,

*Information supplied by Krzysztof Cieszkowski, Curator, Tate Gallery Library, Millbank, London.

$22\frac{1}{2} \times 24\frac{1}{2}''$, publ. by H. Graves & Co, declared 28 Sept. 1889: 375 artist's proofs (5 gns), 25 presentation copies, 300 lettered proofs (3 gns), & undeclared number of prints (2 gns).

Quatre Bras, mixed-media engraving by F. Stacpoole, $40 \times 19\frac{1}{2}''$, publ. by The Fine Art Society, declared 30 Oct. 1876: 500 artist's proofs (15 gns), 25 presentation copies, 250 proofs before letters (10 gns), 350 lettered proofs (7 gns).

Quatre Bras (reduced size), mixed-medium engraving by Richard Josey, $30\frac{5}{8} \times 14\frac{5}{8}''$, publ. by The Fine Art Society, declared 24 Apr. 1888: 125 artist's proofs (4 gns), 25 presentation copies, & undeclared number of prints (1 gn).

Remnants of an army, mixed-media engraving by J. J. Chant, $30 \times 17\frac{3}{8}''$. publ. by The Fine Art Society, declared 7 Nov. 1882: 200 artist's proofs (8 gns), 25 presentation copies, 50 proofs before letters (6 gns), 100 lettered proofs (4 gns), & undeclared number of prints (2 gns).

The return from Inkerman, mixed-media engraving by W. T. Davey, $40 \times 21''$, publ. by The Fine Art Society, declared 8 Apr. 1878: 525 artist's proofs (15 gns), 25 presentation copies, 250 proofs before letters (10 gns), 350 lettered proofs (7 gns), & undeclared number of prints (5 gns).

The Roll Call, line and stipple engraving by F. Stacpoole, $40\frac{1}{4} \times 20\frac{3}{8}''$, publ. by J. Dickinson & Co, declared 13 July 1874: 525 artist's proofs (15 gns), 25 presentation copies, 250 proofs before letters (10 gns), 350 lettered proofs (7 gns).

The Roll Call (reduced size), mixed-media engraving by W. T. Hulland, $30 \times 15''$, publ. by The Fine Art Society, declared 7 Nov. 1882: 200 artist's proofs (4 gns), 25 presentation copies, & undeclared number of prints (1 gn).

Steady the drums and fifes! (the 57th Regiment, the 'Die-hards', on the Ridge of Albuhera in Spain, 16th May 1811), a 'Goupil-gravure' engraved & publ. by Goupil & Co, $31\frac{1}{8} \times 20\frac{1}{4}''$, declared 12 Nov. 1904: 200 artist's proofs on India paper (5 gns), 25 presentation copies, & undeclared number of prints on India paper (1 gn).

CHAPTER 4

OF ENGLAND, HOME AND DUTY
THE IMAGE OF ENGLAND
IN VICTORIAN AND EDWARDIAN
JUVENILE FICTION

J. S. Bratton

Of the institutions which reproduce the dominant culture, the educational system is clearly of central importance, since it addresses the task of disseminating values directly; the public school has been called 'the central institution of the consolidation' of Victorian ideology.[1] The National and later the Board school systems also played their part; and for the study of culture, the history of educational institutions, and the teaching material produced for their use, have been fruitful ground, which is explored in the context of imperialism in the present volume. But the limitations of teaching as indoctrination, even in the ideal circumstances of the Victorian public school, where influence extended beyond the classroom to the playing-field, the dormitory, and the whole ethos self-consciously created around the *alma mater*, are considerable. The ex-schoolboy needed to have become self-motivating, to have internalised the appropriate values to the point where the support of the school community was not only unnecessary, but was actually superseded by a more profoundly personal and conscious commitment to the ideology. This was especially true in respect of the young empire-builder, whose refreshing contact with the old school was likely to be at the best intermittent, and whose ideological grounding might be tested in culturally very alien or acutely challenging circumstances.

Advocates of empire were aware of this problem for the young. Even Henry Newbolt, whose belief in the public school is as well as in the imperial ideal verged on the mystical, knew that the transference from the cricket match in the college close to the broken square in the bloodsoaked desert sand was not a simple matter, and a determination to play up and play the game was not all that was needed. In *The Twymans* (1911), his novel for young men of old families, he offers at an early stage the avowedly Arnoldian doctrine of the power of the 'rhythmic harmony' of the school community to transmute the virtues of 'ancient patriotism', which are

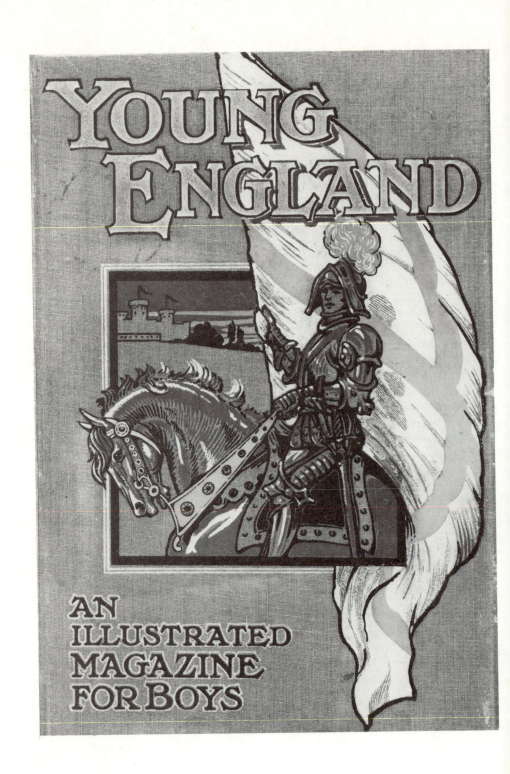

'heroic self-sacrifice', 'passionate devotion', 'pride of patriotism', 'fortitude, self-reliance, intrepidity', 'public spirit' and 'general readiness for united action', to the uses of the 'world-wide society' of which the boys are just becoming members.[2] But the enthusiastic response of the young protagonist to this sermon is at once qualified by his elders, including the naval Commander who is the heroic model in the book, who says he doubts the immortality of societies, even those produced by such classic virtues. This recessional caveat is later reinforced when the boy himself assesses the 'scheme of life' established for him by his school, and finds that while it appeals to him for 'its scientific positivism, its lofty reasonableness, its immense possibilities for power'[3] it excludes or suppresses vital elements of emotion. He finds he must remake the athletic patriotism he learnt at school into a mystical commitment to history and his place within it, 'not an ordinary feeling for the picturesque, but a longing, as it were, for a past that had been his and was forgotten, the desire of a dream long vanished or perhaps never yet dreamed'.[4]

The essential privacy of this dream is also stressed, perhaps unexpectedly, in Kipling's *Stalky and Co.* (1899), where the commitment of the schoolboys who are the future military leaders of the Empire is to an ideal so purely private that it cannot be voiced even between themselves, and official attempts to foster it are met with contempt and loathing. An MP, 'an impeccable Conservative'[5] comes to lecture these boys, 'eighty per cent . . . born . . . in camp, cantonment, or upon the high seas, . . . seventy-five per cent . . . sons of officers . . . looking to follow their fathers' profession'[6] on patriotism. He outrages them, for

the reserve of a boy is tenfold deeper than the reserve of a maid . . . With a large and healthy hand, he tore down these veils, and trampled them under the well-intentioned feet of eloquence. In a raucous voice he cried aloud little matters, like the hope of Honour and the dream of Glory, that boys do not discuss even with their most intimate equals; cheerfully assuming that, till he spoke, they had never considered these possibilities. He pointed them to shining goals, with fingers that smudged out all radiance on all horizons. He profaned the most secret places of their souls with outcries and gesticulations . . . Some of them – the rending voice cut a frozen stillness – might have had relatives who perished in defence of their country. (They thought, not a few of them, of an old sword in a passage, or above a breakfast-room table, seen and fingered by stealth since they could walk.) He adjured them to emulate those illustrious examples; and they looked all ways in their extreme discomfort. Their years forbade them even to shape their thoughts clearly to themselves. They felt savagely that they were being outraged by a fat man . . . they sat, flushed and uneasy, in sour disgust.[7]

He concludes his outrage by waving a glaring calico Union Jack, at which they stare in amazement, as a thing that was occasionally seen down at the coastguard station, or on a box of sweets, but was 'no part of the scheme of their lives . . . a matter shut up, sacred and apart'.[8] So the role of schooling and overt official indoctrination is seen by Newbolt and Kipling to be limited even in the creation of officers and gentlemen; and of course the extension of the public school ethos to those in less privileged forms of education was necessarily indirect; it was only possible through the medium of fiction. Robert Roberts describes the process, the 'Greyfriars' experience.[9] Greyfriars was the public school invented by Frank Richards as the setting for his serial stories in the *Magnet* and the *Gem*, and Roberts and his contemporaries in back-street Salford were 'avid' for the fictional world of the school – it 'became to some of us our true Alma Mater, to whom we felt bound by a dreamlike loyalty . . . the public school ethos, distorted into myth and sold among us weekly in penny numbers, for good or ill, set ideals and standards'. When he at length thought to apply the terms of that idealised world to his own reality he suddenly realised that he was excluded from its promises by class; but the fiction retained power over the imaginations of many who never made that connection.

Many educators consciously turned to fiction to solve problems of the transmission of the ideology. Fiction had the advantage of a much more nearly universal availability: anyone educated to the level of basic literacy was accessible through a story. It was also private, enabling the direct messages inculcating imperial ambitions, and national, familial and racial pride, to be received without a blush; and apparently optional, so that no one need feel repelled by being forced to undergo indoctrination. This last point needs to be qualified by the awareness that just as storybooks are written for the young rather than by them, so they are far more often bought for rather than by their supposed readers; but this element of imposition was absent in some important Victorian and Edwardian printed matter, especially the many magazines which were priced so as to be available directly to the child reader. Perhaps the most compelling virtue of fiction as a vehicle for ideology was (and is) that it appeals to and employs the readers' imagination, the vital element that Newbolt felt was repressed and excluded by the processing of the boy through public school. The elaborated idea of the school itself, or of the battle, or the expedition, when set in the ideal and shapely world of art, may be far more potent than the messy and unsatisfactory reality.

The examination of such fiction which follows focuses upon a particular set of values and motifs in the work of nineteenth-century imperialist writers for children. It is not an argument about the prevalence of imperialist attitudes and intentions in juvenile fiction of the period. Such an argument would be fruitless. There are innumerable Victorian children's books, and while very few seem deliberately anti-imperialist, there are many which do not concern themselves with the matter in any discernible way, and many more whose primary object is, say, religious, or moralistic, but which sometimes repeat in passing current platitudes about the Empire. To attempt to quantify the presence of imperialism in the thousands of juvenile publications appearing year by year would be a hopeless undertaking in such an essay as this.[10] I have chosen instead to look at one aspect of those tales which demonstrably do contain imperialist thought or propaganda.

There is a considerable range of feeling and of seriousness in such writing. At one extreme are the boys' magazines, with their masthead Prince of Wales' feathers and Union Jacks, their cover pictures of big game in furious conflict with white hunters, their pull-out, full-colour charts of the ships of the Navy, the badges of the regiments, the insignia of the chivalric orders, the flags of the dependent world, and so on. Often an overwhelming surface impression is that a blatant reiteration of racial pride, militaristic values and a coarse enthusiasm for conquest characterises serialised adventure stories, whether published in the penny bloods or the *Boy's Own Paper*. Stalky and his friends, indeed, grasping for an epithet to suit the 'swag-bellied flagwagger' who addresses them, call him a 'Bopper', presumably from BOP, an insulting usage which reveals Kipling's view of that supposedly worthy publication. His own stories are much more subtle and serious, and therefore more imaginatively powerful. For both Kipling and the magazine hacks, however, an important element in the pattern is the image of England and the English, and that set of ideas provides an opening for analysis.

Martin Green's account of the rise of imperialist adventure stories posits 'a conflict between the feudal and the modern [cultural] systems'[11] as merchants took power previously held by aristocrats, because the newly powerful immediately sought to adopt the status associated with nobility. 'The merchant castle [was] anxious to dub itself gentlemanly – that is, aristocratic but not military.'[12] He therefore regards the adventure story as peculiarly culturally powerful, in that it was instrumental in this annexation, and became 'the energising myth of Empire'[13] as a consequence. Martin J. Wiener sees the transference and adoption of values rather differently.[14] He argues that the failure of the British economy to maintain its lead in industrialisation is due to this self-defeating cultural manoeuvre. He expresses this, using Donald Horne's terminology, as 'the Southern Metaphor'[15] – the insistence, which he traces through all levels of British society, upon perceiving England as a green and pleasant land, essentially rural and traditional, and therefore upon rejecting the urban and the industrial. Merrie England, a pastoral idyll set in deep meadows and ancient villages, destroyed, he argues, the will to excel in the real world of factories and business. The suggestion of this present study is that the southern metaphor, the image of England, was, at least in children's books, an essential part of Green's 'energising myth'. I find in the fiction for the young over many decades a powerful and multi-faceted presentation of English-ness, as a moral and ethical baseline, and therefore a starting point for the justification of the Empire. It seems necessary to very many writers to present and to praise English or British national characteristics, and the land itself, in order to establish a sense of what is good and to be valued. For the imperialist writer, the extension of this Englishness overseas is a cogent reason for colonial expansion. I also find in much Victorian and Edwardian fiction a feeling that, while readers enjoy exotic adventure stories set in distant corners of the Empire, no significant transference of their messages into the children's own lives will take place unless there is some bridge provided between that fantasy world and the everyday. The presentation of an idealised England as the motive and reward of the Empire-builder provides this activating link.

The creation of English images includes both the land and the people, and both are placed within an historical context. The presentation of the history of England has been studied before, notably by Valerie Chancellor,[16] through the evolution of history textbooks for children. Chancellor's study highlights the change during the nineteenth century from a notion of history teaching as the inculcation of facts and dates, through the recognition that ideas of history may shape attitude and opinion, to the consequent propagandist emphasis in books such as Fletcher and Kipling's *School History of England* (1911) which are avowedly designed to form opinion and inspire action. By the 1870s it is not uncommon to find an historian declaring unequivocally 'God has wonderfully blessed England, though but a speck on this earth; He has made its people known over the whole world for wisdom and just dealing, and has given to it sovereign dominion in almost every part of the globe, so that the sun always shines on some part that belongs to us'. Since this is the case, the author is telling these *Stories of the Land We Live In* with the hope that his book will lead the reader 'to love [his] native land more and more' and to thank God for making him 'a happy English child'.[17] With this teaching aim, however, the formal school method becomes a hindrance, for it was realised that for this purpose 'an ounce of atmosphere is worth a pound of facts'[18] and that some imaginative spur is needed if the pupil is to 'stand, for instance, for half an hour, and breathe the air of Elizabeth's reign, feel [his] own pulses bounding with the fresh young life, the consciousness of power and possibility in which the strong youthful England of that day was rejoicing . . .'.[19] Writers of historical fiction are particularly defeatist about the impact of ordinary history lessons, representing their heroes as hating the strings of dry facts and dates more than any other subject. Some historians resorted to the admixture of fiction with their history, Kipling supplying stirring verses for Fletcher's narrative; H. E. Marshall, writing for little children in Australia, to explain to them how their 'big island' and 'the little island in the West' came to 'belong to each other', declares that the book is 'not a history lesson, but a story-book', including 'stories which wise people say are only fairy-tales and not history. But it seems to me that they are part of Our Island Story, and ought not to be forgotten.' The story therefore starts with Neptune and Brutus of Troy, before arriving at the Romans, and later interjects Arthur – a very useful character model – and presents Wolfe, Nelson and other British heroes almost entirely in terms of myth.[20] The lives of such heroes, particularly figures like Clive of India who could be represented as achieving greatness through a boyish delight in adventure, form a large group of narrative histories formulated to appeal to children 'as a story'. Accounts of battles were often treated in the same way, normally with the conscious intention, voiced by W. H. Fitchett in introducing his stories of *Deeds that Won the Empire*, of making 'an effort to renew in popular memory the great traditions of the Imperial race to which we belong' in order to avoid the danger that 'imagination will take no colour from the rich and deep tints of history', and so produce a 'pallid, cold-blooded citizenship'.[21] But the marriage of information and mythmaking was an uneasy one in books purporting to be factual. Fiction offered a much better medium for eliciting imaginative identification with English history and creating a particular emotional response to it.

The historical novel was one of the first genres in which full-length fiction for children was written, and by the end of the century it was among the dominant forms in boys' books. It normally uses real places and incidents, with a fictional focus, a young person or persons who are to provide both imaginative involvement for the readers and a means of embodying moral and political ideas. The first partisans to exploit the form were probably religious writers, who fictionalised incidents in Christian history, either from the early history of the church in Rome and the East, suitably slanted to match their own sectarian bias, or, more frankly, stories of the rise of Protestantism, and especially the English Reformation. The religious interest normally excludes the specifically imperialist lessons, but does become patriotic when contrast can be made between the behaviour of British Protestants and foreign Catholics. W. H. G. Kingston, a fervent advocate of the Empire as well as a devout Evangelical, sometimes combined the two messages, as in his *Manco, the Peruvian Chief* where he explicitly contrasts the responsible and godly rule of Britain overseas with the wicked exploitation of South American lands by Catholic Spain.[22]

But the evocation of another empire through which to praise or warn against aspects of British imperialism was not a manoeuvre which many of these writers cared to try. The textbooks for small children struggle with the Roman and Norman conquests of Britain:

I dare say every one of our forefathers, when they saw the Romans come first, were discouraged, and thought . . . they should never be happy any more . . . But these very things were meant for their good. Their savage customs and barbarous manner of life were thus changed. There we find the first step on the ladder that has conducted Englishmen to such power and greatness . . . let us heartily thank God for it.[23]

and:

I do not think the English would have allowed Duke William to be king so easily, if he had not told them that Edward the Confessor had promised that he should be king and persuaded them that the prince Edgar Atheling . . . was too silly ever to govern the kingdom well . . .[24]

If the conquests of England by various imperialist powers were impossible to explain satisfactorily to the young in a few simple sentences, they were nevertheless potential vehicles for the lessons of imperialism, if they could be effectively ficionalised for older readers. Few writers accepted the challenge until Kipling did so in *Puck of Pook's Hill* (1905). There he presents, along with several other things, a very skilfully interwoven version of the Roman and the Norman governments in Britain, turning the stories into an exposition of admirable conduct for young men faced with the acute demands of empire.

The method is beautifully contrived: two very young children, Dan and Una, are presented as the inheritors of a piece of England, idyllically described in the first chapter. They inadvertently invoke Puck, the personification of Old England. He shows them moments in the history of the country which have connections with their own place. Of ten tales, eight in some way concern either Hugh and Richard, a Saxon and a Norman knight, or Parnesius and Pertinax, centurions of Rome. One primary message is the public-school dictum that friendship overrides most other ties, and determines moral worth: 'your fate will turn on the first true friend you make . . . I am not pious . . . But I know what goodness means, and my friend, though he was without hope, was ten thousand times better than I'.[25] These pairs of friends are placed at opposite ends of the span of empire. Hugh and Richard, who meet first in heroic manner as enemies in battle, are in on the beginning of England; they stand shoulder to shoulder united by love of place – the manor now owned by Dan and Una's father – and by the bonds of sword-brotherhood, rather perfunctorily reinforced by the marriage of Richard to Hugh's sister. They fight for the future greatness of England, when Saxon and Norman shall be one. The Roman pair are also of different bloods, Parnesius British born and Pertinax from Gaul; but they are united as Roman citizens by the long tradition of power and its responsibility: by caste, like the later pair. They see the end of Rome's empire in Britain – literally see it, as the word 'finish' scratched up on the bricked-over end of the Great North Road under the statue of Roma Dea on Hadrian's Wall. They struggle, quite without hope for the future, for the abstractions which they think the empire stood for, for justice and peace, and so for their personal integrity embodied in that ideal, doomed as it is in its present manifestation. In practice, however, both pairs do the same thing: they fight, against great odds, in the midst of hostile groups defined by race or religion, inspired by loyalty to each other and to a code, and rewarded by the satisfactions of the beloved leader. Richard is given the land that was Hugh's, by his feudal lord, and told to hold it now that 'Fighting is foolishness and craft and cunning all'.[26] His first act is to rush to repel thieves, and he later recalls that 'we ran together, my men-at-arms and the Saxons with bills and bows which they had hidden in the thatch of their huts, and Hugh led them'.[27] Hugh declares that by this practical demonstration of unity in caring for the land first, above all divisions, Richard has gone far to conquer England; and Richard asks for Hugh's help 'to deal aright with these people'.[28] The practical and ideological message for prospective sahibs could hardly be more clearly or more stirringly conveyed. For the Romans too the problems of political power in situations of military occupation are a central issue. They are burdened with the defence of the Wall for three years, to save the Empire for Maximus, a task he knows only they, the men with local knowledge, can do: 'It is always one man's work — always and everywhere'.[29] Solemnly sacrificing to their dead youth, they shoulder the responsibility, rule the Picts with understanding as long as they can, and then fight the Vikings, even after Maximus is dead. They are defending the statue of Roma Dea, all that is left of the border between civilisation and the barbarian horde. They are 'deep in the War as a man is deep in a snowdrift or a dream'.[30] Eventually they are relieved by two legions serving the Emperor Theodosius, and allowed to go home, which is not, of course, to Rome. Whether in Northern Britain or Northern India, the ritual of good government is played out by its doomed devotees.[31] The interleaving of these two tales, and the setting of both of them in England, makes for an emotionally powerful exposition of the idea of empire as an obligation of caste and a responsibility not just to country, but to home. *Puck of Pook's Hill* ends with a hymn, and the lines 'Land of our Birth, our faith, our pride, / For whose dear sake our fathers died'.[32]

Kipling's heroes are devoted to notions of duty, power and responsibility which are the values of an aristo-military caste: they define themselves by birth, by the profession of arms, by the practice of certain sports and games, notably hunting, and by adherence to a set of rules of personal behaviour which can loosely be designated chivalric. In *Puck of Pook's Hill* and *Rewards and Fairies* (1910) this is shown as the brighter, boyish side of a nexus of forces that make up the deep and dark business of government. But it is much more crudely glorified in boys' books which deal with one of the most popular periods of English history, 'the Middle Ages', which means, for this purpose, the period of the wars in France from Edward III's first campaign to the Treaty of Troyes. This setting was often an excuse for a combination of debased Gothicism with the glorification of physical force, as triumphantly demonstrated at Crécy, Poitiers and Agincourt.

The earliest efforts in this genre, obviously reliant upon the model of Sir Walter Scott, can be found in the boys' magazines of the 1860s; an outstanding name is that of J. G. Edgar, whose *Cressy and Poiters; or the story of the Black Prince's page* was the first serial in Beeton's *Boys Own Volume*, midsummer 1863. Edgar is earnest about his historical settings, but his interest in creating an image of Englishness for the modern reader is always evident. The first sentences of the story are an example:

During the long and prosperous reign of the first Edward, Englishmen, while enjoying blessings of freedom and order vigilantly guarded by law, had learned to speak their minds without fear, and with little hesitation . . . they had not yet unlearned the lesson that an Englishman's words should be as free as his thoughts . . . The day . . . was not yet come when a crazy priest, like John Ball, could rouse the populace to a frenzy, or when a rude demagogue, like Wat Tyler, could lead on a rabble to plunder and bloodshed.

Edgar's contemporary Francis Davenant, who supplied Beeton with *A Story of King Richard's Days the Second* in 1865, professed himself deeply concerned with the accuracy of his history, the real existence of his characters, and his adherence to Froissart and Stowe, whom he found 'magnetic' reading. He even undertook to tell his story in a language which would give some flavour of Middle English, but the result was as ineluctably Victorian, in its models for heroism and its reading of history, as Edgar's tales. These earnest practitioners created a model for boys' fiction which was worn threadbare during twenty years use in the cheapest magazines, like Edwin J. Brett's *Boys of the British Empire*, until it rubbed down into vaguely medieval stories of mayhem and romance in doublet and hose, with such titles as *The Young Knight's Revenge* and *Harry of England or the Outlaw's Secret*.[33] The tradition was ready to the hand of G. A. Henty, who produced several medieval adventures, of which *St George for England* (1885) is a fair sample. It is prefaced with a sturdy assertion that 'tales of fighting and bloodshed' will teach the reader 'that determination and enthusiasm can accomplish marvels . . . The courage of our forefathers has created the greatest empire in the world around a small and in itself insignificant island; if this empire is ever lost, it will be by the cowardice of their descendants.'

It is a romance tale of a boy of noble birth brought up by a bowyer and an armourer, both worthy London tradesmen who expect that 'the blood in his veins' will lead him 'to take to martial deeds' and recover his patrimony. He first attracts attention when the Black Prince, aged ten, admires the 'spirit of the knight in him' as he batters other city lads in dunghill brawls. The fights, from this moment to the battle of Poitiers, are all recounted in loving detail. We hear precisely how apprentices break each other's heads, the exact arrangements and strategies of a court and city tournaments (where, though 'these assaults-at-arms rarely end without two or three being killed' the fun is 'rare'[34]) and eventually the numbers, dispositions and casualties of all parties in a series of major battles. Walter regains his lands and titles, of course, but his aristocratic right is only the foundation for his physical courage and prowess in arms and in leadership. When the solid citizen his guardian remarks that 'admiration for deeds of valour and bravery is ingrained in the heart of man, and will continue until such times as the desire for wealth . . . has so seized all men that they will look with distaste upon everything which can interfere with the making of money', and Walter answers indignantly 'Surely that can never be', the reader is supposed to sense and to wish to repudiate an ironic reflection on his own times.[35]

The glorification of boyish physical force, so important in these stories, is often signalled by descriptions of the physique of the hero. Walter is 'an exceedingly fine little fellow' at the age of three, and grows ever bigger, stronger and more handsome. The heroes of magazine stories are often described in glowing terms which combine the values of youth, masculinity and fitness with more abstract qualities of high birth, moral worth and racial type. The boy heroes presented, for example, in the first issues of *The Boys of the Nation* include Jack Fairweather, 'a handsome, well-proportioned English boy; face as brown as a berry, eyes coal-black and flashing, and hair to match in colour'[36] and Tom Allbrass, who 'has a brave, intellectual brow; a pair of piercing, candid, laughing hazel eyes; nose, mouth, and chin finely chiselled, and a head of bonny brown curly hair. Tom is perfectly aware that he is good-looking' but the reader is asked to admire him anyway.[37] The implication is that the boy – the idealised self of the reader – is the highest form of life.

The medieval stories retain, as part of this image of the noble boy, elements of the romance emphasis on birth and breeding, which Kipling also invokes in his own way; but the other favourite setting for historical tales, the Napoleonic Wars and especially Nelson's navy, tends to have a slightly more egalitarian stress. Tom Allbrass is a middy, the apotheosis of the boy as leader. Here qualities of bravery, and of national as opposed to class superiority, are heavily stressed. The officer quality of leadership is not so much feudal or charismatic, connected with the mystique of blood, but rather an exaltation of the gentry qualities of efficiency and intelligence and moral worth. The naval stories highlight two things above all, and both are relevant to the training of the empire-builder. The first is that England is a gallant little nation whose power and whose conquests are obviously the reward of merit, since all her opponents are bigger and uglier than she is. Her naval triumphs are the result of undeniable superiority: it is axiomatic that the small English ships are better sailed, better manned and better fought than those of the enemy, whether French, Spanish, American or pirate. European opponents fail from lack of courage and efficiency, while the Americans and the pirates may be daring and effective, but lack any sense of honour or heroic self-sacrifice. The British tar is superhuman in his bravery, his endurance and his discipline, the last quality partly owing to his officers, who are equally brave (or rather daring, for the different overtones of the word are important). In addition, they are wonderfully good at inspiring their men, and very clever, able to devise and carry out audacious manoeuvres under the noses of lumbering or befuddled foreigners. The emblem of this superiority in the men is the working of the guns, which is normally allowed to be at least twice as fast on an English ship; amongst the officers, the captain is usually wise and silent, and wins battles against great odds by his long familiarity with the sea, while the youngest middy may show his potential by brilliant feats of enterprise, his cheek in charge of a cutter.

Such stress upon cleverness is unusual in boys' books, which normally seek to reassure the reader that he can do his bit perfectly well by being a decent average sort of chap, as long as he internalises the values offered to him completely; too much brain is indeed often said to get in the way of action. But the stress upon outstanding merit is the second feature of the naval tales which contributes something distinctive to the training of the sons of empire. Mental as well as physical excellence and self-development are offered as the path by which the exceptional boy may achieve a dramatic rise in status and wealth. It is a translation of the Samuel Smiles doctrine from commercial to 'gentlemanly' terms. Tales of 'men who have risen' are an identifiable sub-genre in writing for children from before *Self-Help*; but while in America they took the characteristic form of stories of financial and political success, under such titles as *From Log Cabin to White House*, in Britain the entrepreneur was soon overtaken by the national, and especially naval, hero. Typical examples are *From Powder Monkey to Admiral* by W. H. G. Kingston (1883), and *From the Slum to the Quarterdeck* by Gordon Stables (1907), and the mammoth series of stories which translated Kingston's *The Three Midshipmen* (1873) to *The Three Admirals* (1877) by way of most of the ranks in between. All these first appeared as serials, and so were very widely available. The diverting of national energy from business to public service was one of the prime objectives of the public school system[38] and the boys' stories of Nelson's navy served the same end in imaginative terms.

When *From Powder Monkey to Admiral* appeared in volume form, it had a preface by the first editor of the *Boy's Own Paper*, Dr Macaulay. He makes the usual disclaimer about the bad effects of bloodthirsty stories before passing on to tackle at much greater length the possible objection that the story might raise fruitless ambition. He strenuously denies this, and gives a set of examples of boys who have risen from the lowest to the highest rank in naval service, beginning with Benbow and Jean Bart and asserting that there are living examples, whom he conveniently feels he should not name, in case their families object to their humble origins being mentioned. Normally the writers of these tales make it clear that the rise they are talking about is only emblematically from the bottom of society. The hero is a displaced middle-class boy, his true rank often signalled, in the manner of romance since *Oliver Twist,* by his superior speech. 'Reid did not speak the low-caste London dialect', Stables states of his hero in the first chapter of *From the Slum to the Quarterdeck.* The social objective of these stories is to set forth a model for behaviour which offers the middle- or lower middle-class youth a path to the highest distinction, a way in which he can prove himself a gentleman equal to the highest in the land. It is suggested that he can achieve this elevation of caste by means which are available to him in practice – by exercising his energy, intelligence and drive, and indulging in his boyish taste for adventure, in the interests not of personal gain, but of an ideal of service to the nation. Dr Macaulay allows that it is actually impossible, in the late nineteenth century, for a sailor boy to become the Admiral of the Fleet, but he assures us that there are still chances of advancement, to 'what is better than mere rank or title or wealth, – a position of honour and usefulness'. The fictions themselves simply sidestep this disappointment by their setting in a period when conflicts were more desperate and more direct, the structure of the service was less formalised, and the fortunes of war made for rapid advances and reversals. In the narratives, therefore, adventure and ambition could be set out in their most vivid terms, side by side.

The adventure at sea also allows for another dimension in the imaginative patterning of these books which is useful in the transference of their values to the support of the Empire: such adventures necessarily take place far from England, while the inspiration and the ultimate reward lies at home. That home is often, therefore, described and glorified. The ideal boy is given an idyllic, normally pastoral, background; if he comes from an English slum, he will win his way to a place in the shires; if he comes from a quiet village, venturing forth because his family is in need, or has a tradition of service, he can restore the fortunes or the glory of the old home. The remainder of this paper will be concerned with this dimension of the image of England.

There is an evolution in the picture of England in these books, which matches the changing emphasis and direction of imperialist propaganda. Tennyson's 'English Idylls' (1842) may have marked the point at which the Romantic vision gave way to the rural-idyllic in literature for adults,[39] but the dominance of such images in children's fiction did not begin so early.

The advocates of emigration in the 1840s and '50s had another use for their descriptions of England: they are presented for the purposes of contrast, and show squalid, bleak and usually urban situations from which the hero escapes to new worlds of freedom and opportunity, where hard work brings its just rewards, free of the overcrowded slums and limited prospects of English working life. This is the emphasis in, for example, the early works of W. H. G. Kingston, who besides writing a great number of boys' stories was the secretary of the Colonization Society, wrote manuals on emigration for the SPCK and edited the *Colonial Magazine* from 1849–52.[40] He had several imitators who consciously employed their pens in the same cause. In, for example, *Hardy and Hunter*, the author, Harriet Ward, states her hope that the book will be useful, because 'although but a tale of boyish adventure, . . . [it] . . . relates to scenes which will become familiar to many a British settler, now struggling against poverty in our own over-populated island'.[41] Her hero is born in India, son of a British sergeant; he finds himself back in England when his father falls ill, and his mother supports the family by washing and scouring, in 'a dark dismal home at Portsmouth', one room overlooking 'a hideous group of barrack buildings' and beyond that a churchyard 'plated with graves'. It rains, and his sister has Dickensian visions of 'a growth of human heads among the docks and nettles, cumbering the ground, and emitting a steam of noxious vapours', whose stink he remembers all his life.[42] Their fortunes decline still further, and the hero is sent to Gaelic-speaking cousins in Scotland, who mistreat him, working him to exhaustion and looking down on his poverty; all is dingy, antique, sunless and comfortless, and when he can he flees to the hills, where he can read of 'the glories of Africa'. Eventually he and his mother escape as emigrants to the Cape, and conclude the book, after a series of pioneering and military adventures, with a school and a thriving farm in Kaffirland; they buy up the dour haughty Scots.

A minor line of such emigrant adventure stories continues throughout the century, often written either by Canadian or Australian writers, or by hacks borrowing their formulae. These tales frequently ignore England altogether, and begin with the hero arriving in the colony, where his tenderfoot Englishness is quickly rubbed off during a series of colourful adventures in snow or bush, at the maple-sugaring or the kangaroo hunt. The most of England that the reader is likely to be shown by a pulp fiction writer like E. Harcourt Burrage, for example, is in a first chapter where the stress falls upon the straitened opportunities for English youth. In his *Never Beaten!*, Jack resolves to go to Canada as he trudges home from the Post Office after his night's work as a clerk, on a 'cheerless March morning' through gloomy ill-lit streets in a cold and dusty wind. Jack sleeps with two younger brothers; he is still dependant, and foresees that he will be only barely able to support himself when he is thirty. He is away to Saskatchewan on the sixth page, never to return to the land of 'pale-faced boys, earning poor pay, smoking cigarettes and lounging idly about'.[43] But these tales of colonial adventure tend to be among the least complex and gripping of the boys' books, their excitement becoming increasingly one-dimensional and, one would guess, less and less inspiring, as the familiar motifs became threadbare. They were produced by very moderately talented writers, who often seem to lack any genuine concern for the imaginative impact of their factitious pictures of colonial life. More serious writers soon found optimistic stories might do harm by painting the pioneering life in enticing colours without suggesting its dangers, or the standard of fitness it required. By the 1860s Kingston was writing books like *The Gilpins and their Fortunes* (1864) which stress the risks of life in Australia; he was concerned by this stage that only the most suitable and determined should attempt emigration. The focus of imperialist writing for boys shifted, therefore; and in the new pattern the idyllic vision of England became semiotically important as the inspiration and justification of empire. The tension between Old England, its beauty and cultivated fertility, its security, its beloved associations with family or sweetheart left behind, and the new lands of promise, which are exciting, but also hard and masculine, dangerously unfamiliar, lawless and lonely, is a deep structural polarity in the fiction of the second half of the nineteenth century. Its archetype in popular writing is not a boys' book but a sensation novel which became a melodrama, Charles Reade's *It is Never Too Late to Mend* (1856). Apart from the controversial but entirely detachable prison sequence, this story hinges upon the fate of George, typical English countryman, who at the outset is losing both his little ancestral farm and his girl, defeated by the complexities of English systems and the machinations of a villainous financier. He tears himself away from home, and goes with a richer neighbour to Australia, where he has the advantage of his aristocratic companion. He returns with a huge nugget of gold, as well as useful and profitable experience of sheepfarming and land dealing in the outback, rescues his girl and his farm and lives happily ever after. The Merrie England image, a vision of simple countrymen and peaceful rural life, which was used as emblematic of the lost golden age of equality and good in many early nineteenth-century melodramas, is thus deliberately grafted on to the story of imperial adventure and expansion, and becomes an important part of its dynamic. The transference is also a signal that the nostalgia for a rural past is extending from the working-class level of melodrama to become equally influential in middle-class contexts.

An episode Reade uses to symbolise the power of England is the story of the imported lark: the goldminers, scattered across the diggings in cutthroat competition, trek miles one Sunday morning to hear the song of a caged lark, which has been brought from England and reminds them with unbearable but invigorating poignancy of the old home, whose name purifies and justifies their lonely struggles. The episode is so emblematically potent that it is repeated as a true anecdote in several popular publications, including, for example, Eleanor Bulley's *Great Britain for Little Britons* (1879) which aims to inculcate 'a stronger love of the old country' in its readers. She retells the story of the lark, and adds that 'one old digger said that when he heard the bird sing he felt as if he was in church'.[44] Thus England becomes a deity, and the memory of her natural beauties and their innocent and homely associations replaces worship.

The motifs representing England are often as emblematic and unelaborated as this in children's stories. In, for example, *Old Grimshaw's Ghost* by Vernon Fielding, in the first volume of *The Union Jack* (1880), we are immediately introduced to 'the *beau ideal* of an English country gentleman', equipped with a wife who is 'a true English matron, kind, and gentle, and thoughtful, dignified and courteous, utterly above the littleness of common mortals. She was the very antipodes of vulgarity, yet was full of animation, and could keep everyone alive and make them happy.'[45] This adolescent boy's fantasy of motherhood is appropriately blessed with a son at college, one in the army, one a middy, and three younger boys, at present home for the Christmas holiday. This is a wonderland of crisp walks to church, holly berries, turkey and plum pudding, carol singers, mummers, presents, games and mince pies flaming with brandy. Christmas is a favourite image; it occurs again in *For England, Home and Beauty* (serialised in *Boy's Own Paper* in 1888) where Gordon Stables, himself a Scot, embarks upon an almost grotesquely English setting for his naval hero's boyhood, in 1793. Colonel Trelawney and his lady, a handsome pair, are awaiting at the outset both the first snow and the arrival of their Christmas guest, the captain who is to take their son away to sea. Before the sub-Dickensian scenes of skating and dancing parties at their home, Agincourt Hall, Staples takes the reader along the family picture gallery, to appreciate mail-coated ancestors and interspersed scenes: 'an old castle among bright, autumnal-tinted woods, with a river rolling past it . . . the castle is on fire, and the besieged have sallied forth . . . Here is a battle raging on an open plain. Both armies are English undoubtedly . . . a last stand of the brave Saxons . . . the [next] engagement is a naval one, in which the might of Britain is ranged against the floating chivalry of France. What matters it that the war-ships of the latter are as two to one of the former . . . From warlike scenes . . . wander away, and linger with delight on little rustic tit-bits – of peaceful woods and fields in summer time; of rose gardens, of terraced lawns, on which children and dogs gamble [sic] and play; or meadows through which streams meander, where cattle stand or lie beneath the shady pollards, and where the starry ox-eye daisy blooms, and eke the yellow celandine.'[46] The childhood fantasy of the pleasure of Christmas is thus deepened by a context of antique Englishness.

The interconnection of the enjoyment and beauty of the countryside with its rootedness in history is the essential link in turning the merely idyllic into the inspirational. The culminating example is Kipling's evocation of the countryside as a background to the stories in *Puck of Pook's Hill* and *Rewards and Fairies*. Martin Green argues that these books are Kipling's contribution to 'English ruralism' which is 'nonimperialist . . . quietist, cyclical, fertility-oriented' and feels the writer has to accommodate his imperialist interests to this, creating a 'rich mixture'.[47] I would rather say that the evocation of England is an essential element in Kipling's imperial message, bringing to bear the emotional force of the child's devotion to home, love of family and a dawning sense of his place in time and history as both the reward and the motive for the assumption of the white man's burden. Dan and Una, the children in the books, are more intimate with the land than any adult can be; going barefoot in the meadows and streams, they luxuriate in the beauty of the land, and feed their imaginations on memorised Shakespeare and beloved church music as well as games with sticks and boats, the old pony and the nesting dormouse shown them by Hobden. Hobden is the real possessor of the land, if anyone is, a countryman whose ancestors have worked those fields for uncounted generations; through him the children inherit the English earth. Kipling's sense of the meaning of this nexus of values, the history of the interaction between man, nature and place, is encapsulated in the verses which intensify the story-telling: 'Puck's Song' points to the traces of past civilisations that have contributed to the English landscape and rendered it magical:

> Trackway and Camp and City lost,
> Salt Marsh where now is corn;
> Old Wars, old Peace, old Arts that cease,
> And so was England born!
> She is not any common Earth,
> Water or wood or air,
> But Merlin's Isle of Gramarye,
> Where you and I will fare.[48]

The 'Charm' which begins the second volume, *Rewards and Fairies*, elaborates the mysterious power as a compound of the earth itself, and the generations of Hobdens who have contributed to it:

> Take of English earth as much
> As either hand may rightly clutch.
> In the taking of it breathe
> Prayer for all who lie beneath –
> Not the great nor well bespoke,
> But the mere uncounted folk
> Of whose life and death is none

Report or lamentation.
   Lay that earth upon thy heart,
   And thy sickness shall depart![49]

And 'Sir Richard's Song' offers an example and a celebration of the glad devotion which makes potent the image Kipling has created:

I followed my Duke ere I was a lover,
To take from England fief and fee;
But now this game is the other way over –
But now hath England taken me!

I had my horse, my shield and banner,
And a boy's heart, so whole and free;
But now I sing in another manner –
But now hath England taken me![50]

Richard the eager knight of England, the flower of chivalry and the servant of his country, who is simultaneously a worried boy in his first job and an old man in funny clothes talking to Dan and Una, is a creation of Kipling's genius, but the image overlaps with one of the most common symbols of the inspirational power of England: the red-cross knight, St George. This is the home image, the central visual presentation of the idea. It appears in every sort of publication for the young, a handy token of the complex of values discussed here. The picture suggests all that is significant of the traditional story; no narrative needs to accompany it, and so no reading ability is needed for the child to absorb or reaffirm its suggestions.

The connotations of the image are still familiar to most Britons. The most obvious is the popular idea of the chivalric, suggested by the armoured figure on horseback; this includes ideas of honour, bravery, nobility, the mores of the aristomilitary caste reinforced by association with 'the heritage', the literature of romance (somehow vaguely including Shakespeare, through 'God for Harry, England and St George', as well as Spenser, Chaucer and Arthurian legend). Even to the vast majority which has not read *The Faerie Queene*, the poetic link reinforces an association between chivalry and an emblematic goodness and consideration for others. Where St George appears with the maiden he has rescued, the sublimated sexuality of the code of romantic love is also brought into play. The red-cross surcoat is part of the chivalric image and also carries the glamour of heraldry, which is the picturesque side of partisan assertion and aggression, transferable not only to the national flag, but by association to regimental colours, badges and suchlike emblems: a usefully concrete symbolism attracting not only the clubbable and the supporter of the team, but also the juvenile collector and hobbyist. St George's slaying of the dragon is associated with the aristo-military pastime of hunting , much used for pictorial and fictional excitement in boy's magazines, and it has the attractions of the hunt in a concentrated form. It is a killing which is not only allowed but applauded as virtuous as well as valorous; and while one might feel misgivings about venting bloodlust on beautiful birds or animals, this prey is absolutely legitimiate, the distillation of the ugly and dangerous, a representation of evil which frees the desire to conquer and kill from any concomitant guilt or remorse. If there is any religious content in the image at all it lies not in the colourless affix 'St', but here, in the hero as conqueror of a subhuman threat, a devil. The saint's name being George, however, does contribute to the effect, because it is an essentially English cognomen, transforming the obscure foreign martyr into a sturdy, honest, comfortable, reliable English lad of no particular class but conservative inclinations: the ideal imperial servant.

The version of the St George image which first impinged on the present writer's consciousness was in a 'fairy play' by Clifford Mills, *Where the Rainbow Ends*. This originated in 1912, but was revived in 1951, with its references to the Empire made over to the Commonwealth. It is a curiously feeble piece, clumsily adapting pantomime methods to patriotic ends: there is for example a British Lion, called Cubs, kept as a pet pussy by the child hero and heroine at their cousin's house at Maidenhead. St George is similarly emasculated: he is dismounted, and first appears veiled in a grey cloak, because he now exists 'humbly clad, unnoted and unsung, . . . hidden in the hearts of men'.[51] He tells the children the story of Agincourt ('a Patron saint could hardly miss a chance like that') and in Act III he fights the Dragon King; but on the whole his splendour is greatly reduced by his domestication. He is delivered very explicitly into the possession of little children, as if the idea had become tame, rather shrunken, almost like Father Christmas, a desirable notion that unfortunately only convinces the young and innocent.

An element in this impression is the presence of the girl as the one who actually summons the saint. Like Kipling's Una, she marks a change: earlier imperialist indoctrination was chiefly directed towards boys. The notion of Englishness as a personal ideal is gradually transferred to girls' fiction in the years up to and including the First World War, the period of its greatest potency. In *Terry, the Girl Guide* by Dorothea Moore, published, with a preface by Agnes Baden-Powell, in 1912, 'English' is insistently used by the girls as the ultimate word of moral approval, and even the French girl strives to be 'English' (causing some mirth by her perception of the term: she claims 'I am quite English now. When I am an-gry I hit the other person verri hard').[52] At the climax of the tale, one of the first-form Guides gets a verse published in the local paper, which may stand as a conclusion to this examination of the storytellers' attempts to teach the lessons of Empire to the children of England:

> The splendidness of England
> Is ours to have and hold,
> It shan't be just belonging

To the history days of old.
While boys and girls are learning
To be their Empire's fence,
We needn't really be afraid
Of national decadence.[53]

Notes

1   M. J. Wiener, *English Culture and the Decline of the Industrial Spirit, 1850–1980*, Cambridge 1981, 11.
2   H. Newbolt, *The Twymans*, London 1911, 101–3.
3   Newbolt, *Twymans*, 121.
4   Newbolt, *Twymans*, 181.
5   R. Kipling, *Stalky and Co.*, London 1899, 206.
6   Kipling, *Stalky*, 210.
7   Kipling, *Stalky*, 212–13.
8   Kipling, *Stalky*, 213.
9   See R. Roberts, *The Classic Slum*, Manchester 1971, 127–8.
10 For other studies see for example P. Dunae, 'Boy's literature and the idea of Empire, 1870–1914', *Victorian Studies*, XXIV, 1980, and L. James, 'Tom Brown's imperial sons,' *Victorian Studies*, XVII, 1973.
11 Martin Green, *Dreams of Adventure, Deeds of Empire*, London 1980, 18.
12 Green, *Dreams*, 20.
13 Green, *Dreams*, XI.
14 Wiener, *English Culture*.
15 Wiener, *English Culture*, 41–2.
16 Valerie Chancellor, *History for Their Masters*, New York 1970.
17 W. Locke, *Stories of the Land we Live in*, London 1878, 5.
18 E.A.L.K., 'How to study History', *Young England*, 1885, 79.
19 'How to Study History', 79.
20 H. E. Marshall, *Our Island Story*, 1905.
21 First published London 1897, rapidly and frequently reprinted – the quotation is from the twenty-first edition of 1907 (unpaginated introduction).
22 See J. S. Bratton, *The Impact of Victorian Children's Fiction*, London 1981, 123–4.
23 Locke, *Stories*, 9.
24 Lady Callcott, *Little Arthur's History of England*, 2 vols., 1835, I, 85. There were very many reprintings and extensions of this popular history, the last over a century after its first publication.
25 R. Kipling, *Puck of Pook's Hill*, London 1908 (Macmillan Pocket Edition), 76–7.
26 Kipling, *Puck*, 44.
27 Kipling, *Puck*, 48.
28 Kipling, *Puck*, 49.
29 Kipling, *Puck*, 189.
30 Kipling, *Puck*, 221
31 For the dedication of Kipling's imperial heroes to a task which is perceived as ultimately impossible, see A. Sandison, *Wheel of Empire*, London 1967, and the modification of his view in F. Reid and D. Washbrook, 'Kipling, Kim and imperialism', *History Today*, August 1982, 14–20.
32 Kipling, *Puck*, 306.

33 *Boys of the British Empire* No. 1, 9 May 1882, and No. 27, 7 November 1882.
34 G. A. Henty, *St George for England*, London 1885, 80.
35 Henty, *St George*.
36 'Jack Fairweather', *The Boys of the Nation*, 5 September 1895, 8.
37 'The Cheeky Mid', *The Boys of the Nation*, 31 October 1895, 194.
38 Wiener, *English Culture*, 20–22.
39 Wiener, *English Culture*, 49.
40 Bratton, *Victorian Children's Fiction*, 116.
41 Harriet Ward, *Hardy and Hunter*, London, new edition, 1859, V (first published some time in the 1850s; BL copy is dated 1858). The accurate dating of the mass of cheap juvenile publications of this period is immensely difficult.
42 Ward, *Hardy*, 2.
43 Quotations from pp. 7 and 165 of an undated printing by S. W. Partridge; the British Library catalogue assigns it to 1908.
44 Eleanor Bulley, *Great Britain for Little Britons*, London 1879, 8.
45 *Union Jack*, I, 1880, 157.
46 Quoted from the undated volume edition published by Dean & Son, 12–13.
47 Wiener, *English Culture*, 395.
48 Kipling, *Puck*, 4.
49 R. Kipling, *Rewards and Fairies*, London 1910 (Macmillan Pocket Edition), ix.
50 Kipling, *Puck*, 63.
51 C. Mills and J. Ramsay, *Where the Rainbow Ends*, London 1951, 11.
52 Dorothea Moore, *Terry, the Girl Guide*, London 1912, 177.
53 Moore, *Terry*, 278.

CHAPTER 5

SHOWBIZ IMPERIALISM
THE CASE OF PETER LOBENGULA

Ben Shephard

In the late Victorian period journalism was to imperialism as the tick bird is to the rhino. Everywhere that British armies went they bore on their backs correspondents like G. W. Steevens, illustrators like Melton Prior, and professional self-promoters like the young Winston Churchill. Every colonial war was almost instantly replayed for the audience in Britain and soldiers with a talent for public speaking – like Baden-Powell – became public personalities. The arch-imperialist Cecil John Rhodes was a friend of, may even have financed, the Napoleon of the new journalism, Alfred Harmsworth, and Northcliffe's papers, in their turn, 'gloried in the vulgarities' of imperialism.[1]

In the aftermath of the Falklands War, the role of newspapers in imperialism needs re-examination. Just as E. P. Thompson, in an article in May 1982, struck a note new in his work when he wrote that

the whole British people had a part in [the] naval empire. It was not just a preserve of the ruling class. They were the common people who built and manned the ships and whose families awaited their return. Naval victories were a staple of popular ballads and broadsheet. Drake and Nelson were genuine heroes not invented from above . . .

so a way has to be found to assess the popular appeal of imperialism and to gauge the part played in it by the new journalism.[2]

Some recent writers on the subject have dismissed newspaper evidence almost entirely; others, perhaps, have overstressed their role. Richard Price, in his analysis of working-class attitudes to the Boer War, argued that 'the belief in working-class imperial sentiment rests almost entirely upon supposed working class behaviour during the Boer war' and that 'it was upon the newspapers that the prime responsibility for inciting [those] riots was placed'; yet felt little need to look in detail at those newspapers. Rather he saw working-men's clubs as the true expression of the 'indigenous [working-class] subculture within the wider framework of Victorian Britain.' Douglas Lorimer, in his analysis of racialism in mid-Victorian Britain, wrote that 'the press, indulging in senationalism to arouse readers' interest, gives us an exaggerated, distorted view of racial attitudes', and preferred to base his account on 'the reports of an articulate minority from the respectable ranks of society'. And, at the opposite pole, there is the recent assertion by H. John Field, that the *Daily Mail* and G. W. Steevens in particular, 'co-opted the Masses' to imperialism.[3]

My own limited researches and the example of Charles van Onselen's magnificent account of Johannesburg around 1900, have convinced me that it is both senseless and unhistorical simply to dismiss popular newspaper material as Price and Lorimer are inclined to do. 'Sensationalism' should not simply be written off: it should be understood as the vehicle through which many popular perceptions about the world were obtained; the concept of a sealed-off working-class 'sub-culture' (which Raymond Williams more than anyone else has fathered) also needs re-examination. The difficulties in interpreting newspaper evidence are of course colossal, but a way has to be found to accommodate both the forces within newspapers – the interlocking of proprietorial control, commercial pressure and journalistic impulse – and the complex interaction between newspapers and their readers.[4] For, as the story of Peter Lobengula demonstrates, newspapers can give us a uniquely vivid sense of the texture of popular imperialism.

On 12 September 1913, a 'frail-looking negro wearing a band of crêpe on his arm' appeared in Salford Revision Court, claiming that, as 'Prince Peter Lobengula, the oldest son of King Lobengula of Matabeleland, whose country was incorporated in the British domains after more than one difficult campaign', he was entitled to a vote in West Salford. The revising barrister, overriding the objections of the local Liberals, ruled that he was.[5] The next day the *Salford Chronicle* sent a reporter round to get this exotic exile's story. Though 'quiet and kindly in appearance', the Prince claimed to have been a great warrior who had fought in the Matabele War of 1893, personally led the Matabele uprising of 1896 and parleyed with Rhodes in the famous *indaba* in the Matopo Hills afterwards. He had come to England to appear in a show and been left stranded when it flopped on tour in Manchester. Forced to earn his living as a miner, he had soon caught tuberculosis and was now beyond treatment. The Prince, his white wife and four children (a fifth had recently died) were subsisting on a state pension of ten shillings a week, 'lacking the comforts – to say nothing of the delicacies – which are normally enjoyed by a man of his birth'.[6] Over the next few weeks the local press and clergy took up the cause of this 'Prince in Poverty', with such vigour that on 1 November 1913, the Colonial Secretary, Harcourt, asked the British South Africa Company in Salisbury to check his

eligibility for a pension.[7] By then they were already looking into the events of 1899.

'Savage South Africa, a vivid realistic and picturesque representation of LIFE IN THE WILDS OF AFRICA', opened at the Empress Theatre, Earl's Court, on 8 May 1899, as part of the 'Greater Britain Exhibition' put on there by the Hungarian-born impresario, Imre Kiralfy. While the exhibition proper was a worthy assemblage of colonial products, 'Savage South Africa' offered the public 'a sight never previously presented in Europe, a horde of savages direct from their kraals, comprising 200 Matabeles, Basutos, Swazis, Hottentots, Malays, Cape and Transvaal Boers' plus 'Prince Lobengula, the redoubtable warrior chieftain who was taken prisoner in the Matabele war'.[8]

The show's creator, Frank Fillis, was a 'tall, fair, dashing blade of a man, most limber in the saddle', a Londoner who had built up a network of circuses and theatres in the British and Dutch areas of South Africa in the 1880s and enjoyed good relations with both Kruger and Rhodes. He and his wife – a former human cannon ball, now an equestrienne – had recruited the Africans mainly from white farmers in Natal, having been forbidden to enter Matabeleland itself and run into opposition throughout South Africa. A number of the Africans had been induced to join the party under the impression that they were bound for the diamond fields in Kimberley. The Fillises had also advertised in the South African press: 'Wanted: horned animals, baboons, zebras, giraffe, koodoo, springbucks, hartebeestes, young Afrikander girls, good looking and to be slightly coloured'.[9]

When the troupe reached Cape Town, opposition to the enterprise grew louder: 'Matabele' Thompson, Rhodes's former emissary to King Lobengula and the creator of the 'compounds' at Kimberley, warned in a letter to the *Cape Times* that once the 'kaffirs' had been 'exposed to all the vices of a large place', 'nothing but vice in a white skin would satisfy [them] thereafter'. 'How many times', he concluded, 'have I not had it thrown in my teeth by natives from our own big centres who assert that they can get as many white women as they like?'. The Cape authorities did arrest some of the Africans, but with £50,000 at stake and many powerful friends of Rhodes among his investors, Fillis was not to be deflected. His specially chartered liner was allowed to sail and neither a passionate denunciation in the pages of the London *Star*, a campaign by the Aborigines Protection Society, nor Chamberlain's condemnation of the scheme in the House of Commons had any effect. The Colonial Secretary admitted that 'the British government had no power to compel imported natives to return' and could

---

'Prince Lobengula with troop of Matabele. Frank Fillis's Savage South Africa': a contemporary postcard.

only persuade the Duke of Cambridge, in opening the 'Greater Britain Exhibition', to dissociate himself from 'Savage South Africa'.[10]

Once in London, Fillis solved the sensitive question of accommodation for his troupe by putting them on display, at sixpence a look, in an expensive replica of a 'Kaffir Kraal', thus continuing what was by 1899 a long tradition of putting 'savages' on display in England: a 'Hottentot Venus' had caused great excitement as far back as 1811. Where 'primitive' people had once aroused romantic idealisation, by the later nineteenth century the 'philanthropic stereotype' of the negro had declined and his showground appeal was based more on crude pseudo-scientific notions of 'missing links' between men and apes. According to Bernth Lindfors, two broad strands had developed; the one stressing physiological abnormality and usually featuring 'Bushmen' or 'Pygmies' as evolutionary freaks; the other exploiting the martial, bloodthirsty stereotype which came, often rather loosely, to be associated with 'Zulus'. In 1852 a performance given at St George's Gallery, Hyde Park Corner by eleven Zulu from Natal provoked Charles Dickens into a diatribe against 'the howling, whistling, clucking, stamping, jumping, tearing savage'. After the 1879 campaign, in which the Zulu inflicted a major defeat on the British at Isandhlwana, P. T. Barnum offered the British government $100,000 for the right to exhibit the Zulu king Cetewayo for five years. He was unsuccessful but a rival did manage to put the King's nieces on display.[11]

Christine Bolt, in her analysis of Victorian racial attitudes, remarks that 'As one would expect from those who prided themselves on their pluck, Britons admired (perhaps unconciously feared) the war-like individual or tribe . . . The eighteenth-century concept of the noble savage was dead . . . but traces of the mythology remained'. *The Spectator*, in an article in 1898, singled out the Zulu, the Masai and the Matabele as possible recruits to the British Army. (The British preference for African fighting men was to continue, as post-colonial events in Uganda testify.)[12]

By the late 1890s the pace of colonialism had hotted up and so too had the competition for would-be importers of 'savages'. Fillis's real novelty lay in the scale of his enterprise – and in the way he combined the different strands of the tradition: thrilling circus spectacle, ethnography laced with savage exoticism, and grandiose and superficially convincing enactment of the Matabele wars of 1893 and 1896, featuring a son of King Lobengula himself. Dramatic need, rather than strict chronology shaped the programme. The first part of 'Savage South Africa' re-enacted incidents from the 1896 uprising in Matabeleland – a running battle between a stagecoach and Ndebele warriors and an attack on a white homestead, ending with 'the eldest daughter plung[ing] over cliff and river rather than be taken alive'. Then, in the second part, came the scenes from 1893: Lobengula 'reviewing his troops and perform[ing] the ceremony of throwing the assegai in the direction they are to go to annihilate the white man'; and, as the climax of the evening, a re-enactment of the Shangani Patrol, a central episode in imperial and white Rhodesian mythology when Major Allan Wilson and twelve British troopers were separated from the main body and − singing 'God Save the Queen' − cut down by the Ndebele. Fillis played the plum part of the doomed major.[13]

... The savage rite, when performed in a Christian country, is usually interminable and dull [wrote *The Graphic*]. This is not so in the case of 'Savage South Africa', where the natives contrive out of a certain effervesence of vanity always to be in the eye of the spectator. The *indaba* with its rhetorical Lobengula, its hoarsely shouting *indunas* and their war cry rising like the 'husky whispering wave' is one of the weirdest things that London has ever been given the opportunity to see. The fight of Wilson's troopers by the [Shangani] river has, in spite of its gimcrack surroundings a pathos that is undeniable and irresistible.

The Graphic found the show 'an agreeable blend of the Agricultural Hall, Buffalo Bill's Indians, and the March to Chitral, with a dash of the Somaliland natives who appeared a year ago at the Crystal Palace, but . . . a great deal better . . .'

The Times thought it 'a good show, skilfully arranged both in its broad effects and in details'. The Africans in the kraal were 'fine men and many of them have a most intelligent cast of feature' − a verdict echoed by *Reynolds News*, which purveyed its diet of radical politics and divorce court titillation to a working-class Sunday readership:

There has never been landed on these shores a more picturesque horde of savages than these warriors of magnificent physique and in the flower of manhood. This semi-nude band of aborigines . . . with their chocolate coloured bodies gaily decked out with feathers and skins of wild animals formed a striking and original spectacle.

Only the magazine *Rhodesia* struck a note of colonial sourness: 'the warriors are active enough to please an amused London audience but very tame when contrasted with the real thing enacted under the eye of their living and independent chiefs − a sight which is now a thing of the past.'[14]

'Savage South Africa', according to *The Sketch*, was the 'talk of London. It has drawn thousands of people twice a day . . . not only the multitude but the smart people from the West End'. Prince Lobengula achieved overnight celebrity and may even have shared a bottle of champagne with the Prince of Wales when he visited Earl's Court. The press also noticed how 'our womenkind fairly mob the Africans in their anxiety to see them near'.[15]

Then, in late July, rumours emerged that Prince Lobengula was about to marry a young, pretty and respectable white girl, Miss Florence, 'Kitty', Jewell. The news sent an audible smacking of the lips round Fleet Street. 'There is something inexpressibly disgusting', wrote Alfred Harmsworth's *Evening News*, 'about the mating of a white girl with a dusky savage.' The monks of Carmelite House didn't need to be reminded that 'the archetypal figure of the threatening super-sensual dark villain or black beast usually engaged in a life-or-death struggle with a white, godlike hero for the possession of a white goddess is at the heart of all western myth, poetry and literature'. It was a stock theme of contemporary sensational fiction and pornography. (A volume published in Paris in 1901, 'for students of nervous disorders', illustrated acts of interracial sex alongside ones of bestiality.) The supreme expression of this taboo, the film *King Kong*, was of course created by an old *Daily Mail* man, Edgar Wallace.[16]

It may therefore have been something of a disappointment to the reporters who flocked to Earl's Court to discover that Prince Lobengula, for all the savagery of his stage persona, had very pleasant manners and a comparatively good education which, he told the *Church Family Newspaper*, had been acquired from the Wesleyans in Bloemfontein. His father, he said, had sent him there 'to be educated as a civilized man. He wanted me taught English so that I could interpret for him when the concession-hunters came about him.' He claimed to have returned to Matabeleland in about 1891, witnessed the collapse of Lobengula's kingdom, and then fled to South Africa, to work as a valet for a white man. While passing through Bloemfontein in 1898 he had met both Fillis and Kitty Jewell.[17]

Miss Jewell, on whom *The Graphic* conferred 'grey eyes and a frank open expression', was the daughter of a Cornish mining engineer who had emigrated to South Africa. Her meeting with the 'Prince' might have been part of that 'considerable traffic between aboriginal natives and white women' so deplored by white opinion in the Cape in the 1890s, but she sounds too respectable to have been a prostitute. She may well have been a teacher, nurse or patient in Bloemfontein, 'the educational centre of South Africa' and 'another Madeira, another Algiers, another Egypt in regard to English sufferers with weak chests and imperfect lungs'. At all events she followed Lobengula to London.[18]

She emerges from the events of the next week as a fairly determined character. For three days in succession the couple attempted to get married in St Matthias' Church, Earl's Court, and were obstructed, in turn, by the management of 'Savage South Africa', the local vicar, the Chancellor of the Diocese of London, and Kitty's mother – who had read of the intended wedding in the Paris papers. Press coverage was intense throughout, veering between facetious amusement and righteous indignation. On the first day a large crowd of 'young ladies of the neighbourhood, early tradesmen, postmen on bicycles and clerks going to work' saw the couple arrive at the church: 'The Royal South African was dressed in a short jacket and a straw hat . . . Loben is a presentable-looking gentleman, and Miss Jewell was still more presentable. "Oh Lor, I wish I was a nigger", said an enthusiastic admirer of the bride who stood leaning over the churchyard wall.'[19]

Even a turn on the water chute at Earl's Court that night was worth some copy; 'The big Matabele and the little Jewell presented a grotesque spectacle as they came careering down side by side. The lady screamed in quite the orthodox style when the water was reached while the black was as calm as if he had been fording the Limpopo.'[20]

Meanwhile the *Evening News* wrote: 'It is to be hoped that steps will be taken to prevent so disgraceful an occurrence as the projected marriage, the mere mention of which must produce a feeling of disgust in all decent minds.'[21]

Though a marriage certificate was actually filled in on the second day – Lobengula gave his name as 'Peter Kushana Loben' and his father's profession as 'King, Matabeleland' – no ceremony took place. Nor is there any evidence of a civil wedding. Amid a welter of speculation and 'signings' from all over the country, the couple retired to Southampton – Lobengula having broken his contract with the show – as if to return to South Africa.[22]

The intrepid reporter from the *Southern Echo* who tracked Lobengula down three days later, still in Southampton, found the 'Black Prince' in bitter mood:

It's all lies that has appeared about me in the London papers . . . I shall never forget how I have been treated in this country, more like a dog than a prince.' People thought he couldn't understand the language and said all sorts of things about him, but he knew all about it although his father was a savage and had called the English white dogs. He was different. He knew what civilisation was.

He offered no explanation for not catching the boat but was emphatic that 'me and the princess' would be on the next one. He bought a round of drinks for everyone in the restaurant and said dramatically: 'Good bye. I shall never see you again, never see you again'.[23]

By now the London papers had turned to wider issues. 'Miscegenation', wrote *The Spectator*, 'has long been regarded by the Anglo-Saxon races as a curse against civilisation,' Why, it asked, was this 'prejudice' so much stronger with Anglo-Saxons than with Latins?

The white man, being supported in his faith by the whole history of the world, believes firmly, often without thinking about it, that his colour marks him out as belonging to the hereditary aristocracy of mankind and regards any degradation to that aristocracy as a kind of personal insult, to be prevented if possible and, if not, bitterly resented.

The radical *Star* agreed that 'sentiment is generally against such a union'.[24]

The *Daily Mail* congratulated the clergy on their refusal 'to be parties to the consecration of a stupendous act of folly and of physical immorality'. Then it turned to the 'Kaffir Kraal', where the Africans were on display in huts. A South African, H. Lucius Pearce, described, in the true Harmsworth style of genteel innuendo, what was going on there: 'Women, apparently of gentle birth, crowd round the nearly-naked blacks, give them money, shake hands with them, and even go down on their hands and knees in order that they may investigate further the interior of the overcrowded huts.'

Bad enough. But: 'At night it is even worse, for under the cover of partial darkness, the manners of the Matabele grow very offensive and they are encouraged by the behaviour of female visitors whose IMPROPRIETY IS PLAIN' and who: 'shower upon them attentions that were certain to be INTERPRETED IN THEIR WORST SENSE.'[25]

These women, wrote *Vanity Fair*, were not simply 'degrading themselves in the opinion of healthy-minded persons'; they were 'seriously weakening the Empire'. As Lucius Pearce explained in the *Daily Mail*:

All of her race take care that in Africa an English woman shall be respected . . . English people having female relatives in South Africa might well feel some anxiety for the women who live in close proximity to natives who are worse than brutes when their passions are aroused. Colonists know how to keep these passions in subjection by a wholesale dread of the white man's powers and that dread is being dissipated daily by familiar intercourses at Earl's Court.

The real danger would come, the *Daily Mail* added, when 'the Kaffirs return to their own country and convey their impressions to men of their own race'.[26]

In a society in which 'sex, enticing the imagination, remained hidden behind voluminous garments', and 'the naked body was a rare prize all the more luscious for being cunningly wrapped' (as the novelist William Trevor has written), a group of semi-naked Ndebele warriors must have made a powerful image of masculine sexuality, as showmen like Fillis were well aware. But much of the press hysteria derived from white settlers in Africa, with their particular phobia about 'black peril', and from a force that Fraser Harrison has detected in Kipling's work at this time: [his] 'fear, one that he was by no means alone in feeling, that his masculinity was insufficient to stir the blood of the young women who were his contemporaries.' This fear of the new, emancipated woman was overtly and comically expressed by *Vanity Fair*:

Man seldom makes such a show of himself as this amorous woman has been making of herself. The modern woman – superior as she is – affects to adore the highest in man, not the lowest. Yet here is a specimen of her sex most eager to tie herself to a savage. We should like to regard her as an exception but why do so many women take pleasure in touching and patting and even stroking these black persons? These blacks do not represent the highest, but the lowest in man. If the Earl's Court savages were a collection of astronomers or physiologists, if they were in any way noted for their brain power they would create no interest at all among women of this kind. Minds weigh not at all against matter with many women. It is not a pleasant thing to say; but this Earl's Court show has not tended to show the niceness of women.[27]

The Liberal *Morning Leader*, the cheap daily paper most aimed at a working-class readership, enjoyed the ironies of the situation.

The outcry was at first against the danger that these natives would run in a huge city and in a strange land. It looks as though, by the strange irony of fate, some of the 'conquering race' require to be saved from themselves. For some time the monstrous record of drunken orgies, of wild escapes and escapades in the streets [of Earl's Court] went on, and all that was bad enough. But since then it has become notorious that English women have petted and pampered these specimens of a lower race in a manner which must sicken those who know the facts. The gloomy theories preached by those who believe in 'decadence' are, in a general way, it is well to know, 'mere moonshine'. But if ever a champion of that doctrine wants an object lesson in support of his creed he has only to point to 'Savage South Africa'.

IMPERIALISM IN THE WIND

Imperialism! Why the manner in which some of our race have acted with regard to these savages has been a fine thing for prestige. The tales that these black men will take back to their own land about the white men in the capital city of the Empire – in that mysterious city which they have always connected with the power of the Great Queen and of a superior race – will be a precious result of a show supposed to help the Empire.

The *Morning Leader*'s stablemate, *The Star* had attacked 'Savage South Africa' from the start, partly on humanitarian grounds but mainly because of Fillis's links with the 'bright particular stars of Rhodesian finance', men like Rhodes's public relations chief, Rutherfoord Harris. Having defeated the Ndebele on the battlefield they were now exploiting their bodies in a sordid spectacle, 'satyrs for whom no profits smell vile'. The Aborigines' Protection Society stepped up its opposition.[28]

It was probably, however, the *Daily Mail*'s almost daily campaign throughout August to 'close the kraal' which brought about the Earl's Court management's decision, on 29 August, to bar women from the kraal. Some 600 had to be turned away in a single day.[29]

After failing to have the ban overturned in the courts, Fillis moved his show to Olympia, sent half of the Africans back to Cape Town and, to counter charges that they had been roaming the streets, more or less locked up the rest. There was a scandal over the sanitary arrangements and an outcry from missionaries when the Africans were not allowed out at Christmas. The show did less well at Olympia, and closed abruptly on 27 January 1900.[30]

What, meanwhile, of its erstwhile star? Peter Lobengula and Kitty Jewell never caught the boat back to South Africa. Had they done so they would at this time have married (in the Cape, anyway) but would have faced social isolation. Instead, they drifted back to London, living quietly in rented rooms in South Kensington. By 3 December 1899, reality had caught up with them, as it does all fugitive lovers. Kitty's money, on which they had been living, had run out, and in West London Magistrates Court she accused Lobengula of living on her immoral earnings. He accused her of having lovers. The confused press accounts suggest a relationship under unbearable strain.[31]

But there was no immediate parting. Two months later, in February

1900, a still smartly dressed Lobengula was back before the magistrates for arrears of rent owed by Miss Jewell – who had decamped only the previous week. And, four months after that, in June 1900, the couple were still together. Lobengula, by choice or necessity, had returned to the only role in which he could earn a living, as a 'magnificent savage', and had rejoined 'Savage South Africa' for a provincial tour. He and Kitty were the centre of attention as they left Manchester Station in their 'private brougham'.[32]

By then, showbiz imperialism had entered a new phase. In Manchester, the Free Trade Hall was offering 'The War Boerograph – Life Motioned Pictures. Actual Battle scenes taken under fire' and even the Zoological Gardens in Belle Vue were given over to a 'Monster Open-Air Picture of the Siege of Ladysmith'. Fillis's main attraction was now the ten families of Boers he had originally brought over, plus various bits and pieces from the recent battle of Elandslaagte. Prince Lobengula, 'the famous and terrible', etc., got lower billing.[33]

Fillis's staging, in a football ground in Salford, was as slick as ever, and *Savage South Africa* a great success. Prince Lobengula was kept busy giving 'at homes' in his kraal in the interval. The *Salford Chronicle* noticed his 'white bride' watching every performance from a special seat, 'a young lady of rather prepossessing appearance, remarkably pleasant in both demeanour and conversation'. She seemed, though, bored and dissatisfied, and remarked, ominously, 'You know I hate all black people'.[34]

By the time the interview appeared she had gone. There had been a quarrel, Lobengula had attacked her, and 'a letter of a tragic character signed "Kitty Jewell" and addressed to Prince Lobengula, together with some lady's apparel [had] been found on the canal bank between Salford and Bowden'. The suggestion of suicide is not pursued and press references to Kitty cease abruptly. Her end, like her true character, remains a mystery.[35]

'Savage South Africa' played in Salford for eight weeks, then moved to Blackpool, Leeds and Liverpool; but, with overheads of £1,800 a week, broke up before the end of 1900. Fillis sold his props in Manchester and returned to South Africa with most of his Africans. By 1904 he was taking Boer generals to St Louis, Missouri – where they refought their battles with great popularity. Then he fell on hard times, abandoned his human cannon ball of a wife and moved to the Far East. He died in Bangkok in 1922.[36]

Peter Lobengula, however, remained in England. The 'rhetorical Lobengula' may have had a brief outing in a pantomime, *Robinson Crusoe*, in Manchester in 1901, but any theatrical career was short-lived and he was soon obliged to apply to Agecroft Colliery, Salford, for work as a miner.[37]

By 1900 Salford had evolved from Engels' industrial cauldron into the working-class slum recalled by Robert Roberts. A web of community and philanthropy stretched across the worst of the hardship and squalor, extending even to indigent blacks. The size of the Salford – or Manchester – black population at this time is as impossible to assess as that of Great Britain as a whole. Press accounts suggest a small, but definite black community, most of them probably ex-sailors.[38]

Given the absence of any records, Peter Lobengula's experiences among the white working-class of Salford can only be extrapolated from other contemporary accounts, notably *Britons Through Negro Spectacles* (1905) by the West African A. B. C. Merriman Labor, who stresses particularly the ignorance that lay behind popular attitudes.

The people's notion of black men is very limited and even the limited very vague. A good many Britons believe that all Africans and even Indians in Britain are from the same country, that they speak the same language and are known to each other . . . Of the black man's country their knowledge is worse still . . . In the low class suburbs a black man stands the chance of being laughed at to scorn until he takes to his heels. [The Diamond Jubilee of 1897], by bringing hundreds of black soldiers and others into Britain, made black faces somewhat familiar [but] . . . pray even now you never meet a troupe of school children just from school. They will call you all kinds of names, sing you all sorts of songs. Pray also that you never encounter a band of factory girls just from their workshop. Some of these girls will make fun of you by throwing kisses at you when not making hisses at you while others shout 'Go wash your face, guv'nor', or sometimes call out 'nigger, nigger, nigger'.

(Savage South Africa's visit to Blackpool in August 1900 had been marked by similar incidents; a 'sensational affray' developed when one member of the troupe, 'irritated by the taunts from the crowd – "Go wash your dirty faces" and other remarks of a similar nature', had 'commenced to talk in a very wild manner', [declaring] 'that he belonged to Barbadoes, West Indies and was as British as anyone around him'.)[39]

Merriman Labor was even once asked, by a poor beggar to whom he had just given money, to 'show me your tail, your coal-black tail'.[40]

Nor would Peter Lobengula's working environment have been an easy one. The owners of Agecroft Colliery, Andrew Knowles and Son, were very tough employers indeed, the pit's safety record was poor, and the Lancashire coalfield as a whole was marked by a 'history of miserable strikes following miserable strikes in weary and often futile repetition'.[41] When, in 1913, Peter Lobengula re-emerged from obscurity, he had, as we have seen, fathered five children by an Irish girl, contracted severe phthisis, been supported by the local clergy, given his vote to the Tories of West Salford, and gained public attention as 'a Prince in Poverty'.[42]

The British South Africa Company, having been asked by Harcourt to look into the Prince's claim to a pension, came back two weeks later with a crisp reply: 'The man's story has no shadow of foundation'. The Company listed the known sons of King Lobengula and quoted evidence from the organisers of the 1899 show that the theatrical Lobengula had been engaged in Natal and knew nothing about Matabeleland.[43] As quickly as they had taken up his cause, the Salford reporters returned to hound the dying Lobengula. He remained quite adamant in his claim. But the latest excitement was too much for him, and on 24 November 1913, in the arms of the ever-faithful local vicar, he died, reaffirming 'to the last that he was the son of King Lobengula. A man on the point of death would hardly persist in a false statement.'[44]

Two days later, large crowds lined the route of the funeral procession. 'As it passed the pits where the deceased man had worked, his comrades dropped their hats. The body was enclosed in a plain oak coffin. Several coloured gentlemen attended. There were many wreaths.'[45] By 1920, his Irish-born wife and four of his children lay beside Peter Lobengula in Agecroft cemetery – where their graves can still be seen. One son lived till 1977, working mainly as a packer in a local factory and apparently quite uninterested in the 'Prince Lobengula' story when it periodically resurfaced in the Manchester papers.[46]

Was Lobengula genuine? Clearly the version of his past which he gave in 1913 was a pack of lies derived from Fillis's show. The 1899 account, however, is detailed and superficially convincing in its recollections of Matabeleland; but it, too, contains factual errors and confuses episodes between 1893 and 1896. The BSAC's judgment that he was an imposter is supported by the absence in missionaries' and traders' accounts of any reference to a white-educated son, by the indifference of the Khumalo family to his claims, and by the general opinion of contemporaries like Francis Colenso that he was a Zulu. On the other hand, the BSAC was hardly an impartial enquirer, the parameters of Lobengula's family were extensive, and there is some evidence, in documents in Harare that I have not had a chance to see, that children of his were taken to South Africa, perhaps by wives or concubines (apart, of course, from the sons that were educated by Rhodes).[47]

But the operatic power of the story derives not from the Khumalo connection but from the violent juxtaposition of cultural worlds it evokes. Peter Lobengula's character comes through quite clearly: a survivor, a collaborator, a man who adapted easily to the opportunities the white entertainment machine offered, savouring the fancy clothes and the personal broughams, only to find himself trapped in the role of the 'dusky warrior'. Washed up amongst the white proletariat of Salford, he seems to have retained his dignity and adaptability. How far he was accepted by his white fellow miners (like Paul Robeson in the romantic film *The Proud Valley*), whether on his deathbed he was recalling a boyhood in the Matopos or simply re-enacting his greatest role, the historian cannot say.[48]

It is tempting to see 'Savage South Africa' as some latter-day Roman triumph, though of course a 'privatised' one, conducted, like the Charter itself, for gain as well as glory. There are powerful Roman echoes here and there in the press coverage, such as a reference to 'the Matabele consent[ing] to bite the dust in deference to the hot fire of the Maxims' – a ritual prostration before a superior foe. The performance was certainly in part a celebration of racial superiority, but in the particular British indirect way. *The Times* reported

one pleasingly British incident which caused a change in the public programme. At a certain stage in the drama there is an examination of a native prisoner who refuses to tell which way his chief has fled. A file of men with loaded rifles is drawn up before him and he is told that if he still refuses he will be shot. According to the printed outline of the plot he ought to have been shot forthwith. But his repeated refusal drew from the audience such a genuine cheer that the performers wisely altered the course of events and one of them got an additional round of applause by a remark that 'a brave man is a brave man, whatever the colour of his skin'.

(A view not generally held in Matabeleland in 1896).[49]

It was also an explicit piece of economic and physical exploitation, using Africans to project to British audiences a series of stereotypes of savagery, darkness and cruelty. Fillis himself was very much in the 'Zulu' tradition, however: he did not exploit 'bestial' imagery as, for example, P. T. Barnum did. Rather he profited from his Africans' very humanity, the beauty of their bodies, their half-naked masculinity. Peter Lobengula spoiled it all by crossing the fine line that separated a 'magnificent warrior' from a black man who 'mated' with a white woman.

'Savage South Africa' was a loosely slung together set of tableaux, probably culled from newspaper accounts of the time. If there was any dialogue, no one was credited with writing it. The interesting thing about its selection of material is that both the battles depicted – the Gwelo coach in 1896, the Shangani patrol in 1893 – were won by the Ndebele, not by the British. Lord Blake, the historian of white Rhodesia, has explained how the Shangani patrol

has come to be a symbol of Rhodesian history, a symbol of courage, heroism and endeavour, a symbol too of the civilised few among the savage multitude. The fact that it was utterly futile and affected the war in no way whatever is irrelevant. The men who died were not to know this and it does not detract from their gallantry.

It is difficult to say quite why a particular episode becomes part of a nation's folklore, legend and inspiration. The stock cliché – that their 'loss was not in vain' does not apply here, for it obviously was. Perhaps Philip Mason is right [in *Birth of a Dilemma*] in suggesting that man is 'deeply suspicious' of a free gift or anything too easily won. The advance of the Pioneers and the Matabele war had cost scarcely a single life. The heroic legend of the Shangani Patrol met the deep human instinct that great gains are not made without sacrifice.

Whatever the reasons, no one who has been in Rhodesia [Blake was writing in 1975] for even a few days can doubt the impact of Allan Wilson's last stand. It is by far the most prominent feature in the iconography of Rhodesia's history. Paintings galore, sculptures, friezes, tapestries depict it. There is scarcely a public building where one does not see in some medium or other the depiction of a scene which has now become semi-stylised – the troopers firing from behind a rampart of dead horses; Allan Wilson himself, taller than all the rest, shooting an Ndebele warrior with his revolver, the enemy in the background with assegai and gun. There is a flavour of romantic imperialism, *The Boy's Own Paper*, Kipling, Henty and much else which was common coin in the England of the nineties. From there it has long disappeared but in Rhodesia, along with many other pickled pieces of the English past, it lingers on.

It was presumably precisely this mood of adolescent heroism which Fillis sought to tap.[50]

The manipulation of emotion was also at the heart of the new journalism. By adapting the techniques of popular fiction, Northcliffe and his journalists were able to reduce the complexities of life to a few simple formulae, with the oppositions well coloured. The emotional angle of the initial story tended therefore to set the tone throughout – or 'set the agenda' in modern jargon – unless something happened to upset the formula. Peter Lobengula was initially cast as a lovable savage, but his association with Kitty Jewell transformed him into the blackest of villains, while allowing Fleet Street to purvey its favourite mixture of righteous indignation and prurient suggestion. In 1913, however, the dynamic went the other way: the story was 'a Prince in Poverty', and the notion that a man of his station deserved better is implicit even in the *Manchester Guardian*'s stories. Nor did anyone then remark on the fact that he was living with a white woman and had fathered several children by her.

The newspaper coverage in 1899 certainly contains many examples of 'bestial' stereotyping of blacks derived vaguely from mid-nineteenth century scientific views which had by then become discredited among academics. A picture in *The Sketch* of an African holding a monkey carried the caption 'the best of friends'; a letter to the press quoted by J. A. Rogers in his *Sex and Race* refers to 'these hulking and untamed men animals'. On the other hand there are no direct echoes of Douglas A. Lorimer's argument that Victorian popular attitudes to black men derived mainly from the debased North American models propagated first by philanthropists and then by the minstrel tradition. But what of Lorimer's earlier-quoted opinion that the sensationalism of newspapers makes the press an unreliable index of general attitudes and opinions? I hope that this essay has shown that newspaper material is a useful source, provided its full context and implications are explored.[51]

The fact remains, of course, that few of the newspapers quoted here were read by the working class. When the *Daily Mail* was launched in 1896, an old newsvendor outside King's Cross reported that the paper was bought by 'thousands of working men who never bought a newspaper before', but there is no doubt that, even when it reached a circulation of close to a million in 1900, it did not, in Francis Williams' words, appeal to 'the largest public of all, the mass working class ... the last and numerically the greatest of all newspaper publics'. If the 'masses' were 'co-opted' by the *Mail*, it was done indirectly. Robert Roberts's much-quoted remark that 'many of the nationalistic ideas plugged by the *Daily Mail* and similar newspapers filtered into lower working-class minds already imbued with the Imperialistic teachings of school days and found an enthusiastic welcome there' refers, of course, to a later period but is a useful reminder of the indirect effects of newspapers.[52]

A survey of reading habits in working-class areas of Manchester in 1906 contrasted the expectations aroused by the Education Act of 1870 with 'present reality' and reported that

> the kind of reading in which the average working-class men and women of Manchester and Salford delight consists of sporting and ultrasensational newspapers, unclean and illustrated sheets, 'blood and thunder' novelettes, the vulgarest and feeblest attempts at 'comic writing', journals which are merely lottery sheets thinly disguised ... Cut throat blackguardism, the brutality of the strong upon the weak, precocious pruriency, and the most jingo shade of insular 'patriotism' are served up in regular instalments to the rising generation.[53]

What these readers made of Peter Lobengula and his doings cannot with confidence be said. What is striking is that papers aimed at a specifically working-class readership tended to linger on the sensational possibilities of the story – both Harmsworth's *Answers* and Newnes's *Tit-Bits* recounted the stories of previous 'white wives of dusky savages' – without bothering to add the note of racial indignation found in the *Daily Mail*.[54]

That there was an hysterical reaction to the contact between white women and Ndebele warriors will surprise no one who has read Bernard Semmel on Social Darwinism or Michael Howard's recent essay on 'Empire, race and war in pre-1914 Britain'. Sections of the British governing elite did indeed see themselves as an imperial race whose sinews were stiffened and whose loins were girded in a struggle for global supremacy. Events at Earls Court were a deep affront to racial pride, as both *Vanity Fair* and the *Morning Leader* acknowledged.[55]

Whether Prince or Pretender, Peter Lobengula had touched a sensitive nerve in the body imperial.

Acknowledgements

Earlier versions of this article appeared in *History Today* in April 1984 and at an Institute of Commonwealth Studies seminar in May 1984. For generous assistance, I am indebted to Miss Evelyn Vigeon of the Ordshallhall Museum, Salford, Professor R. S. Roberts, Dr Julian Cobbing, Dr Bernth Lindfors and Dr Preben Kaarsholm. For necessary encouragement to Brian Willan, Professor Terence Ranger, Professor Shula Marks, Dr John MacKenzie (for being patient) and my wife, Sue whose idea it was.

Notes

1 R. Pound and G. Harmsworth, *Northcliffe*, London 1959, 206–7. Northcliffe's diary for 1899, now accessible in the British Library, (Add M 63287), has frequent references to Rhodes. S. Koss, *The Rise and Fall of the Political Press in Britain*, I, London 1981, 373.
2 *The Guardian*, 31 May 1982, 12.
3 R. Price, *An Imperial War and the British Working Class*, London 1972, 2, 140; D. A. Lorimer, *Colour, Class and the Victorians*, Leicester 1978, 18–19; H. John Field, *Toward a Programme of Imperial Life: The British Empire At the Turn of the Century*, Oxford 1982. See also Lorimer's article, 'Bibles, banjoes and bones: images of the Negro in the popular culture of Victorian England', in B. M. Gough (ed.) *In Search of the Visible Past*, Toronto 1975.
4 C. van Onselen, *Studies in the Social and Economic History of the Witwatersrand*, 2 vols, Harlow 1982.
5 *The Reporter*, 13 September 1913.
6 *Salford Chronicle*, 13 September 1913.
7 *Manchester Guardian*, 22 October 1913, 24 October 1913 (with a photograph of 'Prince Lobengula'); *Salford Chronicle*, 1 November 1913.
8 Daily Programme, Greater Britain Exhibition, 1899, 5.
9 This account of Frank Fillis's career draws heavily on Carel Birkby, *The Pagel Story*, Cape Town 1948, 91–5. *The Sketch*, 28 June 1899.
10 *The Star*, 14 August 1899; *Cape Argus*, 6 January 1899; *Cape Times*, 8, 21, 22, 27, 28 March 1899; *The Times*, 9 September 1899; *The Aborigines' Friend*, June 1899, 438–9; *Times of Africa*, 21 May 1899.
11 R. D. Altick, *The Shows of London*, Cambridge, Mass. 1980. Bernth Lindfors, 'Circus Africans', *Journal of American Culture*, VI, 2, 1983, 9–14. *Household Words*, 11 June 1853, 337–9.
12 Christine Bolt, *Victorian Attitudes to Race*, London 1971, 144–5.
13 Birkby, *Pagel Story*, 93; *Cape Times*, 27 March 1899; Daily Programme, Greater Britain Exhibition, 1899, 6.
14 *The Daily Graphic*, 9 May 1899; *The Graphic*, 13 May 1899; *The Times*, 9 May 1899; *Reynold's News* 14 May 1899; *Rhodesia*, 20 May 1899. Other descriptions of the show, and illustrations, can be found in *Illustrated Sporting and Dramatic Times*, 13 May 1899; *Black and White*, 13 May 1899; *The Sketch*, 3 May 1899.
15 *The Sketch*, 28 June 1899; *The Graphic*, 24 June 1899.
16 *Evening News*, 12 August 1899. Paul Hoch, *White Hero, Black Beast*, London 1982. Count Roscaud (pseud.), *The Human Gorilla*, Paris 1901. On *King Kong*, Margaret Laing, *Edgar Wallace*, London 1935; and Carlos Clarens, *Horror Movies*, London 1968.
17 Interviews with 'Prince Lobengula' appeared in *The Church Family Newspaper*, 11 August 1899; *The Sketch*, 12 July 1899; *Evening News*, 9 August 1899; and *The Star*, 11 August 1899. *The Star*'s version differs significantly from all the others: 'His mother was the tenth wife who was turned out of the kraal through a misunderstanding in which a Scotch trader was involved. The son was taken to Cape Town and educated by missionaries', but, as it appears under the authoritative byline 'A *Star* man learns', I have felt safe in disregarding it.
18 *The Daily Graphic*, 12 August 1899; *Evening News*, 9 August 1899; *Morning Herald*, 11 August 1899; wedding certificate, St Matthias's Church, Earl's Court (now in Greater London Records Office). Robin Hallett, 'Policemen,

pimps and prostitutes: public morality and police corruption, Cape Town 1902–1904', unpublished paper cited in van Onselen, *Studies*, 136. A. Trollope, *South Africa*, London 1877; Lord Bryce, *Impressions of South Africa*, London 1897. *The Friend of the Free State* and *Bloemfontein Gazette*, 9 September 1898 describes the visit of Fillis's circus.

19 *The Star*, 11 August 1899; *Daily Mail*, 14 August 1899; *Morning Herald*, 11 August 1899.

20 *Evening News*, 11 August 1899.

21 *Evening News*, 10 August 1899.

22 Marriage certificate now in Greater London Records Office. On 12 August 1899, the County Assignation Book of the Diocese of London, now in the Greater London Records Office states: 'A licence having been issued on the ninth day of August instant and being retained by the Rev Curate of the Church of St Matthias Earl's Court who declined to act upon it without the specific directions of the judge and a caveat having been entered by Mrs R. Jewell the natural and lawful mother of the said Florence Kate Jewell Prince Peter Kushana Lobengula and Florence Kate Jewell appeared personally and prayed that the judge would direct that the licence be acted upon – but declined to await the result of Mrs Jewell's evidence in opposition to the directions being given as prayed. The judge thereupon ordered the licence to be revoked.'

23 *Southern Echo*, 15 August 1899; *The Star*, 15 August 1899.

24 *The Spectator*, 19 August 1899; *The Star*, 10 August 1899.

25 *Daily Mail* editorial, 12 August 1899. See also *Evening News*, 12 August 1899; *The Star*, 14 August 1899. *Morning Herald*, 15 August, has the landlady's account of how 'Lobengula and his love-smitten Jewell occupied the same bedroom for three weeks'. 'Mrs Copland says she saw nothing objectionable in their conduct. They behaved at table and kept reasonable hours. On several days they drove out together in a carriage and pair', *Daily Mail* (lead story), 15 August 1899.

26 *Vanity Fair*, 17 August 1899; *Daily Mail*, 15 August 1899.

27 William Trevor, *Guardian* review of Ronald Pearsall, *The Worm In the Bud*, quoted on cover of Penguin edition. On 'black peril', see van Onselen, *Studies*, Harlow 1982, 45–54. On 'black peril' in Rhodesia, see Philip Mason, *Birth of a Dilemma*, London 1959. Fraser Harrison, *The Dark Angel*, London 1975; *Vanity Fair*, 17 August 1899.

28 *Morning Leader*, 14 August 1899; *The Star*, 14, 15, 16, 19 August 1899.

29 *Daily Mail*, 12, 15, 18, 19, 21, 29 August. The *Daily Mail* quoted support from fourteen other newspapers.

30 *The Times*, 9 September, 22, 29 December 1899, 22 January 1900. *The Aborigines' Friend*, April 1900, 526.

31 *The Times*, 4 December 1899.

32 *Kensington Express*, 10 February 1900; *The Times*, 6 February 1900. *Manchester Courier*, 4 June 1900.

33 *Salford Chronicle*, 2 June 1900.

34 *Salford Chronicle*, 16 June 1900.

35 *Salford Chronicle*, 16 June 1900.

36 *Blackpool Times and Fylde Observer*, 10 August 1900; Birkby, *Pagel Story*.

37 *Salford Chronicle*, 13 September 1913.

38 For histories of the black population in Britain see K. Little, *Negroes in Britain*, London, 1947; J. Walvin, *Black and White: The Negro and English Society 1555–1945*, London 1973; N. File and C. Power, *Black Settlers in Britain 1555–1958*, London 1981; and P. Fryer, *Staying Power*, London 1984. None

of these books, excellent though in their different ways they are, has much to say about working-class blacks at the turn of the century.

39   A. B. C. Merriman Labor, *Britons Through Negro Spectacles*, London 1905, 175–7; *Blackpool Times*, 22 August 1900.
40   Labor, *Britons through Negro Spectacles*.
41   W. Challiner, *The Lancashire and Cheshire Miners*, Newcastle 1972.
42   *Salford Chronicle*, 13 September 1913.
43   *Salford Chronicle*, 22 November 1913.
44   *Salford Chronicle*, 29 November 1913.
45   *Salford Chronicle*, 29 November 1913.
46   Information from Miss Vigeon.
47   For an authoritative discussion of the Zimbabwean evidence, see R. S. Roberts, 'Peter Lobengula – a prince or an imposter', *The Herald* (Harare), 19 April 1980.
48   Produced by Michael Balcon and directed by Pen Tennyson in 1939.
49   *Manchester Guardian*, 5 June 1900; *The Times*, 8 May 1899.
50   R. Blake, *A History of Rhodesia*, London 1977, 109–110.
51   J. A. Rogers, *Sex and Race*.
52   Pound and Harmsworth, *Northcliffe*, 202–3; Francis Williams, *Dangerous Estate*, London 1957, 142. R. Roberts, *The Classic Slum*, London 1973, 179.
53   J. Haslam, *The Press and the People*, Manchester 1906, 3–4. See also A. J. Lee, *The Origins of the Popular Press 1855–1914*, London 1976.
54   'I Chat with Savage South Africa', 'White Wives of Dusky Savages', 'The Romance of Strangely Assorted Marriages': *Answers*, 13 May, 2 September 1899; *Tit-Bits*, 5 August 1899.
55   B. Semmel, *Imperialism and Social Reform*, London, 1960; M. Howard, 'Empire, race, and war in pre-1914 Britain', in *History and Imagination*, London 1981.

CHAPTER 6

'THE GRIT OF OUR FOREFATHERS' INVENTED TRADITIONS, PROPAGANDA AND IMPERIALISM

J. A. Mangan

The *Shorter Oxford Dictionary* defines propaganda as 'Any association, systematic scheme, or concerted movement for the propagation of a particular doctrine or practice'.[1] Lasswell placed the emphasis elsewhere, describing it as 'the technique of influencing human action by the manipulation of representations'.[2] As far as they go, both are useful and complementary definitions. However the *Encyclopedia of the Social Sciences* provides a fuller interpretation of the word which more exactly fits the actions of the propagandists we will shortly consider, when it argues that 'propaganda is the relatively deliberate manipulation by means of symbols (words, gestures, flags, images, monuments, music, etc.), of other people's thoughts or actions with respect to beliefs, values and behaviours which these people . . . regard as controversial'.[3]

Sophistication, it has been asserted, characterises twentieth-century propaganda. The modern proponent, it has been suggested, has long disdained the ridiculous lies and outmoded crudities of the past.[4] He deals cleverly in truth of a kind – half-truth, limited truth, truth out of context. His purpose is to focus issues and spur men to effort. Such effort, it has been further maintained, is essentially of two kinds: agitation or integration. Propaganda aims to turn resentment into rebellion or loose coalition into unity. In the immediate context of this chapter there are further dimensions to propaganda worth noting – that whatever the subtleties or lack of subtleties inherent in the various attempts to define the term, it is widely accepted that the propagandist presents a prefabricated and biased argument, that education is not necessarily a prophylactic against propaganda's influence but often a successful instrument ensuring its effective assimilation, that propaganda speaks most effectively to the converted. In the words of Aldous Huxley: 'The propagandist is a man who canalises an already existing stream. In a land where there is no water, he digs in vain.'[5]

THE
EMPIRE YOUTH
MOVEMENT

Finally there is, of course, a close association between propaganda and ideology. Propaganda can be a powerful tool of ideological persuasion propelling men into action.

Imperialism as a period ideology of late nineteenth-century England, was described in 1899 by Lawson Walton, the Liberal Imperialist, as a formula for interpreting the duties of government in relation to Empire. As such he argued, it comprised an emotion, a conviction, a determination and a creed:

The Imperialist feels a profound pride in the magnificent heritage of empire won by the courage and energies of his ancestry, and bequeathed to him subject to the burden of many sacred trusts. This is his emotion. He is convinced that the discharge of the duties of his great inheritance has an educational influence and a morally bracing effect on the character of the British people, and that the spread of British rule extends to every race brought within its sphere the incalculable benefits of just law, tolerant trade, and considerate government. This is his conviction. He is resolved to accept readily the burden of inherited dominion, with every development and expansion to which the operation of natural and legitimate causes may give rise, and to use the material forces of government to protect the rights and advance the just interests of all the subjects of the Queen. This is his determination. He believes that the strength and resources of our race will be equal to the weight of any obligation which the sense of duty of our people may call upon our Government to undertake. This is his creed.[6]

'In as modest language as a necessarily swelling theme will allow' Lawson maintained that the British were imperialists in response to the compelling influence of their destiny. The energy of their race gave them their Empire. Nature then supplemented this bequest with gubernatorial qualities which distinguished their ancestry. In short, race was the basis of imperialism. And the spirit of the people which won empires would never relax its grasp. Its genius would find scope in developing and extending its possessions. In the process of extension, Lawson proposed, the English public schools would furnish an unstinting supply of youth with the stuff out of which great imperial administrators were made; men who would bear their powers and dignities meekly, whose one effort would be to govern with a single eye to the good of the population committed to their charge, and who would ever be ready to sacrifice self to duty.[7]

As a consequence *inter alia*, of such propositions, the last quarter of the nineteenth century saw a close relationship established between the system of secondary schooling, propaganda and the concept of imperialism. It was a relationship substantially restricted to the British public school. Prior to the Balfour Education Act of 1902, and in reality for a long time after, Britain was a nation of two educational systems – the wealthy and well-

---

Chivalry and the Empire Youth movement: from the cover of a report, *The Great Crusade of Youth*, 1948. By courtesy of the Royal Commonwealth Society.

developed private system of preparatory and public schools, and the poor and under-developed state system of elementary, higher elementary and state-owned or state-subsidised grammar schools. The idea and ideals of imperialism were propagated and took root more slowly in the latter. Initially there were more pressing matters than preparation for imperial adventures and responsibilities. State schooling was preoccupied with the creation of a system of organised instruction and with training in the increasingly essential artisan skills of reading, writing and arithmetic.[8] There were also socialist critics of empire who, in the urban areas especially, were often less than enthusiastic advocates of the imperial dream. For many years, it would seem that the proletariat, while nursing a vague pride in the Empire, were less knowledgeable than the middle classes about its dimensions, nature and extent, and less certain of a personal role in its maintenance and survival. It was not until well after the First World War that the Empire became part of the educational consciousness of the state-educated. Of course, well before this time some enthusiastic state teachers took it upon themselves to foster in their charges an ethnocentric vision of imperial greatness, and 'once instructed . . . the indigent remained staunchly patriotic. They did not know whether trade was good for the Empire or the Empire was good for trade but they knew the Empire was theirs and they were going to support it.'[9] Nevertheless imperial propaganda in British education in its earlier years is concerned essentially with the growing awareness of empire among public schoolboys and with a persistent attempt to portray their role as predominantly one of martial self-sacrifice.[10] This conditioning, incidentally, bore remarkable similarity to that of the adolescent educational elite of Nazi Germany and likewise involved a structure of values based on four interlocking spheres of socio-political consciousness – the need to establish an ideal of selfless service to the state, the need to establish a sense of racial superiority as a cornerstone of this selflessness, the need to establish and maintain an imperial chauvinism, waxing and waning in reaction to imperial crises but always persistent, and the need to engender uncritical conformity to the values of the group.[11] As in the case of the Third Reich a major purpose of this interlinked set of values, was to create a 'fighting community,' in this instance ready to serve the nation in the plethora of its imperial struggles, large and small.

In his discussion of 'mass-producing traditions', Hobsbawm claims that they sprang up with 'particular assiduity' in the thirty or forty years before the Great War.[12] The creation of these traditions was undertaken not only by the State but also by organised social or political movements. The reason for this assiduous activity, states Hobsbawm, lay in the dramatic transformation of social groups, environments and contexts requiring new devices to establish or express social cohesion and corporate identity and to create new social relationships. After 1870, rulers and middle-class observers rediscovered the importance of 'irrational' elements in the maintenance of the social fabric and the social order and new 'irrational' traditions were created to ensure social stability. To 'institutionalise' the Revolution and republicanism, the French invented public ceremonies, the most important being Bastille Day, while to emphasise nationalism the Germans, for their part, celebrated Sedan Day. These were the actions and achievements of states but such efforts, argues Hobsbawm, were also the property of international movements – the best example being May Day, which for the International Labour Movement symbolised renewal, growth, confidence and hope.[13] As we shall see shortly, such endeavours were also the property of educational systems and energetic individuals.

'It is with the discovery of patterns of a characteristic kind', suggests Raymond Williams, 'that any useful cultural analysis begins.'[14] Furthermore such patterns can reveal unexpected correspondence between hitherto separately considered activities. In this chapter we will consider two ostensibly autonomous, but, in reality, linked attempts at establishing late nineteenth-century British traditions both associated with the English public school system – the socio-psychological 'tradition' of martial sacrifice and the socio-political 'tradition' of Empire Day. They were, and were intended to be, mutually reinforcing mechanisms, of solidarity and survival. To an extent the latter grew out of, and owed something to the former. In both instances the propaganda of the written word was an important, but not exclusive, vehicle for the transmission and maintenance of subscription.

J. A. Hobson, in his *Imperialism* published in 1909, railed against a 'persistent attempt to seize the school system for Imperialism masquerading as patriotism' and continued:

To capture the childhood of the country, to mechanise its free play into the routine of military drill, to cultivate the savage survivals of combativeness, to poison its early understanding of history by false ideals and pseudo-heroes, and by a consequent disparagement and neglect of the really vital and elevating lessons of the past, to establish a 'geocentric' view of the moral universe in which the interests of humanity are subordinate to that of the 'country' . . . to feed the always overweening pride of race at an age when self-confidence most commonly prevails, and by necessary implication to disparage other nations, so starting children in the world with false measures of value and an unwillingness to learn from foreign sources – to fasten this base insularity of mind and morals upon the little children of a nation and to call it patriotism is as foul an abuse of education as it is possible to conceive.[15]

He saw the clerical school masters of the public schools in the forefront of this enterprise, and warned that it was but a single step from the muscular Christianity of the last generation to the imperial Christianity of the next. Mark Starr for his part, in his savage attack on imperial jingoism in *Lies and Hate in Education*, wrote a little later: 'The text books may be chauvinist, the furnishings of the school include six-inch shell cases . . . the military pictures abound, yet they are passing factors compared to the influence of the teacher'.[16] Both men had a point. Public-school staff were persuasive and persistent propagators of imperialism. Headmasters, for example, espoused British imperialism with a simple-minded, single-minded fervour. The roll-call included some of the most successful of their day: Warre of Eton, Welldon of Harrow, Almond of Loretto, Thring of Uppingham, Moss of Shrewsbury, Norwood of Marlborough (and Harrow) and Rendall of Winchester. They shared a shallow complacency, attached priority and permanence to the idea of empire, were righteous in their conviction and arrogant in their ethnocentricity. And in their zeal they proved forceful disseminators of persuasive propaganda effectively playing the part of 'agents of hegemonic persuasion serving in the role of Gramsci's "intellectuals" spreading and legitimising dominant convictions, winning over youth and "creating unity on the contested terrain of ideology" '.[17] They were able to spread their influence and enthusiasm throughout the schools in a variety of ways: chapel sermons, prize day speeches, magazine editorials, classroom lectures and informal 'jaws'. As institutional autocrats, they were also excellently placed to restrict the propagation of alternative views. Furthermore they had access to positions of administrative influence in the wider society. Four public school headmasters, for example, were included in the Schools Empire Tours Committee: C. Norwood (Harrow), F. Fletcher (Charterhouse), M. J. Rendall (Winchester) and E. H. Stevens (Westminster): 'Such men were the coupling mechanisms linking two interdependent spheres – school and society; they were the critical ingredients of a hegemonic paradigm; they fostered a passionate adherence to the propriety of imperialism.'[18]

Cowper has suggested that public school imperial propaganda was of 'a very gentle kind'.[19] In reality, in the hands of such men it was, on occasion, aggressive, bigoted and extreme. Some indication of the less than gentle propagandising of headmasters within the schools in promulgating the concept of empire can be gained from the strenuous efforts of H. W. Moss, headmaster of Shrewsbury School from 1872 to 1908. Moss was a keen imperialist.[20] In his certain view God entrusted to England unique opportunities for disseminating the knowledge of His will and for holding up before mankind the saving light of the gospel. World-wide dominion was the appointed field of the nation's service. Moss was also an enthusiastic militarist.[21] In boyhood, he 'had read all the histories of wars in the nineteenth century, and thought much about the causes and developments of strife among nations'.[22] In maturity, England's amateur attitude to military matters irritated him. He was fond of Napier's comment in his *History of the Peninsular Campaign*:

Why were men sent thus to slaughter when the application of a just science would have rendered the operation comparatively easy? Because the English Ministers, so ready to plunge into war, were quite ignorant of its exigencies; because the English people are warlike without being military, and under the pretence of maintaining a liberty which they do not possess, oppose in peace all useful martial establishments. Expatiating in their schools and colleges upon Roman discipline and Roman valour, they are heedless of Roman institutions; they desire, like that ancient republic, to be free at home and conquerors abroad, but start at perfecting their military system as a thing incompatible with a constitition which they yet suffer to be violated by every Minister who trembles at the exposure of corruption. In the beginning of each war England has to seek in blood the knowledge necessary to ensure success . . .[23]

After the Boer War, Shrewsbury was one of the first schools to set up a Cadet Corps. Practically every boy became a member. Despite considerable anxieties over a decline in excellence at athletics which held a prominent place in Shrewsbury life, 'the Headmaster's constant ideal of patriotism and the duty of service for England put games in their proper place'.[24] They yielded to training for defence of King and country: 'The competition in shooting, the marches, the drills in uniform, the field-days and reviews by important generals, the summer camp, all became part of Shrewsbury's life'.[25] For Moss, the creation of a Cadet Corps was only the beginning. He recommended a compulsory scheme for training army officers at school with scholarships for those who could not afford to stay on to acquire the training. Recruits would be selected by examination, thus boys of brain and character would then be available for the preservation of England's dominions in time of war. And their public school ideals would permeate through the ranks in a manner unavailable to professionally trained officers in a military academy whose whole time and attention had to be given to military subjects.[26]

Moss was obsessed with England's military unreadiness to defend its possessions: 'Do we wish to retain our Empire', he asked in an address entitled 'National Defence', 'even at the cost of much trouble, or are we completely indifferent whether it holds together or is wrested from us, or drops away from our nerveless grasp?'[27] The permanent nightmare of a European 'challenge to combat' on a far larger scale than the Boer War haunted him. He cast himself in the thankless role of a Micah. He prophesied the catastrophe of raw, ill-organised levies thrown against the machine-like armies of the Continent, castigated ignoble motives, selfishness, greed and pleasure and warned his fellow countrymen not to be like Esau who, for a mess of meat, sold his birthright. He hoped the words that with 'ineffable stigma, branded the name of Belshazzar, the Chaldean King, would never apply to . . . Englishmen of the twentieth century of the Christian era: "They praised the gods of silver and gold, of brass, iron, wood and stone" '.[28] Commitment and sacrifice were the prerequisites of the honour and profit which accrued to imperial pre-eminence. His preoccupation with the militarism and associated sacrifice was shared by others and brings into question the gentleness of a propaganda which urged the ultimate concession of life from its audience.

Another who gives the lie to Cowper's assertion is Hely Hutchinson

Almond, headmaster of Loretto school on the outskirts of Edinburgh from 1862 to 1903. He too was a committed imperialist. Every year on 19 June, sandwiched purposefully between the anniversaries of Waterloo and Victoria's accession, he delivered to staff and pupils, his 'Waterloo Sermon' as it was colloquially termed. In his published sermons, it was more elegantly and immodestly entitled 'The divine governance of nations'. It was an arrogant, bigoted and chauvinistic piece. God's divine purpose for the British, asserted Almond, was nothing less than the guiding of the world's history. Lorettonians, as preordained upper-class leaders, would play their part. They would accept unhesitatingly the beneficent gift of the Almighty – the glorious iron crown of Duty. They would carry the banner of the Cross to the colonies, and with strong arm, iron will and earnest purpose guard the empire from those dual evils of degeneracy: effeminacy and vice. Through 'the contagion of their vigour' Britain's righteous destiny would be assured. The cost would be willingly paid – blood was the price of glory. The blood of heroes, he informed his congregation, was the life of nations. He urged on his pupils the Pauline concept of the body as a living sacrifice to God: 'He no more shirked pain of disfigurement, or loss of life or limbs, in fighting the battles of his King, than any of you would do if the dream of the alarmists shall some day or other be fulfilled and you find yourselves at no holiday review, but for the first time hear shots fired in anger.'[29] The imperial role of the public schoolboy was sacrificial and the purpose of a public school education was to create the 'neo-imperial warrior: untroubled by doubt, firm in conviction, strong in mind and muscle'.[30] We shall return to this point.

On 14 May 1895, at the Whitehall Rooms, Hotel Metropole, J. E. C. Welldon, then headmaster of Harrow, read a paper at a Royal Colonial Institute gathering, entitled 'The imperial aspects of education'. In it he argued that education must relate to the administration of the empire. Consequently, the purpose of the public schools was not the production of classicists and mathematicians, but of governors, generals, philanthropists and statesmen:

The boys of today are the statesmen and administrators of to-morrow. In their hands is the future of the British Empire. May they prove themselves not unworthy of their solemn charge! May they scorn the idea of tarnishing or diminishing the Empire which their forefathers won! May they augment, consolidate, and exalt it! May it be given them to cherish great ideas, to make great efforts, and to win great victories! That is my prayer.[31]

Their role arose out of the colonising genius of the English – the product of racial superiority. The source of this superiority was to be found largely in team games:

Englishmen are not superior to Frenchmen or Germans in brains or industry or the science and apparatus of war; but they are superior in the health and temper which games impart . . . I do not think I am wrong in saying that the sport, the pluck, the resolution, and the strength which have within the last few weeks animated the little garrison at Chitral and the gallant force that has accomplished their deliverance are effectively acquired in the cricket-fields and football fields of the great public schools, and in the games of which they are the habitual scenes. The pluck, the energy, the perseverance, the good temper, the self-control, the discipline, the cooperation, the *esprit de corps*, which merit success in cricket or football, are the very qualities which win the day in peace or war. The men who possessed these qualities, not sedate and faultness citizens, but men of will, spirit, and chivalry, are the men who conquered at Plassey and Quebec. In the history of the British Empire it is written that England has owed her sovereignty to her sports.[32]

Welldon was the persistent propagandist of the banal argument that British imperialism owed its continued existence to English games. In his view, their potential for moral training gave them a higher value than intellectual studies. The Anglo-Saxon capacity for sound imperial government was created out of participation in this instrument of ethical education. It was for this reason he once wrote, that 'no well-wisher of the British Empire . . . would not desire that sport should retain its lofty place in the esteem of all Britons'.[33]

Cowper considers Welldon an exponent of the gentle propaganda typical of the public schools.[34] This is a kindly assessment. Welldon was often crudely insular, opinionated and insensitive in his declamations on imperial matters. He exhibited a naive and uncomplicated confidence in his ethnocentric pronouncements. At Harrow he once dismissed a boy from his presence unpunished with approval and satisfaction on hearing that the black eyes he had given an Egyptian Harrovian were because the upstart had had the temerity to say 'something bad about the British race'.[35] On another occasion he asserted with sublime self-assurance that the moral superiority of the white instinctively recognised by yellow and brown inferiors was the basis of a right to govern others: 'The Oriental man respects superiority; it respects moral superiority most of all, and it yields instinctive obedience to a Power which is recognised as morally superior'.[36] As Archbishop of Calcutta, *c.* 1900, his ambitions for India included nothing less than its conversion to Christianity for reasons of moral elevation – an objective which brought his friendship with Curzon, then Viceroy of India, to an end and destroyed Welldon's promising ecclesiastical career. And as we shall discover later, Welldon was as firmly enamoured of a sacrificial vision of the public schoolboy as Moss and Almond.

Moss, Almond and Welldon were energetic and compelling propagandists. Their vision was clear, their instincts uncomplicated, their conviction complete, their natures uncompromising. They uttered simple slogans, spoke with sincerity and exuded certainty. And their messages were far from pacific. They spoke fervently of duty (unto death), discipline and self-abnegation.

Ideological indoctrination into the ethic of self-abnegation was not exclusively the task of headmasters. It was also undertaken by assistant masters the length and breadth of the British Isles, frequently through the medium of emotional doggerel. These men constructed desirable images of robust boyhood and imperial manhood for internal consumption within the schools. They had a self-assumed and self-assured didactic purpose. Their verse constituted 'morality with emotion'. They willingly interpreted the moral world for their pupils, framed moral laws for their use and were in fact, the metaphysicians of a Victorian and Edwardian educational sub-culture[37] preaching the metaphorical character of the games field and issuing mimetic statements about ultimate imperatives. They sang elegiacally whenever the opportunity presented itself, of school heroes transported from playing-field to battlefield and performing logical and preordained acts of heroism. Theirs was the Homeric view that battle provided the most searching test of a man – his strength, courage, resource, decisiveness. And they had their influential counterparts in the wider society reinforcing their sacrificial message, in patriotic versifiers such as Henley, Aylward, Doyle, Barlow, Austin and above all, Newbolt. Newbolt gloried in the sacrificial role of the schoolboy athlete on the battlefield:

> Our game was his but yesteryear;
> We wished him back; we could not know
> The selfsame hour we missed him here
> He led the line that broke the foe.

> Blood-red behind our guarded posts
> Sank as of old the dying day;
> The battle ceased; the mingled hosts
> Weary and cheery went their way.

> 'To-morrow well may bring', we said,
> 'As fair a fight, as clear a sun.'
> Dear lad, before the word was sped
> For evermore thy goal was won.[38]

The sacrificial refrain however, found its most frequent expression in the magazines of the schools. In their pages, time and again the 'crown of self-sacrifice' was handed to the public schoolboy to place on his brow. By the turn of the century he was in no doubt as to one essential imperial role – if required he was to guard the Empire with his life. As early as 1885, as I have written elsewhere of the Eton, Haileybury and Cheltenham magazines, there had developed 'an awareness of empire in the boldest terms of "glory won and duty done". The foremost image of the public schoolboy was defined and constant: the warrior-patriot. His purpose was noble and sacrificial – to fight and die for England's greatness overseas.'[39] This comment is no less true of other magazines of the period.

The propaganda role of the school magazine in the promotion of sacrificial imperialism is well illustrated by a Scottish exemplar – *The*

Fettesian. Throughout its pages can be found what Raymond Williams has called 'selective tradition'; a process which bears full witness to the accuracy of the observation that the study of educational knowledge is frequently a study in ideological manipulation and often an investigation into what the dominant groups and classes consider legitimate instruction in specific institutions at specific historical moments.[40] Institutional priorities can only be fully understood in their determination when viewed within the wider social, cultural and political context. In all societies at all times specific social interests are invariably served through education by the careful filtering of knowledge to be disseminated and assimilated. School knowledge, more often than not, serves in this manner as an instrument of social control and conformity and assists in sustaining the status quo. The external world is portrayed as an intractable reality[41] and an ideology is created and perpetuated sustaining this portrayal and demanding a specific response. The extent to which its absorption is successful must often be a matter of conjecture but in the case of the Victorian and Edwardian public school imperial propaganda, on the evidence of hundreds of biographies, autobiographies and memoirs, the least that can be said is that such conditioning was not ineffective. In fact, widespread concord and sparse dissent suggest that it was remarkably effective, reflecting period class ambitions, concepts of high status occupations and national jingoistic tendencies. Pedagogic conservatism is the best ally of social and political conservatism, argues Bourdieu, contributing both directly and indirectly to the maintenance of the social order. It constitutes a process of functional reinforcement assisting in the creation of individuals with durable, transposable thoughts and actions – themselves standardised instruments of conservatism.[42] *The Fettesian* is a good example of an institutional instrument of propaganda assisting in this process.

From 1878, when the magazine was introduced, up to the time of the Great War, its consideration of Empire falls broadly into three parts: familiarisation with empire and incipient jingoism, more strident jingoism at the time of the Boer War and then a decreasing concentration on imperial affairs and a shift towards domestic preoccupations. A belligerent 'Hercles' (sic) contributed 'Britannia Rediviva' to the first number and set the tone for an era:

When once she knows her cause is right
Britannia never shuns the fight,
Then Victory crowns the race.
Unconquered country! Every way
Britannia o'er the land holds sway,
Britannia rules the waves![43]

A little later 'Hercles' celebrated the obligatory public school themes of duty, sacrifice and endurance. All was well with Britannia:

As long as England's sons
In life, in death, in peace, in war;
By land or sea; or near or far;
    Stand steady at their guns.[44]

Over the next twenty years a steady stream of letters from Old Fettesians in
every part of the Empire familiarised the pupils with all its many and diverse
regions. It is plain from occasional statements from the editors that there
was a careful attempt to familiarise its readers with as many different
geographical areas of the Empire as possible. In addition, descriptions of
imperial actions and armies – skirmishes in the Khyber Pass, route marches
in the Punjab, a bayonet charge at Tel-el-Kebir and episodes from the
Burma campaign – were presented in terms reminiscent of Henty.[45]
Occasionally school debates during this period were another means of
raising imperial matters and providing information on the empire. An early
motion in 1879 – 'That the present war with Afghanistan is unjustifiable'
allowed a full and detailed examination of British policy on the North-west
Frontier.[46] However such judicious balance was rare. Further motions of
this kind included 'That the system of emigration had proved inadequate to
the needs it was designed to supply',[47] and 'that the Colonies should assist
the Mother Country in time of War'.[48]

    While the military aspects of imperialism received much attention,
cultural, industrial, commercial and economic matters were virtually
ignored. Army heroes such as H. L. J. Maclean – 'Self-forgetful, on to
Death, he hurl'd / True to his Corps, a Guide to all the world,'[49] were
eulogised – teachers, medical practitioners, administrators, engineers,
technicians were overlooked. The image of empire was a young soldier's
empire. There was little or no attempt to present careful factual geographical, political and economic information. If there were lectures on such topics
they were not reported; if articles of this nature were submitted they were
not published. It is hard to avoid the impression that the image promoted
was one of a carefully cultivated romantic heroism well summarised in 'The
Adventurers' which appeared in 1899:

    For her we wandered, and for her we died,
    And to her feet we brought our trophies real.
    For her we bargained, fought and strove and tried
    That unto her our honour might be wed.

    By land we lost our lives amid the snows
    That lie above the sunny Indian plains;
    Backwards we rolled the war-might of our foes
    Or left our bones to rot 'neath Burma's rains.

    We brought her merchandise, we brought her gold.
    Our chosen strength we sold to work her will.
    By war, red war, the lands we won we'll hold
    Through storm or fair, through good report or ill.

We are her power, hers to hold us in her hand;
So shall it be until the end of all.
With hand on sword we guard our native land,
And gladly die, if once we hear her call.[50]

It is hardly surprising that in such a vehicle for imperial glory, bitter thoughts of the fate of Gordon of Khartoum lingered long in the memory, in fact until Kitchener's defeat of the Mahdi in 1899, inspiring these lines:

'Remember Gordon' do those rivers cry?
Yea, we remember: for the goal is won
The vengeance is complete, for which we
   looked.[51]

Hard on the heels of such jingoistic verse came the Boer War which produced the inevitable elegies for sacrificial youth:

Thy country craved thy strength and thou didst go
To fight her battle, should this hour allow.
Already hadst thou seen stern fights enow:
We marvelled at thy prowess, thews and speed;
Thou wast not as thy fellows, and the wreath
Of larger worth seem destined for thy brow.
Thou has not failed us: in the roll of fame
Among the elect there is not first nor last;
Who nobly does, does best in small or great
And when the last call to duty came
And thy young life was on the waters cast,
Well, didst thou strive, we know and take thy fate.[52]

Subsequent numbers throughout the war are full of battle and bravery, and the period fittingly saw the erection of a 'Memorial to Fettesians who have died in the active service of their country'.[53]

It would seem that the Boer War acted as a catharsis for vicarious patriotism or possibly the futility of the expensive, exhausting and unglamorous struggle produced reaction. It was certainly a turning point. Subsequently, at least until the Great War, references to heroes were few and far between, mention of the Empire was more infrequent, debates were insular or frivolous. The school's attention, at least on the evidence of magazine content, like the nation's, turned increasingly to Europe and the growing threat of German militarism. The Cadet Corps, established in 1909, received increasing attention as the headmaster and the school dwelt upon the importance of putting the country in a right state of mind as well as a right state of body for effective national defence. It seems that the Empire was now taken more for granted, and scenes so assiduously presented earlier were now tediously familiar. Whatever the causes, the magazine at this time ceased to be an overt vehicle of propaganda for imperial ideals and delights; yet the Empire was omnipresent. Its influence remained pervasive – in the Old Fettesian Column which provided information of imperial births, deaths, marriages and awards;[54] in the lists of service appointments such as that of Captain A. L. Thomson, 58th Vaughan Rifles (Frontier Force) Indian Arms, to be Major;[55] in snippets of news from colonial newspapers on the doings of old boys, such as the tribute to B. O. Storey of the Colonial Civil Service from the *Straits Times*;[56] in the presentation of news of public-school dinners in Empire such as an Annual Scottish Schools Dinner at Baluchistan which was graced by five Fettesians – Colonial W. C. Macpherson, CMG, PMO Quetta Division, Captain J. C. Macrae, 19th Punjabis, Lieutenant T. A. S. Morgan, Royal Artillery, Lieutenant D. S. R. Macpherson, 7th Gurka Rifles and 2nd Lieutenant T. L. Leslie attached to the 1st Essex Regiment;[57] and in the recounting of imperial Fettesian sporting success such as the occasion when a Fettesian team reached the final of the Indian Polo Association Championship in 1913.[58]

The Great War inevitably saw a resurgence of the impulse dormant since the South African Campaign, to honour martial sacrifice in verse. In 'Revally', Lauchlan MacLean Watt wrote of the early volunteers of 1915:

> They have gone, like men, before us
> Where the dawn was breaking grey,
> See their shadows, crowned with glory,
> Pointing onwards to the fray.[59]

And in 1919 in an anonymous verse entitled 'Sacrifice' the fallen heroes have returned to their Alma Mater with their gift of life for the next generation:

> Bravely ye triumph yet, and comfort give;
> Gaily ye whisper as we hurry by –
> 'This is not death that helps new life to live,
> Be glad to live as we are glad to die.'[60]

From the evidence of the *Fettesian* and other magazines, it is suggested tentatively, as a proposition for more detailed examination, that attitudes to empire in the public schools in the late nineteenth and early twentieth centuries were concerned with 'the propagation of national myths, social Darwinism and imperialistic fervour'[61] It was the imperialism of Dilke, Seeley and Cramb – inspirational in purpose, visionary in scope, biased in argument. Its function appeared to be to engender a narrow, militaristic patriotism. In the case of Fettes its emotional success can be estimated to some extent perhaps, by this recollection of his schooldays by R. H. Bruce-Lockhart, a Fettesian shortly after the Boer War:

The orchestra and the choir performed on Founder's Day and at the School Concert . . . The set piece which I remember best was Kipling's 'The English Flag' set to Bridge's music. There was a splendid bass chorus of four lines beginning with 'Look – look well to your shipping', and this always produced an impressive roar. But the verse which stirred my emotions almost to the verge of tears was:

'Never the lotus closes, never the wild-fowl wake,
But a soul goes out on the East Wind that died
   for England's sake.'

It was sung pianissimo by the trebles and altos, and the singing filled me with strange longings. Kipling had just entered my life, and the Boer War lent an added poignancy to tales like 'The Drums of the Fore and Aft'. I was something more than a little patriot who was ready to die for England's sake. I wanted to see the world, and, with uncles in Malaya and Singapore sending me home strange stamps with tiger's heads, vaguely I felt the call of the East. I knew all about wild-fowl, but I longed to see that lotus close.[62]

In the early years of the twentieth century, the public school socio-psychological 'tradition' of duty, discipline and self-sacrifice was given wider social sanction, visibility and expression. As MacKenzie has made clear this 'tradition' inspired a host of associations and organisations in an effort to give it wider focus, stimulus and momentum. These included the Boy Scouts, the Boys' Brigade, Empire Youth Movement and lesser groups such as the Navy League, the Legion of Frontiersmen, the National Service League, the Girls' Patriotic League, the League of Empire, and the British Empire Union.[63] The 'tradition' was promoted with special determination by the tireless efforts of Reginald Brabazon, twelfth Earl of Meath (1841–1928)[64] through three social movements – the Lads' Drills Association, the Duty and Discipline Movement and the Empire Day Movement. The latter was by far the most publicised and influential and represents an attempt to create a Hobsbawm mass tradition equivalent to Sedan Day in Germany and Bastille Day in France. Meath (1841–1928) was educated at Eton and served in the Diplomatic Corps, which took him to Germany in 1868. Towards the end of the century concern over Germany's imperial ambitions led him to the conclusion that the nation's youth required a further and deeper understanding of the glory which was the British Empire in order to ensure its survival. By the turn of the century he had found his life's work and devoted much of his time and energy to imperial organisations. In time he became Vice-President of the Navy League (1909), a member of the Executive of the Council of the National Service League (1910–14), the General Council of the Legion of Frontiersmen (1911), the League of Empire and a Commissioner for the Boy Scouts Association (1910). These various bodies were all involved with schools and the National Service League in particular, was closely connected with the public school system. It was through these various organisations that many middle- and working-class boys developed a consciousness of empire.[65]

Meath's post-diplomatic life, we are told by Springhall, can be conveniently divided into two parts: 'philanthropic in the 1880s and 1890s and imperialist in the 1900s'. There was a logic in this progression. It was his view that only a healthy and fit working class would be fully receptive to the gospel of imperialism. Once committed, his involvement was total: 'His quasi-religious attachment to Empire . . . brought him either as Chairman, President or Vice-President, into nearly every movement organised by the military imperial caste that was active before 1914'.[66]

As already mentioned, Meath's considerable energy and motivation were harnessed to two movements which clearly illustrate his obsession with concepts of duty, discipline, self-sacrifice and patriotism. These were the Lads' Drill Association and the Duty and Discipline Movement. The Lads' Drill Association was an attempt to promote the means of 'systematic physical and military training of all British lads, and their instruction in the art of the rifle'. Meath never spared himself in his patriotic endeavours, and in his advocacy of the Association he mounted a powerful, but ultimately ineffective, campaign, involving deputations to the government, questions in the House of Lords, published speeches, annual reports and memoranda to the Board of Education.[67] The campaign failed at the barricades of Labour and Liberal Members of Parliament anxious to avoid the emergence of militarism in British education. But it was not for want of trying on Meath's part. The Duty and Discipline movement had Meath as Inaugural Chairman and President from 1912 to 1919. It had a complementary function to the Lads' Drill Association. It was to preach patriotism in place of politics and recreate a nation in his view increasingly divided by political sectarianism. Once again, the energy expended in propagating the message of the movement was impressive – leaflets, tracts and books were issued replete with warning of the dire consequences to the Empire if the degeneracy of the young continued unabated. The spirit of the Movement is caught in *Essays on Duty and Discipline: A Series of Papers.*[68]

The tone of this tract is far from gentle. It is chauvinistic, severe and puritanical. To the various contributors, the issue under discussion was of the utmost seriousness. As the preface dedicated 'to British Men and Women who love their country and its children' put it, the level of juvenile indiscipline was a serious social danger and a peril to the permanent security of the Empire. The list of these eminent personages makes interesting reading: it included the Earl of Cromer, Lord Curzon, Viscount Esher, the Archbishop of Canterbury, Baden-Powell and Winston Churchill; while those who wrote in strong support included Viscount Milner, G. R. Parkin, Edward Lyttelton and Howard Marsh. This was not a fringe group of obsessive zealots but the Establishment on the attack. The churches were well to the fore. The Archbishop of Westminster ('The Paramount Need of Training in Youth'), the Archbishop of Dublin ('Lack of Discipline in the Training of Children – and the Remedy'), the Bishop of Durham ('An Open Letter to Parents') and the Bishop of Down and Connor ('The Best Men are the Men who aim at the Best') all contributed. Their titles, however pompous to the modern eye, were restrained in comparison to those of Lord Meath ('Have we the "Grit" of our Forefathers?'), Edward Lyttelton

('Endure Hardness') and Mrs Arthur Phillip ('The Value of a Certain "Hardness" of Education').

Meath, too, relished the idea of 'hardness'. 'The survival of the fittest', he wrote, 'is a doctrine which holds as good in the political and social as in the national world. If the British race ceases to be worthy of dominion it will cease to rule . . . Britons have ruled in the past because they were a virile race, brought up to obey, to suffer hardships cheerfully, and to struggle victoriously.' The white men and women of the British race would not rule well if they were idle, soft, selfish, hysterical and undisciplined.[69] In 'Have we the "Grit" of our Forefathers?' he looked back with relish to a Golden Age somewhere in the not too distant past. 'Grit' he defined as 'that virile spirit which makes light of pain and physical discomfort, and rejoices in the consciousness of victory over adverse circumstances, and which regards the performance of duty, however difficult and distasteful, as one of the supreme virtues of all true men and women.'[70] He was greatly concerned with the moral deterioration of the Anglo-Saxon woman. Once upon a time duty demanded of women subordination to parents, husband and state. Her first duty was to marry and produce children. Honour demanded that she should face the obligations of the marriage tie and the sufferings and dangers of childbirth 'with as much coolness and courage as was expected of the man on the field of battle'.[71] Society, he asserted, was rightly 'merciless to those of either sex who failed in the exhibition of courage in the face of their respective duties.' Yet, 'the desire for pleasure and for personal ease' appeared to have taken a firm hold on the minds of many well-to-do women. Some girls had been known to decline suitors unless they provided them with luxuries unheard of by their mothers. He had his anxieties about men too. They showed an increasing tendency to enjoy sport as a spectacle rather than 'submit themselves to even the mild severities of amateur training, or take the rough and tumble of the game itself'.[72] Such attitudes threatened the 'national and individual successes of former times . . . won by the unrelaxing "grip" which our ancestors, as a rule, kept on themselves in the performance of duty' and reinforced 'by the stern discipline of the day, which never failed to visit with instant and condign punishment of any dereliction of duty, or even innocent failure in the execution of superior orders'.[73] As for the young, slackness, weakening of moral fibre, ws one of the most potent signs of lack of grit among them. He advocated strict and unquestioned discipline, the encouragement of the slipper and a Spartan-like upbringing in order that the Empire, obtained by hard struggle, should be retained by the strength of a strong right arm and a disciplined demeanour. The value of hardness in education, was reiterated by Mrs Arthur Phillip, who advised mothers to avoid making children pets and playthings. The path of duty was the road to glory:

We must avoid creating a false idea in the minds of children that pleasure and happiness are the ultimate end of life, the one thing to seek and pursue, in distinct contradiction to our Lord's doctrine that they who seek their life shall lose it; and to the teaching of all experience, that they who pursue happiness choose a fleeting shadow which ever eludes their grasp; while to those who forget it, and are guided by duty and right, it comes unasked, walking ever with them, a welcome and blessed, though unsought companion.[74]

Inevitably, that pre-eminent propagandist of Empire from the public school system, J. E. C. Welldon, put in his pennyworth, quoting admiringly the Aristotelian axiom: 'To serve the State, to honour the State, to live, and, if need be, to die for the State – that is the office of a good citizen'.[75] He regretted the advance of 'political individualism' and insisted upon the inculcation of 'a sense of obligation to the State'.[76] Welldon had been greatly impressed by his recent Japanese experiences, where he was informed that eight out of ten schoolboys would choose 'the happiness of laying down their lives for their country'. He too, urged the cultivation of 'a certain hardness of character', wished to see the promotion of 'a true imperial grit' and deplored the lydian tendencies of the sons of the rich. The sacred words of the Apostle rang continually in his ears: '. . . endure hardiness as a good soldier of Christ'. He ended his homily with these words: 'God has endowed the British race with a world-wide Empire, an Empire transcending all imperial systems which the world has known, not for their own aggrandisement but that they may be executants of His sovereign purpose in the world. The citizens of the Empire should then cultivate a sense of a mission to humanity . . . the fear of God, as Froude says, made England great . . . It is, therefore, in the spirit of Mr Kipling's great Recessional Hymn, and in no other spirit, that the Empire can be consecrated and conserved.'[77] In the chapter on 'Duty and Discipline in the Training of Children' Meath drew specific attention to the relationship between the formation of character which so concerned his fellow-authors and the 'Empire Day Movement' itself, which preached the gospel of good citizenship and laid a special stress on the training of youth in order to build up an imperial race 'worthy of responsibility, alive to duty, filled with sympathy towards mankind and not afraid of self-sacrifice in the promotion of lofty ideals'.[78]

The history of the movement is briefly told. It was founded by Meath in the early 1900s. Simultaneous with a colonial conference in London in July 1902 Meath wrote to the Colonial Secretary Joseph Chamberlain:

For years I have advocated the establishment throughout the Empire of a day to be called 'Empire Day', on which, by State regulation, in each portion of the Empire, a whole holiday shall be given to all scholars attending schools entirely or partially maintained out of public funds, with the exception of a couple of hours in the morning, these to be spent by the children in exercises of a patriotic and agreeable nature, and in listening to lectures and recitations on subjects of an Imperial character. Such a holiday should be held on the same day throughout the whole of the Dominions of the King-Emperor; if possible, I would venture to suggest, on May 24th, the birthday of our late Sovereign, Queen Victoria, Empress of India.[79]

The first public meeting took place in St James Hall on 24 May 1904. Meath's opening address described in his *Memories of the Twentieth Century* provides a flavour of the grandiloquence of his hyperbolic rhetoric. Meath wished that no pains might be spared to inculcate into the minds of all, but youth in particular:

the importance of acquiring a thorough knowledge of the history, extent, power, and resources of the great Empire to which they belong, of the conditions, moral and physical, which rule in the different portions of that Empire, of the nature of the climates, productions, commerce, trade, and manufactures, and of the characteristics, religion, customs, and habits of thought of the various races, peoples, creeds, and classes, which owe a common allegiance to King Edward.[80]

Such an inculcation of loyalty to a common sovereign, patriotism towards a common Empire, self-sacrificing devotion towards fellow-citizens 'must inevitably tend towards the universal reign of righteous dealing between man and man, between nations and nation'. The promotion of Empire Day, he proclaimed, had nothing in common with the condition of mind popularly known as jingoism. Proponents had no desire to flaunt the glorious standard which had braved for a thousand years the battle and the breeze defiantly in the face of potentate and people. They sought only peace and amity with the whole world. While it was no occasion for boasting, 'they were conscious of the magnificence and power of the Empire, of its absolutely unique character, of its extent and almost boundless resources, of the loyalty of its populations, by the unrivalled freedom and liberty of person they enjoyed'.[81] In 1920 in response to the Editor of the *Daily Mail* for a message for Empire Day, with similar exaggeration and carefully ignoring the efforts of France and United States among others, he wrote:

We fought for our lives, and they, and all that makes life worth living, were gained by Imperial unity. Without it, Europe would probably today be under the heel of a military despotism, intoxicated by victory, uncontrolled by public opinion, whilst violence and brute force would have crushed the last remnants of independence and of just and Christian feeling amongst the demoralised survivors of the cowed races of Europe.[82]

Everyone knew, he continued, that Empire union meant peace, freedom, justice, personal liberty, Christian conduct between man and man, and happiness, not only for British subjects, but for the whole of mankind.

Meath ran the whole effort himself until 1913 when with money and energy in increasingly short supply, he set up an Empire Movement Committee. From 1922 the movement occupied rooms at the Royal Colonial Institute; by 1945 it had moved into its own premises with a new director. Finally, in 1958 Empire Day was changed to Commonwealth

Day.[83] For many years Meath promulgated the idea single-handedly against Labour and Irish Nationalist opposition. It was only in 1916 that he was supported by the government. As early as 1908 the House of Commons rejected a proposal for official recognition. In fact 'it was the war rather than Meath's incessant propaganda efforts which brought recognition'.[84] 24 May was designated Empire Day, and it was agreed that the government would fly the Union flag from public buildings. It was the intention that local education authorities would foster the concept of Empire Day. Many did. The movement was far from ineffectual and it had a wide appeal. In 1905, 6,000 schools throughout the Empire were said to have participated[85] and by 1922, the year of Meath's retirement from active involvement and his valedictory essay in the *Dominions Yearbook*, the 6,000 schools had grown to 80,000.[86] In Britain in 1928 the *Morning Post* claimed that five million children participated in the Empire Day Ceremonies, and by the late forties it involved some 1,200 schools. As a school organisation it went from strength to strength until the mid-1950s, by which time it had become far more than a middle-class phenomenon.

Behind Empire Day, wrote Springhall, there was a 'coherent social and moral doctrine'.[87] We have explored it through the utterances of several advocates of the Duty and Discipline Movement. In essence, it comprised a belief in the qualities of self-denial, discipline, subscription to duty, fealty to the state. It involved the submission of individualism to corporatism, a doctrine consistently endorsed in the pronouncements of several earlier generations of public school masters. In the specific context of the Empire Day Movement, subscription to the doctrine was carefully described in the *Court Journal* of February, 1910. 'Personal service rendered to the individual', wrote Antony Guest in his review of Meath's philanthropic work, 'leads naturally to service to the community, and hence it is but a step to self-sacrificing devotion to the Empire. This is a duty that Lord Meath had taken special measures to enforce through the "Empire Movement".'[88] He went on, echoing Welldon, 'It is a noble conception, to some extent foreshadowed in Mr Rudyard Kipling's "Recessional" hymn, and it is to be carried to fruition by instilling it into the minds of the young'.[89]

In Meath's plan of things it was to be engendered through powerful and reiterated ritualistic acts and by possession of appropriate symbols. Empire Day, for example, would begin by the hoisting and saluting of the flag; it would include a recitation from Kipling and the singing of the national anthem. During Empire Day week, imperial topics in schools were to predominate. In time, a whole battery of instruments of indoctrination came to exist – 'schools could choose from among an Empire Service, the performance of an Empire play or pageant, an exhibition of Empire products, film and slide lectures, a school concert, a recitation of heroic

English poems, an Empire Day wireless programme, a display of imperial flags in the playground and the observance of the slogan 'Empire Meals on Empire Day'.[90] To these, were added by the 1930s special booklets on empire, an Empire Day Community Song Sheet, samples of imperial products and even picture postcards of the Empire's industries. Meath's fervour proved to be a sword with two edges. The movement was received with some disquiet in various quarters, and not merely in local authorities with strong socialist traditions. The unapologetic militarism of its founder was a continual source of anxiety for many,[91] while in the public schools the ostentatious ceremonial, rather curiously for institutions which made so much of these things in other areas of life, seemed to embarrass some authorities. Certainly the movement was never celebrated at Fettes throughout the entire period from its creation to World War II.[92]

The Lads' Drill Association, the Duty and Discipline Movement and the Empire Day Movement, as Springhall has remarked, were all 'expressions of Meath's imperialism'. In promoting this imperialism, he indulged in foolish and simplistic assertions, nostalgia for a mythical Golden Age, stern and joyless puritanism and ethnocentric chauvinism. His speeches and essays were uncritical and eulogistic. They comprised the purest propaganda. And this propaganda was constantly revised and expanded: 'Letters were sent to the press, posters were distributed and the Movement supplied speakers and Union Jacks to the schools. It concentrated mainly on the secondary schools since it was assumed that there was a "better" audience among the pupils. Certainly it was considered more appropriate for children to learn about the Empire once they had some concept of it.'[93] By the 1920s there was a wealth of material available. The *Teacher's World* of 19 May 1926, offered in response to enquiries from many teachers who found difficulty in obtaining material for their Empire Day celebrations, a wide range of plays, poems, pageants and songs of a patriotic nature. Playlets included *Britannia and her daughters*, *Birth of the Union Jack*, *Masques of the Children of the Empire*, *John Bull and his Trades* and *The British Lion*; songs included 'The British Flag', 'Songs of the Union Jack', 'Songs of the British Empire', 'What is the Meaning of Empire', 'British Empire Song', 'Hymn for Empire Day', and 'The Flag of Empire'; poems included Henley's 'England, My England', Kipling's 'English Flag', Cowper's 'England' and there was an anthology, *The Empire Day Reciter*.[94] Such material was not always appreciated. In *The Educational Worker* in 1927, one antagonist remarked in a sardonic article 'Gramophone records of royal speeches, special radio lessons, plus the efforts of the Press and the cinema are all being used to standardise the mental goose-stepping, miscalled education'.[95] He quoted with exasperation, 'a touching picture of the affection of the coloured worker Sambo for the British Empire' in the playlet, 'Britannia and her Daughters':

> Now all de black men lub de British name,
> Look on de white man – den work de same
> Lib on cornpatch, merrily sing
> Playing on de Banjo, God Sabe de King![96]

Other songs such as the 'Flags of the Nations' rang with similar, complacent congratulations:

> With the life-blood of my bravest
> I have writ the tyrant's doom
> From Hong Kong to Colombo,
> From Cairo to Khartoum.[97]

England itself was portrayed as an idyll of delight, success and prosperity. *John Bull and his Trades* begins 'O, happy are the hours of the home of the great John Bull' and 'Britannia's Court' has a verse of 'quite remarkable self-esteem':

> The nations not so blest as thee
> Must in their turn to tyrants fall;
> While thou shall flourish great and free,
> The dread and envy of them all.[98]

While 'What is the Meaning of Empire Day' rejoiced in simplistic patriotic militarism:

> What is the meaning of Empire Day?
> Why do the cannons roar?
> Why does the cry 'God save the King'
> Echo from shore to shore?
> Why does the flag of Britannia float
> Proudly o'er fort and bay?
> Why do our kinsmen gladly hail,
> Our glorious Empire Day?
>
> *Response*
>
> On our nation's scroll of glory,
> With its deeds of daring told
> There is written a story,
> Of the heroes bold,
> In the days of old
> So to keep the deeds before us,
> Every year we homage pay
> To our banner proud
> That has never bowed,
> And that's the meaning of Empire Day.[99]

The impulse behind Empire Day, it is suggested, was linked to an earlier public school 'tradition'. Both arose out of a need to create a sense of imperial commitments and new patriotic imperatives. The circle was closed when the public schools themselves celebrated the occasion with pomp and pageantry. Shrewsbury under Moss, was one of the earliest. Moss strongly supported the Empire Day Movement believing that 'it did more to cement the ties between the Mother-country and her sons overseas than any other organisation'. Moss, in fact, in his enthusiasm for empire, had been inspired directly and personally by Meath, who had attended the Church Congress at Shrewsbury in 1896 and shared a platform with him.[100] Empire Day at Shrewsbury was celebrated 'in a way quite after its founder's heart':

... there was always a half-holiday, a patriotic address from the Head Master, the Corps was paraded, 'Rule, Britannia' and other patriotic songs were sung by a band of boys on the top of the School roof; these could be heard across the river in the Quarry. For some years it was made an occasion to invite representatives of Secondary Schools and private schools in the town to a children's Patriotic Play, or Tableaux, in the School House garden, where the company marched in procession, saluted the Flag (on the School), and sang Empire songs. Part of the proceedings was to watch the parade of the School Corps and listen to the Head Master's address. Some of the elementary school teachers were asked, too, as their schools had a half-holiday, their Empire festivities having taken place in the morning.[101]

By the 1920s, a public school 'tradition' had merged into a national 'tradition' and had become 'an ideal for emulation in State schools and youth organisations alike'. A homogeneous ideology had been established which promoted common characteristics – 'social discipline, national consent and Social Darwinian superiority'.[102] 'Empire Day' was eventually held in schools of every kind all over Britain. The *Daily Herald* in May 1927 reported:

Empire Day was celebrated in all parts of the country yesterday. At the London Guildhall 1,000 children assembled to celebrate the day, some of them making speeches while their elders sat and listened. Speeches were also made by the Lord Mayor and Sir James Parr, High Commissioner for New Zealand. In the London schools children were presented with small Union Jacks. At night in Hyde Park there was community singing. Dame Clara Butt sang the solos.[103]

A British tradition had been created out of a political reality. As long as the reality survived, the 'tradition' survived.

This chapter suggests two hypotheses for further consideration. The invented traditions of late nineteenth- and early twentieth-century Britain included both public school and public imperial 'traditions' which had common elements and which were related. The latter to an extent grew out of the former through the strong concern and energetic efforts of members of the upper middle classes imbued with the values and attitudes of the public school system. In this specific context there is a need for detailed scrutiny of the public schools themselves in the first half of the twentieth century, in order to acquire a clearer, more accurate understanding of their response to the Empire Day Movement. Similarly there is a need for an examination of the manifestations of Empire Day in the state system, to determine the extent of the influence of public-school educated staff, governors and councillors as well as the role of others in stimulating its celebration. In addition, what has been further suggested in this chapter, is that imperial propaganda in the public schools prior to the Great War was frequently of a limited, crude, militaristic nature. It, too, is a hypothesis to be more widely investigated. In both contexts this chapter raises many questions and highlights a shortage of both investigation and information. Intensive, comprehensive and comparative studies of general attitudes to imperialism within the schools are required; to locate the disseminators and the responses to their dissemination, to establish the nature and extent of dissent, to discover the ritualistic and symbolic instruments of persuasion, to examine the relationship between the various mechanisms of propaganda and their relative efficacy, to trace the nature of the association between public school and state school in the promulgation of imperial enthusiasm, and to discern the changing nature of school attitudes to imperialism as the twentieth century progressed.

The British Empire was run by former public schoolboys. As yet we know extraordinarily little about the general attitudes to imperialism within the schools of their youth and the methods of indoctrination adopted. We know even less about variation in emphasis and response between schools. Arguably the public school system has received closer attention from scholars than any other aspect of British schooling. Yet enquiry into this significant aspect of its history is still in its infancy.

Acknowledgements

I am indebted to Jordanhill College of Education Research Committee for funds which enabled me to undertake the research for this chapter.

Notes

1 'propaganda', *Shorter Oxford Dictionary*, 1466.
2 H. D. Lasswell, 'Propaganda', in E. R. A. Seligman (ed.), *The Encyclopedia of the Social Sciences*, New York 1933, XII, 521, quoted in Julius Gould and William C. Kolb, *A Dictionary of the Social Sciences*, London 1964, 547.
3 'Propaganda', *Encyclopedia of the Social Sciences*, New York 1933, XII, 579.
4 Konrad Kellen in his introduction to Jacques Ellel, *Propaganda: The Formation of Men's Attitudes*, New York 1973, V.
5 David Welch (ed.), *Nazi Propaganda: The Power and the Limitations*, London 1983, 7.
6 J. Lawson Walton, 'Imperialism', *Contemporary Review*, LXXV, 1899, 306.
7 Walton, 'Imperialism', 308.
8 Frank Smith, *A History of English Elementary Education 1760–1902*, London 1931, Chaps XI and X.
9 Robert Roberts, *The Classic Slum* quoted in Henry Erskine Cowper, 'British education, public and private', and the 'British Empire 1880–1930', unpublished PhD thesis, University of Edinburgh 1979, 194.

10 J. A. Mangan, 'Images of Empire in the Victorian Edwardian public school', *Journal of Educational Administration and History*, XII, No. 1, January 1980, *passim*. See also J. A. Mangan, 'Moralists, metaphysicians and mythologists: the 'signifiers' of a Victorian sub-culture', Mark Harris Address, Inaugural Conference, Sports Literature Association, University of California (San Diego), July 1984.

11 Welch, *Nazi Propaganda*, 182. See also J. A. Hobson, *Psychology of Jingoism*, London 1901, 48.

12 Eric Hobsbawm, 'Mass-producing traditions: Europe, 1870–1914', in Eric Hobsbawm and Terence Ranger, *The Invention of Tradition*, Cambridge 1983, 263.

13 Hobsbawm, 'Mass-producing traditions', 283.

14 Raymond Williams, *The Long Revolution*, London 1961, 47 quoted in Martin J. Weiner, *English Culture and the Decline of the Industrial Spirit 1850–1980*, Cambridge 1981, x.

15 J. A. Hobson, *Imperialism*, London 1902, 115.

16 Mark Starr, *Lies and Hate in Education*, London 1929, 85.

17 See J. A. Mangan, 'Public school propagandists, proselytizers and publicists' in *The Games Ethic and Imperialism: Aspects of the Diffusion of an Ideal*, Harmondsworth 1985.

18 Mangan, *Games Ethic and Imperialism*, Chap. 1.

19 Cowper, 'British Education', 18.

20 Mrs H. W. Moss, *Moss of Shrewsbury*, London 1932, 139.

21 J. Basil Oldham, *A History of Shrewsbury School 1552–1952*, Oxford 1952, 150.

22 Moss, *Moss of Shrewsbury*, 130.

23 Ibid., 130.

24 Ibid., 131.

25 Ibid., 131.

26 Ibid., 136–7.

27 Ibid., 135–41.

28 Ibid., 141. See also his sermon at Great St Mary's Church, Cambridge, reported in the 'Supplement to the Cambridge Review', XXVI, Thursday, May 11 1905, LXXVII–IX.

29 R. J. MacKenzie, *Almond of Loretto*, London, 1905, 326, quoted in Mangan, *Games Ethic and Imperialism*, Chap. 1.

30 Hely Hutchinson Almond, 'The Consecration of the Body', in *Christ the Protestant and Other Sermons*, Edinburgh 1899, 150, quoted in Mangan, *Games Ethic and Imperialism*, Chap. 1.

31 J. E. C. Welldon, 'The imperial purpose of education', *Proceedings of the Royal Colonial Institute*, XXVI, 1894–5, 839, quoted in Mangan, *Games Ethic and Imperialism*, Chap. 7.

32 Ibid., 829.

33 J. E. C. Welldon, *Forty Years On*, London 1935, 254.

34 Cowper, 'British Education', 18.

35 Welldon, *Forty Years On*, 262.

36 J. E. C. Welldon, *Recollections and Reflections*, London 1916, 239 quoted in J. A. Mangan, ' "Gentlemen Galore", imperial education for tropical Africa; Lugard the ideologist', *Immigrants and Minorities*, I, No. 2, July 1982, 159–60.

37 Mangan, 'Moralists, metaphysicians and mythologoists', *passim*.

38 Henry Newbolt, *Poems New and Old*, London 1912, 80.

39 Mangan, 'Images of Empire', 32.
40 M. Apple & N. King, 'What do schools teach', in J. B. Macdonald and W. Gephant (eds), *Humanism and Education*, Berkeley 1977, quoted in *School, Knowledge and Social Control*, Course E202, Schooling and Society, Open University 1977, 41. For a further discussion of this subject, see Michael B. Apple, *Education and Power*, London 1982, especially Chap. 1.
41 Ibid., 41.
42 Pierre Bourdieu & Jean Claude Passeron, *Reproduction in Education, Society and Culture*, London 1977, 196–8.
43 *Fettesian*, I, No. 1, April 1878, 13.
44 *Fettesian*, 1, No. VI, April 1879, 124.
45 *Fettesian*, 1, No. VI, April 1879, 103–6; 1, No. II, July 1878, 50–2; V, No. 2, December 1882, 28–34; and VIII, No. 6, July 1886, 151–4.
46 *Fettesian*, 1, No. VI, April 1879, 109–12.
47 *Fettesian*, IV, No. 2, December 1881, 37.
48 *Fettesian*, XI, No. 2, December 1886, 33.
49 *Fettesian*, XX, No. 1, November 1897, editorial. H. L. J. MacLean, in an attempt to rescue the body of a fellow officer, was killed in a skirmish at Landokai, 17 April 1897.
50 *Fettesian*, XXI, No. 3, March 1899, 53.
51 *Fettesian*, XXI, No. 4, April 1899, 75–6.
52 *Fettesian*, XXII, No. 4, April 1900, 85. Anonymous poem to 'D.B.M.'. For typical outbursts of jingoism see XXI, No. 5, June 1899, 100–1 and XXII, No. 3, March 1900, 1, 55 and 73.
53 *Fettesian*, XXII, No. 3, March 1900, 49.
54 For a good example, see the *Fettesian* XXXIII, No. 1, November 1910, 29–32.
55 *Fettesian*, XXXIV, No. 2, December 1911, 55.
56 *Fettesian*, XXXIII, No. 3, March 1911, 86.
57 *Fettesian*, XXXIV, No. 1, November 1911, 24.
58 *Fettesian*, XXXV, No. 3, March 1913, 51.
59 *Fettesian*, XXXVIII, No. 2, December 1915, 24–5. See also 'The Elect' by R.H.P., XXXIX, No. 3, March 1917, 45.
60 *Fettesian*, XIII, No. 1, November 1919, 11.
61 Cowper, 'British Education', 229.
62 R. H. Bruce-Lockhart, *My Scottish Youth*, London 1937, 290–1.
63 J. MacKenzie, *Propaganda and Empire*, Manchester 1984, 232. The National League was linked closely to the public schools, see Cowper, 'British Education', 190.
64 *DNB 1922–1930*, 100–1.
65 Cowper, 'British Education', 284.
66 J. H. Springhall, 'Lord Meath, youth and Empire', *Journal of Contemporary History*, V, No. 4, 1975, 99.
67 Ibid., 100.
68 *Essays on Duty and Discipline. A Series of Papers on the Training of Children in relation to Social and National Welfare*, London 1910.
69 Lord Meath, 'Duty and Discipline in the Training of Children', *Essays on Duty and Discipline*, 9.
70 Lord Meath, 'Have we the "Grit" of our forefathers?', *Essays on Duty and Discipline*, 1.
71 Ibid., 2–3.
72 Ibid., 7.

73 Ibid., 8.
74 Mrs Arthur Phillip, 'The Value of a Certain "Hardness" in Education', *Essays on Duty and Discipline*, 13.
75 J. E. C. Welldon, 'The Early Training of Boys into Citizenship', *Essays on Duty and Discipline*, 3.
76 Ibid., 8–9.
77 Ibid., 12–13.
78 Meath, 'Duty and Discipline in the Training of Children', 12.
79 Reginald, 12th Earl of Meath, KP, *Memories of the Twentieth Century*, London 1924, 43. See also his reference to 'the year [1896] when the Germ of the future Empire Day Movement took up residence in my brain' in *Memories of the Nineteenth Century*, London 1923, 337–8.
80 Ibid., 77–8.
81 Ibid., 76.
82 Ibid., 289.
83 MacKenzie, *Propaganda and Empire*, 236.
84 Springhall, 'Lord Meath, youth and Empire', 101.
85 Starr, *Lies and Hate in Education*, 67.
86 MacKenzie, *Propaganda and Empire*, 233.
87 Springhall, 'Lord Meath, Youth and Empire', 107.
88 Antony Guest, 'Social ideals: The Earl of Meath', *Court Journal*, 16 February 1910, 212.
89 Ibid., 213.
90 Cowper, 'British Education', 222.
91 See Starr, *Lies and Hate in Education*, 68–93. See also Cowper 'British Education', 223–6.
92 Letter to the author from Mr R. A. Cole-Hamilton, Archivist, Fettes College, dated 20 November 84.
93 Springhall, 'Lord Meath, youth and Empire', 108.
94 *The Teachers World*, 19 May 1926, 267.
95 Mark Starr, 'Lesson material for Empire Day', *The Educational Worker*, 5.
96 Ibid., 5.
97 Ibid., 5.
98 Ibid., 5.
99 Robert Roberts, *The Classic Slum*, Manchester 1971, 143.
100 Moss, *Moss of Shrewsbury*, 133.
101 Ibid., 134.
102 MacKenzie, *Propaganda and Empire*, 249.
103 Starr, *Lies and Hate in Education*, 65.

CHAPTER 7

BOY'S OWN EMPIRE
FEATURE FILMS AND IMPERIALISM IN THE 1930s

Jeffrey Richards

Historical orthodoxy has it that the masses were indifferent to the British Empire in the inter-war years. Recently, however, a number of important studies have appeared which have challenged that view and sought to restore the imperial dimension to domestic British history.[1] What clues do we have, in the matter of Empire or indeed anything else, to that great intangible 'the national mood'? I suggest that we need to turn above all to popular culture.

There were, roughly speaking, three cultures in the inter-war years. There was the high culture of the intelligentsia, whose background was predominantly upper or upper-middle-class, but who rejected established conventions in matters moral, sexual, artistic and political. There was working-class culture, which was fundamentally non-literary and unofficial. It was defined by George Orwell as 'the pub, the football match, the back garden, the fireside and "the nice cup of tea" '.[2] But this culture was closely linked with the third, and most dominant strand, which by contrast with the high culture was anti-intellectual, middle-class and largely right-wing. Its chief outlets were mass-produced popular fiction and the movies, but it was precisely these outlets, along with the wireless, that attracted the mass popular audiences. Thus the truly popular culture tended to be controlled and disseminated by the middle-class but consumed by middle and working classes alike.

George Orwell wrote in 1937: 'It is quite likely that fish and chips, art-silk stockings, tinned salmon, cut-price chocolate, the movies, the radio, strong tea and the football pools have between them averted revolution'.[3] If this sounds fanciful, examine the contents of that list more closely – cheap food, cheaply produced luxuries, gambling and the popular mass media. The movies and the wireless in particular were tightly controlled and programmed to middle-class values. The values and virtues they promoted were summed up by Orwell as 'patriotism, religion, the Empire, the family, the sanctity of marriage, the old school tie, birth, breeding, honour and discipline'.[4] The movies, whose average weekly audience rose from 18 millions to 23 millons during the decade, and whose most assiduous attenders were the working-class urban young, were thus one of the most potent means for propagating such values.[5]

The films were made against a background of sometimes conflicting impulses. They were produced and distributed by men who were concerned to gain prestige and respect for themselves and their parvenu industry and to maintain the legislative protection which ensured that a fixed minimum quota of British films had to be shown on British screens every year. Hence, there was a concern to dramatise the dominant ideology, to promote consensus and class harmony, and to remove from the screen by the means of self-imposed censorship anything morally, politically or ideologically offensive. But these same men also wanted and needed to make money with their films. This meant giving people what they wanted, within limits, and paying attention to box-office returns, which indicated popular approval of particular themes, genres and star types. It is extremely unlikely that they would have continued to invest heavily in the production of expensive imperial epics if these had not met with popular approval.

People's reading had a great influence on what they saw on the screen, as producers hastened to provide film versions, 'cinematisations' as they were called, of bestselling books and authors. Although the 1930s saw the revolutionary introduction of Penguins, the formation of the Left Book Club and a vogue for realistic authors like J. B. Priestley, A. J. Cronin and Winifred Holtby, these were not the everyday reference points for the mass readership. As Mrs Q. D. Leavis discovered to her horror in 1932, the names most prized by the mass readership were Warwick Deeping, Marie Corelli, Hall Caine and P. C. Wren, all of whose best-known books enjoyed cinematic success too.[6] The inter-war years in particular saw the apogee of the thriller, an unending stream of fast-moving adventure and crime yarns from Edgar Wallace, Sydney Horler and Sapper, which were one of the staples of cinema, theatre, library and bookstall. Their heroes were invariably public-school educated and subscribed to the class system, middle-class values and love of country and Empire. In stories featuring the likes of Bulldog Drummond, Tiger Standish, Berry and Co., foreigners were murderous and sinister, servants knew their place and were devoted and usually comic, and intellectuals were effete and dangerous. Popular fiction presented an entire and self-contained world view reinforced to a large extent by the cinema, which drew on it for source material. Edgar Wallace was the single most filmed author of the decade, and Sapper's Bulldog Drummond featured in a string of movies made both in Britain and America.

This inevitably meant that there was a great gulf between attitudes in the high culture and attitudes in the mass culture. As Orwell pointed out, 'the really important fact about so many of the English intelligentsia is their severance from the common culture of the country'.[7] Interestingly, Orwell laid particular stress on patriotism as a feature of the common culture. 'In the general patriotism of the country they form a sort of island of dissident thought. England is perhaps the only great country whose intellectuals are ashamed of their own nationality. In left-wing circles it is always felt that there is something slightly disgraceful in being an Englishman and that it is a duty to sneer at every English institution from horse-racing to suet pudding.'[8] The hostility of the largely left-wing intelligentsia has resulted, as Hugh Cunningham has demonstrated, in patriotism being composed of conservatism, monarchism, militarism, racialism and imperialism.[9]

It is therefore extremely dangerous to take the high culture as being representative of anything other than the views of a narrow, isolated elite. The high culture was remorselessly hostile to the public schools, for instance. 'At school I lived in a Fascist state', wrote W. H. Auden, setting the tone for his generation, and in the 1920s and the 1930s writers like Wells, Forster and Orwell castigated the public schools in their novels, depicting them variously as hotbeds of philistinism, racism, snobbery, bullying and homosexuality.[10] Those, as it happens, were more or less the characteristics of the popular fictional heroes like Bulldog Drummond, celebrated and eulogised in books and films. But this hostile view of the public schools was not the one purveyed by popular culture, where the public schools were celebrated lovingly and promoted assiduously for readers who had never been to and would never go to them, in best-selling books like James Hilton's *Goodbye Mr Chips*, turned into an award-winning and successful film in 1939, and the indefatigable boys' papers like *Magnet* and *Gem*. An image of an essentially benign public school system and all that that entailed was thus inculcated early and rooted deep.

The same was true of the Empire. 'Serious literature' was uniformly hostile to the Empire, which was depicted as a hollow, repressive and hypocritical sham. But this was not how the general public saw it. For ordinary people, the Empire was the mythic landscape of romance and adventure. It was that quarter of the globe that was coloured red and included 'Darkest Africa' and 'the mysterious East'. It was in short 'ours'. It may have been true, as H. G. Wells claimed, that nineteen Englishmen out of twenty knew as much about the British Empire as they did about the Italian

---

Defending the British Raj against native rebels. Cary Grant, Victor McLaglen and Douglas Fairbanks Jr. in *Gunga Din* (1939), directed by George Stevens for RKO Radio Pictures. By courtesy of the Jeffrey Richards Collection.

Renaissance, but most people were not bothered about actual conditions in the Empire.[11] It was the imagery which they absorbed and endorsed and that imagery was romantic, adventurous and exotic.

By the 1930s, the image of Empire was already established, hallowed by the popular imperial melodramas of the Victorian theatre, by the paintings of Lady Butler and the heroic engravings of the war artists, examined elsewhere in this volume by John Springhall. As these media of expression were overtaken in popularity by the cinema, so the imagery was transferred intact to the broader and more immediate canvas of the screen.

It was always the imagery and never the history that was important in the cinema. The myth transcended the reality. As Walter Webster wrote in his review of *The Charge of the Light Brigade* (1936):

The film is not history. It does not pretend to be history. In a foreword it disclaims any pretensions to be history. And why not? Is there any good reason why films should be faithful to this or that historian any more than plays or novels or poems or paintings . . . Of course it is not true but it does give Hollywood the chance to present to the world a magnificent picture of the splendour of British rule in India . . . Honestly I do not like it but what can I do but tell you that *The Charge of the Light Brigade* is a very great film when that is the plain truth . . . I am not worried about filmgoers going away with their history jumbled as the result of seeing this film. I rely rather on their being profoundly moved.[12]

It is the unique power of the cinema to evoke and channel emotion which makes it such an important propaganda medium. Beside this, history, reality, authenticity pales. Bertolt Brecht testified to the effect on him of the film *Gunga Din* (1939):

In the film *Gunga Din* . . . I saw British occupation forces fighting a native population. An Indian tribe . . . attacked a body of British troops stationed in India. The Indians were primitive creatures, either comic or wicked: comic when loyal to the British and wicked when hostile. The British soldiers were honest, good-humoured chaps and when they used their fists on the mob and 'knocked some sense' into them the audience laughed. One of the Indians betrayed his compatriots to the British, sacrificed his life so that his fellow country-men should be defeated, and earned the audience's heart-felt applause. My heart was touched too: I felt like applauding and laughed in all the right places. Despite the fact that I knew all the time that there was something wrong, that the Indians are not primitive and uncultured people but have a magnificent age-old culture, and that this Gunga Din could also be seen in a very different light e.g. as a traitor to his people, I was amused and touched because this utterly distorted account was an artistic success and considerable resources in talent and ingenuity had been applied in making it.[13]

The propaganda had no effect on Brecht, whose views on imperialism were already formed and developed. But its effect on those who had no previous view must have been immense.

For anyone predisposed to accept its message, then, the imperial epic was an undilutedly moving and stirring experience. This even applied to those who might have had other reasons for being dissatisfied. The success of

Major Francis Yeats-Brown's *Bengal Lancer* (1930) led Paramount Pictures to buy the film rights. But Yeats-Brown's book was a work of non- fiction, a collection of travel and sporting sketches and a sympathetic depiction of Hindu religion. So Paramount, using the book only as a source of local colour and background detail, produced a rip-roaring imperial melodrama, which owed more to Kipling and Henty than to Yeats-Brown. It was filmed mainly in Lone Pine, California, Hollywood's perennial stand-in for the North-West Frontier. Hollywood had little compunction about sacrificing authenticity to sweep and star charisma. Director Henry Hathaway shot for three weeks with the British actor Henry Wilcoxon in the leading role, but finding him 'authentic but dull', he halted production and brought in Gary Cooper to replace him. Cooper was anything but authentic, one of the great incarnations of Americana, star of *The Virginian*, *The Plainsman* and *Mr Deeds Goes to Town*. Cooper was initially reluctant to do it, but Hathaway turned his role into that of a Canadian and 'got Gary to think of it as a western set in India'.[14] The resulting film, *The Lives of a Bengal Lancer*, (1935) was a smash hit on both sides of the Atlantic. What was the view of Major Yeats-Brown? He wrote to a friend on 6 February 1935:

I must say it is a wonderful 2 hours entertainment. There is something of the spirit I tried to convey in the early chapters of my book: It is nothing to do with the text as I wrote it, but it does have something which was in my mind . . . Curious that such a patriotic film should have been made in Hollywood . . . the Frontier atmosphere . . . is very good and genuine by the way. Do go and see it. Here there is always a long queue at the Carlton, waiting to get in.[15]

Something similar happened with Alexander Korda's production of *The Four Feathers* (1939). During filming, Korda discovered that in the sequence of the regimental ball the actors wore dark blue uniforms. This was militarily correct, according to the technical advisers. Korda insisted that they be put into scarlet, commenting tersely: 'This is Technicolor'.[16] The result was a swirl of colour, a sequence of eye-catching splendour, factually inaccurate but emotionally satisfying. *The New York Times* called the film 'an imperialist symphony' and observed:

The news this morning – in spite of what you hear about British colonial difficulties – is that Alexander Korda has retaken the Sudan. In fact, Mr Korda, the Kipling of the kinema, has retaken the already twice-filmed *Four Feathers* of novelist A. E. W. Mason – and a fine, stirring, gorgeously Technicolored job he has made of it too. In a week rich in action epics, African locales and good remakes, Mr Korda has managed to plant the British flag higher than all the rest.[17]

R. C. Sherriff, who had adapted the novel for the screen, later admitted to having had some anxiety at the film's premiere: 'Among the invited guests was an old officer who had actually commanded a company at the battle of Omdurman forty years before. I thought he would be critical, but he was bubbling with enthusiasm, and when I said: 'How did our battle on the screen compare with the real ones?', he clapped me on the shoulder and said, 'Better, my dear fellow, much better.'[18]

So far I have been discussing British and American imperial epics interchangeably, but before looking in rather more detail at the common features that make this possible, I want to look at the British and American epics separately in the context of their respective cultures. In the case of Britain, there were some half a dozen films actually set in and dealing with the Empire, as opposed to films detailing imperial attitudes, of which there were considerably more. The Gracie Fields South African Gold Rush musical, *We're Going to be Rich* (1937) glamourised the profit motive of imperialism, for instance, while Edgar Wallace's thriller *The Four Just Men* (1939) centred on a plot by an unnamed enemy to block the Suez Canal and seize control of the British Empire.[19]

The key British imperial films, however, are the Korda trilogy: *Sanders of the River* (1935), *The Drum* (1938) and *The Four Feathers* (1939), and what might be called the Balcon trilogy, produced by Michael Balcon at Gaumont British: *Rhodes of Africa* (1936), *The Great Barrier* (1936) and *King Solomon's Mines* (1937). The Balcon trilogy is interesting because it deals essentially with economic aspects of Empire. This is worth noting because we sometimes get the impression, due to the overwhelming military emphasis of the Hollywood imperial epics, that imperial films are about India, the Army and specifically the scarlet and gold heroics of the North-West Frontier.

Rhodes of Africa is a whitewashing biographical film about Cecil Rhodes, stressing his Imperial vision and his paternalistic concern for the natives. *The Great Barrier* is the story of the building of the Canadian Pacific Railway, with heroic feats of exploration and engineering, and a personal story of redemption of two wastrels by work and sacrifice. *King Solomon's Mines* is the classic Rider Haggard tale of the search for the legendary diamond mines of Central Africa.

It is worth noting that all three films are based on books and more importantly that all three are firmly set in the nineteenth century. They look back to the pioneering days of exploration, construction and profit, construed and legitimised as adventure. They evoke the romance of engineering, the romance of exploration, the romance of profit, and take care, at least in the first two cases, to stress the imperial dimension – Rhodes acquires his diamond mines in pursuit of his dream of an Africa united under British rule and the Canadian Pacific is built to ensure that British Columbia remains within Canada.

This romanticisation of the economic aspects of imperialism is in line with the post-World War One re-orientation of imperialism, via the British Empire Exhibitions, the Imperial Institute and the Empire Marketing Board, to centre on the positive benefits it produced rather than the sacrifice it demanded. The result was what might be called 'produce imperialism' – the idea that the Empire meant cocoa from the Gold Coast, diamonds from South Africa, rubber from Malaya, tea from Ceylon and the Prince of Wales sculpted life-size in Canadian butter. But films took care to ally this dimension to an older, nobler and altogether more potent concept, 'The White Man's Burden' – hard work, self-sacrifice, duty and death.

For the Balcon films, like the Korda films, are first and foremost adventure stories. Little attention has been paid to discussing the ethic of adventure in films. Martin Green's admirable pioneering work on the literature of adventure, *Dreams of Adventure, Deeds of Empire*, is illuminating for adventure films.[20] Green rescues a vital part of British literary heritage from the neglect into which it has been thrust by left-wing Little Englander 'Eng. Lit.' intellectuals, by establishing a 'great tradition of adventure', robust, masculine and direct, as opposed to the essentially feminine, delicate and refined 'Great Tradition' of F. R. Leavis. Counter-pointing Leavis' choice of Jane Austen, George Eliot, Henry James and D. H. Lawrence, Green selects Daniel Defoe, Walter Scott, Rudyard Kipling and Joseph Conrad.[21] The countervailing images speak for themselves. Put very simply, it is the primacy of action as opposed to the primacy of feelings, and moreover action which is frequently imperially-based as opposed to specifically England-based, and the exaltation of the warrior-explorer-engineer-administrator-imperial paladin at the expense of the wilting provincial spinster. It is only right and proper to restore this missing dimension to the official record of our art and culture, if only because the last two artists of genius to have touched the hearts of the mass of the public – Kipling and Elgar – were deeply rooted in that imperial ethos.[22]

Martin Green sees the writers of his 'Great Tradition' and a host of minor writers in the same vein energising and validating the myth of Empire as a vehicle of excitement, adventure and wish-fulfilment through action. In the nineteenth century literature provides the vehicle by which the middle-class mercantile exploration-colonisation tradition, epitomised by Robinson Crusoe, is reconciled with the chivalric aristo-military tradition, revivified by Scott. It is possible to see films continuing Green's 'Great Tradition' and in particular the Balcon and Korda trilogies representing different strands. According to Green, the crucial images of the mercantile tradition are precious metals, mines and explosions, the combination of technology and wealth. These images run through the Balcon films, which are punctuated by sandstorms, rockslides, forest fires, volcanic eruptions, explosions, the energy of nature being overcome and harnessed by the energy of Imperial Man, with the Canadian Pacific Railway smashing through the great barrier of the Rockies, Rhodes plucking diamonds from the earth of the Cape and vanquishing the Matabele with the aid of firearms, and the Curtis

expedition discovering the fabled wealth of King Solomon's Mines and
cowing the Kukuana by use of their superior technology.

It is worth noting too that this is a man's world, in which romance and
women play a subsidiary role. There is no romantic interest in *Sanders* or
Rhodes. The women in *The Drum* and *The Four Feathers* are brisk, no-
nonsense mother-substitutes, incarnating the imperial ethic, as stand-ins for
the Great White Mother, Victoria herself. In the American films *Bengal
Lancer* and *Gunga Din* the role of women is positively destructive, a threat
to the carefree bachelor life of the trio of male heroes. The appelation 'Boy's
Own yarn', often applied to these films, is more revealing than it intends to
be. The reference is to the archetypal Victorian boys' paper. But as Green
points out, 'it is a striking feature of late Victorian culture that its emotional
focus was on boys'.[23] Boys' fiction was born in the nineteenth century and
gave wide currency to the ethic of adventure and of Empire. Ballantyne,
Kingston, Henty and so forth popularised the ideas of Empire in easily
assimilable images. It is surely more than coincidence that many of the great
imperial heroes were devoted to boys or to young men – Gordon, Rhodes,
Kitchener, Stanley, Baden-Powell. The philosopher Santayana knew what
he was talking about when he described the Briton as 'the sweet, just, *boyish*
master of the world' (my italics).[24] So did Sir Henry Newbolt, who summed
up the Empire's public school code of behaviour in poetic form in *Vitai
Lampada*, describing a battle in which 'the voice of a schoolboy rallies the
ranks: 'Play up! Play up! and play the game!' The central relationships of
the Empire in reality, in literature and on film are between men, with the
whole presided over by an almost deified Mother. If Kim is perhaps the
archetypal hero of this world of boys and overgrown boys, it is surely Peter
Pan, the boy who never grew up, who mythically expresses the whole
psychological orientation.

Baden-Powell, with his love of practical jokes, amateur theatricals, music
hall ditties and comic disguises, was perhaps the most extreme example of
what Piers Brendon calls 'the boy-man' – 'a perennial singing schoolboy, a
permanent whistling adolescent, a case of arrested development *con brio*'.[25]
But it was this permanent adolescence which enabled him to understand so
thoroughly the unalloyed romanticism of boyhood adventure which he was
to channel so successfully into the Scouts. B.-P. was writing from the heart
when he declared in *Scouting for Boys*:

Boys are full of romance, and they love 'make-believe' to a greater extent than they
like to show. All you have to do is to play up to this, and to give rein to your
imagination to meet their requirements . . . To stand on the right footing for getting
the best out of your boys you must see things with their eyes. To you the orchard
must, as it is with them, be Sherwood Forest with Robin Hood and his Merry Men in
the background; the fishing harbour must be the Spanish Main with its pirates and
privateers; even the town common may be a prairie teeming with buffaloes and Red

Indians, or the narrow slum a mountain gorge where live the bandits or the bears . . . Think out the points you want your boys to learn, and then make up games to bring them into practice. Bacon said that play-acting was one of the best means of educating children, and one can quite believe him. It develops the natural power in them of imitation, and of wit and imagination, all of which help in the development of character; and at the same time lessons of history and morality can be impressed on their minds far better by their assuming the characters and acting the incidents themselves than by any amount of preaching of the same on the part of the teacher.[26]

The Empire was the perfect vehicle for the dramatisation of adventure, chivalry and character-forming. So we find B.-P. advocating historical pageants based on such classic imperial episodes as 'Major Wilson's Last Stand' and 'the Wreck of the *Birkenhead*', games based on the storming of Badajoz in the Peninsular War and the capture of Delhi during the Indian Mutiny and a tableau enacting the verses and sentiments of Newbolt's *Vitai Lampada*.[27] Imperial films were almost an extension of this world. Both the books and the films which celebrate and legitimise Empire are ballads of boyhood, innocent, exciting, pure and true.

If Balcon's films represent the mercantile tradition, Korda's represent the aristo-military and they also represent a chronologically later period than that of exploration and exploitation. They deal with the period of administration; their themes are government and defence. In making the films, Korda seems to have had three main motives. He was a businessman and wanted to make financially successful films. He had a policy of signing up popular authors and acquiring the rights to bestselling books to this end. Edgar Wallace's *Sanders of the River* stories and A. E. W. Mason's *The Four Feathers* were longstanding bestsellers and therefore obvious candidates for cinematisation. Korda wanted to capture a larger share than he had of the lucrative Empire market and thought films set and filmed in the Empire would contribute to this. He also sought deliberately to stress the virtues of the British imperial system, the doctrines of fair play and moral authority at a time when the rise of fascism was threatening those ideals and offering a different sort of world government. As Korda's biographer Karol Kulik has written: 'He was a confirmed Anglophile who saw the Empire builders as the embodiment of all the most noble traits in the English character and spirit'.[28]

'Character' and 'spirit' are key words here. Looked at in outline the plots of all three films are strikingly similar. In *Sanders*, District Commissioner Sanders puts down a native uprising in Nigeria and rescues his faithful ally Chief Bosambo from the evil King Mofalaba. In *The Drum* Captain Carruthers joins forces with the Indian Prince Azim to put down an uprising led by his uncle, the wicked Ghul Khan. In *The Four Feathers* a disgraced British officer Harry Feversham redeems his honour, assisted at the end by the pro-British chieftain Karaga Pasha, by helping to put down the revolt of the Khalifa in the Sudan.

These three films unquestionably championed the continuation of the

British Empire. In each of the films, the exercise of power by the British is supported by the consent of the governed, as represented by Bosambo, Prince Azim and Karaga Pasha, and is defined by the opposition of self-seeking, power-hungry native despots, who, if left alone, would prey unmercifully on their own people – King Mofalaba, Ghul Khan and the Khalifa.

Korda's films offer no concrete political, economic or constitutional justification for the Empire's existence. There is no indication of the state of flux that the Empire actually found itself in during the interwar years, when it seemed to be evolving into something rather different – the Commonwealth. The Empire is justified in the apparent moral superiority of the British, demonstrated by their adherence to the code of gentlemanly conduct and the maintenance of a disinterested system of law, order and justice. As long as the British regarded it as their God-given duty to ensure fair play for all the world, then the maintenance of the Empire was inescapable. It was this lofty view that the Korda films projected and since all three films were made with the active cooperation of the colonial authorities and the British Army, the scripts must have been officially approved and the image one which the authorities endorsed. The Korda films and indeed their Hollywood counterparts depict British rule as timeless and eternal. The inevitable result was to foster what Francis Hutchins has called 'the illusion of permanence' – the idea that whatever they might say about progress towards ultimate independence, the British in fact expected and believed that their Empire would last for a thousand years.[29] As Russell Ferguson put it in a witheringly ironic review of *The Drum*: 'A magnificent record of life in Northwest India, the same yesterday, today and tomorrow'.[30]

I mentioned earlier Korda's belief in the character and spirit of the Empire-builders. This is supremely what the films are about. To take *Sanders* as an example, the eponymous hero Commissioner Sanders is seen as the ideal colonial administrator and the story of the film is so constructed as to demonstrate these attributes. Quiet, pipe-smoking, good-humoured and authoritative, Sanders has virtually singlehanded brought law and order to the River Territories over the previous ten years. He has banned slavery and the running of gin and guns, 'the most dangerous gifts of civilisation to the natives'. Having brought peace and order, he now seeks to maintain it. Backed only by a handful of white officers and a single regiment of native troops, he rules largely by force of personality.[31]

Sanders is the embodiment of the character and spirit that Korda so much admired. His character is the justification for British rule. The man is the message. It was a message that could readily be understood and endorsed by the mass viewing public. But what relationship do these films have to the many articulations of imperial ideology and imperial theory? All three are adaptations of books, though in two cases pre-war books. Edgar Wallace's

Sanders stories were first published in 1909 and *The Four Feathers* by A. E. W. Mason in 1902. *The Drum* was a novella by Mason specially written for the screen and published in 1938. It is books like these which dramatised the idea of altruistic imperialism developed by the young imperial visionaries at the end of the nineteenth century.

To this extent, the role of the popular film based on the popular book seems to me to be admirably summed up by P. J. Keating, writing about the relationship between popular novels about the East End of London and theories of class and class relationships. Keating says of the popular novelist:

His concern is not merely to purvey the ideas of other more informed and perceptive men than himself but rather to refine and simplify those ideas and perceptions into symbolic images capable of entering the public consciousness with a minimum of opposition and thought. It would be impossible for him to exist without the ground already having been prepared by, for instance, the conscientious analyst or dedicated reformer, but they, in their turn, can only communicate with a large uninformed public by using the special techniques and understanding of the popular novelist. By crystallising complex issues into oversimplified but still valid images the popular novelist becomes an invaluable middleman, skirting rational debate, of which he is an offshoot and appealing, often in the name of reason directly to the emotions.[32]

I suggest that this is true of popular films. Indeed it is echoed in Basil Wright's critical review of *The Drum*, published in *The Spectator*. He complains that the film 'could have told us something of the fundamental importance of the Empire and in particular of the political and social problems which the British Raj represents' but instead it appeals to the 'shallower herd instinct, the instinct which prefers with double instinctiveness to mistake melodrama for tragedy and is too willingly moved to tears by a regiment marching'.[33] But I suggest that it is precisely by doing this rather than engaging in intellectual debate that the film made its point and achieved its success.

What are the simplified images that Keating talks about with regard to *Sanders*? They are Sanders and his handful of Houssas defying the numerically superior might of the Old King Mofalaba, reading him the riot act and dismissing him with 'the palaver is finished'. They are Sanders, riddled with malaria, ordering his ancient paddle-steamer up the river to the Old King's country on a journey never before undertaken. They are Sanders and his men racing ashore amidst bursts of machine gun fire to rescue Bosambo in the nick of time from the Old King. They are the finale, with Sanders, pipe in mouth, leaning on the rail of the boat, the Union Jack fluttering over his head, with Paul Robeson and his warriors hymning his virtues from their canoes.

The left-wing critic and film-maker Paul Rotha poured scorn on the film: 'It is important to remember that the multitudes of this country who see

Africa in this film are being encouraged to believe this fudge is real. It is a disturbing thought.'[34] But much more typical of the reviews it received was that in *The Sunday Times*, which declared that Alexander Korda, the producer, and his brother Zoltan, the director, revealed in the film 'a sympathy with our ideals of colonial administration, giving us a grand insight into our special English difficulties in the governing of savage races and providing us with a documentary film of East African nature in its raw state, a picture which could not be improved upon for the respect it displays to British sensibilities and ambitions'.[35] The usually perceptive trade paper, the *Kinematograph Weekly*, whose business it was to assess a film's potential selling points, described the film as 'a fine tribute to British rule in Africa' and said: 'Not only is the film a glorious piece of clean, engrossing entertainment, but it has in its title, cast and ready-made public, represented by the popularity of the author's work, unprecedented box-office creden- tials.'[36] The importance of reviews in assessing audience reaction to films should not be underestimated. For as Mass Observation noted in 1941: 'The advance press analysis of the film was an important influence in conditioning the approach of the audience to the film. Favourable reviews exert social sanction, disposing people favourably towards the film before they have ever seen it.'[37]

But how far was the government directly involved in feature-film making to propagate its imperial message? There were certainly continuous calls for the use of the cinema to promote the cause of the Empire. Sir Philip Cunliffe-Lister, President of the Board of Trade, encapsulated the view in the Commons when referring to the unanimous resolution of the 1926 Imperial Conference that imperial film production should be increased: 'It is based on a realization that the cinema is today the most universal means through which national ideas and national atmosphere can be spread . . . Today films are shown to millions of people throughout the Empire and must unconsciously influence the ideas and outlook of British people of all races.'[38]

Nevertheless, there was considerable reluctance on the part of the government to become directly involved in feature film production. When in 1938 a committee was set up to coordinate propaganda under the chairmanship of Sir Robert Vansittart, Permanent Under-Secretary at the Foreign Office, it called for the use of feature films to influence the mass audience, because 'they strike subconscious chords and reinforce or modify prejudices or opinions already held, and thus in the long run make a more lasting impression' than newsreels or documentaries.[39] But the government remained unconvinced, that it should take on this job and there was no official use of feature films until the Second World War.

Vansittart, however, put into practice what he was preaching. When, because of his opposition to Chamberlain's appeasement policy he was shunted aside and given the nebulous post of Chief Diplomaic Adviser to the government, he plunged into the world of commercial film-making. He signed a contract with Alexander Korda to provide scripts for imperial epics and co-wrote Herbert Wilcox's film *Sixty Glorious Years* (1938), the biographical film about Queen Victoria, which according to *Today's Cinema* 'acclaims the greatness of the British Empire and its peoples'.[40] Vansittart contrived to insert in the film several speeches calling for national preparedness as well as depicting the British Empire as a potent force for peace in the world.

But Vansittart could not go too far in his criticism of the government because there was one area where there was official involvement in the film business – censorship. Although the British Board of Film Censors was not a state-run organisation, it maintained close links with relevant government departments to ensure that nothing undesirable reached the screen. The Presidents of the BBFC were appointed in consultation with the Home Office and during the 1930s they were successively Rt. Hon. Edward Shortt, a former Home Secretary, and Lord Tyrrell of Avon, a former Ambassador to Paris and Chairman of the British Council. The bulk of the censors' work was moral censorship, the preservation of middle-class standards of propriety and decorum. But in political matters, they enforced a policy of 'no controversy', thus virtually excluding from the screen any discussion of such current issues as fascism, pacifism and industrial unrest. The maintenance of the status quo was the aim. It is clear that the government's primary interest was not so much in the constructive use of feature films to put across their policies as the negative factor of fear, fear of causing offence and inflaming public opinion. When it came to the Empire, the government was on the whole content to leave things to the BBFC. The Board operated according to a strictly defined code which expressly prohibited films which reflected adversely on the British army, British colonial administration or the white race. On the basis of this, it was able to reject all but six of the eleven imperial projects submitted to it at script stage. The government was, however, prepared to intervene when it was politically necessary, as when two films proposing to deal with the Indian Mutiny were banned by the BBFC after consultation with the India Office. Sir Samuel Hoare, the Home Secretary, defended the decision in the Commons in 1938, saying: 'to produce a film depicting scenes of the Indian Mutiny would be undesirable at this time when we are just embarking on a new chapter in the constitutional development of India, and when we want to get rid of the differences which there have been between us in the past'.[41] The government's concern was not without foundation, as there had been riots in Bombay and Madras when Alexander Korda's film *The Drum* was shown there.[42]

Even if the government was not directly involved in the production of feature films, however, there was the possibility of indirect involvement by the exercise of influence on friendly producers. In a memorandum on propaganda sent in April 1934 to Neville Chamberlain, Joseph Ball, Deputy Director of the National Publicity Bureau, suggested that 'it should . . . be possible to ensure the adoption by some of the more enlightened producers of scenarios dealing with e.g. historical or Imperial subjects in such a way as to enlist the sympathies of the audiences on the side of the present government'.[43] There can be little doubt that Korda was one of these 'enlightened producers'. For in 1938 Ball was reporting to Chamberlain: 'I have cultivated close links with the "leaders" of the British film industry and I am satisfied that I can count upon most of them for their full support to any reasonable degree'.[44] He specifically mentions Korda in this context. It is also known that Isidore Ostrer, Head of Gaumont British, offered in 1935 to place the whole of his organisation at the government's disposal.[45] It could well be, then, that hints were dropped to Korda and Balcon that the government would not be averse to an imperial epic, something which coincided with their patriotic film-making aims. This would certainly explain why Korda's and Balcon's film units received full cooperation from the colonial authorities in India and Africa.

But we should not assume that even if there was government-inspired propaganda in British imperial feature films, it was out of tune with the opinions and attitudes of the mass cinema-going public. Further, it is not likely that the films would have preached a different message if there was no government involvement. For they were drawing on an already accepted body of imagery and emotional commitments, as were the American films of Empire. It is unlikely that the British government had much influence on Hollywood film producers and yet they produced a stream of imperial epics every bit as propagandist as their British counterparts. Of *Lives of a Bengal Lancer* (1935), the *New York Times* declared, 'it is so sympathetic in its discussion of England's colonial management that it ought to prove a great blessing to Downing St.',[46] and *The Daily Mail* suggested 'the film paid a remarkable tribute to the wisdom and courage which have marked British government in India. It is a powerful and popular argument for the continuance of that rule.'[47] *The New York Times* similarly declared that *Clive of India* was 'a handsome tribute to the glory of British rule in India'.[48] All this led the London *Times* to declare in 1937: 'The Union Jack has in the last few years been vigorously and with no little effect waved by Hollywood'.[49] It was precisely this which prompted the banning in Mussolini's Italy of the Hollywood films *Lives of a Bengal Lancer*, *Charge of the Light Brigade*, *Clive of India* and *Lloyds of London*.

It has been said with some justice that the mass working-class audience in Britain in the 1930s preferred American to British films, though a steady improvement in quality and appeal of British films can be traced throughout the decade. But it is not true to say that Hollywood promoted a coherent and attractive alternative world view that was democratic, egalitarian and classless. Some films certainly fell into this category. But for every *Mr Deeds Goes to Town* Hollywood produced a *Cavalcade*, glorifying the British class system, and for every *Grapes of Wrath*, it produced a *Charge of the Light Brigade*, a paean to romantic and militarist imperialism. In fact, throughout the 1930s Hollywood produced a stream of films promoting a deeply conservative, romantic and admiring world picture which included a class system, imperial values and aristocratic ideals.

Nothing is more indicative of this fact than the films of Shirley Temple. Shirley Temple was a world-wide phenomenon. The top box office attraction both in Britain and America from 1935 to 1938 inclusive, she had single-handedly saved the Fox Film Company from bankruptcy, won an Academy Award at the age of seven and become a millionairess before entering her teens. Her star only waned when she began to grow up and by 1940 she was finished, 'a superannuated sunbeam' as one critic put it.[50] Her films included handsome versions of childhood classics such as *Heidi* and *Rebecca of Sunnybrook Farm* and 'little miss fix-it' pictures in which she reconciled estranged couples, humanised crusty grandfathers and generally spread sweetness and light (*Dimples*, *Bright Eyes*, *Curly Top*). But she also made a trio of films glorifying the nineteenth-century British Empire, which were every bit as lavish and admiring as *Lives of a Bengal Lancer* and *Charge of the Light Brigade*. *Wee Willie Winkie* (1937), based on Kipling's short story, featured Shirley as Priscilla Williams, who is taught the meaning of England's mission in India by her grandfather, the commanding officer of a North-West Frontier fort: 'The Empire wants to be friends with everybody, to keep the Pass open and to bring peace and prosperity'. On the basis of this, Shirley intervenes in a frontier war to reconcile a rebel Khan to the Raj. A similar plot was provided for *Susannah of the Mounties* (1939) in which the Royal Canadian Mounted Police stand in for the British Indian Army and a Red Indian tribe for the tribes of the North-West Frontier. *The Little Princess* (1939) featured Shirley as a spirited Victorian girl, reduced to poverty when her adored father is believed killed in the Boer War. She is rescued from her plight by a kindly aristocrat and reunited with her father by the intervention of Queen Victoria herself. The film, opening with the departure of the troops for South Africa to the strains of 'Rule Britannia' and 'Soldiers of the Queen', including the popular celebrations of the relief of Mafeking and ending with the divine intervention of the Queen-Empress and the playing of the national anthem, is a wholehearted and quite entrancing affirmation of aristocracy, monarchy and Empire.

But significantly Shirley also appeared in *The Little Colonel* (1935) and *The Littlest Rebel* (1935), post-American Civil War dramas, in which Shirley acts as reconciler of North and South, black and white, but on the basis of a surviving *antebellum* world of Southern aristocrats, cotton plantations and faithful negro servants. In all her films, Shirley acts as a reconciling figure, but she is in these films reconciling subject peoples to the status quo, be it a beneficent British Empire or an idealised Old South. It is no coincidence that this popular star's work embraced such apparently diverse film subjects. For in fact they are not as diverse as they appear.

The thirties were pre-eminently Hollywood's imperial decade, when the ethos and rituals of British imperialism were given glamorous celluloid life. The pattern was definitively set by Paramount's *Lives of a Bengal Lancer* (1935). This film, made with all the pace, polish and excitement of the best of Hollywood action films, exalts the life of service and obedience to discipline as the ideal and a 'Three Musketeers' all-male camaraderie as the behavioural norm for heroes. It brings this home to the audience by tracing the process by which two outsiders are initiated into it. The outsiders, who serve as perfect vehicles for audience identification, are Lt. McGregor, the self-styled 'Scotch Canadian' (Gary Cooper) and Lt. Stone (Richard Cromwell), the half-American son of the Commanding Officer of the Lancers. The important thing to note about them is that they are not *pukka* Indian Army Officers, and they, along with the audience, have to be taught the meaning and value of service, duty and discipline. But also they are both North Americans and therefore particularly useful identification figures for United States audiences. Initially, they resist the ethos but by the end of the film, they have learned the message. Even though McGregor is killed, he is awarded a posthumous VC and the playing of the National Anthem signals the triumphant fusion of the individual with nation, crown and Empire.

The box office success of this film inspired a stream of imitations and follow-ups, with Warner Bros. contributing *Charge of the Light Brigade* (1936), United Artists *Clive of India* (1935), Fox *Wee Willie Winkie* (1937), Republic *Storm Over Bengal* (1938), Universal *The Sun Never Sets* (1939) and RKO Radio *Gunga Din* (1939). The outbreak of World War Two put a definite halt to the imperial cycle. Several Imperial projects which studios had initiated were abandoned, such as Fox's projected sequel to *King of the Khyber Rifles* and Warner Bros.' *South-East Frontier* about the siege of the British Embassy in Kabul in the 1920s. The war promoted a new dominant ethos, eclipsing imperialism and rendering imperial epics suddenly and dramatically out of fashion. The war, which the United States entered in 1941, was a war for democracy, a crusade which preached racial equality, self-determination and freedom. Its enemies were the cruel and racist tyrannies of the Third Reich and the Italian and Japanese Empires. It would be wrong to equate in any way the British Empire with the Axis powers. But they did share a fundamental belief in a racial hierarchy, in which one race was superior to another. This became an embarrassment when expressed in Hollywood films at a time when for instance India's role as a bulwark against Japanese aggression in Asia was crucial. Consequently the Office of War Information in America scotched MGM's plans for a film version of Kipling's *Kim* and banned re-issues of *Gunga Din*, which had been banned in India, Malaya and Japan on its initial release because it offended 'racial and religious susceptibilities', and *The Real Glory*, Samuel Goldwyn's tribute to American imperialism in the Philippines.[51]

The reasons behind these bans throws significant light on the consistency with which Hollywood produced and American audiences accepted films about the British and indeed other Empires, when the United States had been born in revolt from the British Empire and had long prided itself on its democratic traditions. The militarist, racist and imperialist ethic of these films found a responsive echo in American society. This is perhaps demonstrated best by *The Real Glory* (1939), a stirring epic directed by Henry Hathaway and starring Gary Cooper. It is not just that the film reunited the team responsible for the success of *Bengal Lancer*. It is also the fact that in its handling of the story of a military garrison in the Philippines putting down a native revolt and in the celebration of a trio of military heroes, it demonstrates that American imperialism sprang from the same roots as its British counterpart. It was after all about America that Kipling originally wrote 'The White Man's Burden'.

The Real Glory is simply the most obvious manifestation of a wider trend in Hollywood cinema, reflecting a pervasively racist society. It produced in large numbers and with uncritical approbation sagas of the gentlemanly paternalist Old South in which benign white planters sipped mint juleps on the verandahs of their mansions while faithful singing 'darkies' toiled in the cotton fields.[52] *Gone With the Wind* (1939) was only the biggest and most spectacular representative of the genre. Hollywood also produced rousing, flag-waving westerns, hymning the 'westward march of Empire', with wagon trains full of white settlers moving across the continent to dispossess the red man of his ancestral lands and with regiments of the United States cavalry waging genocidal war against the Indians. It is again not without significance that at least three of the epics of British India (*Lives of a Bengal Lancer*, *Four Men and a Prayer* and *Gunga Din*) were remade as cavalry westerns, entitled respectively *Geronimo*, *Fury at Furnace Creek* and *Sergeants Three*. Indeed, considering that the message of the epics of British imperialism was that the British were in their colonies and dominions for the protection of the native inhabitants, American imperial epics centring on the extermination of the inconvenient native populations are even more blatantly and stridently racist.

It was not just the Indian who occupied an inferior place in the American racial hierarchy. There was also the blacks, linked in the popular mind with the Indian, sometimes called 'the red nigger'. The symbol of all black actors in the thirties was Stepin Fetchit, a consummate comic actor but the archetype of the slow-witted menial. His counterparts were the legion of shoeshine boys, railway porters and domestic servants which constitute the only image America's blacks had on the thirties screen. This is one key to the links between the British Empire and the often unspoken and unarticulated ethos of American imperialism. Whether he was called *sahib*, *tuan* or *massa*, the white man ruled. Whether English or American, he was head of a divinely instituted hierarchy, whose lower rungs were occupied by the red, yellow, brown and black races.

But there was another and equally important link, and it was one that was perceived at the time. Noting the phenomenon of the Hollywood imperial epics, Margaret Farrand Thorp wrote in 1939 in her study of the American film industry:

The immediate explanation of this burst of British propaganda is a very simple one. As continental audiences dwindled, Britain, which had always stood high, became an even more important section of the American movies' foreign public. It was highly desirable to please Great Britain if possible, and it could be done without sacrifice, for the American public too, seemed to be stirred with admiration for British Empire ideals. Loyalty as the supreme virtue no matter to what you are loyal, courage, hard work, a creed in which *noblesse oblige* is the most intellectual conception; those ideas are easier to grasp and very much easier to dramatise on the screen than social responsibility, the relation of the individual to the state, the necessity for a pacifist to fight tyranny, the nature of democracy, and the similar problems with which the intellectuals want the movies to deal.[53]

What Margaret Thorp is here describing as 'British Empire ideals' is in effect chivalry. The nineteenth century had seen a massive revival in matters medieval and chivalric as part of the whole Romantic reaction to the measured, passionless classicism of the eighteenth century. In the wake of the novels and poems of Sir Walter Scott, with their stylised and idealised picture of medieval chivalry, and of the dramatic return to favour of the Arthurian legends, celebrated in poetry and painting, a living and meaningful code of life for the nineteenth-century gentleman had been fashioned. The image of the gentleman was reformulated as a latterday version of the medieval knight, the embodiment of the virtues of bravery, loyalty and courtesy, modesty, purity and honour, and endowed with a sense of *noblesse oblige* towards women, children and inferiors social and racial. By the middle of the nineteenth century the language and imagery of chivalry had been so far absorbed into the fabric of Victorian life and thought that it was automatic to see the gentleman exclusively in terms of the medieval paladin.[54] This process was not accidental. Chivalry was deliberately promoted by key figures of the age in order to produce a ruling elite for the nation and the expanding Empire who would be inspired by noble and selfless virtues. The public schools were a vital instrument in the propagation of the new chivalry and it was they, who became in E. C. Mack's words, 'mints for the coining of Empire-builders'.[55] Baden-Powell drew on chivalry for the code of his Boy Scouts, who were originally to have been called 'Young Knights of the Empire'. The new chivalry even had its own imperial patron saint in General Gordon, of whom one of his many nineteenth century biographers wrote: 'Doubtful indeed it is if anywhere in the past we shall find figure of knight or soldier to equal him, for sometimes it is the sword of death that gives life its real knighthood, and too often the soldier's end is unworthy of his knightly life; but with Gordon the harmony of life and death were complete.'[56] The identification of the Empire with the ideals of chivalry removed it totally from the squalid business of economics and power politics, placed it on an altogether higher and nobler plane and enabled it to be hymned as a timeless vehicle for adventure.

But exactly the same proliferation of chivalry took place in the United States, where in the nineteenth century gallantry, honour and *noblesse oblige* became deeply embedded in the national psyche. As John Fraser has written in his masterly study of this phenomenon:

The chivalric was the magical kingdom of castles and greensward, and twisting cobbled streets at midnight, and sun-baked islands and jostling wharves, and graceful Southern plantations, and velvet tropical skies, and the majestic spaces of the Western landscape, an enchanted composite realm of the imagination in which picturesquely garbed figures coped with the everchanging configurations of warfare or cattle drives, or the intricate rituals and plottings of aristocratic society . . . The family of chivalric heroes has been by far the largest and most popular one in twentieth-century American culture, and its members, in whole or in part, have entered into virtually everyone's consciousness. They include, naturally, the legion of knightly Westerners in print and celluloid sired by Owen Wister's *The Virginian* and their Indian counterparts. They include Robin Hood . . . and Zorro, and the Scarlet Pimpernel, and gentlemen buccaneers, like Rafael Sabatini's Captain Peter Blood . . . They include the officers and gentlemen of *Lives of a Bengal Lancer*, and the gentlemen rankers of *Beau Geste*, and the First World War aviators of *The Dawn Patrol*, and clean-cut American fly-boys like Steve Canyon. They include honest cops like Dick Tracy, and fearless investigative reporters, and incorruptible district attorneys, and upstanding young doctors like Doctor Kildare. They include battered but romantic private eyes like Raymond Chandler's Philip Marlowe, buoyant ones like Jonathan Latimer's Bill Crane and Richard S. Prather's Shell Scott, efficient ones like Alex Raymond's Rip Kirby, depressive ones like Ross Macdonald's Lew Archer. They include John D. MacDonald's battered, rangy knight errant Travis McGee. They include gentleman knights like Prince Valiant, and Nature's gentlemen like Tarzan and Joe Palooka, and miscellaneous *samurai*, and the martial-arts experts of Bruce Lee. They include Superman and Buck Rogers. They include men about town like Philo Vance, the Saint, and Dashiell Hammett's Nick Charles, and the figures played by Fred Astaire . . . They include gentlemanly English actors like Ronald Colman and George Sanders, and gentlemanly American ones like Douglas Fairbanks Jr. and William Powell, and those immortals Gary Cooper, Spencer Tracy and the rest, who have epitomised native American gallantry and grace.[57]

In the light of these comments, it is less surprising to see Gary Cooper starring in *The Lives of a Bengal Lancer* and *Beau Geste*. Proof of the pervasiveness of the chivalric ideal can be found in the career of Errol Flynn, who moved with ease from swashbucklers like *Captain Blood* and *The Adventures of Robin Hood* to imperial dramas like *Charge of the Light Brigade* and *Another Dawn*, to Westerns like *Dodge City* and *Virginia City*, to Civil War cavalry epics like *Santa Fe Trail* and *They Died With Their Boots On*. What Flynn's Captain Blood, Robin Hood, Geoffrey Vickers, Jeb Stuart and George Armstrong Custer have in common is a shining, pure, uplifting and transforming chivalry.

How did audiences in Britain react to these imperial films? Almost all the films I have been discussing were box office successes, seen and enjoyed by millions. It is not necessarily that they went to see the films because they were about the Empire. They were probably more interested initially in escapist entertainment, bestselling writers, stars, and where it was used, technicolor. They would see thoroughly satisfying adventure stories, with a ritual of events (chases, fights, escapes, battles, rescues) and a display of pageantry (dances, processions, parades, formal banquets). Both elements are wedded to personal dramas and firmly anchored within a framework of beliefs in which the chief characters embody ideals and attitudes. By a process of identification with the leading characters, the audience automatically identify with the factors which motivate them. How long they continue to do so once the film is over depends on the individual spectator. For it has long been evident that the old hypodermic idea – that a film injected its message directly into the audience as a whole – is wrong. How a film works on an audience depends on the age, sex, class, health, intelligence and preoccupations of that audience both collectively and individually.

It would therefore be simplistic to suggest that against their better judgment the working classes were directly injected with the Establishment message and accepted it lock, stock and barrel. The fact that there has been a predominantly Tory press for the past fifty years has not stopped Labour governments being elected. There is the important element of subjective perception to be taken into account: audiences do not necessarily take away from a film what the film-maker expects them to. The case of Alf Garnett is a classic one. Constructed by the writer Johnny Speight as a figure of hatred and ridicule, the ultimate working-class racist bigot, he became a popular folk hero. There is a constant subtle interplay of forces at work between film-maker and audience. The media validate certain issues and institutions by depicting them in a favourable light and equally suppress or distort alternative viewpoints. But they must also respond to perceived audience moods, tastes and needs in order to survive financially.

In the last resort, we should perhaps remember three things. First, the anthropologist Hortense Powdermaker observed that on the whole people will accept depictions of something they know nothing about. But they will reject as inaccurate faulty depictions of things they know about at first hand. By that definition the working classes, who knew nothing much of the reality of the Empire, would be likely to accept these cinematic views of what was happening as authentic.

We need to recall the character of the mass cinema-going audience. As John Buchan wrote:

Remember how the average man, who ultimately rules the country, looks at things. He has, as a rule, no special political creed. He has never troubled himself to think out the type of commonwealth he prefers. His convictions are mainly negative . . . He has a number of little reforms which he should like to see effected and he vaguely wants to live under better conditions. But he does not intend to upset present conditions by any violent measures, for he is desperately afraid of losing what he has. He wants to see his way quite clearly before he changes, and he wants to change by degree. He likes to feel that he is progressing, but woe betide the man who hurries him too fast. As a rule no positive measure will rouse him to a keen interest in politics, but if he is once frightened he will go in his might to the polls to defend the *status quo*.[58]

The status quo of the interwar years very definitely included the Empire. None of the major political parties advocated its dissolution. Throughout the 1930s, the majority of the electorate voted for the mainly Conservative National Government. The population at large has been and still is, according to all reliable indicators, conservative (with a small 'c'), racist, male chauvinist, and above all, patriotic, and on one level the Empire can be seen as an institutional expression of these values. On another, the Empire can be seen as a vehicle for the expression of chivalry and those inspired by the purity of noble values would find reason to support the Empire in this guise.

It is also worth adding that, partly as a result of the emergence of the Empire, and therefore implicitly involving it, the Crown and the Royal Family from the 1880s onwards have moved out of and above political and class differences. The genuinely joyous national celebrations of King George V's Silver Jubilee in 1935 and George VI's Coronation in 1937 are merely two of the many manifestations of this, with on the one level their official ceremonial and on another, their unofficial communal gatherings in the form of street parties and outings: a chance to rejoice in the essential soundness of Britain, her Empire and her institutions. The Empire thus moved with the monarchy above the narrow connotation of class and sectional interest to be seen as a symbol of the nation and thus an object of the general patriotism.

Third and last the audience is not a helpless and inert mass, bound hand and foot and forced to digest unpalatable messages. It has the ultimate sanction in its own hands – the cash paid out at the box office. Whatever else it does and whatever other influences it labours under, the cinema industry existed and exists to make money. If the public shuns its films and rejects its stars, it loses money and eventually collapses. So it needs to monitor the national mood, public opinion and popular tastes. There are too many examples of failed blockbusters for this to be doubted. The box office never lies and the Empire throughout the thirties was big box-office. The working class is not of course monolithic. It is clear that there was an element in the working class that was cynical of and disrespectful of authority. There was also an element which was drawn to the American dream of democracy, freedom and equality of opportunity. But, and this is often overlooked, there was a large section which unthinkingly endorsed the dominant ideology and for whom the Empire was a natural and integral part of Britain in the world. I would venture to suggest that the success at the box office of the imperial epics is powerful evidence for what Arthur Marwick calls 'the unwitting testimony' of films, the reflection on the screen of genuinely and generally held attitudes and views. There must have been many who would have echoed the twenty-two-year-old female clerk writing to *Picturegoer* magazine in the 1940s who declared that films like *Charge of the Light Brigade*, *Lives of a Bengal Lancer* and *Sixty Glorious Years* gave her 'an exultant pride in my own country and her achievements'.[59]

Notes

1   John M. MacKenzie, *Propaganda and Empire*, Manchester 1984; Martin Green, *Dreams of Adventure, Deeds of Empire*, London 1980; Stuart Hall *et al.*, *Policing the Crisis*, London 1980. See also Hugh Cunningham, 'The language of patriotism 1750–1914', *History Workshop* XII, 1981, 8–33, the implications of whose arguments stretch beyond his terminal date.
2   George Orwell, *Collected Essays, Journalism and Letters* II, Harmondsworth 1970, 78.
3   Orwell, *The Road to Wigan Pier*, Harmondsworth 1962, 80.
4   Orwell, *Collected Essays* I, 564.
5   Jeffrey Richards, *Age of the Dream Palace: Cinema and Society in Britain 1930–39*, Routledge 1984.
6   Q. D. Leavis, *Fiction and the Reading Public*, London 1932.
7   Orwell, *Collected Essays* II, 95.
8   Orwell, *Collected Essays* II, 95.
9   Cunningham, 'The language of patriotism'.
10   Graham Greene, ed., *The Old School*, Oxford 1984, 9. See also John Reed, *Old School Ties*, Syracuse 1964.
11   Jan Morris, *Farewell the Trumpets*, London 1978, 299.
12   *Sunday Pictorial*, 27 December 1936.
13   John Willett, ed., *Brecht on Theatre*, London 1964, 151.
14   James Bawden, 'Henry Hathaway', *Films in Review*, XXXV, 1984, 146.
15   Evelyn Wrench, *Francis Yeats-Brown 1886–1944*, London 1948, 192.
16   Karol Kulik, *Alexander Korda: the man who could work miracles*, London 1975, 214.
17   *The New York Times*, 4 August 1939.
18   R. C. Sherriff, *No Leading Lady*, London 1968, 293.
19   For a complete discussion of the Empire and imperial attitudes in British and American films, see Jeffrey Richards, *Visions of Yesterday*, London 1973.

20 Green, *Dreams of Adventure*.
21 Both traditions claim Conrad but each would stress a different aspect of his work. Conrad clearly provides a fascinating point of intersection.
22 Even if working-class people did not read Kipling *in extenso* or go to Elgar concerts, they absorbed their essence through the mass media: the music hall, the pub, the wireless, films. 'Gunga Din', 'The White Man's Burden', 'The Road to Mandalay', 'Land of Hope and Glory' were integral parts of the informal folk culture.
23 Green, *Dreams of Adventure*, 389.
24 George Santayana, *Soliloquies in England*, London 1922, 32.
25 Piers Brendon, *Eminent Edwardians*, London 1979, 201–2.
26 Robert Baden-Powell, *Scouting for Boys*, London 1916, 314.
27 Baden-Powell, *Scouting for Boys*, 284–5, 315.
28 Kulik, *Alexander Korda*, 135.
29 Francis Hutchins, *The Illusion of Permanence*, Princeton 1967.
30 *World Film News*, May–June 1938, 57.
31 For a detailed discussion of *Sanders of the River*, see Jeffrey Richards and Anthony Aldgate, *Best of British*, Oxford 1983, 13–27.
32 P. J. Keating, 'Fact and fiction in the East End', H. J. Dyos and Michael Wolff, eds, *The Victorian City*, London 1973, 585–6.
33 *The Spectator*, 9 April 1938.
34 *Cinema Quarterly* III, spring 1935, 175.
35 *The Sunday Times*, 7 April 1935.
36 *Kinematograph Weekly*, 4 April 1935.
37 *Mass Observation* File Report 967, 17 November 1941.
38 *Hansard* 203, 2039.
39 Philip Taylor, *The Projection of Britain*, Cambridge 1981, 232.
40 *Today's Cinema*, 14 Oxford 1938.
41 *Hansard* 342, 1306–7.
42 On the censorship of imperial film projects see Jeffrey Richards, *Dream Palace*, 134–52.
43 Neville Chamberlain Papers, NC 8/21/9, 14 April 1934. I owe this reference to Dr Stephen Constantine.
44 Chamberlain Papers, NC 8/21/9, June 1938.
45 T. J. Hollins, 'The Conservative Party and film propaganda between the wars', *English Historical Review*, XCVI, April 1981, 359–69.
46 *The New York Times*, 12 January 1935.
47 *The Daily Mail*, 1 February 1935.
48 *The New York Times*, 18 January 1935.
49 *The Times*, 12 April 1937.
50 Lester and Irene David, *Shirley Temple*, London 1984, 107.
51 Clayton Koppes and Gregory Black, 'What to show the world: the Office of War Information and Hollywood', *Journal of American History*, LXIV, June 1977, 87–105.
52 For details see Thomas Cripps, *Slow Fade to Black: the Negro in American Film 1900–1942*, New York 1977.
53 Margaret Farrand Thorp, *America at the Movies*, New Haven 1939, 294–5.
54 Mark Girouard, *The Return to Camelot*, London and New Haven 1981.
55 E. C. Mack, *Public Schools and British Opinion 1780–1860*, London 1938, 400.
56 Girouard, *Return to Camelot*, 229.
57 John Fraser, *America and the Patterns of Chivalry*, Cambridge 1982, 12, 16.

58	John Buchan, *Comments and Characters*, London 1940, 174.
59	J. P. Mayer, *British Cinemas and their Audiences*, London 1948, 84.

CHAPTER 8

'IN TOUCH WITH THE INFINITE'
THE BBC AND
THE EMPIRE, 1923–53

John M. MacKenzie

It is a surprising fact that although the BBC's administrative and organisational history has been subjected to minute analysis,[1] and there has been some attempt to discern the Corporation's social penetration and influence in Britain,[2] there have been few studies of the ideological content of its domestic output.[3] In general terms, no one has been in any doubt that it projected the Christian morality and middle-class values of its begetter, Reith. But although the cartoonist David Low identified 'Sir John Blimp of the BBC' as one of Colonel Blimp's many influential relatives in 1938, Reith's assertions of political independence have often been taken at face value.[4] His heroic defence of the comparatively weak Company against a predatory Churchill during the General Strike of 1926 seemed ample confirmation of that, even if the price of freedom was adherence to the Establishment line. Reith was even then fighting free of the commercial interests that had spawned him, trying to reach his goal of an independent public service broadcasting authority. Moreover, Reith's own belief that he blighted his career by holding out against the more aggressive politicians who demanded access to his microphones has been accepted by his biographer and others. Most notably, his long-running battle with Churchill, particularly exacerbated by Indian affairs between 1930 and 1935 and by the Abdication in 1936, ensured that he would secure little of the political preferment he so desperately desired during and after the Second World War.[5] If he was seen by many on the right as a quasi-socialist, his attitudes to strikers, staff associations in the BBC, and his good relations with Baldwin, MacDonald and other members of the Establishment would equally ensure that he was *persona non grata* with the left.

Reith believed, of course, that his role at the centre of affairs was vital to the survival of the BBC, but his friendships with Prime Ministers, his love of honours, his reverence for – and capacity to publicise – the monarchy, and

his connections both cordial and stormy with all who mattered in London, fed his sense of self-dramatisation. Nevertheless, according to Asa Briggs, Reith always knew the difference between news and propaganda: 'Sir Robert Vansittart, at the Foreign Office, was never sure about the difference between the two: the BBC inspired by Reith, to its own glory and the glory of the country, saw the difference clearly. The perception of the difference depends not so much on subtlety of intelligence as on qualities of character.'[6] This article proposes to test this proposition with regard to the British Empire and imperialism. How prominent was the BBC's projection of Britain's imperial role to the domestic population between 1923 and 1953? Which individuals and organisations were given access to the studios and outside broadcasting? How far did Reith's influence predominate during his period as Director-General and how enduring was his legacy? How lively was the debate within the Corporation on the appropriateness of imperial programmes?

The period selected embraces fifteen years of Reith's command of the BBC to 1938 and fifteen years after his departure. Early in its history, the BBC developed a tradition of what might be described as flagship programmes. These were programmes that marked days of national ritual. They often involved members of the Royal Family and permitted politicians to make what seemed like non-partisan speeches. They invoked imperial traditions, and, given the nature of the medium, made particular use of evocative prose, poetry and music to highlight their patriotic and historical content. Although there is very little audience research until 1936 – and it is even then only fragmentary until the fifties – these programmes were often described as being extremely popular, and all attempts by BBC programme planners to kill them off were thwarted. They frequently caused embarrassment within the Corporation, but they seemed to provide it with an admiring national audience, a good press, and social and political respectability, as well as firmly establishing the BBC in its role as reverent chronicler of royal and 'patriotic' events which it has maintained into the eighties. These programmes included those for Empire Day, Armistice Day and Christmas Day, as well as the broadcasts of imperial exhibitions, royal jubilees and coronations.

Before examining each of these in detail, it is perhaps necessary to explain the manner in which the establishment of the various BBC stations tended towards 'national' broadcasting.[7] Early broadcasting was purely local, but simultaneous broadcasting from all transmitters was common from 1923. With the opening of the Daventry transmitter (5XX) in 1925, national

---

Lord Jellicoe broadcasting to the children of the Empire on Empire Day; from the Empire Day Movement annual report for 1935. By courtesy of the Royal Commonwealth Society.

broadcasting became possible. In 1927 a new high-powered transmitter (5GB) at Daventry inaugurated the misnamed 'Regional Scheme'. In fact this was regional only in its administration and in relaying the transmissions from Daventry. Although the idea of limited regional choice was introduced in 1927 it was not until 1930 that a full distinction was made between the 'National' and the 'Regional' programmes. But the concept of regionalism was blunted in a number of ways. First, the regions were exceptionally large (for example, north-west and north-east England were combined, as were, at first, Wales and the West Country). Second, the 'regional' stations generally relayed programmes from London and carried strictly 'local' programmes for only a limited amount of air time. This partly resulted from Reith's insistence on the creation of a national audience which could be put in touch with metropolitan culture and events, a metropolitan bias shared by most of the BBC staff. It should also be remembered that press hostility ensured that curbs were placed on BBC news broadcasts in the early days of broadcasting. Until 1927, 'news' could only be broadcast after 7.00 pm. This restriction was progressively relaxed to 6.30 and, in 1928, to 6.00 pm. A separate news department was not set up until 1934. The opportunity to broadcast 'national' events was therefore a convenient way in which the BBC could overcome these inhibitions on news gathering. The maintenance of the national audience was re-emphasised during the Second World War. In 1939, the 'national' and 'regional' programmes were amalgamated into the 'Home' service; the Forces Programme was established in 1940; and the Empire Service, which had been started in 1932, became the Overseas Forces Service (later the General Overseas Service) in 1943. It was only after the Second World War that the BBC came to recognise the existence of different audience tastes and established the tripartite division of Home, Light and Third programmes. The entire broadcasting philosophy between the wars, therefore, tended towards reaching a 'national' audience and laying emphasis on national ritual and royal events.

Empire Day is now largely a forgotten festival. It was the brainchild of one man, the Earl of Meath, who had suggested in 1896 that the Queen's birthday, 24 May, should be made a school half-holiday (the morning to be used for raising the flag and an appropriate ceremony or service) and a day of patriotic celebration.[8] In 1903 he founded the Empire Day Movement (EDM) and in the following year it held its first public observance. 24 May became a national holiday in Canada in 1897, in Australia in 1905, in New Zealand and South Africa in 1910, and in India in 1923. In 1908, however, the House of Commons rejected a proposal for an official ceremony and holiday on that day and it was only in the patriotic atmosphere of the First World War, in 1916, that it received government support. John Springhall has noted that public interest in Empire Day seemed to increase during the inter-war years.[9] Perhaps the influence of radio goes far to explain this.

Empire Day was in fact given great prominence in the twenties and thirties. There were invariably supplements in the national newspapers. Empire shopping weeks were hitched to it during the period of the activities of the Empire Marketing Board (see the contribution of Stephen Constantine in this volume), and local newspapers throughout the country gave considerable attention to both its civic and commercial observances. In London, the *Daily Express* organised Pageants of Empire with community singing in Hyde Park. The singing was led by Dame Clara Butt in the twenties and was conducted on several occasions by Sir Edward Elgar. The EDM issued a message to schools in Britain and the Empire and organised an Empire Day service, as well as concerts and rallies, often at the Royal Albert Hall. The BBC, for its part, devoted an extraordinary proportion of air time each 24 May to Empire observances.

The tone and content of much of this activity had been set by the Empire Exhibition at Wembley in 1924. This was the first great national event – and outside broadcast – on which the young British Broadcasting Company could cut its teeth, and it did a great deal to popularise broadcasting. The opening ceremony, including the speech of George V, was broadcast, and Reith noted in his diary that 'Everything went most successfully, including the broadcast which went all over the country and was the biggest thing we have done yet.'[10] This was the first of several broadcasts from the Exhibition. On 24 May, broadcasting time was filled almost entirely with events from Wembley. Between 3 and 5.30 in the afternoon there was a programme of massed bands and choirs from the stadium, and in the evening, in a simultaneous broadcast to all regional stations, two and a quarter hours were devoted to what seems to have been a preview of the Wembley Pageant of Empire which opened later in July.[11] There were songs, stories, and episodes of Empire history, poems specially written by Alfred Noyes, music by both military bands and symphony orchestra, with messages from the Viceroy of India, dominion premiers and colonial governors following each episode. A feature in the *Radio Times* described the historical sequence thus: 'The Spirit of England rises from the waves. She summons the spirits of Scotland, Ireland, and Wales. The four sisters fly through sea and storm across the world to found new nations and colonies.'[12] The same issue announced that listeners, having heard the King and the Prince of Wales at Wembley, would be able to hear the Duke of York at the Empire Day banquet at the Royal Colonial Institute on 23 May.[13]

Empire Day was featured on the front pages of the appropriate Radio Times in 1925. The Earl of Meath contributed a two-page article (starting on the front cover) in which he ecstatically hailed the power of radio as 'an Empire force' and its capacity to influence millions.[14] He went on to lay out the EDM's ideology, and its belief that the virtues of loyalty, patriotism and obedience should be instilled into the young. These had ensured the growth of the Empire and would give assurance to its permanence. Empire Day fell on a Sunday that year, and the BBC carried two Empire services, in the afternoon and the evening. Meath broadcast an 'Empire call to boys and girls' on the 25th, and in the evening a concert of imperial music had as its interval an address by the Prime Minister. This pattern became standard for many years. Meath's address to children was frequently followed by an Empire Day programme for schools on the Empire. The *Daily Express* Empire Day Festival and community singing from Hyde Park was broadcast in whole or in part each year, usually in the early evening. Later there would be an Empire Day concert and possibly a documentary on Empire communications or the like. Baldwin, an early convert to the power of radio, broadcast a Prime Minister's message to Britain and the Empire either in the interval of the concert or as part of the documentary programme, a duty willingly taken over by Ramsay MacDonald from 1929. The speeches of the annual Empire Day banquet were often broadcast. More than three hours of broadcasting, a high proportion of the limited air time of the day, were annually devoted to Empire Day ceremonies and programmes.

The pattern established in the twenties was gradually modified in the thirties. The *Daily Express* event was carried until 1932. The broadcasting of the Empire Day message of the EDM continued until 1935. The Prime Minister broadcast each year until 1933. The Empire Day speeches at the Royal Empire Society (as the Royal Colonial Institute had become in 1928) banquet were carried in 1933 and 1934. There were special documentary programmes each year except 1938. As well as the annual Empire Day services, there were special Royal Command concerts in 1935 and 1938.

In 1932 the Empire Day programme was designed as a prelude to the Ottawa Conference on imperial economic relations which was held later that year. It bore all the marks of the Empire Marketing Board and was described in *Radio Times* as 'A Prospect of Economic Unity in a World at Economic War'.[15] This final essay in the old-style Empire Day documentary programme was clearly inspired by contemporary propagandist concerns. In the following year, the BBC programme makers produced a new design inspired by the Empire Service which had opened in December 1932 and by the development of broadcasting services within the Empire.[16] In 1933, the Empire Day programme was entitled *News from Home* and featured an hour-long tour of characteristic British institutions and homes. In future years it was to be followed by similar programmes from the Dominions. Australian broadcasters contributed the programme in 1934, and Canada, South Africa, India and Ceylon provided the feature in succeeding years. In 1936 there was an additional Empire Day programme of readings from the works of Kipling. He had opposed such a broadcast during his lifetime and this one was made possible by his death in 1935. In both 1935 and 1938 the

Empire Day command concerts were broadcast in their entirety from the Royal Albert Hall. In 1938 only half the concert was to have been taken by the National Service of the BBC, but under pressure from the Master of the King's Musick, Sir Walford Davies, the controller of programmes, Cecil Graves, was forced to take the lot.[17] He had to issue an apology to station controllers and producers for the considerable readjustment to schedules this entailed. In 1939 the Empire Day programme consisted of a sound tour of the Empire in which 'The Empire unites in a tribute of loyalty and affection to their Majesties the King and Queen'.[18]

The BBC programme staff did not accept this concentration on Empire Day and Empire broadcasting with equanimity. In 1930, E. J. King-Bull, a member of the BBC's research department, described Empire Day as a 'dead letter day'.[19] A great deal of the music and literature of artistic and sentimental value to the Empire theme, he went on, is no longer effective or evocative. In any case, it had all been used too often. In 1931, Lindsay Wellington, who was concerned with programme policy and planning, suggested to Roger Eckersley, the Assistant Controller (Programmes) – also known as the Director of Programmes – that 'none of us like the Empire Day programme'.[20] He went on to assert that 'the Daily Express show in Hyde Park' was 'not worthy of us or of any public occasion'. In 1932, the Assistant Director of Talks objected that Empire Day programmes offended the 'League of Nations and internationalist people', while the EDM's ideas (for example in their choice of songs) were ultra-patriotic and aggressive.[21] The replies to these complaints are interesting. In 1930, King-Bull was informed by the Assistant Controller in charge of public relations, Gladstone Murray, that 'politically it is of growing importance that the Corporation should identify itself more definitely with Empire sentiment and activity'.[22] In 1931, Eckersley told Wellington that the Empire Day programmes were 'the sort of popular thing with the *poloi* that we ought to do on occasion'.[23]

Whether the BBC celebrated the Empire because of political expediency or popular demand, Reith certainly approved. On several occasions he pressed his subordinates to 'boost Empire Day'.[24] In 1930 the Director of Programmes accepted the difficulties surrounding Empire Day, but minuted that there was pressure from the Director-General.[25] Moreover, Reith had strenuous supporters within the Corporation. J. C. Stobart, who was associated with the Empire Marketing Board throughout its history, annually prepared the schools Empire broadcast to go with Meath's address, and argued that the research staff should be able to come up with inventive ideas for more Empire Day programmes.[26] The Controller of Programmes between 1933 and 1936 was Colonel Alan Dawnay, a man unlikely to sanction any departure from time-honoured patriotic broadcasting. He supported the introduction to the Corporation of John Coatman, former Chief of the Indian Police and Professor of Imperial Economic Relations at the London School of Economics, in 1934. Reith brought him in as 'right-wing offset', as Asa Briggs put it, to balance the direction of news and talks.[27] Although it is difficult to prove, this could well have been a reaction to the known anti-imperial views of some of the staff.

The reasons for Reith's insistence on an extensive broadcast celebration of Empire Day and of patriotic ceremonies associated with the Empire are, like the man, complex. That he himself was an imperial idealist and patriot is beyond doubt. But as Andrew Boyle has written, Reith was also 'in love with symbolism, pomp, dressing-up and orders'.[28] He was a devotee of hierarchical values, a self-dramatist and a conformist. The Empire programmes appealed to all these sides of Reith's nature, and provided for him a sense of participating in great national ritual. After the Wembley Exhibition success, he was already in search of a knighthood.[29] The message constantly reiterated by Meath and the EDM's watchwords of 'Unity, Responsibility, Duty, Sympathy, Self-Sacrifice' must have appealed to him greatly. But he also saw this projection of the Empire as a route to respectability for the Corporation, a means of demonstrating that it could through national and patriotic symbols be a consensual and not a divisive body. Such broadcasting perfectly fitted Reith's desire to protect the listeners from anything he considered to be harmful, contentious or dangerous. The annual Empire Day broadcasts by Baldwin came at a time when Reith's relationship with him was maturing into friendship, when the emollient Baldwin was anxious to heal the wounds of the General Strike. Reith also came to be on good terms with Beaverbrook, who had seemed at first to be an enemy of the nascent Company, but had eventually supported Reith's monopolistic, public service idea.[30] As Reith consolidated the Corporation's place in national life and his own in the Establishment it is perhaps not surprising that he used Empire Day as a seemingly non-partisan platform for Baldwin and as a commercial for the imperial patriotism of Beaverbrook's *Daily Express*.

Nevertheless, the BBC's relationship with the EDM caused great embarrassment within the Corporation. In the twenties, in the aftermath of Wembley, the broadcasters seem to have found it easier to stomach the venerable Earl of Meath. Meath's successor as President of the EDM was Earl Jellicoe, and the chairman of the movement was a military man, Sir William Wayland. The schools broadcasters were perennially anxious to avoid all hint of militarism and suppressed ideas for programmes of music and poetry associated with imperial wars in the past. The Central Council for Schools Broadcasting never accepted responsibility for the EDM address and the Empire schools programme which went with it. It was one schools programme which was always organised by the Corporation itself. Until his death in 1933, J. C. Stobart 'who had been very much in favour of school celebrations of the Empire', organised the Empire Day schools programme.[31] But as the thirties wore on, resistance to the EDM and to this kind of programme grew.

Earl Jellicoe took over the EDM's broadcast message to schools in 1931, and his handling of it generated increasing discontent. He continued to make it until 1935. 'It does no harm', the Director of Talks minuted in response to the disquiet of some members of his department, 'and it is appreciated by the Empire Day Movement.'[32] The Empire programme which had in the past followed the EDM's message was dropped. In 1935 the Central Council on Schools Broadcasting insisted that the address should be described as the Empire Day message 'to schoolchildren' and not 'to schools' in order to dissociate it from normal schools broadcasting. In 1936, after the deaths of Jellicoe and his successor Earl Beatty (who was President of the EDM for only a few months), the redoubtable Director of Schools Broadcasting, Mary Somerville, made a determined effort to abandon the EDM. In the absence of a President, the movement had suggested that the chairman, Sir William Wayland should make the broadcast. 'I don't like this business of chairman of societies broadcasting – as such', she wrote, 'we got pretty heavily criticised at some meetings last year for Lord Jellicoe's speeches which were "of a dullness" to defeat their very object.'[33] She was overruled by the Controller of Programmes, Cecil Graves, who commented wearily, 'We had better have him'.[34]

In fact, Wayland was invited to compère a half-hour programme on the Empire to avoid his actually making a speech. Miss Somerville and Wayland exchanged happy letters after the broadcast, but in 1937 she was on the warpath again. It was decided to broadcast an Empire Day service from St Paul's, which the new King was to attend, and use this as an excuse to escape the obligation to the EDM. Wayland was duly informed. The new President of the EDM was Viscount Bledisloe, former Governor-General of New Zealand. He wrote to Reith, and the EDM's slot was promptly restored. In 1938, the year of Reith's downfall, the schools broadcasters at last thwarted the EDM. One minuted that the kind of message favoured by Bledisloe could do nothing but 'harm to the Empire'. Another wrote that the 'EDM favours the wrong kind of unimaginative flag-waving'.[35] In any case, several local authorities had banned Empire Day celebrations in their schools in 1937.

The victory of this group was, however, short-lived. It had been achieved in the teeth of a resurgence of patriotic programmes associated with the Coronation of 1937. In that year the EDM had been joined by a new Empire pressure group, the Empire Youth Movement (EYM), founded by a Canadian, Major Frederick Ney.[36] It too had remarkable success in prevailing on the BBC. Ney took advantage of the fact that large numbers of young people from the Empire were in London at the time of the

Coronation to organise an Empire Youth Rally at the Royal Albert Hall on 18 May and a service of Empire youth at Westminster Abbey on 19 May. Directors of Education throughout the country were invited to send representative children to both these events, and the Albert Hall rally was so well attended that an overflow hall had to be arranged. The former Colonial Secretary, L. S. Amery presided over the committees which organised both these events. The literature of Ney's organisation, founded soon afterwards, marked it out as a right-wing movement which was fiercely anti-socialist, used the symbolism of chivalry in all its activities and publications, and argued for race purity in migration to the Empire. It is clear that the fact that in Canada the population of British stock had already fallen below 50 per cent was a source of great anxiety to Ney. In founding the EYM, he pointed to this fact, and argued that there was a greater need than ever before to people the Dominions with youth from Britain, particularly in the face of Hitler's demands for colonies.[37] Youth, he suggested, would always be romantic, and Empire appealed to the innate romanticism and love of adventure of the young. They should be dedicated to Empire, health, and recreation, using the techniques of Nazi youth movements to nobler ends. In the atmosphere of the Coronation, Ney was able to persuade the Archbishop of Canterbury and the Dean of Westminster to address the service, while the rally was attended by the Duke of Gloucester, Leopold Amery, Malcolm MacDonald, W. Ormsby-Gore, the Dominion premiers present in London, and Stanley Baldwin.

Ney roped in the BBC too. At first the Controller of Programmes, Cecil Graves decided to take only the service, arguing that the rally would only anticipate this Empire service, and in any case speeches seldom made good broadcasting.[38] Graves was, however, overruled, and the BBC broadcast both the service and the rally. He conceded the rally only on condition that the broadcast of the speeches at the Royal Empire Society banquet on 24 May should be cancelled.

The outbreak of the war ensured an immediate revival in the flagging fortunes of the EDM. The King became its patron in 1941 and Winston Churchill was soon coopted as vice-patron. Membership and funds grew dramatically and the movement was soon able to afford a permanent staff and new premises. A full-time director, R. Huntley-Davidson was appointed, and an assistant director, Stella Monk, was soon added to the strength. The war-time climate favoured the resurgence in Empire broadcasting. Empire Day achieved a new significance when so many Dominions and colonial troops were in London and broadcasting naturally reflected the fact. Although the broadcasting of the EDM message by the President never resumed, Empire Day services, in which the Empire Day message was read out, were taken. Commander Anthony Kimmins, a member of the Admiralty's naval intelligence staff, became a frequent broadcaster, not just in explaining the naval aspects of the war, but also on Children's Hour and on Empire Day programmes. Kimmins, a former naval officer, had been a successful playwright and scriptwriter of films (including the George Formby successes) in the 1930s, and was highly regarded in the BBC.

The Empire Day documentaries returned and were described in the BBC as programmes of 'first-class importance'.[39] In 1940 and '41 Empire Day on the radio featured a programme called 'Brothers in Arms', about the forces of the Empire meeting in London. In 1941, the Empire Day concert included, among all the usual patriotic music, a piece called *Motherland* by George Dyson, the Director of the Royal College of Music. This was a setting of William Watson's poem 'England and her Colonies' written in 1892. It included the words:

> Children of Britain's island breed
> To whom the Mother in her need
> Perchance may one day call.

Although the *Radio Times* described it as 'singularly appropriate', dominion nationalists may have thought differently.[40] In 1942, one of the Empire Day programmes, consisting of the poetry of Kipling set to music by Elgar, produced a number of ripostes. Both the Director of the Indian broadcasting service and the Indian High Commissioner in London protested that this would be very poorly received in India.[41] In 1944, both the Home and General Forces programmes carried 'Empire music' and Empire programmes almost throughout the day, including a major programme entitled *The Empire Speaks*.[42] The Dominion premiers, Smuts of South Africa, Curtin of Australia, and Fraser of New Zealand all took part, though Mackenzie King of Canada steadfastly refused to do so despite repeated requests.

The new director of the EDM, Huntley-Davidson, claimed friends at the broadcasting court, in the shape of John Coatman and the Rev J. W. Welch, the Director of Religious Broadcasting. Both favoured broadcasting about the Empire and the proper observance of Empire Day. But Huntley-Davidson established a reputation as a meddler, who attempted to arrogate to himself an influence over Empire Day broadcasting which the BBC would not accept. He had a habit of consulting ministers like Attlee and broadcasters like Kimmins about possible Empire Day programmes in a manner which incurred the wrath of B. E. Nicolls, the programme controller.[43] Both Huntley-Davidson and his assistant and successor, Stella Monk, were to fall into disfavour at the BBC, but for the moment the fervour of victory gave them their last great fling.

Between 1944 and 1946 the EDM was strong enough to be able to capitalise on the euphoria of victory by organising Festivals of Empire at the Royal Albert Hall. In 1944 and 1945 the King, Queen and the princesses were present, and in 1946 Princess Elizabeth actually participated. These events were organised in association with Lord Kemsley and his paper the *Sunday Empire News*, which provided considerable subsidies to the EDM in these years. The BBC broadcast all of these rallies, although once again there was anxiety in the Corporation. In 1945, the BBC stipulated that the message should be a 'contemporary' one, the brotherhood of nations, 'not colonies, colonials, or Empire-builders'.[44] C. Day Lewis contributed an opening ode, which proved acceptable to the Corporation despite references to 'an emigrant, a settler − bold' and to 'heroes' who 'flash and fall like swordbeams through the gloom'. The image of the swordbeam was taken up in a chivalric central episode. This was entitled 'The Vigil' and was described as follows:

in which the Soul of the Empire dedicates itself anew to the Service of God and Mankind and prepares for the Great Crusade against the forces of Evil. A knight in shining armour is seen kneeling before an altar − sword uplifted − eyes directed to the Great Beyond. While he kneels and prays men and women from every walk of life gather behind him expectantly awaiting a signal. After some moments the knight rises and proceeds to move down the hall signalling to others to follow. Later he again signals and they come on faster and faster, finally passing on with him to the Great Adventure.[45]

Lindsay Wellington in the BBC reflected that 'a knight in shining armour in 1945 is pretty grim, but I suppose we can't help it'.[46] He insisted that the BBC commentator would describe the vigil in the BBC's terms, and the result was as follows: 'In which the Soul of the Empire, symbolised by a knight, dedicates itself anew to the service of God and Mankind and prepares for the Great Crusade against the forces of evil. As the knight kneels in prayer men and women gather behind him offering themselves in service. The knight rises, and, followed by the people, goes forth to the Great Adventure.' The vigil was followed by a performance of Ketelby's *March of the Knights*. The Festival contained a march past of representatives of all the Empire forces to the appropriate 'Empire' music, a tableau by students, 'Britannia and her Empire', as well as a 'Salute to Empire Makers' spoken by Valentine Dyall, all accompanied by the usual patriotic music.

The use of chivalric motifs and ritual was typical of all the Empire movements, particularly the EYM. Mark Girouard has traced the re-emergence of chivalry in the nineteenth century and its harnessing at the end of the century to imperialism and right-wing movements.[47] Girouard, like so many other writers, makes a break at the First World War, and suggests that chivalric symbolism died in the carnage of the Western Front. In fact, it lived on in a variety of ways. The chivalric overtones of the annual Albert Hall extravaganzas of the Primrose League with its knights, dames, habitations and tributes, lived on in the Festivals of Empire and Remembrance held annually in the Royal Albert Hall between the wars.[48] Marching, banners, and the breaking of flags played their part in those solemn occasions as well as in the *Daily Express* Hyde Park pageants. In 1936 the Festival of Empire and Remembrance opened with a performance of Elgar's Froissart overture and the *Radio Times* contained a paragraph on Elgar's fascination with chivalry.[49] Reith again forms an interesting connection here. Membership of cadet corps had formed the brightest part of his unhappy childhood and schooling. When he became a transport officer during the First World War, he took an inordinate pride in 'winning his spurs'. In 1921 Frances Stevenson recorded that he presented Lloyd George with a 'quaint little picture of St George and the Dragon'.[50] The membership cards and the literature of the uniformed youth movements as well as the Empire youth organisations invariably bore images of knights in armour.[51] Major Ney used chivalric notions in his writings as well as in the EYM's iconography. He called the exchanges of Empire youth 'Quests' and called for the idealistic firing of youth as in Nazi Germany.[52] It is an interesting fact that chivalric ritual was used by the Nazis and by the Vichy regime in France.

Another Festival of Empire was held in 1946.[53] The programme bore on the cover a picture of a Chelsea Pensioner with his arm round a Boy Scout pointing out the path to duty. Although the chivalric 'vigil' had apparently disappeared, the flags, patriotic tableaux and imperial music were still prominent. Princess Elizabeth gave an address to the youth of the Empire. Again the Festival was broadcast, part of it in a simultaneous transmission on both the Home Service and the Light Programme. The commentator was Wynford Vaughan-Thomas who seems to have had a friendly relationship with the EDM.[54] In both 1945 and 1946 the BBC paid fees to the EDM and the profits were devoted to the dissemination of Empire knowledge in the schools.

It was in this area that the EDM was able to report some success. In 1945 it claimed that 600 schools were receiving EDM literature, lecturers and the like.[55] By 1947, more than 1,000 schools were said to be affiliated to the movement. This growth in schools' interest in the Empire had undoubtedly been fostered by the BBC itself. The Ministry of Information in association with the Ministry of Education had inaugurated a campaign to improve public information about the British Commonwealth and Empire, particularly through schools broadcasting. This campaign had been promoted by Professor Vincent Harlow at the Ministry of Information and Professor W. M. Macmillan in the Empire Intelligence Section of the BBC.[56] The campaign was continued after the war and the BBC submitted lists of Empire programmes which had been broadcast to schools during the years 1940–5. The propaganda aims behind all this activity can best be summed up by the stated philosophy of one sixth-form series. This was that: 'England is the single country in the world that, looking after its own interests with meticulous care, has at the same time something to give to others'.[57]

Despite all the schools activity, the EDM was near the end of its privileged run. There was an Empire Day school programme in 1948 – on emigrants and the ties they still felt for the mother country, a poignant subject in a period of renewed emigration. The BBC refused, however, to take the EDM's annual concert. The Controller of Programmes, Wellington, dismissively minuted in 1950 that there was 'nothing very entertaining about a Maori singing Mozart or a Zulu singing Grieg'.[58] The secretary of the Central Council for Schools Broadcasting tartly informed the EDM, still importunate, in 1952 that 'It is against the general policy of my Council to ask the BBC to broadcast special messages from outside bodies to the schools'.[59]

Empire Day broadcasting by now had a very different flavour, the Home Service concentrating on talks and discussions by figures like Vincent Massey, the Canadian High Commissioner in London, Jan Smuts and Sir George Dunbar. The historians Margery Perham, Cyril Philips, Gerald Graham and John Hatch took part in a series of 'taking stock' discussions about Commonwealth developments. These were obviously designed for a tiny middle-class audience, while the masses could hear programmes of patriotic music on the Light Programme, assuming that they had not fled to Radio Luxembourg by now. Pre-war echoes were, however, provided by the indefatigable L. Du Garde Peach, who had written 400 radio plays, many of them of a patriotic nature, before the war, had contributed innumerable Children's Hour programmes, as well as writing his Ladybird versions of British history. In 1948, Children's Hour broadcast his programme for Empire Day, 'The Great Family'.

Although the Coronation of 1953, like its counterpart in 1937, produced a spate of programmes of the Empire Day/Christmas Day type, by 1954 the leading members of the EDM were expressing 'surprise and indignation' that the movement's message was no longer being carried in BBC newsbulletins and that the 'Empire Day' page heading had been dropped from the *Radio Times*.[60] The Director-General of the BBC, Sir Ian Jacob, declined to see anyone from the EDM, and the director of the movement refused to accept an invitation to meet the Director of News. There were still one or two people in the BBC who would have liked to promote Empire Day broadcasts. Franklin Engelman offered some suggestions for such programmes in 1951.[61] The balance he suggested was surely still on the side of noble achievement rather than exploitation. There was still scope, he thought, for a programme which focused on Empire-builders. There could be an Empire play from the drama department, an Empire Day edition of *Woman's Hour*, a variety show reflecting the wealth of talent from the Empire. Or, he wrote, we could broadcast a jamboree, 'for if there's anything inoffensively Empire, it's the Scouts'. In fact, Empire Day that year was celebrated only with an Empire Day edition of a light music and variety programme called *Welsh Rarebit*. In 1952, Malcolm Sargent conducted the BBC Opera Orchestra with Webster Booth in a Light Programme concert of Empire music for Empire Day. In 1959, the sole recognition of Common-wealth Day, as by then it had become, was in a question on the Commonwealth on the 'Brains Trust', and BBC employees were somewhat bemused that the EDM had succeeded in giving a mid-week appeal for funds on the radio both in 1957 and in 1959.[62]

For the sake of coherence it has been necessary to trace the fortunes of Empire Day to the 1950s. An examination of Armistice and Christmas Day broadcasts now requires some retracing of our steps. The second important national programme each year was Armistice Day, 11 November. It was consistently given prominence in the broadcasting schedules, not just in the form of the remembrance service still conducted today, but also in additional programmes. The *Radio Times* without fail carried Remembr-ance Day as its cover feature in the appropriate issue (Empire Day was displaced from this place of honour during the thirties), and there were invariably articles on the various programmes associated with the festival. The British Legion's Festivals of Empire and Remembrance were broadcast each year from 1927 to the Second World War, and resumed after the war, though with the word 'Empire' dropped from its title. This consisted annually of march pasts and calls to service from the uniformed youth organisations, veterans and members of the armed forces. There were patriotic tableaux and the ceremonial breaking out of the flags of the Empire. From 1932 the BBC also carried an annual programme of war poems set to the music of Elgar.

Empire Day concerts and Empire music generally form a very interesting study in themselves. The concerts were often conducted by Edward Elgar in the twenties and early thirties and also by Adrian Boult, Henry Wood, Hugh Allen, Walford Davies and, nearer the Second World War, Malcolm Sargent. The music played constituted an aural equivalent of an iconogra-phy, consisting of the patriotic and imperial music composed by a great range of composers in the period 1890 to 1920.[63] On several occasions there were attempts to create programmes of music which featured colonial composers, like Percy Grainger for Australia, Alfred Hill for New Zealand, and Coleridge-Taylor for Africa, among many others. The orientalist music of composers like Ketelby, Lehmann and Bantock was used to illustrate Egypt and India. Elgar naturally figured most prominently. His 'Imperial March', written for the 1897 Jubilee, the 'Pomp and Circumstance' marches (including of course 'Land of Hope and Glory'), 'the Banner of St George', the 'Crown of India' suite, and his 'Empire March' of 1924 made frequent appearances, although the jingoistic final chorus from *Caractacus*, much used in Empire Day concerts before the First World War seems to have been banished in the inter-war years. Walford Davies's 'Solemn Melody', Parry's

'Jerusalem', Arne's 'Rule Britannia' were staple patriotic musical fare, together with the Hallelujah chorus from Handel's *Messiah*, which was hijacked into the patriotic canon.

The idea repeated by all Elgar's biographers[64] that this kind of music was unfashionable and rejected by the time of his death may be true of intellectual and musicological circles, but it is decidedly not true of broadcasting. Indeed patriotic music provided for serious composers an extensive and popular audience such as they could not have commanded without these national occasions which were so frequently broadcast. It is, however, a fascinating fact that these concerts, so essential a part of patriotic broadcasting on the National Service before the Second World War, were relegated in the late forties and fifties from the Home Service to the Light Programme. This reflects, perhaps, both the growing contempt in which this material was held by the Home Service establishment and the extent to which the BBC, by that time, was out of touch with what was really wanted by Light Programme listeners.

Reith clearly saw this patriotic music as a vital adjunct of national life. In 1920, he arranged that at the end of Baldwin's broadcast during the General Strike the words of Parry's 'Jerusalem', intoned by himself, should be taken up by a swelling chorus in a great crescendo of sound.[65] MacDonald was outraged, although later he was only too happy to be involved himself in this kind of broadcast. Big Ben was also a vital part of the aural iconography, preceding every royal broadcast, all national and imperial events. Again Reith recognised and promoted its significance. Through Big Ben, he wrote, rural areas are brought into direct contact with great Empire institutions like Parliament and the Royal Observatory at Greenwich: '. . . the clock which beats time over the Houses of Parliament, in the centre of the Empire, is heard echoing in the loneliest cottage in the land'.[66]

The outpouring of national music by the BBC throughout the period was matched by the remarkable tradition of popular poeticising which had marked the political and artistic convergence associated with imperialism. Elgar's settings of the words of A. C. Benson and Laurence Binyon were repeatedly used. Elgar's music was performed as a backing to broadcasts of war poems. Fitzgerald's *Rubáiyát* and Laurence Hope's *Indian Love Lyrics* reached an even wider public through the music of Liza Lehmann and Amy Woodford-Finden. Sir Henry Newbolt wrote and presented the Empire Day programme in 1929. Kipling was closely associated with the BBC and may well have advised on the King's broadcasts. His poetry was frequently broadcast after his death, usually on days of Empire celebration. Alfred Noyes, who had written a number of poems for the Wembley Empire Exhibition – set to music by Elgar – wrote a special poem for the *Daily Express* Pageant of Empire. Sir John Squire wrote a poem about the King's broadcasts, including the line 'Speaking in rich deep tones to all Humanity'.

It was reproduced on the front cover of *Radio Times* at Christmas 1934, as was a patriotic poem by A. A. Thomson at Christmas 1940.

1932 was a significant turning-point in Christmas Day broadcasts. It was in that year that George V made the first royal Christmas broadcast, a tradition maintained ever since.[67] The broadcast was partly prompted by the inauguration of the BBC's powerful new short-wave transmitter at Daventry, and the opening of the Empire Service on 19 December of that year. It was perhaps natural then that the King's address should be preceded by an hour-long broadcast of greetings from the Empire entitled *All the World Over*. This was later described as having done more in a brief hour than years of humdrum propaganda to inform the public about the Empire.[68] In 1933, the BBC took this didactic purpose further by suggesting in the *Radio Times* that listeners would enjoy the programme better if they had an atlas at hand to follow it. In that year, the programme was called *Absent Friends* and consisted once more of greetings round the Empire. Something much more ambitious was attempted in 1934, when the Christmas Day broadcast was described as the 'principal high-spot programme of the year'.[69] In *Empire Exchange* episodes from Britain and the Empire were used in an alternating sequence, with items from India, South Africa, Australia and Canada, reaching a climax at Ilmington Manor in the Cotswolds. Christmas Day programmes in these years benefited from the fact that the Palestine mandate had brought Bethlehem into the Empire, and so there were normally relays from the Holy Land. Reith demonstrated his power over the details of programme making in 1934 by insisting that a favourite hymn 'All Hail the Power of Jesus' Name' should be broadcast to the furthest reaches of the Empire.[70]

As with the Empire Day programmes, it was not long before dissident voices were being heard in the Corporation. In 1935, a number of suggestions were put up as a means of getting away from 'the imperialistic type of Christmas Day programme'.[71] One member of the features department described the broadcasts of the past as being 'better suited to Empire Day than to the anniversary of the birth of Christ'. Ideas put forward included a history of Christmas, a religious drama, or a programme entitled *Spirit of Man*. Laurence Gilliam, the producer of imperial and patriotic programmes from the thirties to the fifties scotched these ideas. To cancel the by now traditional Christmas Day Empire programme, he wrote, would be an affront to the Empire, would offer an easy opportunity for criticism of the Corporation by the imperialistic press, and in any case it would be difficult to find a more fitting prelude to the King's speech.[72] A Christmas Day programme entitled *This Great Family* duly became the main broadcast of the Christmas schedules of that year. But the imperial flavour of the programme had already driven one nominal member of the Empire away. The Irish Free State had participated in the programme in 1934, but refused to do so thereafter.

The Christmas Day programme disappeared in 1936, since there was no royal broadcast in the aftermath of the Abdication. The 1937 broadcast was clearly a strain to George VI, having to be coached through his stammer at every point, and Neville Chamberlain relieved him of the ordeal in 1938.[73] There were therefore no 'imperialistic' broadcasts in these years, but in 1939 they returned when a programme 'The Empire Greets the King' was used to bring the Empire together in the opening months of the war. Laurence Gilliam and Leonard Cottrell produced Christmas Day broadcasts for the rest of the war, although the imperial content was inevitably diluted by the need to involve the Allies and from 1942 the United States. In 1942, Gilliam described the programme as 'the most important and widely diffused programme of the year, being re-broadcast in practically every Empire country and the USA'.[74] The tradition continued after the war and resumed the predominantly imperial flavour. That these continued to be 'flagship' programmes was symbolised by the fact that they were narrated by Laurence Olivier in 1947, Robert Donat in 1948 and 1950, and John Gielgud in 1951, with music composed by William Alwyn (1945, 1950 and 1951), Benjamin Britten (1947), and Alexander Goehr (1948). During the war (and again in 1949) they had been narrated by Howard Marshall, who was Director of Public Relations at the Ministry of Food, 1940–3 and Director of War Reporting at the BBC 1943–5.

The images presented by these programmes are interesting. The England (and the Scots repeatedly complained of the BBC's use of 'England' rather than 'Britain') depicted was always the England of the country village, the England of bucolic charm, frothing pewter mugs of ale, folk tales and songs around the firelight, seldom the 'England' of the industrial city. In this respect the BBC projected the rural image so favoured by Baldwin and neatly confirms the points made by Martin Wiener on the English stereotype.[75] Cotswolds locations like Ilmington Manor, whose owner was a friend of the BBC's Freddie Grisewood, were used repeatedly, as were other farming locations in the north of England and Scotland. In 1945, the programme opened in Sussex, among 'Kipling's wooded hills'. The only industrial location in one of these programmes appears to have been in 1935 when the Town Clerk of Sheffield persuaded the BBC to feature a steel worker's family since the smelters had to work through the Christmas season.[76] The images drawn from the Empire were equally stereotyped. India was always the India of the North-West Frontier and tea planters in the Nilgiris Hills (conveniently close to a studio in Madras) together with the bells of the Afghan Memorial Church in Bombay. New Zealand and Australia were outsize farms producing food for Britain with Bondi Beach packed with unseasonal (for Britain) bathers making almost annual appearances. Canada was all frost and snow, with fishermen of the maritime provinces and lumbermen of British Columbia the favourite 'types'. But it was Africa that provided the greatest opportunity for stereotyping. 'Historic farms' of Cape Province, Natal sugar planters, Transvaal miners, and Southern Rhodesian settlers were used repeatedly, always to a background of happy Africans dancing and singing. In 1934, a section of the programme on Southern Rhodesia, *Greetings from the Zambezi*, featured a background of 'native tom-toms' and 'loyal farewell salutes' from 'the Matabele and other tribes of the million native of Southern Rhodesia who live and work on farms, mines, and ranches'. Moving south, 8,000 labourers of the City Deep Mine in Johannesburg were to be heard celebrating Christmas Day with drums and African pianos. 'Mdingi, induna, chief of the Xhosa, had composed a special ode', followed by 'a strange and stirring sound as Chief Mdingi and his sturdy chorus recite the salute that is given only to Kings . . . while the drums roll in stirring crescendo'.[77] At the end of that the commentator announced that the thoughts of the world turned to the English countryside.

The projection of a confident mutually beneficial economic imperialism continued after the war. In 1947, the groundnut scheme in Tanganyika was described as offering 'solid ground for hope, hundreds of miles of jungle cleared by science and the bulldozer with a real promise of a better life for African and European'.[78] In 1948 the 'groundnutters' reappeared – 'English families under canvas or in huts' to a background of African drumming and chanting. They rubbed shoulders on the air waves with 'hard-pressed planters in up-country Johore, Malaya'.[79] In 1951, the programme, entitled *The Gifts of Christmas* featured 'Zulu voices raised in thanksgiving' as well as a section on the Gold Coast – 'once the white man's coming here meant terror and slavery; now he comes bringing gifts – gifts of healing, of learning – spelling the way to a fuller life'.[80]

The Christmas Day programmes of the 1940s represent the victory of the Empire of peace and economic regeneration over the historic Empire of conquest and settlement, national greatness and patriotic revival in the images presented to the British public. The former seems always to have been more respectable in the minds of the BBC programme makers, and it was the identification of the EDM with the latter which made their message increasingly unacceptable. The EDM Empire was thought to be that of the officer heroes, the conquerors and warriors of the past, while the 'peace' Empire was that of the ordinary settler and worker, 'Empire-builders' rather than 'Empire-makers'. Even during the Second World War, a peace-loving Empire devoted to economic renewal was of course the most potent propaganda message. Schools and other broadcasts projected the Empire of Lugard and the 'dual mandate', the Empire in which, conveniently, self-interest and altruism converged. It was an image, however, which increasingly diverged from the reality. Crises in commodity prices, producing, for example, cocoa hold-ups in the Gold Coast (when the producers refused to market their crop), riots in Jamaica, miners' strikes in Northern Rhodesia, the economic and social turbulence of the postwar period in the forties, the growing independence of the dominions, the failure of the groundnut scheme, all made it increasingly difficult to sustain.

If the economic image had been relatively uncontroversial in the thirties, the growing power and pursuit of self-interest by white settler groups in eastern and southern Africa, the revolt of a peasantry in the Mau Mau campaign in Kenya and other revolts in South-east Asia, rendered it highly controversial in the fifties. The old image of Empire became increasingly at odds with the BBC news bulletins. While it is true that nationalist revolt and insurgency were invariably depicted as forces of darkness, nonetheless, it was no longer possible to celebrate an Empire of peace and prosperity when it was patently at war with itself and the old colonial economic altruism was revealed as a hollow sham. Moreover, dominion independence would no longer brook the sentiments of the Empire programmes of the interwar years. The Imperial Institute in South Kensington was so wedded to the economic image that it was indeed destroyed by its demise.[81] In future, the variety of cultures and customs of the Empire/Commonwealth, and the training of peoples in democratic institutions were to come front of stage in the new propaganda. Since these concerns involved neither the excitements of colonial war and settlement nor the readily familiar images of food production and consumption, it was much more difficult to stimulate public interest. They were the sorts of issues which would be treated in discussions and talks intended for a minority elite audience.

But patriotic programming associated with the monarchy survived. Just as the imperial re-evaluation was taking place in the early fifties and the BBC turned its face against those who had propounded the old visions of Empire, the coronation of a new monarch brought a fresh wave of national events centred on the monarchy. Anachronistically, the coronation of 1953 was just as 'imperial' an event as its predecessor in 1937, and extensive Commonwealth tours made good broadcasting for schools and in documentary and Christmas programmes. In all of these, however, the BBC was beginning to tread much more warily.

It is considerably easier to survey this programme content of the national broadcasts of the BBC than it is to assess their social penetration or ideological influence. The statistics at any rate are readily available. George Orwell wrote in *The Road to Wigan Pier* that 'Twenty million people are under-fed but literally everyone in England has access to a radio'. In 1923 over two million licences had already been taken out; in 1939 the figure stood at more than nine million.[82] By that year there were seventy-three licences for every hundred households. In the later thirties, audience research suggested that Children's Hour reached 3.75 million listeners out of potential audience of six million. Of the latter, 1.2 million had no access to sets. The sales of the *Radio Times* constituted one of the most dramatic publication successes of the interwar years. The first issue in September 1923 sold quarter of a million copies, and that figure had more than trebled by the end of 1925. Its circulation had passed one and a half million by 1931 and reached 2,588,433 in 1939. The Coronation issue in 1937 sold more than three and a half million copies, a record for any weekly. The best-selling daily paper, the *Daily Express*, had barely reached two and a half million in 1939, and only Sunday papers like the *News of the World* and *The People* had larger circulations than *Radio Times*. None of its buyers in the twenties and thirties could have been unaware of the major patriotic programmes, for they were always given great prominence, usually front-cover treatment together with articles and photographs.

It is of course true that the constant complaint of the listening public – reflected indeed in a letter in the very first issue of *Radio Times* – was that the BBC was too highbrow. It was this which drove listeners to the light music and variety programmes of Radio Luxembourg and Normandie, particularly on Sundays when the BBC's drab fare continued to be influenced by Reith's sabbatarianism. Audience research after 1936 clearly demonstrated the primacy of the demand for variety and music-hall-style entertainment, but the questionnaires never included the 'national' prog-rammes, which were 'once-off', though annual, events.[83] It is interesting that in the second random sample of 1939 military band music scored third in order of priority (72 percent approval) after variety and theatre and cinema organs. In any case, the patriotic programmes were frequently attacked in the BBC as being not 'serious' enough. They were both despised and promoted as a result of their great popularity. The King's Christmas talk rated the highest recorded audience, over 91 percent.[84] It may well be that the Empire programme which preceded it conflicted with the plum pudding in many homes, but the programme makers repeatedly referred to it as the most important programme of the year, a claim re-asserted in wartime. The Christmas Day programme of 1952, *The Queen's Inheritance* was said to have secured the largest audience and the highest appreciation rating since the war.[85] Certainly press reactions to these programmes were generally ecstatic. Moreover, it is a surprising fact that American networks invariably took the Christmas Day programmes and royal broadcasts, and sometimes even transmitted the Empire Day documentaries and concerts. They were said to have a considerable following in the USA, to have excited much press comment, as well as a considerable transatlantic mailbag for the BBC.[86] Many Americans, partly prompted by the material served up to them by Hollywood and by an awareness of their own imperial role were fascinated by the British Empire and its monarchy. Supporters of these programmes argued that they had done a great deal to promote American sympathy for Britain. The oft-repeated assertion that Americans bore a considerable animus for the British Empire by the late thirties is simply not borne out by the evidence of popular culture.

It is perhaps not surprising that the prime medium of the age should project both historic achievement and a spurious sense of an enduring present greatness to the population of an imperial power which had just been one of the victors of a great war. Images of stability and strength, of self-confidence and even complacency were more likely to cultivate support and affection for the BBC than anxieties about weakness and dissension. Moreover, the particular character of radio and the developing wizardry – as contemporaries saw it – of long-distance transmission was perfectly adapted to imperial contacts – 'spreading a great invisible net over the world' as one programme called it. It was this connection between broadcasting and Empire which helped to give radio a mystical and religious power both to its practitioners and its listeners. As always, Reith took this to its limits. In *Broadcast over Britain* of 1924 he dubbed one chapter 'In Touch with the Infinite'. Broadcasting', he wrote, 'would cast a girdle round the earth with bonds that are all the stronger because invisible.'[87] For him the creation of the Empire Service in 1932 was part of this great internationalist process under Anglo-Saxon leadership. Broadcasting had a moral power to unite nation, Empire and ultimately mankind. The connections with the contemporary visions of Jan Smuts, Robert Baden-Powell, even George Bernard Shaw, are immediately apparent. No wonder that Reith was anxious to thwart a breakdown into parochial broadcasting and was concerned to unite national and world audiences through imperial ritual. Broadcasting duly played its part in the fashionable projection of Empire as a form of internationalism, a vision which did much to promote Anglo-Saxon complacency in the superiority of their culture.

The problem was that Reith was never quite clear about the image of Empire which ought to be projected. The lively debate on this was left to his subordinates with Reith frequently intervening to re-assert traditionalism. The peace Empire, the Empire of internationalism and economic harmony was acceptable to most BBC employees. This was the Empire of the Empire Marketing Board and of the British documentary film movement which it nurtured. Although it was an Empire of stereotypes, climatic, national and racial, which bore little relation to the colonial reality of the thirties, it seems to have won considerable support across the political spectrum. Despite the dramatic changes that took place in Colonial Office and Ministry of Information propaganda during the Second World War, it was an image which continued to be projected in the forties.[88] But if the angels of the peace Empire predominated in Christmas Day programmes, the militarist devils of the historic, heroic Empire had all the best tunes. Despite intellectual anxieties at Savoy Hill and the Langham, there was a continuing popular and Establishment demand for patriotic spectacle and sentiment, and there were always some in the BBC who were only too anxious to supply it in the knowledge that Reith approved and the populace listened. If this old-style imperialism seemed to be in decline by the later thirties, it was stimulated afresh by the Coronation and the War.

The activities of the BBC cast a very curious light on the notion that popular imperialism was killed by the First World War. Spectacular patriotic events, a recently created tradition of national music, even chivalric symbolism, all contributed to the BBC's role as an instrument of a peculiarly slanted, and nationally self-deluding 'consensus'. On the one hand, Churchill's fierce opposition to constitutional change in India was kept from the studio, but so was any organised anti-imperialism.[89] On the other, the EDM was allowed privileged access, while the educational authorities which banned Empire Day ceremonies from their schools were, like strikers and hunger-marchers, kept firmly out.[90] If it is argued that the 1945 Labour landslide proved that all of this was irrelevant where it mattered, at the ballot box, it can equally be objected that Labour leaders like Attlee had presented a safe consensual image through participation in these national, broadcast events. Patriotic programming no doubt seemed to many to be above politics, although the organisations which promoted it were identifiably right-wing, as some BBC employees were uncomfortably aware. The broadcasts surely helped to ensure that the language, music and symbols of nationalism lay firmly with an imperial/royalist right. At the very least they contributed to a political climate in which the British public would not tolerate any party which was anti-monarchical or which seemed to attack Britain's complacent sense of superiority.

Acknowledgements

I am grateful to the Senate Grants Committee of the University of Lancaster for financial assistance which enabled me to undertake the research for this article, and to the staffs of the Written Archives Centre of the BBC at Caversham and of the Royal Commonwealth Society and University of Lancaster libraries who made available the records and books on which it is based.

Notes

1   Asa Briggs, *The History of Broadcasting in the United Kingdom*, four volumes, Oxford 1961, 1965, 1970, 1979.
2   Mark Pegg, *Broadcasting and Society*, London 1983.
3   Paddy Scannel and David Cardiff have examined the manner in which talks policies, news broadcasting, and approaches to contemporary issues were carefully controlled during the 1930s. Their contributions can be found in various volumes of *Media, Culture, and Society*, and most usefully summarised

in their article, 'Serving the nation: public service broadcasting before the War' in Bernard Waites, Tony Bennett and Graham Martin (eds), *Popular Culture: Past and Present*, London 1982, 161–88. The modern role of the BBC in seeking the consensual ground has been exposed in Krishan Kumar, 'Holding the middle ground: the BBC, the public and the professional broadcaster' in James Curran, Michael Gurevitch and Janet Woollacott (eds), *Mass Communication and Society*, London 1977, 231–48. An account of the setting up of the BBC's Empire Service and of the preparations of the BBC for wartime propaganda can be found in Philip M. Taylor, *The Projection of Britain*, Cambridge 1981. See also Kenneth M. Wolfe. *The Churches and the BBC 1922–56*, London 1984.

4 Quoted in Peter Mellini, 'Colonel Blimp's England', *History Today XXXIV*, October 1984, 33.

5 J. C. W. Reith, *Into the Wind*, London 1949, part 3. Andrew Boyle, *Only the Wind Will Listen, Reith of the BBC*, London 1972, 270 and *passim*. At least one observer had a rather different view: Hamilton Fyfe, *Britain's War-time Revolution*, London 1944, 55, 103.

6 Briggs, Vol. II, *The Golden Age of Wireless*, Oxford 1965, 370.

7 Briggs, Vol. I, *The Birth of Broadcasting*, 223–4 and Vol. II, 25–6, 29 and *passim*. Pegg, *Broadcasting*, 18–31.

8 John M. MacKenzie, *Propaganda and Empire*, Manchester 1984, 231–6.

9 J. O. Springhall, 'Lord Meath, youth, and Empire', *Journal of Contemporary History*, V (1970), 107.

10 Charles Stuart (ed.) *The Reith Diaries*, London 1975, 133.

11 The Pageant opened in the Stadium on 25 July and ran, with more than thirty matinee and evening performances, to the end of August.

12 *Radio Times (RT)*, 16 May 1924, 322. Except in the case of direct quotations, future references to *RT* will not be footnoted as the date will in each case be obvious from the text.

13 The *RT* pointed out that the other speaker at the banquet was J. H. Thomas, who had risen 'from errand boy to Secretary of State'. Nothing better represented the imperial respectability of the Labour Party in office.

14 *RT*, 22 May 1925, 385–6.

15 *RT*, 20 May 1932, 488.

16 Harding to Assistant Controller of Programmes, 30 January 1933, BBC Written Archives Centre (WAC), R34/213/1, Empire Day 1928–38.

17 C. Graves, 24 March 1938, WAC (no file number), Royal Albert Hall, Empire Day (1938–46). See also WAC R44/122. An indication of the regard in which Walford Davies was held at the BBC can be secured from the admiring article on him in the *BBC Yearbook*, 1931, 157–8.

18 *RT*, 19 May 1939.

19 King-Bull to Gielgud, 22 February 1930, WAC R34/213/1.

20 Wellington to Director of Programmes, 10 February 1931, WAC R34/213/1.

21 Assistant Director of Talks, 20 April 1932, WAC R34/213/1.

22 Gielgud to King-Bull, 25 March 1930, WAC R34/213/1.

23 Minute, Director of Programmes, 10 February 1931, WAC R34/213/1.

24 Reith to Assistant Controller (Programmes), 15 March 1929, WAC R34/213/1.

25 Director of Programmes to Gielgud, 3 March, 1930, WAC R34/213/1.

26 Stobart to Director of Programmes 20 February 1931, WAC R34/213/1.

27 Briggs, Vol. II, 147.

28 Boyle, *Only the Wind*, 20.

29 Boyle, *Only the Wind*, 161.

30 Boyle, *Only the Wind*, 133–4. Stuart (ed.) *Reith Diaries*, 131 and 134.
31 Mary Somerville to Secretary, Central Council for School Broadcasting, February 1938, WAC R51/134/1.
32 Minute, Director of Talks on Sir William Wayland, Chairman Empire Day Movement (EDM) to D.T., 15 March 1934, WAC R51/134/1.
33 Minute by Mary Somerville on Wayland to D.T., 30 January 1936, WAC R51/134/1.
34 Graves to Somerville, n.d., WAC R51/134/1.
35 Lloyd Williams to Mary Somerville, 7 January 1938. Minute by Mary Somerville on Director External Services to Controller of Programmes, 11 January 1938, WAC R51/134/1.
36 MacKenzie, *Propaganda*, 236–9.
37 Correspondence between the Empire Youth Movement and the BBC can be found in WAC (no file number) OBs, Royal Albert Hall, Empire Youth 1937 (WAC OBs RAH Empire Youth).
38 Minute of Graves on Ney to Graves, 15 February 1937, WAC OBs, RAH Empire Youth 1937.
39 Laurence Gilliam, 25 April 1941, WAC R19/305, Empire Day (ED), 1941–50.
40 *RT*, 16 May 1941.
41 These remarks were sent to the producer, Cecil McGivern on 30 April 1942, WAC R19/305. Leopold Amery exerted pressure on the BBC throughout the war to give more attention to the Empire.
42 Correspondence on this programme can be found in WAC R34/213/3.
43 R. Huntley-Davidson to George Barnes, Director of Talks, 14 February 1944. Huntley-Davidson to Nicolls, 11 April 1944. Nicolls to Huntley-Davidson, 12 April 1944. Huntley-Davidson to Nicolls, 14 April 1944. WAC R51/134/1.
44 Minute by Wellington, 25 April 1945, WAC OBs RAH ED, file 1, 1938–46.
45 This is taken from the programme in WAC OBs RAH ED, file 1.
46 Minute by Wellington, 25 April 1945.
47 Mark Girouard, *The Return to Camelot*, New Haven and London, 1981.
48 For the chivalric aspects of the Primrose League, see J. H. Robb, *The Primrose League, 1883–1906*, New York 1942. For the adoption of these symbols by the Festivals of Empire and Remembrance and by the *Daily Express* rallies, see successive *RTs* for 24 May and 11 November each year.
49 *RT*, 6 November 1936.
50 Boyle, *Only the Wind*, 117.
51 This is true of the membership cards and prize book plates of the Boy's Brigade, for example. For the Scouts and chivalry, see Girouard, *Return to Camelot*, 254–7.
52 MacKenzie, *Propaganda*, 238.
53 The programme and other materials relating to this rally are in WAC OBs RAH ED, file 1, 1938–46.
54 Evidence on the connection between W. Vaughan-Thomas and the EDM is in WAC OBs RAH ED, file 1.
55 These figures are to be found in the EDM *Annual Reports*, Royal Commonwealth Society Library and in EDM correspondence with the BBC in WAC files R51/134/1–2.
56 WAC R34/350/2, Empire, Schools Broadcasting Department, 1940–6.
57 This was the rationale of a series of sixth-form programmes listed in 'Programmes on the British Empire, 1940–46' in WAC R34/350/2.
58 Minute by Wellington on the programme for the Empire Day concert at

Kingsway Hall on 24 May 1950, WAC R51/134/2, EDM file 2, 1947–54. The Maori in question was Inia te Waiata.

59 Secretary, CCSB, to Stella Monk, 29 April 1952, R51/134/2.

60 John H. Carrow, Chairman EDM to Sir Ian Jacob, 24 May 1954, WAC R51/134/2. Carrow conveyed the disappointment of the agents general of the colonies and pointed out that Empire Day was more widely appreciated and observed in the Commonwealth than in Britain. Also Carrow to Jacob, 6 September 1954. Harman Grisewood, Director of the Spoken Word, advised Jacob, 13 September 1954 that it would be a waste of time to see Carrow. Grisewood described the movement as having a pre-1914 flavour about it. 'It is not a day that arouses much enthusiasm or affection in the hearts of the people . . .' Jacob advised Carrow (15 September 1954) to make an appointment with the news department. The head of news output offered to see Carrow in a letter of 27 September 1954, but Carrow did not reply.

61 Memorandum by F. Engelman, 29 January 1951, WAC R34/213/3.

62 Memorandum by J. C. Thornton, 20 April 1959, WAC R34/213/3.

63 These ideas on an imperial aural iconography were elaborated by me in a 'Music Weekly' talk, BBC Radio 3, 4 November 1984.

64 For example, M. Kennedy, *Portrait of Elgar*, London 1982, 182–3, 297, 331. Jerrold Northrop Moore, *Spirit of England*, London 1984, 161–2.

65 Boyle, *Only the Wind*, 205.

66 J. C. W. Reith, *Broadcast Over Britain*, London 1924, 220.

67 Tom Fleming, *Voices Out of the Air, The Royal Christmas Broadcasts, 1932–81*, London 1981.

68 Draft text for *RT*, Christmas 1934, WAC R19/166.

69 Gielgud, 21 September 1934, WAC R19/166.

70 A reference to the Director General's desire appeared in the planning for the 1934 programme, WAC R19/166.

71 Memorandum by Whitworth, 14 May 1935, R34/299/1.

72 Memorandum by Gilliam, n.d., R34/299/1.

73 Stuart (ed.) *Reith Diaries*, 196–7.

74 Gilliam to Graves, 17 November 1942, WAC R34/299/4–5.

75 Martin Wiener, *English Culture and the Decline of the Entrepreneurial Spirit, 1850–1980*, Cambridge 1981.

76 All the correspondence and extensive preparations for the 1935 programme can be found in WAC R34/299/1.

77 WAC R19/166 contains correspondence, preparations, and draft *RT* text and programme script for the 1934 programme. For recurrence of the stereotypes see WAC files R34/299/1–11.

78 *RT*, 19 December 1947, 21.

79 *RT*, 24 December 1948.

80 *RT*, 21 December 1951.

81 MacKenzie, *Propaganda*, 141–3.

82 For licences statistics and *RT* sales, see Briggs, Vol. II, 253 and 281. Also Pegg, *Broadcasting*, 7 and 106.

83 Pegg, *Broadcasting*, 124 and 139.

84 Briggs, Vol. II, 272.

85 Audience figures for the 1953 Christmas broadcast are in WAC R34/299/11.

86 Information on American reactions can be found in WAC R34/213/1 and R19/166. In 1935 the British Consul-General in Chicago wrote of the binding effect of the 1934 Christmas Day programme and forwarded some highly favourable correspondence from American listeners.

87 Reith, *Broadcast Over Britain*, 219.
88 Rosaleen Smyth, 'Britain's African colonies as subject and object of British propaganda During World War II', unpublished paper given at conference of African Studies Association of Australia and the Pacific, August 1983.
89 Correspondence on Churchill's demands for broadcasting time and his clashes with Reith can be found in WAC R34/429.
90 Reith reprimanded the North Region programme head for allowing some interviews with hunger-marchers to go out on the air. Boyle, *Only the Wind*, 253.

CHAPTER 9

'BRINGING THE EMPIRE ALIVE'
THE EMPIRE MARKETING BOARD
AND IMPERIAL PROPAGANDA, 1926–33

Stephen Constantine

It was never very convincing to argue that imperial enthusiasms entered on their long goodnight during or shortly after the First World War. The thesis seemed to assume that commitment to Empire was jaded by the prolonged embarrassment of the Boer War and pushed on to the defensive and into retreat during the Great War when the Allies, prodded by the USA, embraced the principles of national self-determination, collective security, mandates and, seemingly, implicit pledges to ultimate decolonisation.

Much work, especially recently, has shown on the contrary the prevailing preoccupation of those who governed Britain in the 1920s and 1930s with maintaining, utilising and developing Empire links and resources. The preservation of imperial control over India, the Middle East and the Colonial Empire remained a priority. The attitude of self-assertive dominions required adjustments in imperial political relations but not their termination. The business of extracting economic benefits for Britain from imperial connections involved British ministers in obsessive concern with migration, tariff and colonial development policies. Such an agenda, though with different emphases, was adopted by Labour and Liberal parties as well as by the Conservatives (and the British Union of Fascists), and was endorsed consistently by such organisations of industry and commerce as the Federation of British Industries and not infrequently by the Trades Union Congress.[1] Moreover, the period shows no diminution but if anything an increase in the amount of propaganda which pressed upon the British public through a wider range of media the virtues and values of Empire.[2]

So pervasive is this material that it is tempting to see imperialism between the wars as forming part of the dominant ideology of the day. The dominant ideology is normally taken to be that which is expressed by or on behalf of the dominant economic and political class, and in the early twentieth century it might be expected to emphasise principally the values of individualism, private property and profit-making and to legitimise consequent social and income inequality. The dominant ideology thesis argues that the impression which these values makes upon subordinate classes defuses their resentment at social injustice and explains, or helps explain, their toleration of inequality and the resulting stability of capitalist society.[3] It could be argued that imperialism did not endorse precisely similar values and was not seeking directly to legitimate and consolidate capitalism and the incorporation of the working class within it. But imperial ideology supported the same purpose in an indirect fashion. Firstly, it justified an economic system which provided opportunities for individual enterprise and profit-making and therefore helped to maintain the capitalist economy and social stability. And secondly, it offered for ideological approval the notion of an Empire which was both an economic asset and a civilising mission: it set out to appeal to the perceived economic self-interest and the moral instincts of all social classes, and to create a set of common allegiances and shared beliefs to bind up and swaddle social disharmony. Even if it failed to carry complete conviction and achieve the total commitment of subordinate classes, imperial ideology might still aim to confuse and inhibit the development of a counter-ideology antagonistic to the dominant class.

If imperialism is to be seen as an effective part of the dominant ideology, three characteristics of the interwar period need to be demonstrated. It has to be shown, firstly, that imperial ideals were indeed the consensus among the dominant class in government and in the economy, secondly, that the means of transmitting the ideology to subordinate classes existed and were utilised for this purpose, and thirdly, that imperial ideals did penetrate popular culture particularly among the working class and that this did affect mass perceptions and behaviour.

The Empire Marketing Board had only a brief existence, formed in 1926 and abolished in 1933, and it would be foolish to claim that this is a sufficient vehicle to carry a general assessment of imperialism as a dominant ideology. Nevertheless, the EMB has certain characteristics which make a study of its origins and activities peculiarly suitable as a contribution to a larger analysis.

To begin with, its establishment in 1926 does suggest that imperialism was in the 1920s a central preoccupation of major sections of the dominant class. Several economic pressure groups with imperial interests appeared during and after the First World War, such as the British Empire Producers Organisation (formed in 1916), the British Commonwealth Union (1916), the Empire Resources Development Committee (1916), the Empire Development Parliamentary Committee (1920), the Empire Development Union (1922), the Empire Industries Association (1924) and the Empire Economic

HIGHWAYS OF EMPIRE

BUY EMPIRE GOODS FROM HOME AND OVERSEAS

Union (1929). They represented colonial economic interests and sections of British industry especially vulnerable to competition at home and in overseas markets. Members were responding to what they saw as the inevitable collapse of that nineteenth-century free-trading international economic system which had for a while apparently served the interests of a uniquely advantaged British economy, but which, they believed, suited Britain ill when other nations industrialised. It was particularly unacceptable when from the later nineteenth century and more punishingly after the First World War so many of those industrial nations discriminated against British imports by erecting tariff barriers, while continuing to flood the home and colonial markets of free-trading Britain with their products. The onset of economic depression late in 1920, pushing unemployment rates between the wars almost continuously above 10 per cent of the insured labour force, confirmed the point and won much more widespread support for an imperial solution. The need to protect threatened sterling by reducing the dollar gap caused by trade with and debts to the USA was an additional incentive to trade with sterling areas especially in the Empire. The general aim proposed by many imperialists since the days of Joseph Chamberlain was the creation of a more economically self-sufficient British Empire. Britain, it was claimed, linked to her Empire of the dominions, India and the colonies, could be made less vulnerable to foreign competition. Specific programmes were also advanced for the imperial government to provide funds for colonial development schemes and scientific research into problems of empire production, to assist settler migration from Britain to the white dominions, but especially to introduce tariff protection with imperial preferences which would obstruct foreign imports, encourage inter-imperial trade and foster economic recovery.[4]

These bodies on the whole looked to the Conservative Party for the satisfaction of their aims, since that party had not only come closest to embracing tariff reform before the First World War, but had also been most explicit, if generalised, in its commitment to imperial solutions for the postwar depression. The Conservative Party manifesto in 1922, for example, claimed that 'The markets . . . we have lost in Europe, can best be replaced by further development of trade with overseas countries, and especially of trade within the British Empire'.[5] The pressure groups also found certain Conservative ministers particularly sympathetic, for example Sir Philip Cunliffe-Lister who had been a member of the British Commonwealth Union and who was President of the Board of Trade in the Bonar

---

'Highways of Empire', a poster by MacDonald Gill, published by the Empire Marketing Board in 1927: the map was also reproduced for use in schools. By courtesy of the Victoria and Albert Museum and HMSO.

Law and Baldwin governments in the 1920s. 'The solution of unemployment', he wrote in 1924, 'depends on finding and developing new markets
for our industry. The great opportunity for this lies within the British
Empire.'[6] Even more deeply committed was Leo Amery. He was a young
recruit to Chamberlain's tariff reform campaign in 1903, had approved the
aims of the Empire Resources Development Committee as a junior minister
after the war, had endorsed the message of the British Empire Producers'
Organisation, had helped create the Empire Industries Association and was
a founder member of the Empire Economic Union. As Secretary of State for
the Colonies 1924–9 and for the Dominions 1925–9, he was a strategically
placed and unstoppable mouthpiece for imperial causes. He announced in
his election manifesto of 1924 that 'the Conservative and Unionist Party
stands for increasing Empire Trade as a means of providing work for our
unemployed', and to the honouring of this obligation he devoted his not
inconsiderable energies.[7]

For Amery, imperialism offered a solution to more than economic
problems. It is highly relevant to note, given the purpose and effects of the
dominant ideology claimed by the dominant ideology thesis, that imperialism was often regarded as the only effective antidote to the poisonous
doctrine of socialism. Imperialism and patriotism had been consciously used
before and during the First World War to try to distract a working-class
electorate from notions of class conflict and anti-capitalism.[8] The extension
of the franchise in 1918, the impact of the Russian Revolution, trade union
militancy in the 1920s and the growing support for an ostensibly socialist
Labour Party reinforced Amery in his view that only a Conservative Party
which adopted a constructive imperialist policy with attendant ideals would
be able to resist socialist advance in a period of high unemployment.
Orthodox economic liberalism, with its commitments to *laissez-faire*, free
trade and limited government activity, he denounced as an inadequate
response to the economic and political crisis. He argued in speeches,
writings and in the numerous letters with which he bombarded Baldwin, his
party leader, that the real choice facing British society was between
moribund liberalism and either of its two vigorous challengers, the ideology
of socialism on the one hand and of imperialism on the other. In 1906
Amery was describing tariff reform as part of an imperial policy which 'will
be capable of detaching the working people in this country from the anti-
imperialist leaders of Socialism', and in 1923 he was claiming that 'the real
healthy and natural division of parties in this country is between
construction Conservatism on the one side, with a policy of Empire
Development and national economic organisation, and on the other hand
Labour Socialism with its ideas of levelling up by taxation, nationalisation
etc'.[9] In similar fashion, Neville Chamberlain was quick to interpret tariff
reform in ideological terms when Baldwin adopted the policy in 1923: 'He

has offered the discontented worker and the unemployed an alternative to Socialism which will not merely keep our own followers within our ranks but will seriously disorganise labour'.[10]

The suggestion that imperialism was being proposed in the 1920s as a solution to Britain's economic difficulties and as a counter-ideology to socialism may be supported by the manoeuvrings which lay behind the foundation of the Empire Marketing Board. After the general election of 1922, the Labour Party, with 142 MPs and nearly 30 per cent of the vote, clearly emerged from the shadow of the Liberals as the principal party of opposition. When Baldwin became Prime Minister for the first time in May 1923, imperial enthusiasts in his cabinet, especially Amery and Cunliffe-Lister, and their supporters on the backbenches, hoped to see the new Conservative government strike a radical note in response and adopt a policy of tariffs and imperial preferences. The governments of the dominions also for the most part urged this policy, and they persuaded the British government at the Imperial Economic Conference in the autumn of 1923 to agree to alter the duties on British imports of a limited range of foodstuffs so as to give greater preferential treatment to dominion products. The set-backs which then followed are well-known. When Baldwin cautiously announced a programme of selected tariff reforms, the opposition argued that prices would inevitably rise, and at the election in December 1923 the Conservatives lost their overall majority. In January 1924 the first Labour government was formed. In spite of Amery's protestations that a constructive imperial policy was still needed and that negative anti-socialism was inadequate,[11] Baldwin accepted the political need to reduce the emphasis on tariffs at least for the time being and the stunned Conservative Party on the whole agreed.[12] In the next election campaign in October 1924, although the Conservative manifesto claimed that 'the best hope of industrial revival lies . . . in the development of the resources and trade of the British Empire', Baldwin pledged that there would be no large-scale tariff protection.[13] To his dismay, Amery found the free-trader Winston Churchill appointed as Chancellor of the Exchequer when a new Conservative government was formed late in 1924. This symbolised Baldwin's public recantation of economic heresy.

However, this relapse into economic liberalism was unacceptable to Amery and Cunliffe-Lister, and they insisted that something should be done to satisfy the disgruntled dominions governments, denied their tariff preferences. Cunliffe-Lister proposed that the British government should instead spend money improving the marketing of Empire foodstuffs in Britain, and thus reduce a reliance on foreign imports, as a non-tariff way of encouraging inter-imperial trade. Amery accepted this as a second-best, and, rather surprisingly in view of his later hostility, Churchill too was persuaded to accept the plan. To a Cabinet divided over the political wisdom of tariffs and yet anxious to operate an imperial policy, to relieve economic depression and to redeem pledges made to the dominions, this was an acceptable compromise. Instead of the preferential duties previously promised, a rough cash equivalent of up to £1 million a year of British taxpayers' money was to be used to promote the sale of Empire foodstuffs in Britain. It was assumed that the consequent increase in the purchasing power of the overseas Empire would in return benefit British exports of manufactured goods. But settling the details was hard-going, and the office to administer this fund, the Empire Marketing Board, was finally established only in May 1926. It was the surprising by-product of an unsuccessful campaign for tariff reform.[14]

Tariffs remained controversial aspects of an imperial economic policy. By contrast, it is striking how much endorsement the EMB seemed to receive although its imperial purposes were similar. The Board was established as part of the official machinery of state. All its finances came from an annual parliamentary vote, and it was served by a civil service staff. There were about 120 people employed by the Board at its maximum.[15] Technically it was an advisory committee of the Secretary of State for the Dominions, Amery in the first instance, but in practice it operated as an executive body with remarkable freedom from normal Treasury financial control. But its advisory character allowed the Secretary of State to co-opt a wide range of members, thus demonstrating the breadth of support for its imperial mission. The Parliamentary Under-Secretary of the Colonial Office (later of the Dominions Office), ministers representing English and Scottish agriculture and the Financial Secretary at the Treasury were *ex officio* members, but the others, and there were around twenty on the Board altogether, included in 1926 representatives from the dominions, India, the colonies and the United Kingdom and, strikingly, Sir Archibald Sinclair representing the Liberal Party and J. H. Thomas representing the Labour Party. The Board spawned a number of committees to direct its detailed operations, especially a Research Grants Committee and a Publicity Committee, and further appointments to these committees confirmed the non-party character of the EMB which Amery was delighted to achieve. He wrote, for example, in his diary: 'J. H. Thomas to breakfast ... He was keenly interested in the EMB, and disposed to accept my invitation to come on himself, and suggested Johnston for the Publicity Committee. I think this is a good move.' Amery was to write later that J. H. Thomas, Tom Johnston and William Graham, another Labour Party representative, were 'most helpful'.[16] It is symptomatic of the consensus support for imperial strategies by the major political parties that when a Labour government took office in June 1929 the EMB was preserved under a new chairman, Lord Passfield (Sidney Webb). He assured the Board that 'the new Government would be no less interested in the work of the Empire Marketing Board than their predecessors in office had been. They had every confidence in the work of the Board.'[17] Moreover, and as remarkably, Labour's ostensible political enemy, Leo Amery, received and accepted an invitation to retain his place on the EMB. William Graham, Labour's President of the Board of Trade, wrote to Amery at the same time confessing that there was no real difference between the parties on Empire development: 'I know that irrespective of Party we can depend on your generous help in that sphere; and I should like to see a united House of Commons making the very most of our Empire resources'.[18] Furthermore, William Lunn, who since 1929 had served *ex officio* on the Board as Labour's Under-Secretary at the Dominions Office, continued as a representative of the Labour opposition after August 1931 even when his erstwhile Labour colleague, J. H. Thomas, became chairman as Secretary of State for the Dominions in the National Government. On one occasion Thomas announced publicly: 'There are no politics in this . . . the Empire Marketing Board is an official non-political body'.[19] There is more than a hint here that if imperialism was part of the dominant ideology, it was not without its influence beyond the confines of industry, commerce and the Conservative Party: it embraced also the hierarchy of the Labour Party.[20]

The dominant ideology thesis also demands proof that the means of transmitting the ideology to subordinate classes existed and were employed for this purpose. The general means by which Empire foodstuffs were to increase their share of the British market to the exclusion of foreign products were naturally much debated by the Board. It is true that Amery concluded that a substantial portion of the Board's annual budget, some 85 per cent, should be spent not on publicity but on scientific research into problems of production and into improved marketing services. Grants were indeed made to research institutions in Britain and in the overseas Empire such as the Rowett Research Institute at Aberdeen, the Ontario Agricultural College and the Amani Research Station in Tanganyika. A range of problems concerned, for example, with animal husbandry, entomology, plant breeding, dietetics and mycology was investigated. In addition, weekly or monthly information bulletins were also issued to inform trade organisations in Britain about the quality, quantity and price of British, overseas Empire and foreign foods such as meat, fruit, grain crops and dairy produce currently on the market. The informed trader should be able to order more Empire products and reduce a traditional reliance on foreign sources.[21] A total of £1,962,639 was spent on research and marketing services from 1926 to 1933 and the work absorbed much of the EMB's money and energy. But contrary to the impression left by Amery's memoirs, expenditure on publicity was £1,224,562, not much less. As Amery admits, 'the conspicuous success of our publicity schemes tended to impress the general public with the idea that they were the main part of our work'.[22]

From its inception in 1926 to its closure in 1933, the EMB was rapidly and rightly identified in public and political eyes as a propaganda organisation. As a major part of its duties, it sought to influence consumer choice, not by financial means – tariff barriers – but by propaganda.

Here, then, was an official government department formally charged with impressing aspects of an imperial ideology upon the general public. The difficulty of this task was not lost upon the Board. Traditionally Britain had been the centre of an international and not just an imperial economic system. The percentage of British imports coming from the Empire had increased substantially since before the First World War, but the overwhelming predominance of foreign imports was still apparent and consumer ignorance an obstacle: Amery recalls that it was difficult to persuade shopkeepers and customers that California tinned fruit was not an Empire product.[23] As was pointed out to the Cabinet, 'Forty millions of people had to be induced to change their habits'.[24] This, the Board concluded, could only be done by 'bringing the Empire alive'.[25]

The EMB's expectation that propaganda might have a sufficiently powerful impact reflects the remarkable development and extension of the range of media available for communications and persuasion since the end of the previous century. Even the well-established techniques of paper-making and printing had experienced such technical changes as to substantially cheapen the cost and ease the process of producing large runs of printed books, pamphlets, leaflets, postcards and other printed materials. The invention of the rotary press and the improved capacity to introduce pictures into text contributed to the development of cheap mass circulation newspapers, both nationals and locals. *Lloyd's Weekly News*, a Sunday paper, was in 1896 the first newspaper to reach sales of one million. In the same year the *Daily Mail* appeared, costing a halfpenny, and reached average sales of 750,000 a day in the Edwardian period, to be emulated and even overtaken by the *Daily Express* and especially by the *Daily Mirror* which sold one million copies for the first time in 1912. There were also 121 English provincial dailies by 1910 and a proliferation before and after the First World War of popular magazines like *Woman's Weekly*, first published in 1911, aimed at the working class.[26] Similarly, colour lithography and offset printing techniques revolutionised the design and production of eye-catching coloured posters.[27] The 1890s also saw experiments with radio which in 1922 were to produce the British Broadcasting Company and in 1926 the British Broadcasting Corporation. Radio was rapidly established as a mass medium, especially when the biggest transmitting station in the world was opened at Daventry in July 1925 to embrace 94 per cent of Britain in its range. Licences increased from over two million or nineteen households in every hundred in 1926 to nearly six million or forty-eight households in one hundred by 1933.[28] This rapid expansion paralleled the development of that other exciting new medium, the cinema, progressing from a fairground novelty in the 1890s to crafted silent movies before 1914 and to the introduction of 'talkies' in 1929. The estimated 3,878 cinemas in operation in 1925 had risen to 4,448 by 1935 by which date annual admissions topped 900 million tickets a year.[29]

Developments in the media in an age, generally, of rising living standards, opened up the prospects for salesmanship and mass consumerism which were not lost upon commercial companies and advertising agencies. EMB staff were inevitably conscious that newspapers, local and national, were heavy with advertising and indeed absorbed the vast bulk of expenditure on advertising by businesses. But some companies, like Cadbury's and Lever Brothers, were not slow to employ picture postcards to advertise their operations, and it was business patronage which transformed the advertising poster on the public billboard into vivid coloured products, artist-designed. And while the BBC avoided explicit commercialism, the potential of radio for advertising had been widely recognised when public broadcasting was being planned, and wireless owners could shortly tune in to Radio Normandie and Radio Luxembourg which did carry advertising. Some businesses even experimented with film as a medium to publicise their products. The National Milk Publicity Council, set up by representatives of the dairy industry to increase milk consumption, was just one organisation which in the 1920s explored the use of posters, the press, films, recipe books and a range of entertaining publicity stunts to improve their business.[30] The growing importance and self-consciousness of the advertising industry in exploiting the media and marketing their skills is indicated by the formation of its own professional bodies, the Association of British Advertising Agents in 1917 and the Advertising Association in 1925. Commercial appreciation of the value of advertising is shown by the increased expenditure on it from an estimated £31 million in 1920 to £57 million by 1928. The 1920s have been described as 'the golden age of advertising', and its charms inevitably appealed to the EMB.[31]

It might also be noticed as a model for EMB activities that the value of the media for political purposes had not gone unrecognised. The development of a mass electorate in Britain after franchise extensions in 1867, 1884 and especially 1918 obliged political parties to contemplate new ways of contacting, persuading and holding the allegiances of voters. Sympathetic mass circulation newspapers were regarded as essential political assets, as witnessed by Lloyd George's wooing of the press barons Northcliffe, Rothermere and Beaverbrook and by the relaunching in 1922 of the *Daily Herald* as a voice for the Labour Party. Printed material, especially posters and leaflets but also picture postcards of party leaders and personalities, deluged the public, overwhelmingly at election times. Party political broadcasts on the radio began in the general election of 1924, and the skill the Conservative Party and Baldwin demonstrated in handling this medium was matched by their effective pioneering of the use of film. The Conservatives employed a fleet of daylight cinema vans to expound their message from 1925 and commissioned their own propaganda films from 1926.[32]

Given this extensive use of the media by commerce and to a lesser extent by political parties, what is striking is how little was the experience gained in their use by government departments. There was not much expertise within the government service upon which the EMB could draw. Prewar precedents were particularly thin. There had for some time been regular use of the press and public posters but mainly to advertise state loans and to issue legal proclamations and notices. The Post Office, as one of the first government departments to offer a commercial service to the public, was also the first, from the 1850s, to advertise and market its facilities. Lloyd George had dispatched a corps of lecturers around the country in 1912 to explain the operations of the new National Insurance Act, and the War Office employed an advertising agency in 1913 to improve its recruiting. These operations were conspicuous by their rarity. For specifically imperial purposes, the Colonial Office Visual Instruction Committee had been set up in 1902, with inadequate funding, to offer to audiences in Britain and overseas a series of anodyne lectures illustrated with lantern-slides, a technique becoming rapidly obsolete. Its material was abandoned to private hands in 1914. The Imperial Institute, sited in South Kensington, was partly funded by the state from 1902 and housed a collection of imperial artefacts, especially of colonial economic products, in increasingly dusty and largely unvisited displays – until revitalised at the same time as the EMB's propaganda machine swung into operation. Not until the First World War had vastly increased the responsibilities of government and the need to ensure public conformity with its policies, was a recognisable system of state publicity and propaganda devised. Then the wartime government organisations culminating in the Ministry of Information in 1918 explored the full range of available media, from the publication of books, pamphlets and exhortatory posters to the production of official propaganda films like *The Battle of the Somme*. But whereas in the Soviet Union and in fascist Italy in the 1920s totalitarian governments continued to extend their official propaganda activities, the armistice brought the rapid end of the Ministry of Information and the virtual elimination of overt official propaganda or even publicity operations. The Foreign Office continued to maintain on a modest scale some press and propaganda work; the Department of Overseas Trade, established during the war, survived to provide some trade news and became involved in exhibition work; a Government Cinematograph Adviser seems to have performed modest duties looking after the small stock of official films; and one or two government departments like the Ministry of

Health, War Office and Air Ministry appointed press officers and engaged in some publicity work. The only spectacular recent propaganda event to impress the EMB was the British Empire Exhibition at Wembley in 1924–5, and while this was guaranteed by an Act of Parliament and the government met half the costs, it was organised by a specially-constituted committee on a semi-official basis and was not directly a responsibility of the government service.[33] Members of the EMB correctly concluded at their first meeting in June 1926 that they 'had to explore ground that was at some points still unprospected, and would be working on a scale of which no Government, except perhaps in war time, had had experience'.[34]

Not surprisingly, therefore, Amery and the Board turned at once to experts from outside government service. The Publicity Committee, appointed after the very first Board meeting, was chaired by the Under-Secretary of State for the Colonies, and its members included the Comptroller-General at the Department of Overseas Trade, the Deputy Controller at the Stationery Office and the Director of the Imperial Institute. But more interesting was the inclusion of Sir Woodman Burbridge, Chairman and Managing Director of Harrods, Viscount Burnham, President of the Empire Press Union (and a member of the Overseas Settlement Committee) and J. C. Stobart, Director of Education at the BBC and a member whose support for Empire broadcasting to schools is well-attested elsewhere in this book.[35] Another appointment was Frank Pick, Assistant Managing Director of the London Underground and General Omnibus Company from 1921 and Managing Director from 1928. He had transformed the publicity of the company by, especially, the employment of artists in the design of advertising posters, and is described in one source as 'the nearest approach to Lorenzo the Magnificent that a modern democracy could achieve'.[36] Even more striking was the appointment in 1926, firstly, as a full member of the Board and, secondly, as Vice-Chairman of the Publicity Committee of William Crawford, head of one of the two major British advertising agencies in the 1920s. He is described by his biographer as an Empire man by conviction and was already a member of the Imperial Economic Committee: 'Everything that is richest and best can be garnered from the soil of the Empire. All that is needed to sell it is skilled marketing and advertising.' The establishment's approval of Crawford's talents and allegiances is indicated by his knighthood in 1927.[37] Later members of the Publicity Committee included two directors of the Co-operative Wholesale Society (one a woman to give the 'woman's point of view'), a representative of the National Chamber of Trade and the Publicity Manager of the Gas, Light and Coke Company (a company soon to make a lasting reputation in its sponsorship of documentary films).[38]

These professionals brought to the EMB their faith, as clients or practitioners, in the persuasive power of the modern media. Pick and

Crawford, the dominant forces behind the EMB's publicity work, were convinced for example that the employment of artists to design advertising introduced an aesthetic element into the product which hugely increased its effectiveness. They and their colleagues drew upon their business experience to argue that it was through such methods that the mass consumer could be influenced. Crawford was to argue that 'Advertising is education. It makes people think. And thinking leads to action.'[39] In expressing such views they found a perhaps surprising ally in a career civil servant of most unusual character whose ideas happily blended with theirs. Stephen Tallents translated the message of the advertising profession into a language of government service. It was, he argued, essential in a modern mass democracy, in which the functions of government were increasing, for departments of state to keep the public informed of government services, educate them in their use, persuade them to comply. The need to justify government action by publicity was explicitly recognised by Tallents as one of the obligations upon a government public relations service. It is probable that Tallents' earlier work in handling food rationing during the First World War, in serving on the postwar relief commission in the Baltic provinces, as Imperial Secretary in Northern Ireland, and, most recently, as secretary to the Cabinet committee dealing with the General Strike had made him unusually sensitive to the need to assess and to massage public opinion. His reward, too, was a knighthood in 1932.[40] What he, Crawford, Pick and others had acquired through practical experience, insight and, in part, the knowledge of methods pioneered in the USA was the notion that publicity could have a constructive impact upon public opinion, leading to public approval, consent and action. It was a tool of management, for use by government as well as business, to secure managerial requirements, be they political or commercial. The manipulative power expected of modern advertising and public relations work made members of the EMB confident of their ability to achieve their ideological and economic targets.

Even when the Board took up well-established propaganda techniques, the scale of their operations was still unique for a government department in peacetime. For example, the Board launched a nationwide series of public lectures, dispatching its own speakers and also subsidising other societies and institutions which arranged talks on approved topics. The audiences were said to be predominantly women, but the range was wide and included members of literary societies, the YMCA, working-men's clubs, cooperative societies, adult and army schools, training colleges, Women's Institutes, Rotary Clubs, Grocers' Associations and meetings in public libraries. The programme began in 1927 and at its peak in 1929 about 2,400 lectures were given in the year to over 500,000 people at a cost to the Board, and the British taxpayer, of almost £10,500. Thereafter as the Board's budget was cut this work was reduced, but in total from 1926 to 1933 it had cost £35,320 and had offered talks on such topics as 'The British Empire and

What it Means to You', 'Airways of Empire', 'Economics of Our Empire', 'Lower Burma and its Pearl Fisheries', 'Life in the British West Indies', 'Rhodesia, the Land of Promise' . . .[41]

At the same time a lot of effort was put into the writing, design and distribution of EMB books and pamphlets: its seventy-two major reports, mainly scientific, for example *The Behaviour and Diseases of the Banana in Storage and Transport* (maximum price 1s 6d), its twenty-four reports on the production and trade of individual British Empire territories, ranging from Canada to the Falkland Islands (price 2d), its seven reports on particular commodities such as dairy produce, oilseeds, fibres and fruit. But much more widely distributed, and a tribute to technology, were the booklets and leaflets which the Board could produce in large numbers and distribute cheaply or free of charge. There was *A Handbook of Empire Timbers*, a *Calendar of the Fruits and Vegetables of Empire* of which 180,000 copies were distributed in 1929 and for which a reprint was needed, *A List of Empire Tobaccos*, *A Book of Empire Dinners* of which a first edition of 10,000 was exhausted in a few weeks, and explanatory leaflets such as *Why Should We Buy from the Empire?*, *Why Every Woman Ought to Buy British*, *What is the Empire Marketing Board?* There was also a range of recipe leaflets available from the Board, including a very popular one for the King's Empire Christmas Pudding, made entirely out of Empire ingredients: Canadian flour, South African raisins, Demerara sugar, English eggs, Jamaica rum and so on. 15,000 copies of that were exhausted at once when first offered and a further 20,000 had to be printed. There were thirty-two new leaflets published in 1929 alone and eight new ones in 1930. Altogether 2 million leaflets were distributed in 1929, another 2 million in 1930 and a further 1 million in 1931. A final report in June 1933 reckoned that by then 10 million leaflets and pamphlets had been issued.[42]

The EMB also made extensive use of the press. Like commercial advertisers, they turned to the network of national and local newspapers as a means of making contact with the masses. At its peak in 1928, the press campaign cost £106,066 in the year and altogether the use of this medium absorbed £364,280 of the Board's funds. Crawford's expertise proved invaluable in guiding copy-writers. In 1929 advertisements placed by the Board drew attention to home fisheries, Scottish oats, Canadian and New Zealand apples, Australian dried fruits, South African citrus fruits, Irish dairy produce, Indian rice, Southern Rhodesian tobacco, East African coffee and Empire eggs. A monthly page was taken in *Punch* in 1927, items were regularly placed in trade journals and a particularly strong emphasis was placed on the local press, often encouraging local shopkeepers to add similar Empire-inspired advertisements. This was most apparent when the EMB responded in the balance of trade crisis in the autumn of 1931 with a special 'Buy British' campaign. So, for example, a single page of the *Durham*

County Advertiser for 20 November 1931 carried a general message from the EMB plus Buy British or Buy Empire advertisements from a local brewer, local grocers, local butchers, a local stationer and a local draper. 'Greenwell's have wonderful value to offer in Empire produce. Best Australian Currants . . . Pure Empire Honey.' On the previous day and across the Pennines, the *Lancaster Guardian* carried the first of a series of large advertisements placed by the Board which ran through to Christmas Eve, urging the public to buy and shopkeepers to sell British and Empire goods. One by-product of the EMB's press campaigns was the encouragement it seems to have given other advertisers to stress the imperial origins of their products: 'No Foreign Wheat in Allinson Flour and Bread . . . Home and Empire Wheat Only . . . Constipation is naturally corrected by Allinson Flour and Bread.' Or more crisply from Shredded Wheat: 'Britons Make It – It Makes Britons'.[43]

The Board had been quick to appoint a press officer, still comparatively rare in government service, and he was able to draw newspaper attention to other EMB activities, thus gaining additional, and free, publicity for the campaign. Naturally many of the EMB's publicity stunts attracted press attention. Spectators travelling to the Wembley Cup Final in 1927 were greeted with a huge canvas sign urging them to buy Empire products, draped on the outside of the stadium. Travellers to the West Country in November 1931 found their GWR train decked out as a Buy British special. If you had gone into Trafalgar Square at night that month you would have found it illuminated by a large sign bearing the words 'Buy British' in letters fifteen feet high. If you gazed overhead in the daytime, aircraft painted with the same slogan, one flown by Amy Johnson, might have momentarily blotted out the sun. And even attendance at major football matches could be diverted by parades of Boy Scouts, recruited to the imperial cause, carrying large cut-out letters with that inspiring injunction. Even the sober *Times* reported enthusiastically on the mixing and cooking of a King's Empire Christmas Pudding at the Olympia Cookery Exhibition in December 1928. They might well cheer: this particular beauty was cooked in about one hundred sections and then assembled. When formally unveiled by Mrs Amery it stood seven feet high. Nor should we forget the effort of the Morecambe and Heysham Corporation who celebrated Boxing Day 1931 with the formal slicing of the Morecambe and Heysham Empire Christmas Pudding, portions to be sold in 'dainty cartons, 6d each'.[44]

The Olympia Cookery Exhibition was only one of the seventy or so different exhibitions at which the EMB mounted a display, usually erecting its specially-designed eye-catching pavilion. It appeared at the annual British Industries Fair, the Imperial Fruit Show, the Bakers' and Confectioners' Exhibition, the Ideal Home Exhibition and at a host of provincial city exhibitions such as in 1927 the Belfast Empire Week Exhibition, the

Edinburgh Imperial Exhibition, the Liverpool Commerce and Industry Exhibition, the Birmingham Grocers Exhibition and the Norwich Grocers Exhibition. It attended nineteen different exhibitions in 1928 including the Cardiff Empire Exhibition in October–November at which the 70,833 visitors to the EMB pavilion were said to have been a record at a Cardiff exhibition. The Board also encouraged and partly funded a huge number of local Empire Shopping Weeks. For the space of a week, retailers in different towns around the country were persuaded to plaster their shop windows with advertisements for Empire products and to press Empire goods on their customers. The Board provided advice and material, and prizes were awarded for the best display. There were pre-war precedents for this kind of activity, some organised by a shadowy All British Shopping Movement in 1911,[45] but there had never been anything on the scale of the EMB's activities. Altogether some two hundred Empire Shopping Weeks were sponsored, in sixty-five towns in 1930 alone. Fifty different shop window posters were printed by the Board and seven million copies issued. Expenditure on exhibitions and shopping weeks topped £61,000 in 1929 and totalled £277,771 during the EMB's life-time.[46]

The immediate appointment of a BBC representative to the EMB's Publicity Committee indicates the Board's receptivity to the potential of this new medium. Indeed, it is interesting to note that in addition to Stobart, that first meeting of the Publicity Committee was also attended by Gladstone Murray, Director of Public Relations at the BBC from 1924 to 1935. The EMB appeared to face no difficulties gaining access to the airwaves. Most regular from 1928 onwards were the brief morning bulletins broadcast to housewives either fortnightly or weekly, mainly describing Empire produce in season. Recipes too were broadcast, emphasising Empire ingredients. Over 20,000 listeners wrote in for copies in 1929 and a similar number in 1930. Of related interest were the eight morning talks given in 1930 under the general title 'Where Your Food Comes From' which appeared to indicate that what was not home grown came invariably from South Africa, Australia, Canada, New Zealand or India. Other items broadcast included in 1930 a talk on 'The Empire Marketing Board', one on 'Why We Should Buy from the Empire', a series on Empire Trade and a fascinating disquisition with an EMB slant by J. H. Thomas called 'Insects and Empire'. Even the Empire Day programme for that year, 'How the Sun Never Sets', was devised by its producer as 'a sort of audible version of a series of Empire Marketing Board posters'. Heavier fare was provided in 1932, nine fifteen-minute talks on a Friday evening called 'The Empire and Ourselves', delivered by Professor John Coatman. His chair in Imperial Economic Relations at the London School of Economics was funded by the EMB, and in addition to conducting research, supervising postgraduate students, lecturing and extra-mural teaching he was obliged to expound his subject and carry his message to the general public. The BBC helped. His lectures, like several other Empire talks, were published in *The Listener*. One might add in this context that the EMB also placed full page advertisements in the *Radio Times*, encouraging in June 1929 for example the consumption of East African coffee, Irish dairy produce and Australian dried fruits. When the BBC published its *Household Talks* of 1928 in a one shilling paperback it was done in collaboration with the EMB, who provided not only illustrations with appropriate messages but also plenty of information and advice about Empire products and injunctions for their use. But perhaps the most striking contribution of the BBC to the work of the Board came during the economic crisis late in 1931. The news service announced the Buy British campaign and reported on its progress, special items were added describing its aims, and major speeches were broadcast by the Prince of Wales, J. H. Thomas and Lady Snowden, the wife of the Chancellor of the Exchequer. Reference to the campaign even featured in that winter's vaudeville entertainment programmes and in the Grand Good-Night which concluded the year's broadcasting on New Year's Eve.[47]

By 1926 the power of film to influence public opinion, action and consumer taste was widely assumed in official circles. Approval of the operations of the British Board of Film Censors since its creation in 1912 was one negative indication of that. The sponsorship of propaganda films by the state for home consumption during the First World War is a more positive acknowledgment.[48] The Imperial Conference of 1926 accepted a sub-committee report which claimed that 'the Cinema is not merely a form of entertainment but . . . a powerful instrument of education . . . and even when it is not used avowedly for purposes of instruction, advertisement or propaganda, it exercises indirectly a great influence in shaping the ideas of the very large numbers to whom it appeals'. The commercial implications of this were spelled out the following year when Cunliffe-Lister moved the Cinematograph Films Bill essentially to reduce the American domination of British cinemas said to be responsible for the increased consumption of American goods to the detriment of British and Empire producers: 'From the trade point of view', he said, 'the influence of the cinema is no less important. It is the greatest advertising power in the world.'[49] It is not therefore surprising that the EMB should investigate the use of films for its purposes. In the summer of 1926 Tallents discussed film propaganda with Rudyard Kipling, who, incidentally, thought 'television . . . would soon be a practical thing and very valuable for our work'. The provisional Publicity Committee reported in favour of the use and even of the making of films in June 1926; this was immediately accepted by the Board and was written into the terms of reference of the properly constituted Publicity Committee: 'the inclusion in cinema performances of short educational or propaganda films dealing with Empire products might be secured'.[50] These decisions had been made and work begun before John Grierson, the legendary creator at the EMB of the British documentary film movement had returned to Britain in January 1927. Moreover, when after meeting Tallents, Grierson did submit to the EMB his views on films, largely derived from his studies and experiences in the USA, they conformed to the managerial and educational concepts of public relations and propaganda which members like Crawford, Pick and Tallents had already developed. Hence his sympathetic hearing. 'Cinema', he wrote, 'is recognised as having a peculiar influence on the ideological centres to which advertisement endeavours to make its appeal . . . it is an ideal medium for all manner of suggestion.' Cinema had 'a practical monopoly over the dramatic strata of the common mind in which preferences, sympathies, affections and loyalties, if not actually created, are at least crystallised and coloured'. To reinforce his point and to set up some models for emulation, Grierson arranged for EMB staff to see, among other things, the classic Soviet propaganda films like *Turksib*, *Earth* and *Battleship Potemkin*. By 1933, he was to write, with some exaggeration: 'the EMB is the only organisation outside Russia that understands and has imagination enough to practise the principles of long-range propaganda. It is not unconscious of the example of Russia.'[51]

We must not over-stress the EMB's emphasis upon films. It always remained a small unit: expenditure at its peak in 1929 was £17,748 and totalled only £35,320 over eight years. Much of its work had of necessity to be done on the cheap. It began at once, before Grierson arrived, by cadging copies of films made by various other official and semi-official bodies in Britain and in the overseas Empire, such as *Solid Sunshine*, made in New Zealand about butter production. A major activity throughout the Board's career was then the re-editing of this footage into new films, such as *Axes and Elephants*, a six-minute short about the lumber business of New Zealand and Burma. It was making films, rather than commissioning them from commercial companies outside, which made the EMB especially distinctive as a government office. Preparations were already under way, before Grierson arrived, to shoot footage for a specially written film, *One Family*, a story designed to reveal some of the riches of the Empire by sending a boy on a shopping expedition around the world gathering ingredients for a King's Empire Christmas pudding. Production of this film was overtaken by the more modest but manageable shooting of Grierson's *Drifters*, depicting the herring fleet at work in the North Sea. Many more films followed from different directors including *The Country Comes to Town* (London's food and milk supplies), *Cargo from Jamaica* (bananas), *Shadow on the Mountain* (pasture experiments in Wales), *Windmill in Barbados* (sugar) and *Industrial Britain* (shot by Flaherty, edited by Grierson). By the end of its operations, the film unit had made from stock or its own material about one hundred films.[52]

It was originally the intention of Grierson and the Board to show these films to a mass public through the usual commercial cinema circuits. *Drifters*, although a 'silent' film, did, indeed, make an initial impact in 1929 and six films were eventually sold to Gaumont-British for inclusion in their programmes. But *One Family*, having cost £15,740 to make, received only fifty-four theatrical bookings in Britain and made £2,865. It was panned by one critic: 'We have waited for a march-past of the British Empire on the screen, and now that we get it we find it allied to a Christmas shopping-tour conducted by a little boy with ungracious manners and a squeaky voice'. Harry Watt called it 'abysmally vomit-making'. The main problem was not, however, the quality of individual films, which on the whole, while not high, contained products of distinct worth, but the reluctance of the circuits to include in their programmes documentary films, especially short ones and 'silents'. That British documentary films were not always recognised as 'quota' films under the 1927 Cinematograph Act was another discouragement. It was, then, need more than choice which obliged the EMB to turn to non-theatrical outlets.[53]

The EMB therefore opened a film library in 1931, published a catalogue of films available for free borrowing (a total of 176 in 1932) and was soon busy: there were 6,000 borrowings in 1932 reaching an audience of perhaps 800,000, and some 800 organisations were using the service in 1933.[54] An earlier initiative was consistently popular. In July 1926 the Publicity Committee began negotiations leading to the construction and opening in June 1927 of a cinema at the Imperial Institute for the free showing to organisations and general public of films from the EMB library. Eventually twenty-six film shows a week were being staged (four on each weekday and two on Sundays) and audiences increased from nearly 215,000 in 1928 to a peak of 357,000 in 1930 to accumulate a total audience of 1,603,000 by the autumn of 1933. The EMB also showed films itself, for example, at exhibitions and Empire shopping weeks, making them multi-media events, and it equipped a pantechnicon as a travelling cinema. Moreover, it produced a special film as part of the Buy British campaign in the autumn of 1931, featuring exhortatory speeches by the Prime Minister Ramsay MacDonald and, interestingly, by his former colleague and now political enemy George Lansbury, the new leader of the Labour Party: this was shown in over 1,000 cinemas to approximately 12,000,000 people.[55] But perhaps one of the EMB's most cost-effective enterprises was the production out of old stock or new film of a large number of short loop films running for only a few minutes, the forerunners of television commercials. They advertised, for example, Gold Coast cocoa, Burma teak, Home herrings, New Zealand dairying, Canadian apples. They were often displayed on daylight cinema screens in public places and evidently impressed. A film about milk attracted such crowds when shown at Victoria Railway Station that it disrupted the running of the Southern Railway and had to be temporarily abandoned.[56]

Much public interest at home and overseas also seems to have been aroused by the EMB's use of posters to advertise its message. Like advertisements in the press, this was regarded as an effective way of contacting directly the largest mass audience, and it proved even more expensive, topping £103,000 in 1927 and costing altogether £426,879. Here, of course, the Board was drawing most directly on the proven expertise of advertising professionals like Crawford and especially of Frank Pick who was made chairman of a poster sub-committee. While working for the London Underground, Pick had developed useful personal contacts with artists. He it was who commissioned, criticised, rejected or approved the designs presented by a wide range of artists. The high quality of much of the work drew critical acclaim. There was an exhibition of the first designs at the Royal Academy of Arts in Burlington House in 1926, the German art magazine *Kosmos* asked permission to reproduce some of them in 1927, and they were made the subject of an approving leading article in *The Times*.[57] The high costs are partly explained by the employment of some artists who had already made distinguished names for themselves in the art world, particularly but not exclusively as poster artists: they included McKnight Kauffer, Charles Pears, F. C. Herrick, Paul and John Nash and Clive Gardiner. The latter's strikingly modernist sequence of industrial scenes cost the Board 280 guineas. Costs were also high because of the enormous number of designs reproduced. Most posters were displayed in a series of five: in 1927 nineteen changes of programme were planned for the year, there were the same number in 1928, eighteen in 1929, seventeen in 1930, thirteen in 1931, twelve in 1932. One source reckons that 836 different posters were published in six years.[58] Further expense resulted from the Board's determination to give particular prominence to its advertisements by displaying them on solus sites, that is, on specially erected billboards isolated from the mass of other commercial advertising. During 1926, 450 oak-framed EMB hoardings were erected and this had risen to a total of 1,800 in 450 towns by 1933. Here were displayed the five sequential posters, together stretching some twenty feet in width and about four feet in height, topped by a commanding letter press heading: 'Let the Empire Flourish', 'Ask for the Produce of New Zealand', . . . In addition to the standard pattern several other posters were designed for shop window displays and for posting in factories, and during the 'Buy British' campaign over 4,000,000 copies of two special posters were issued. To give wider dissemination to some designs and their message, some were made available to George Philip and Son Ltd for use in an Empire Card Game, others were reprinted in postcard sizes, some were offered as the design for jigsaw puzzles, 5,000 sets of eight posters were reproduced as Christmas cards in

1929 (with 'Best Wishes for a Happy and Prosperous New Year from the Empire Marketing Board' printed on the envelope), and a quarter of a million particularly attractive animal designs bearing Buy Empire messages were printed in cigarette-card sizes in sets of twelve to be collected by children from an EMB shop in Glasgow in 1930.[59]

The jigsaws and cards to be collected by children are not frivolous indications of the EMB activities. On the contrary, they are enormously revealing of its propagandist and ideological intentions. It is worth emphasising what the evidence suggests was one major strategy of the Board, the propaganda it aimed at children. The evidence is significant because more than anything it indicates that the Board's aims in practice embraced more than the immediate economic objective of boosting inter-imperial trade.

At the second meeting of the Publicity Committee in July 1926, it was decided to explore the possibilities for publicity work in schools, and later that month at a conference with representatives of the EMB, the President of the Board of Education agreed that the dissemination of information on Empire topics to schoolchildren and their teachers 'could be valuable'. In November the Poster Sub-Committee concluded that the reproduction of posters in a smaller size for schools as well as the general public 'might form the basis of effective propaganda'. This interest was sustained. In December 1927 the Publicity Committee expressed itself as keen on further work in schools, and in 1930 the Board argued in its published annual report that 'if the habit of Empire buying is to be permanently established, educational publicity is essential'. By then, an Education Sub-Committee had been formed, chaired by Sir William Furse, Director of the Imperial Institute, and including Stobart from the BBC and a representative from the Board of Education and the Scottish Education Department. In July 1932 they concluded 'that teachers as a whole offered a most promising field for propaganda work'. EMB staff were not unaware of the delicacy of this intrusion if material were pressed upon schools, and instead it adopted a policy of making it known that EMB material was freely available for the classroom. The NUT's official journal *The Schoolmaster* noted this method approvingly.[60]

The EMB's 'softly-softly' approach was nevertheless conspicuously successful. In its first year of operation, there were over 9,000 requests from schools for copies of EMB posters, and by May 1933 some 27,000 schools, the vast majority of the schools in Britain, were on the EMB's mailing list, and they received free reproductions of the posters for use in classrooms. Accompanying leaflets on Empire territories and products were specially written as explanatory teaching aids by, for example, John Buchan and Sir Henry Newbolt.[61] The material dispatched was generally warmly received. It was blessed by the NUT, endorsed by the Consultative Committee of the

Board of Education, and favourably reviewed by *London Teacher*. 'The Empire Marketing Board', wrote the last, 'has made available for teachers . . . an enormous amount of valuable material . . . Most teachers agree that the EMB posters have been an excellent visual aid to the teaching of geography.'[62] This viewpoint was certainly endorsed by those letters from staff which the EMB received and chose to preserve. One poster, a world map with the British Empire conspicuously and centrally displayed, was variously described as 'a wonderful help both in Geography and History lessons', 'admirable for illustrating school geography', 'a splendid means of showing our boys . . . the links of Empire', 'invaluable for British Empire lessons'. The way the EMB nurtured the Empire-centred nature of much inter-war teaching was much appreciated by several correspondents. 'The posters are of real value educationally and nationally, and quite fit in with my idea of teaching geography, history and economics.' Another teacher made this quite explicit: 'Your posters have been a god-send to us. They vivify and intensify the very impression we wish our pupils to receive with respect to the resources and potentialities of our Empire.' They enabled teachers, wrote another, 'to impress on the minds of our future Empire citizens the vast resources of our great Empire'. The Board prided itself that endorsements ranged from humble elementary schools to masters at Eton (and the Department of Geography at the University of Birmingham).[63] Interestingly, twenty-five EMB posters were reprinted in 1932 by Macmillan as part of a collection of pictures for use in geography lessons: the set plus teachers' handbook went into its fourth reprint in 1939.[64]

But not only posters were aimed at children. Many of the lecturers the EMB despatched with their slides and specimens addressed school audiences, on 'The White Man in the Dark Continent', for example. Some lucky Belfast children found themselves in 1930 entering for an essay competition, on predictable themes, as part of the local EMB-arranged British Empire Week. And the EMB attended the Schoolboys' Own Exhibition in 1929, distributing 26,000 miniature copies of its 'Highways of Empire' poster and having the rails round its stand knocked down by some of the 100,000 visitors who crushed in.[65] Given that the power of film to influence children, for good or ill, was part of the conventional wisdom of the day, given also the enormous numbers of children who were already regular cinema attenders (over half the children of London according to a survey published in 1932),[66] it is not surprising that the EMB rapidly turned its attention to film as another way of presenting its message to children. Tallents discussed the display of Empire films to schoolchildren with the Chief Inspector of Schools and reported that 'the field was undoubtedly a promising one'. He later recorded that 'the making of films for schools was treated as an essential element in [the EMB's] programme'. Films were made using stock donated by overseas Empire governments or edited down from larger films shot by the film unit. There were over forty such films available in 1932–3, including *Wheatfields of the Empire*, *The Great St Lawrence*, *Farming in South Africa*, and *The English Potter* (the last being footage shot by Flaherty for *Industrial Britain* and collected from the editing-room floor). There were even some cartoon films. One substantial film, *Conquest*, about the settlement of the Canadian prairies had been put together by Grierson in 1930 from a variety of sources, including Hollywood feature film footage. There was also a monthly film magazine for schools called *Empire Journal*. The films were available free of charge from the EMB film library and encouragement to use this source had some effect: some 70 per cent of library users in 1932 were schools.[67]

All this activity should not over-impress us. The substantial limitations to film propaganda in schools were the scarcity of film projectors in schools and teachers trained to use them. After much official encouragement including the offer of sizeable Board of Education grants, it was reckoned in 1935 that there were only about 1,000 projectors in the 32,000 schools and colleges in Britain. Cost, ignorance and hostility significantly blunted this EMB strategy.[68] However, there were attempts to circumvent the obstacle. For example, in 1929 arrangements were made with the local education authority for 46,000 schoolchildren in Newcastle and Gateshead to be shown special displays of Empire films in local cinemas during school hours. Something similar was arranged for 15,000 Belfast children in 1930, and again, in co-operation with the Senior Chief Inspector at the Board of Education, a film programme was mounted for 42,000 children and teachers in Birmingham in 1931, teaching notes being issued to schools in advance.[69] Finally, there was the use of the Imperial Institute cinema to see EMB films: the director in 1933 reckoned that about half the audiences were children, drawn from 1,477 schools, 'many of which have sent their classes for their instruction in Empire geography term after term'.[70] It perhaps needs little emphasis that using teachers and schools for propaganda work was a particularly appropriate way of disseminating a dominant imperial ideology: it was obviously less concerned with influencing the imperial consumers of today than with moulding the minds of the imperial citizens and consumers of tomorrow.[71]

So much for the media, what about the message? According to the Board's secretary, Stephen Tallents, the EMB 'has engaged in the mobilisation and distribution of ideas'.[72] Like most effective propagandists, the EMB emphasised only a limited number of themes during its career. Goebbels later wrote that 'the nature of propaganda lies essentially in its simplicity and repetition. Only the man who is able to reduce the problems to the simplest terms and has the courage to repeat them indefinitely in this simplified form . . . will in the long run achieve fundamental success in influencing public opinion.'[73] The EMB aimed by the repetition of simple but central themes to lay down a foundation, stressing in the minds of its audience the values and virtues of the Empire. Upon this base, individual Empire governments and Empire producers could construct their own publicity.[74]

To begin with there was an emphasis upon the territorial extent of the Empire. The EMB leaflet *Why Should We Buy from the Empire?* explained that it 'embraces a quarter of the world's surface and a quarter of its population'. The same point was made by the Prince of Wales in his Buy British broadcast speech in November 1931, drafted by Tallents: 'The British Empire . . . offers you the resources of a quarter of the world'. It was given visual effect in the popular world map, originally designed by MacDonald Gill as a poster, which placed the British Isles in the centre of the frame and projected, in red, the overseas Empire around them, in somewhat distorted and exaggerated size.[75] The importance of trade routes connecting this Empire was frequently stressed.[76] But more important than simply size was the natural wealth of the individual units. Echoing traditional imperial assertions, one published EMB report claimed that the Empire can 'grow almost every kind of natural product'. In 1926 the Publicity Committee approved as a theme for a series of press advertisements the claim that 'There is nothing the Empire cannot provide, if you encourage it to do so'.[77] Each territory seemed to have its contributions to offer. The film *Drifters* emphasised the fertility of the North Sea. Posters displayed the agricultural abundance of the dairy regions of New Zealand, the orange orchards of South Africa, the tea plantations of India, the flax of Northern Ireland. There was sago from Borneo, copra from Fiji, sugar from Mauritius, and little St Vincent could provide you with all the arrowroot you ever wanted. The *Handbook of Empire Timbers* informed readers that the Empire incorporated some 2,000,000 square miles of forest and that more than 2,500 different kinds of trees were found in India alone. The teacher's notes accompanying Macmillan's reproduction of EMB posters echoed this approach, noting that 'India is the natural home of rice', that in the Gold Coast were 'the largest plantations of cacao trees in the world', that Jamaica 'has advantages over every country in the world for banana cultivation'. (Its assets included, it was noted, an abundance of cheap negro labour.)[78] The EMB's apparent obsession with Christmas puddings was not altogether misjudged since such a sphere, rich with a wide range of ingredients from all round the Empire, was an appropriate image for the imperial globe they were trying to present.

It was also stressed that the British Empire included the United Kingdom as well as the overseas Empire. The promotion of home food products within the terms of reference of the EMB had been added in a late stage in its planning, in response to complaints from British farmers and the Minister of Agriculture who feared that otherwise the work of the EMB would serve to increase dominion competition at the expense of home producers. It was agreed that Empire producers at home should have first share of the market followed by Empire producers from overseas.[79] The EMB was loyal to this extended concept of Empire and from the beginning repeatedly claimed that 'The Empire is at home as well as overseas'. Posters consistently urged the public to 'Buy Empire Goods from Home and Overseas'.[80] British citizens were to be made aware that they were part of an imperial society: there was no place for Little Englanders.

Moreover, there was a vital mutual dependence between the Empire at home and the Empire overseas: the prosperity of one depended upon and fuelled the prosperity of the other. No theme was given greater emphasis. 'Empire buying', ran the slogan, 'brings prosperity to you.' The appeal to the enlightened self-interest of the British consumer was given detailed prominence in one poster which combined a portrait of a New Zealand family with the following commentary:

The people of the Empire Overseas are Britain's best customers. In New Zealand a family of five will spend on average at least £90 a year on buying goods imported from the United Kingdom . . . The average European only pays about 12 shillings a year for British goods . . . By buying Empire produce . . . you are directly helping to create employment and prosperity for your own people in your own country.[81]

An interdependence between the manufacturing sector of the British imperial economy and the agricultural sector was also stressed. The leaflet *Why Should We Buy from the Empire?* argued that as a great industrial country dependent for its prosperity on exporting manufactured goods, Britain needed to turn in an increasingly competitive world to the expanding markets of the overseas Empire. The further growth of those markets depended on the British consumer: 'Everyone who buys Empire products is helping to win, both now and in the future, orders for our home factories and employment for our own people'.[82] The posters put it more crisply: 'Empire Buying Makes Busy Factories'.[83] One series combined illustrations of a Lancashire cotton mill, old ladies drinking tea, bales of Lancashire cotton goods bound for India, and crates of Indian tea stacked in a British warehouse.[84] The EMB also issued a special series of posters for display in British factories. One example was headed by the announcement that a contract for the overseas Empire was currently in hand in this factory, and contained the following exchange:

Question: How can you help to secure further contracts from the Empire?
Answer: By buying, and by getting your wife to buy, the produce that the Empire sends us.[85]

The benefits to employment in Britain were naturally emphasised. That imperial development and trade would relieve the endemic unemployment problem of inter-war Britain was a commonplace and the poster issued by the EMB as part of the 'Buy British' campaign in 1931 was only an unusually stark indication: 'Remember the Unemployed, They are Your Brothers'.[86]

The notion that citizens of the Empire at home and overseas constituted a single community was a recurrent element in much of this propaganda, employing frequent references to family ties. 'Keep Trade in the Family' and 'Remember the Empire, Filled with Your Cousins' were other slogans used in the 1931 crisis, but these only echoed the title of the EMB film *One Family* and the cheery Christmas message on posters in 1927: 'The Empire is One Large Family. God Bless us Every One'.[87] But it should be apparent that roles within this family were being defined by the EMB. Only the United Kingdom appeared to have a mixed economy, combining industrial production and wealth from agriculture and fishing. Territories in the overseas Empire were categorised solely as primary producers. The emphasis upon their agricultural production was unavoidable, given the brief the EMB was to follow, but the images the Board presented strongly suggested that this was the inevitable economic order of the present and of the future in which a natural economic harmony between British and overseas Empire interests existed and would prevail.

In addition to these readily comprehensible economic messages went two unexpected moral claims. The art critic in *The Times* wrote in 1934: 'Until the Board began advertising, the words "Empire" and "Imperial" were for all sensitive people fatally compromised'. Empire had become linked with unsavoury money-grubbing schemes and Jewish capitalist finance, for example during the tariff reform campaign. But, thanks to the EMB, 'Words and symbols which had become tainted by unfortunate associations were redeemed by art'.[88] What the EMB evidently did was to deny, at least implicitly, connections between Empire and exploitation. What was being encouraged was, apparently, the economic development of the Empire bringing benefits to all its citizens not merely profits to its businessmen. The beneficiaries of this enterprise were the heroic figures of labour, Indian tea-pickers, Scottish shepherds, English industrial workers, Canadian lumbermen, North Sea fishermen, who featured in many of the posters and in such documentary films as *Drifters* and *Industrial Britain*.[89] 'Empire buying makes for fair wages and conditions' was an EMB slogan of 1926, a claim re-used in 1930, incorporated in the leaflet *Why Should We Buy from the Empire?* in 1928, and cited in Lady Snowden's speech in the Buy British campaign in 1931. Here, then, was a vision of Empire as a system of co-operative development bringing mutual benefits in which the image of the family had a moral as well as economic dimension. Grierson claimed in 1933 that the EMB's 'principal effect in six years has been to change the connotation of the word "Empire". Our command of peoples becomes solely a co-operative effort in the tilling of soil, the reaping of harvests and

H

the organisation of a world economy. For the old flags of exploitation it substitutes the new flags of common labour.'[90] Such at least was the EMB's claim.

There was also a second moral theme, implicit more often than explicit: that the Empire being developed by this co-operative effort was a force for international peace. Traditional late nineteenth-century imperial images of jingoism and military conquest, the iconography of battle, were significantly avoided. No explicit references to the military advantages of greater imperial economic development and self-sufficiency have been detected. Instead, we have images of pastoral calm, harmonious trade, industrial and agricultural progress. One striking poster sequence, whose message seems tangential to the ostensible economic purpose of the EMB, carried under the slogan 'The Fishing and Rural Life of Peace' appropriate pictures and a quotation from Isaiah: 'They shall beat their swords into plowshares and their spears into pruning hooks: nation shall not lift up sword against nation, neither shall they learn war any more'.[91] Stephen Tallents included among the slogans for press advertisements he recommended to the Publicity Committee: 'A Well-Built Empire Means the Peace of the World'. 'I am told', he added, 'by those who are accustomed to address meetings of women that no theme appeals more strongly to them than this.'[92] The attempt to harness Empire to the cause of international peace made good sense to propagandists in the decade after the First World War.

Propaganda has been usefully defined as 'an attempt to influence the attitudes of a specific audience, through the use of facts, fictions, argument or suggestion – often supported by the suppression of inconsistent material – with the calculated purpose of instilling in the recipient certain beliefs, values or conclusions which will serve the interests of the author, usually by producing a desired line of action'.[93] It is the precision with which the EMB's activities match this definition, plus the frequency with which members used the word themselves, which allows us to describe their products as propaganda. Much was inevitably distorted in their presentation of the case for Empire, in their selective handling of statistics and in their partial depiction of inter-imperial economic and racial relations. The bulk of this material, the impressive range of media employed, and the mass audiences, young as well as old, at which they aimed strongly suggest that this propaganda is evidence of an attempt by the dominant class to impose through official means an important imperial aspect of their dominant ideology upon subordinate groups. The EMB appeared to express part of the dominant ideology and had the means to hand for its transmission.

The problem with such a simple conclusion is, of course, that the EMB was abolished in 1933. Could imperialism be a part of the dominant ideology if its official propagandist mouthpiece was so swiftly stopped? It is necessary to explore briefly the reasons for this abolition and their implications.

Certainly the EMB had not enjoyed a trouble-free existence before 1933. But to a very considerable extent this simply reflected the novelty of the Board's work as publicist and propaganda body. The excesses of official propaganda during the First World War had left lasting distaste for such work within government service and outside.[94] Tallents, looking back, remembered the opposition: 'the feeling was prevalent that we were introducing a discreditable element into Whitehall'. The Board 'felt itself sometimes an unwanted child in the Government service'. Even mere publicity work by government departments remained restricted: this was an extension of government service which other officials were reluctant to accept. It involved a more positive role for government and a closer contact between officials and the general public. Tallents saw this 'new and more creative conception of government' colliding with 'the older view of government as a negative function, preventing the bad rather than promoting the good'. The future troubles which Tallents was to experience after 1933 as head of the GPO's publicity unit strongly suggest that it was the administrative novelty rather than the imperial message of the EMB which some in government and outside found intolerable.[95] It is also worth noting that many of the scientific research grants previously funded by the EMB were later continued by the Colonial Development Fund, set up in 1929, and that the Imperial Economic Committee continued to produce reports on marketing issues and to publish the weekly or monthly intelligence notes on food products first issued by the Board: only the explicit and public propaganda novelties were abandoned.

The usual way to suppress unwanted government activities was to stress the pressing need for economies in government expenditure. Economic conditions in the 1920s and 1930s were ripe for such an appeal to draw support, given the persistence of economic depression, measured by high levels of unemployment, and given also the established orthodox belief that balanced budgets, lower taxes and reduced government expenditure were the royal routes to recovery.[96] Throughout the existence of the EMB, Chancellors of the Exchequer repeatedly pressed, and successfully, for some savings on the EMB account, and in fact the Board never received the £1 million a year originally promised by the Cabinet. The highest annual grant received was only £612,500 in 1930–1, and altogether only £3,681,500 was granted in the eight financial years in which the Board operated.[97] To the Treasury's institutionalised hostility were added critical reviews of EMB expenditure each year by the Public Accounts Committee and more criticism of costs and of the Board's freedom from detailed Treasury control in two reports by the Select Committee on Estimates.[98] The demands for economy were strong and inevitably intensified as the cyclical downturn accelerated after 1929. The Committee on National Expenditure (May Committee), set up to propose public expenditure cuts in the depths of the depression in 1931, concluded that the Board was 'unjustifiable in existing circumstances'.[99] The Board survived instant execution, but the depression left the financially struggling National government obliged to keep looking for further economies in government activities, and a body like the EMB which could not be regarded as a traditional, well-established operation remained obviously vulnerable. When the Board was finally abolished, a correspondent to *The Times* described this as 'a piece of national economy long overdue'.[100]

The timing of the Board's abolition was determined, however, not by any worsening of the government's financial problems but by their adoption at last, in the economic crisis, of tariff protection, and their signing of the imperial preference agreements with the dominions at the Imperial Economic Conference at Ottawa in 1932. Most enthusiasts for Empire had always preferred tariffs as the more effective means of securing closer imperial economic ties, and with their erection the original explicit *raison d'être* of the EMB disappeared. The EMB was more aware of its wider ideological role, and argued in its own defence that 'whilst the Board was started in lieu of certain proposed Imperial Preferences, it had now become an essential instrument of Imperial co-operation in research, in marketing and in propaganda'.[101] But majority opinion in government and business seemed to accept that with the shift to the new imperial strategy, the need for economy in government expenditure could now demand the termination of the official propaganda experiment. It would have survived only if the dominion governments had agreed to share the financial cost. Such a request was put to them by the British government at Ottawa and received a dusty response. The sum involved was pretty insignificant, but the dominions also preferred tariffs to persuasion. They retained in any case, particularly the governments of Canada, South Africa and the Irish Free State, a lingering suspicion of a centralised imperial organisation like the EMB which seemed to detract from that autonomy within the British Empire which the dominions between the wars were anxious to declare.[102]

There were evidently problems in translating an imperial ideology into something as specific as a practical administrative operation. The EMB did not offend because of its imperial assumptions and claims. It aroused the opposition which led to its closure because its duties disturbed those in the dominions who were anxious to demonstrate national autonomy within the imperial system and those in Britain who disliked novel government responsibilities and the taxation necessary to pay for them and who preferred tariffs as the way to exploit imperial connections and opportunities. The EMB was a symptom of the dominant ideology, one of several policies seeking to achieve imperial economic aims but a unique experiment in trying to impose an imperial ideology on the public by official propaganda means.

A final question obviously remains. Was the experiment successful and did an organisation so fertile in its exploitation of modern media succeed in impressing imperial beliefs upon the public and affecting their behaviour? The dominant ideology theory requires such an inquiry.

It must be conceded at once that in spite of the great volume of propaganda designed by the EMB for mass audiences, there were problems of transmission. While it is doubtful if contemporaries could avoid being made aware of the existence of the Board, we should not exaggerate the share of public attention which it could monopolise. Its financial resources were by no means great, and it is necessary to put the EMB's output into context. We should compare the £278,414 spent by the EMB at the peak of its publicity activities in 1928 with the estimated £57 million spent altogether on national advertising in Britain that year. EMB advertisements may be located in most local and national newspapers, but they took up only a modest proportion of newsprint, even at the height of its campaign. The numerous special EMB billboards and posters, while distinctive, were unlikely to have regularly outfaced the great bulk of ordinary commercial advertising. The EMB hardly dominated the BBC's broadcasting, and the substantial volume of EMB leaflets and reports provided only a modest proportion of the reading matter produced in Great Britain at the time. The scarcity of film projectors in schools and the failure of EMB films to gain full access to the commercial cinema circuits have already been mentioned. The EMB was an exceptionally vigorous and enterprising body even by the standards of commercial operators, but we need to keep its activities in perspective. Of course, the general imperial ideology and some of the specific economic aims of the Board were expressed and supported by other unofficial or semi-official organisations, some of which are examined elsewhere in this book. This must have reinforced the impact of the EMB, while making it impossible to disentangle the specific effects of the Board's own work.

Some contemporary scepticism was expressed about the effectiveness of the Board's activities in achieving its explicit economic aim. In two investigations in 1928 and 1932 the Select Committee on Estimates pressed Tallents hard to demonstrate the effects of the Board's publicity work, and the Public Accounts Committee returned year after year to the question. In 1930, for example, the committee conceded that *Drifters* was 'a very good show, but does it make a man eat an extra fish?'[103] Often Tallents had to concede that it was very difficult to measure the consequences of the Board's work. The Board, of course, was convinced of the efficacy of its actions and it routinely collected testimonials of support from those who should have been able to assess prevailing commercial trends from their own experience, for example, the Australian Dried Fruit Board in 1928, the Association of British Chambers of Commerce in 1929, the Australian Association of

British Manufacturers, Melbourne, in 1931 and the Associated Chambers of Commerce, New Zealand, in 1932.[104] When dissolution was imminent the Board was defended not only by several national newspapers – *The Times, Financial Times, Observer, Manchester Guardian, Glasgow Herald, Irish Times* and even *Punch* – but also by trade journals like the *Bakers' Record* and the *Fruit, Flower and Vegetable Trade Journal* and by trade organisations like the Federation of Grocers' Associations, the Scottish Grocers' Federation and even the Sydenham and District Grocers' Association. (Not even the latter could deflect the implacable governments of the British Empire from their decision.)[105]

Many of these defenders picked up the claims made in the EMB's own annual reports which regularly listed record levels of overseas Empire imports into Britain (comparable figures for home production do not seem to have been kept). Twenty-two records were logged in 1928, twenty-five in 1929, sixteen in 1930, twenty-five in 1931, twenty-four in 1932 in a wide range of products such as Australian sultanas, New Zealand lamb, Rhodesian tobacco, East African coffee, Palestinian grapefruits, South African wines, Malayan canned pineapples and so on.[106] Moreover, the EMB conducted inquiries among selected retailers around the country and often published their conclusions about patterns of consumption of selected Empire and foreign foodstuffs, not the least interesting of the Board's innovations at a time when market research in Britain was embryonic. These seemed to show, for example, an increase in the consumption of Empire butter in the northern counties after a special campaign in 1931, and a similar displacement of foreign by Empire butter was recorded between 1928 and 1931 in two surveys conducted in Nottingham. Tallents told the Select Committee on Estimates that the consumption of foreign butter in Britain had increased by 9 per cent between 1929 and 1932 but of Empire butter by 50 per cent.[107]

The difficulty lies in interpreting such figures. Not even the EMB claimed that such trends were due solely to the Board's propaganda. We know that the percentage of United Kingdom imports coming from the Empire rose from 30 per cent of the total in 1926 to 37 per cent in 1933, but the percentage had already risen from a mere twenty per cent of total imports in 1913 in the years before the EMB was established and it then remained fairly steady at around 30 per cent until 1932 (and it was then to rise to 39 per cent in 1938 in the years after its demise). Two main factors probably explain these trends. The first is the increase in supply of certain products such as Australian dried fruits and New Zealand meat and dairy products. This enabled British retailers to offer customers increasingly large and regular quantities to rival established European or American products. Britain was already absorbing 91 per cent of New Zealand butter exports in 1926 and took 99 per cent in 1933, but the volume had more than doubled.

The other, not unconnected, element was price and the relative movements between Empire and foreign prices. EMB reports showed that between November 1928 and November 1930 wholesale prices fell by 30 per cent for Danish butter but by 38 per cent for New Zealand butter. Commenting on the increased share of the Nottingham market taken by Empire butters, the investigators concluded: 'it may be of some significance that Australian and New Zealand are slightly less highly priced butters than Danish'.[108]

These points suggest the limitations to the effectiveness of mere publicity. Other surveys confirm this. It was reckoned that the Buy British campaign of 1931 had led to a definite increase in public unwillingness to buy foreign products, but subsequent inquiry suggested that the effect was on the wane probably as the factors of supply and price reasserted their influence. Even more revealingly, a census of 1,000 retail grocers around the country in 1928 disclosed that though there had been an overall increase in demand for Empire goods, this was recognised mainly by retailers in better class areas, where surplus income may be presumed to have existed, and was much less apparent in poorer districts, where the exigencies of price probably prevailed.[109] This was a society in which even by contemporary standards substantial numbers lived on or below the poverty line, and in which many experienced a worsening of living standards in the depression of 1929–32. A sizeable portion of the population could not afford to have their patterns of consumption affected by ideological considerations. There were barriers, then, to the effectiveness of propaganda, and it may be that in this respect tariff preferences, which affected prices, were a more effective method of imperial economic engineering.

How far the EMB managed to intrude a more general imperial ideology into popular culture is even more difficult to determine. Where hard data on popular attitudes towards Empire and the wider world is lacking, speculation must take over. It is very doubtful whether imperial propaganda by the EMB and from other sources was much responsible for the social cohesion which must, on balance, be said to have existed between the wars, in spite of growing electoral support for the Labour Party, a substantial and occasionally militant trade union movement, and national and local demonstrations against unemployment and the dole. It is likely that that consensus was mainly effected by a rising standard of living for most of the employed, by a system of unemployment relief which did not break down (unlike in Germany), by the threat of unemployment which encouraged quiescence, and by the operations of industrial discipline and of the forces of law and order which demanded conformity. Suitable social, economic and political conditions had to exist before ideological persuasion could play its own subordinate supplementary role.[110]

It is, however, difficult to disprove the contention that the EMB confirmed in the minds of the majority a world view, a broad conception of the nation's status and power in the world as the centre of a legitimate and uniquely favoured imperial system. The concepts of the wider world presented by the EMB conformed to those emanating from other official and unofficial sources. Together they dominated the media and infiltrated the educational system. Moreover, their views were not greatly challenged by alternative, conflicting interpretations of Britain's Empire and its characteristics. Besides, the affairs of the wider world, in the Empire and outside, were remote from the intense everyday experiences of most people, the activities of the family circle and the patterns of earning and spending. Accordingly the messages written on the mind by imperial propagandists may indeed have been absorbed, if passively and with indifference. It may well be true, as one teacher told the Board, 'Your posters have created a new "Idea of Empire" in the minds of these poor little slum children here'.[111] It may not have been an achievement which had much practical effect upon the activities of the masses, but it does suggest one conclusion. Whereas the EMB's economic importuning to 'Buy Empire Goods from Home and Overseas' had a modest, limited effect because the message conflicted with the realities of supply and price, the EMB's general ideological message on the validity and virtue of Empire was implanted more successfully in the popular mind because of the absence of contradictory data.

Notes

1　John Darwin, 'Imperialism in decline? Tendencies in British imperial policy between the wars', *Historical Journal*, XXIII, 1980; I. M. Drummond, *British Economic Policy and the Empire 1919–1939*, London 1972; R. F. Holland, *Britain and the Commonwealth Alliance 1918–39*, London 1981; P. S. Gupta, *Imperialism and the British Labour Movement 1914–1964*, London 1975; Stephen Constantine, *The Making of British Colonial Development Policy 1914–1940*, London 1984.

2　John M. MacKenzie, *Propaganda and Empire*, Manchester 1984.

3　N. Abercrombie, S. Hill and B. S. Turner, *The Dominant Ideology Thesis*, London 1980, an excellent statement of the thesis and a critique.

4　See especially Drummond, *British Economic Policy and the Empire*, pp. 36–88 and Constantine, *British Colonial Development Policy*, 9–194.

5　F. W. S. Craig (ed.), *British General Election Manifestos 1918–1966*, Chichester 1970, 11.

6　Sir Philip Lloyd-Greame, *The Imperial Economic Conference*, Unionist Workers' Handbook, National Unionist Association, Westminster 1924, 6. See also his autobiography, Lord Swinton, *I Remember*, London 1948, 30–7, and J. A. Cross, *Lord Swinton*, Oxford 1982, 14–81. The Swinton Papers, Churchill College, Cambridge, contain little of direct relevance to this study. He changed his name from Lloyd-Greame to Cunliffe-Lister on inheriting property in 1924 and became Lord Swinton in 1935: for the sake of convenience he is referred to throughout this essay as Cunliffe-Lister.

7　For his career and connections see L. S. Amery, *My Political Life*, 3 vols., London 1953–5, especially II, 291, III, 19, 24; J. Barnes and D. Nicholson (eds.), *The Leo Amery Diaries*, I, London 1980; Amery Papers, in particular Box G.84 correspondence between Amery and BEPO, H.121 material on EEU and F.79 election manifestos. I am grateful to the Rt. Hon. Julian Amery MP for permission to examine and to quote from the Leo Amery Papers.

8   G. R. Searle, 'Critics of Edwardian society: the case of the radical right', in A. O'Day (ed.), *The Edwardian Age: Conflict and Stability 1900–1914*, London 1979, 79–96; J. O. Stubbs, 'Lord Milner and patriotic labour 1914–1918', *English Historical Review*, LXXXVII, 1972.

9   Amery, *My Political Life*, I, 253–6, 331; Baldwin Papers, University of Cambridge Library, XLII, Amery to Baldwin, 21 Dec. 1923. See also Amery to Baldwin, 28 Jan. 1924, *ibid.*, and for his criticism of negative anti-socialism, *My Political Life*, II, 240–1, 488. His views on imperialism as constructive anti-socialism were also aired in lectures he gave to the Conservative Party's Philip Stott College in 1923, printed subsequently in *The National Review* and published as *National and Imperial Economics* by the National Unionist Association, Westminster, 1923: a second edition in 1924 with an emphatic new foreword followed the party's electoral setback in December 1923.

10   Neville Chamberlain Papers, NC 18/1/415, N. Chamberlain to Ida Chamberlain, 11 Nov. 1923. I am grateful to the Head of Special Collections at the University of Birmingham Library for permission to consult and to quote from the Neville Chamberlain Papers.

11   Amery Papers, Box G.82, Amery to Baldwin, 11 Feb. 1924.

12   For Chamberlain's reluctant acquiescence see N. Chamberlain to Ida Chamberlain 12 Jan. 1924 and to Hilda Chamberlain 24 Jan. 1924, NC 18/1/422 and 423.

13   Craig (ed.), *British General Election Manifestos*, 30.

14   The detailed origins of the EMB may be traced in Baldwin Papers, XCIII 'Memo. on encouragement of Empire production' and covering letter by Cunliffe-Lister 5 Dec. 1924, XXVII Churchill to Baldwin 6 Dec. 1924, XCII Amery to Baldwin 28 Jan. 1926; Amery Papers, Diary 1925 and 1926; Cabinet Papers, CAB 24/169/CP 543, CAB 24/175/CP 446, CP 458, CAB 24/178/CP 31, CP 54, CP 60, CAB 24/179/CP 112, CP 115; Cabinet Conclusions, CAB 23/49/CAB 60(24)3, CAB 67(24)11, CAB 23/52/CAB 3(26)11, CAB 5(26)1, CAB 7(26)3, CAB 11(26)6; *Hansard*, Debates, House of Commons, CLXXIX, cols. 1065–8; *Report of the Imperial Economic Committee*, Cmd.2493, 1925. Drummond, *British Economic Policy and the Empire*, 65–6, provides a brief account and Amery, *My Political Life*, II, 346, a partial one which ignores the role of Cunliffe-Lister.

15   Tallents Papers, Institute of Commonwealth Studies, File 25, 10. J. M. Lee, 'The dissolution of the Empire Marketing Board, 1933: reflections on a diary', *Journal of Imperial and Commonwealth History*, I, 1972, 51 gives a figure of 172.

16   Amery Papers, Diary, 19 Oct. 1926; Amery, *My Political Life*, II, 347.

17   CO 760/12, minutes of 37th meeting of Board, 17 July 1929. Quotations from Crown copyright material kept at the Public Record Office appear by permission of the Controller of HM Stationery Office.

18   Amery Papers, Box G.90, Webb to Amery 18 June 1929, Amery to Webb 20 June 1929 and Graham to Amery 13 June 1929.

19   *The Times*, 17 Nov. 1931, p. 11. Membership of the EMB was printed as an appendix to the annual *Empire Marketing Board: Note on the Work and Finance of the Board*, Cmd.3158 1928, Cmd.3372 1929, Cmd.3637 1930, Cmd.3914 1931, Cmd.4121 1932.

20 Analysis of Labour's colonial development policy in 1924 and 1929–31 supports this view: Constantine, *British Colonial Development Policy*, 109–11, 136, 183–7.

21 For a detailed listing of grants for research see *Report of the Imperial Committee on Economic Consultation and Cooperation*, Cmd.4335, 1933, table 3, and for a selected description of some activities see Amery, *My Political Life*, II 348–51.

22 Amery, *My Political Life*, II, 348; figures calculated from annual *Appropriation Accounts* in Parliamentary Papers.

23 Amery, *My Political Life*, II, 340; and see Tallents Papers, File 25, 4.

24 CAB 23/52/CAB 3(26)11, 3 Feb. 1926, quoting CP 458.

25 Tallents Papers, File 25, 4.

26 Donald Read, *England 1868–1914*, London 1979, 45, 93, 164, 430–1.

27 H. F. Hutchinson, *The Poster. An Illustrated History from 1860*, London 1968; B. Hillier, *Posters*, London 1969.

28 Keith Robbins, *The Eclipse of a Great Power. Modern Britain 1870–1975*, London 1983, 164–5; Mark Pegg, *Broadcasting and Society 1918–1939*, London 1983, 7.

29 Jeffrey Richards, *The Age of the Dream Palace*, London 1984, 11–12; P. Perilli, 'Statistical Survey of the British Film Industry' in J. Curran and V. Porter (eds), *British Cinema History*, London 1983, 372, 375.

30 Alan Jenkins, *Drinka Pinta*, London 1970, 80–104.

31 T. R. Nevett, *Advertising in Britain*, London 1982, 145; see also E. S. Turner, *The Shocking History of Advertising*, Harmondsworth 1965.

32 K. Middlemas, *Politics in Industrial Society*, London 1979, 351; A. Briggs, *The Birth of Broadcasting*, London 1961, 268; T. J. Hollins, 'The Conservative Party and film propaganda between the wars', *English Historical Review*, XCVI, 1981; J. Ramsden, 'Baldwin and film' in N. Pronay and D. W. Spring (eds), *Propaganda, Politics and Film, 1918–45*, London 1982.

33 M. Ogilvy-Webb, *The Government Explains: A Study of the Information Services*, London 1965, 47–51; M. L. Sanders and P. M. Taylor, *British Propaganda During the First World War 1914–18*, London 1982; Cate Haste, *Keep the Home Fires Burning: Propaganda in the First World War*, London 1977; P. M. Taylor, *The Projection of Britain*, Cambridge 1981; Nevett, *Advertising in Britain*, 141–3; MacKenzie, *Propaganda and Empire*, 107–17, 122–46, 162–6; K. Walthew, 'The British Empire Exhibition of 1924', *History Today*, XXXI, 1981, 34–9; Tallents Papers, File 32, 6. The covert activities in 1918–22 of Lloyd George's coalition government in employing front organisations and planting anti-Bolshevik and anti-trade union material in newspapers remained too shadowy to provide a model to guide the EMB, Middlemas, *Politics in Industrial Society*, 131–2, 153–4, 158, 351–4.

34 CO 760/12, minutes of 1st meeting of Board, 2 June 1926.

35 CO 760/23, minutes of 1st meeting of Publicity Committee, 8 July 1926; *Who Was Who*.

36 Turner, *The Shocking History of Advertising*, 245; see also C. Barnam, *The Man Who Built London Transport*, Newton Abbot 1979.

37 G. H. Saxon Mills, *There is a Tide . . .*, London 1954, 129, Nevett, *Advertising in Britain*, 145, 148.

38 For membership of Board and Committees see appendices to the annual reports *Empire Marketing Board*, EMB Nos. 9, 19, 28, 41, 53 and 63.

39 William Crawford, *How to Succeed in Advertising*, 1931, quoted in Paul

Swann, 'The British documentary film movement, 1926–1946', University of Leeds PhD, 1979, 4.

40 Sir Stephen Tallents, 'Salesmanship in the public service', *Public Administration*, II, 1933, 259–66: this essay is more relevant in this context than his more famous *The Projection of England*, London 1932, which is principally concerned with the influencing of consumers in overseas markets. For his career see *Who Was Who* and Amery, *My Political Life*, II, 347. He was to work subsequently for the Post Office, the BBC and the Ministry of Town and Country Planning, and he became the first President of the Institute of Public Relations in 1947.

41 Annual *Note on the Work and Finance of the Board*; annual *Appropriation Accounts*; CO 760/3/289; CO 760/25/ESC 18; Tallents Papers File 33, 16.

42 EMB Nos. 9, 19, 28, 41, 53, 63; *Note on the Work and Finance of the Board*, Cmd.3637 1929, Cmd.4121 1930; CO 760/12, minutes of 21st meeting of Board, 3 Nov. 1927.

43 Annual *Appropriation Accounts*; Tallents Papers File 33, 10–11; *Note on the Work and Finance of the Board*, Cmd.3637 1930, 15; CO 760/12, minutes of 12th meeting of Board, 8 Dec. 1926; *Durham County Advertiser*, 20 Nov. 1931, 12, 1 Jan. 1932, 12; *Lancaster Guardian*, 12 June 1931, 3, 20 Nov. 1931, 5, 4 Dec. 1931, 6, 11 Dec. 1931, 16, 18, 24, 18 Dec. 1931, 3, 7, 24, 24 Dec. 1931, 13–14.

44 CO 760/12, minutes of 15th meeting of Board, 12 April 1927; Tallents Papers File 6, File 14, 21–2; *Note on the Work and Finance of the Board*, Cmd.4121, 1932, 17; EMB 53, 108; *The Times* 24 Nov. 1928, 9, 3 Dec. 1928, 16; *Lancaster Guardian* 24 Dec. 1931, 4. The Empire Day Movement's sponsorship and ceremonial mixing of the first King's Empire Christmas Pudding to an EMB recipe was reported in *The Times* 20 Dec. 1926, 9, 21 Dec. 1926, 9 (photo., p. 16), 23 Dec. 1926, 12. There was a similar performance in 1927.

45 Michael J. Winstanley, *The Shopkeeper's World 1830–1914*, Manchester 1983, 78–9.

46 Annual *Note on the Work and Finance of the Board*; EMB Nos. 19, 28, 41, 53 and 63; Tallents Papers File 33, 9, 14–16; annual *Appropriation Accounts*.

47 CO 760/23, minutes of 1st meeting of Publicity Committee, 8 July 1926; annual *Note on the Work and Finance of the Board*; EMB Nos. 19, 28, 41, 53 and 63; Tallents Papers Files 6 and 14, 20 and 33, 17; *The Times*, 17 Nov. 1931, 11; *The Listener*, I, 767, IV, 207–8, 700–1, VI 900, 928, 976, VII 42–7, 94–5, 178–9, 215–16, 251, 269, 321–2, 359, 396; *Radio Times*, XXIII 583, 645, 697; XXVII, 411; *BBC Household Talks 1928*, London, 1929; BBC Written Archives Centre R 34/213/1, Harding to Gielgud 24 April 1930.

48 N. Pronay, 'The political censorship of films in Britain between the wars', in Pronay and Spring (eds) *Propaganda, Politics and Film*; Richards, *The Age of the Dream Palace*, 89–107; Haste, *Keep the Home Fires Burning*; Sanders and Taylor, *British Propaganda in the First World War*.

49 *Imperial Conference 1926, Summary of Proceedings*, Cmd.2768, 1926, 53, *Appendices*, Cmd.2769, 1926, 403; *Hansard* CCIII, col. 2040. Very similar sentiments may be found in *Imperial Conference 1930, Summary of Proceedings*, Cmd.3717, 1930, 77, *Appendices*, Cmd.3718, 1930, 238.

50 Tallents Papers File 28, see also File 26, 7, File 35, 3; Co 760/1/8 11 June 1926; CO 760/12 minutes of 3rd meeting of Board 16 June 1926; CO 760/22/EMB/PC/1 29 June 1926; CO 760/23 minutes of 2nd meeting of Publicity Committee 16 July 1926 and minutes of 5th meeting 16 July 1926.

51   CO 760/37/EMB/C/2 (Grierson's memo. was warmly endorsed by John
     Buchan, former Director of the Department of Information, CO
     760/37/EMB/C/3); John Grierson 'The EMB Film Unit', *Cinema Quarterly*,
     summer 1933, 204; F. Hardy, *John Grierson, A Documentary Biography*,
     London 1979.

52   CO 760/12 minutes of 3rd meeting of Board, 16 June 1926. Film lists in R.
     Low, *The History of the British Film 1929–1939: Documentary and
     Educational Films of the 1930s*, 211–27 and see 51–67, and in A. Lovell and
     J. Hillier (eds), *Studies in Documentary*, London 1972, 37–46. For the
     making of *Drifters* see Hardy, *John Grierson*, 49–54 and Paul Rotha,
     Documentary Diary, London 1973, 25–9.

53   Low, *Documentary and Educational Films*, 52, 67; A. Cooke (ed.) *Garbo and
     the Night Watchmen*, London, new ed. 1971, 36–9; E. Sussex, *The Rise and
     Fall of British Documentary*, Berkeley and Los Angeles 1975, 5, 13; Rotha,
     Documentary Diary, 22; The Arts Enquiry, *The Factual Film*, London 1947,
     57.

54   Tallents Papers File 35, 16; EMB No. 63 (giving 960,000 as the size of
     audience in 1932); Low, *Documentary and Educational Films*, 66; Sir
     William Furse, 'The Imperial Institute and the films of the Empire Marketing
     Board', *Sight and Sound*, II, autumn 1933, 79.

55   CO 760/23 minutes of 3rd meeting of Publicity Committee 22 July 1926; CO
     760/12 minutes of 18th meeting of Board 7 July 1927; EMB Nos. 19, 28, 41,
     53, 63; Furse, 'Imperial Institute', 79; Tallents Papers File 35, 8–9, File 14,
     19–20; *Note on the Work and Finance of the Board*, Cmd.3372 1929 16,
     Cmd.4121 1932 17.

56   CO 760/37/C 47, Progress Report of the Film Committee 17 July 1930; EMB
     Nos. 28, 41 and 53 for lists of such films; CO 760/23 minutes of 16th meeting
     of Publicity Committee 1 Feb. 1928; CO 760/12 minutes of 23rd meeting of
     Board 15 Feb. 1928; Sussex, *British Documentary*, 8–9, 14; Rotha,
     Documentary Diary, 49.

57   Annual *Appropriation Accounts*; Royal Academy, *Empire Marketing Board
     Posters 1926*, catalogue and photographs of exhibits, in the Victoria and
     Albert Museum Library; CO 760/12 minutes of 12th meeting of Board 8 Dec.
     1926; *The Times* 6 Jan. 1927, 11.

58   *Note on the Work and Finance of the Board*, Cmd.3372 1929, Cmd.3637
     1930; EMB Nos. 28, 41, 53 and 63; CO 760/1/54; CO 760/26 minutes of
     Poster Sub-Committee 15 Dec. 1927; Mark Haworth-Booth, *E. McKnight
     Kauffer*, London, 1979, 44–8. The PRO's collection, which is incomplete,
     lists 733 items, CO 956, and the Victoria and Albert Museum Department of
     Prints and Drawings includes posters and/or preliminary paintings by F. C.
     Herrick, V. Polunin, J. K. Lawson, C. Gardiner, C. Pears, MacDonald Gill, C.
     Leighton, H. Taylor, E. McKnight Kauffer, P. Nash and J. Nash: some of
     these appear not to be in the PRO collection.

59   *Note on the Work and Finance of the Board*, Cmd.2898 1927 9, Cmd.4121
     1932 16–17; Tallents Papers File 6 and File 33, 8; CO 760/22/EMB/PC/2
     Notes on a Scheme of Poster Display; CO 760/23 minutes of 2nd meeting of
     Publicity Committee 16 July 1926; CO 760/26 minutes of Poster Sub-
     Committee 9 Feb., 16 May, 4 Oct. 1928, 7 Feb., 16 May, 5 Dec., 19 Dec.
     1929; the design for the poster frame is shown in Royal Academy *Empire
     Marketing Board Posters 1926*.

60   CO 760/23 minutes of 2nd meeting of Publicity Committee 16 July 1926; CO
     760/12 minutes of 8th meeting of Board 21 July 1926; CO 760/26 minutes of

Poster Sub-Committee 11 Nov. 1926; CO 760/23 minutes of 15th meeting of Publicity Committee 5 Dec. 1927; appendix to EMB No. 19; EMB No. 28, 7; CO 760/25 minutes of 23rd meeting of Education Sub-Committee 1 July 1932; CO 760/23 minutes of 31st meeting of Publicity Committee 12 Dec. 1929; CO 760/22/PC/93 10 Dec. 1928.

61 *Note on the Work and Finance of the Board*, Cmd.2898 1927 10; EMB No. 63, 103; Tallents Papers File 14, File 33, 8–9. There were 31,783 schools in England and Wales in 1930: A. H. Halsey (ed.), *Trends in British Society*, London 1972, 166.

62 CO 760/22/PC/93 10 Dec. 1928; Tallents Papers File 7, EMB News No. 156.

63 CO 760/22/PC/29 1 March 1927, PC/130 23 Jan. 1930.

64 *Macmillan's Class Pictures: Reference Book, History, Geography and Literature*, London 1932. I am grateful to Rachel Hasted of the Lancashire County Museums Service for showing me a copy and accompanying posters in the Museum of Childhood, Judges' Lodgings, Lancaster.

65 CO 760/23 minutes of 15th meeting of Publicity Committee 5 Dec. 1927; CO 760/3/289; CO 760/22/PC/146; CO 760/23 minutes of 24th meeting of Publicity Committee 23 Jan. 1929.

66 Richards, *The Age of the Dream Palace*, 48–9, 67–85; Low, *Documentary and Educational Films*, 7–47.

67 CO 760/37 minutes of 13th meeting of Film Committee 24 June 1930; Tallents Papers File 35, 16, 23, 28; CO 760/37/C/27 23 Oct. 1929; EMB Nos 41, 53 and 63; Rotha, *Documentary Diary*, 49, 58, 60; Sussex, *British Documentary*, 9–10; advertisement for EMB's film catalogue in *Sight and Sound*, I, autumn 1932, 87.

68 J. A. Lauwerys (ed.), *The Film in the School*, London 1935, 13–15; Low, *Documentary and Educational Films*, 39–41; Arts Enquiry, *Factual Film*, 21, 105–27.

69 EMB No. 28, 88. *Note on the Work and Finance of the Board*, Cmd.3637 1930 17, Cmd.4125 1932 16; CO 760/22/PC/146; CO 760/37 minutes of 16th meeting of Film Committee 8 Jan. 1931; CO 760/37/C/58 16 July 1931 and C/64 11 Dec. 1931.

70 Furse, 'Imperial Institute', 79. His figures for attendances by children are higher than those given in EMB Nos. 28, 41, 53 and 63 which suggest that children formed just over 25 per cent of total audiences. Most must have come from schools in the Greater London area.

71 The Board also discussed exchanges between teachers in Britain and in the dominions, CO 760/1/9, 16 and 32, CO 760/12 minutes of 8th meeting of Board 21 July 1926, and ways of improving the supply of suitable school textbooks on Empire history and geography, CO 760/4/334, CO 760/12 minutes of 8th meeting of Board 21 July 1926, CO 760/22/PC/104. Both proposals were thought, on balance, to be beyond the brief of the EMB.

72 Sir Stephen Tallents, 'Empire Marketing Board 1926–1933', *United Empire*, XXIV, 1933, 484.

73 Goebbels Diary, 29 Jan. 1942, quoted as the epigraph in Haste, *Keep the Home Fires Burning*, vi.

74 CO 760/12 minutes of 1st and 15th meetings of Board, 20 May 1926 and 12 April 1927; Tallents Papers File 33 1.

75 CO 760/3/247; Tallents Papers File 6.

76 See, for example, the routes marked on the MacDonald Gill poster-map and the sequence of posters designed by Charles Pears under the title 'The Empire's Highway to India', CO 956/688–93.

77 EMB No. 28, 8; CO 760/1/23.

78 *Macmillan's Class Pictures*, notes to illustrations 111, 118, 128. There you will also learn that 'The pig is the great friend of the Irish peasant', note to illustration 136.

79 CAB 24/169/CP 546; CAB 24/175/CP 481; CAB 23/49/CAB 67(24)11; CAB 23/52/CAB 3(26)11; *Hansard* CLXXIX, col. 1067; *Imperial Economic Committee Report*, Cmd.2493, 1925, 4.

80 CO 760/1/23; CO 760/1/7; Tallents Papers File 2, File 42, 5.

81 This poster was reproduced and praised in *Advertising World*, LI, Jan. 1927, 440.

82 CO 760/3/247; Tallents Papers File 26 11–12.

83 Caption to Gardiner's series of posters, which also declared that 69 per cent of the products of the motor industry and 63 per cent of the products of the electrical industry were exported to Empire countries in 1926, CO 956/258–63.

84 CO 956/181–6.

85 Reproduced in EMB No. 19.

86 CO 956/238.

87 CO 956/236, 237, 510; CO 760/26 minutes of Poster Sub-Committee 31 Aug. 1927.

88 *The Times*, 20 March 1934, 11.

89 As poster examples see the Gardiner set referred to above and Frank Newbould's vivid illustration of Canadian lumbermen placed between the texts 'Let us now praise famous men' and 'And some there be which have no memorial' in his sequence entitled 'The Empire is still in Building', CO 956/223–8.

90 CO 760/1/23; EMB No. 41, 45; CO 760/3/247; *The Listener*, VI, 976; Grierson, 'The EMB Film Unit', 205.

91 Designed by J. K. Lawson, CO 956/127–32.

92 CO 760/22/PC/11, 30 August 1926. A similar slogan was used in 1930, EMB No. 41 45.

93 Taylor, *Projection of Britain*, 4–5.

94 Sanders and Taylor, *British Propaganda in the First World War*, 248–50, 264.

95 Tallents Papers, File 25, 5–6.

96 Stephen Constantine, *Unemployment in Britain between the Wars*, London 1980, 45–84.

97 Annual *Appropriation Accounts*. For Amery's sometimes entertaining battles over EMB funding with Churchill, Chancellor of the Exchequer, see Barnes and Nicholson (eds), *The Leo Amery Diaries*, 17 Oct. and 17 Nov. 1925, 26 Jan. and 1, 2, 11 and 24 Feb. 1926, 16 June and 11 and 20 July 1927, 28 Nov. 1928; Baldwin Papers XCII Amery to Baldwin 28 Jan. and 1 Feb. 1926, IV 19 July 1927; CAB 23/55/CAB 42(27)6 20 July 1927, CAB 23/57/CAB 9(28)9 17 Feb. 1928; CAB 24/178/CP 31; Chamberlain Papers NC 2/22 Diary 21 July 1927; Amery, *My Political Life*, II, 486-91. For Amery's later attempts to defend the Board's finances see Amery Papers Box H111, Amery to Passfield 22 Nov. 1929, Diary 21 Jan., 19 March, 22 April and 6 and 20 May 1931; CO 760/12 minutes of 37th, 42nd, 46th, 51st, 57th meetings of Board.

98 Annual *Reports from the Select Committee of Public Accounts*, 1926–7 to 1932–3; *Reports from the Select Committee on Estimates*, 1928 and 1932.

99 *Report of the Committee on National Expenditure*, Cmd.3920, 1931, 131–2.

100 Sir Edward Parry, retired judge, *The Times*, 24 Aug. 1933, 6.

101 CO 760/12 minutes of 60th meeting of Board 13 April 1932; similar arguments in CO 760/7/699, CO 760/8/725 and 797.

102 See Canadian criticisms of the Imperial Economic Committee in *Imperial Economic Conference 1923*, Cmd.2009 1923, 573 and Baldwin Papers XCIII, MacKenzie King to Baldwin 20 April 1926; South African opposition to increasing the role of the EMB in *Imperial Conference 1930*, Cmd.3717 1930, 53; Canadian, Irish and South African objections to the maintenance of the EMB voiced at Ottawa, *Imperial Conference at Ottawa 1932*, Cmd.4174 1932, 14 and *Report of the Imperial Committee on Economic Consultation and Co-operation*, Cmd.4335 1933, 79–92. See also A. C. D. Rivett, 'The Empire Marketing Board: a tribute, a lament and a hope', *The Australian Rhodes Review*, March 1934, 15–19.

103 *Select Committee of Public Accounts*, March 1931, question 2592.

104 *Select Committee on Estimates*, 1928, question 1287; CO 760/12 minutes of 36th meeting of Board 1 May 1929; Tallents Papers File 5; CO 760/7/696.

105 Tallents Papers Files 7 and 12. *Punch* published a Bernard Partridge cartoon, 16 Aug. 1933, 183, depicting the Prime Minister as a schoolmaster in a classroom embellished with an EMB poster-map. 'Mrs Britannia: "I'm so disappointed, Mr MacDonald. Just when my little Johnny was getting so interested in his geography lesson I hear you are going to discontinue them next term." '

106 EMB Nos. 19, 28, 41, 53, 63.

107 CO 760/7/655; *Further Changes in the Demand for Butter*, EMB No. 48, 1932; *Select Committee on Estimates*, 1932, question 304. Other EMB reports dealt with the demand for cheese in London EMB No. 22, canned fruits EMB No. 37, honey EMB No. 50, canned vegetables EMB No. 56 and South African fruits EMB No. 70.

108 Figures calculated from *Statistical Abstract for the British Empire 1925–34*, Cmd.5016, 1935 and from Drummond, *British Economic Policy and the Empire*, 20–1; also see *Changes in the Demand for Butter* EMB No. 39, 1931, *Further Changes*, EMB No. 48, 1932.

109 Tallents Papers File 14 29–30; CO 760/22/PC/78; CO 760/3/226; *Select Committee on Estimates*, 1928, xvii and question 1631.

110 This argument echoes that in Abercrombie, Hill and Turner, *The Dominant Ideology Thesis*.

111 CO 760/22/PC/130, 23 Jan. 1930.

CHAPTER 10

CITIZENS OF THE EMPIRE
BADEN-POWELL, SCOUTS AND GUIDES AND AN IMPERIAL IDEAL, 1900–40

Allen Warren

'Imperialism is above all who share it a form of passionate feeling; it is a political religion, for it is public spirit touched with emotion.' (A. V. Dicey, *Lectures on the Relation Between Law and Public Opinion in England during the Nineteenth Century*, 2nd edn, 1914 London, 457.)

'Imperialism if we regard it properly is not a creed or a principle, but an attitude of mind.' (John Buchan, *A Lodge in the Wilderness*, London 1906, 77.)

'Imperialism, we decided, was the realisation of new conditions for all our problems, an enlarged basis, a fuller data ... Imperialism, so ran our conclusion, is a spiritual change.' (*Ibid.*, 251.)

'But better than the civilisation and weary routine of business and social life at home, I like the fact that "over there" there are still new open spaces to be explored and developed, adventure and hardship to be faced and then the unique joy and satisfaction that results from successfully overcoming them ...'

'Empire is not a Jingo term meaning that we want to spread ourselves aggressively over vast territories in rivalry with others – it stands for team work of free young British nations growing up in different parts of the world in friendly comradeship of goodwill and co-operation.' (R. S. S. Baden-Powell, draft contribution to *Empire Book: Your Empire* in The Scout Association Archives, Baden-Powell House, Queensgate, London, subsequently referred to as SAA.)

The historian of any aspect of British imperial experience immediately faces a perplexing problem as he begins his researches. On the one hand he has a vast literature of what the British Empire actually meant in administrative, strategic, diplomatic, military and economic terms. As a result, he quickly becomes enmeshed in the thickets of historical debate about the imperialism of free trade, or the 'blue water' versus the continental theories of defence, or the Hobsonian and anti-Hobsonian arguments over economic determinants of Empire. On the other hand, few historians have studied the nature of imperial sentiment itself as a bundle of cultural modes, each extending and reinforcing one another, and which clearly became one of the dominant (if at times unarticulated) elements in popular thinking between 1890 and 1950. And should the historian be blamed for neglecting the big questions, when the records of the Foreign, War, Colonial and Indian Offices remain so unexplored and so pleasingly concrete? Furthermore would a study of the nature of the imperial frame of mind get the researcher very far, given the quotations at the head of this essay? If intelligent and discriminating contemporary imperial enthusiasts could only articulate vague 'feelings' or 'emotions' about the relations between Britain and the various elements of her Empire what hope the humble and distanced historian of such a protean phenomenon?

There are of course honourable exceptions to the picture just described – historians who have attempted to articulate the unspoken assumptions behind the imperial attitude. The work of Koebner and Schmidt in 1964 was a pioneering attempt at the history of cultural language. The late Eric Stokes was certainly appraised of the problem as he demonstrated in his sensitive and illuminating inaugural lecture on 'The political ideas of English imperialism', published in 1960. Stokes there made the crucial point that 'Imperialism was above all an unformulated philosophy of life and politics' and one feels that Stokes could have been a guest of Francis Carey in John Buchan's *A Lodge in the Wilderness*. Similarly, A. P. Thornton has explored the intellectual substructure of imperial activity in numerous books and articles emphasising, amongst much else, that imperialism became a central part of the ideology of the British governing classes from at least the early 1890s until the 1950s. Sir Nicholas Mansergh has also emphasised, in his studies on the evolution of the Commonwealth, the variety of imperial moods and their contradictions and more recently Dr Thomas Dunne amongst others has presented imperialism as part of a distinctive English nationalism.[1]

This connection with national sentiment also helps to make the familiar point that imperialism, as a set of popular responses, had both an outward and inward eye, both an external and domestic dimension and that any exploration of its meaning needs to take account of each of its aspects. As a result connections can be made across the line which too frequently divides historians of foreign and colonial policy from domestic political and social practitioners. Thus Bernard Semmel and H. C. G. Matthew have shown in different ways how the pervasive imperial sentiment of the Edwardian years was used both by those who wished to encourage ideas of social reform untinged with the charge of radicalism or socialism and also by those trying

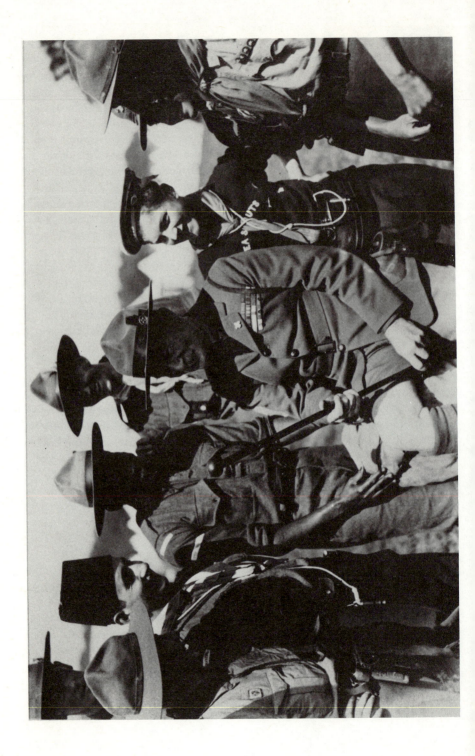

to refashion a comprehensive Liberal ideology in the place of what was seen as a narrow and disabling Gladstonianism. Amongst social historians also, there has been an increasing interest in the popular manifestations of imperial enthusiasm – Mafeking crowds, the Empire Day organisation and youth movements – as well as in the more difficult question of how far this many faceted phenomenon became a significant feature of the popular mind. Recent research in this area has included work on the nature of the educational syllabus, the style and content of children's literature and the social influence of an upper class governing ethic, some of which is reflected in the contributions to this volume. Much of this social history has tended to concentrate upon the years prior to 1914 and perhaps not surprisingly has emphasised the introverted and defensive aspect of imperial attitudes at home in the years of anxiety and introspection which followed the Boer War.[2]

It is this interest in the social aspects of the imperial frame of mind that has prompted this essay, since there are few developments of the years before 1914 that seem to exemplify more clearly the popular face of imperialism than the twin creations of the defender of Mafeking – the Scouting and Guiding movements. The content of the first edition of Baden-Powell's handbook, *Scouting for Boys*, published in early 1908, and his later collaborative work with his sister Agnes, *The Handbook for Girl Guides or How Girls can help build the Empire*, published in 1912 seem to confirm fully an impression of an essentially defensive domestic ideology underpinning both of these organisations for children and young people. It has certainly seemed so to most historians. Sidney Hynes was in no doubt when he wrote that *Scouting for Boys* represented 'a crude and insistent expression of Tory Imperialism' and John Springhall was only slightly less confident in his portrait of the youth movements founded before 1914 as being essentially concerned with 'the problem of establishing the hegemony of the dominant ideology over the rising generation'. More recently, in one of the few comments from feminist historians about the largest single sex organisation for girls, Carol Dyhouse places the Girl Guide movement firmly within a pattern of conservative and social Darwinian assumptions.[3]

Undoubtedly, there are elements of a defensive domestic imperialism to be found in the early writings of Baden-Powell and in some of the social sentiments which responded to his ideas about the need for boy training. But as with other aspects of popular imperialism, historical attention has tended to be concentrated rather exclusively upon the years before 1914 and upon Great Britain itself and this has had the effect of obscuring the variety

---

Baden-Powell symbolising the international fellowship of scouting at the Imperial Jamboree, Wembley, August 1924. By courtesy of The Scout Association.

of imperial sentiment and opinion. In addition, too close attention to the earliest writings of Baden-Powell ignores the fact that his own opinions, imperial or otherwise, were not static but proved to be capable of evolution and development in response to changing perceptions about the purposes of Scouts and Guides. It is also sometimes forgotten that as organisations for the young they proved to be both genuinely imperial and international, attracting adults and children throughout the English speaking world as well as in Europe. Similarly, as organisations they survived the reactions against popular patriotism which followed the First World War, the Guide movement in particular experiencing a rapid expansion both at home and abroad throughout the 1920s. In fact, the Scout and Guide movements were in many ways at their most 'imperial' between about 1920 and 1955 which suggests that their ideological underpinnings may be a little more complex than they have seemed to those who have confined their attentions to the years before 1914. Finally, both organisations were in a real sense 'popular' drawing support and membership, if differentially, from all levels of society from royal patrons and presidents alongside powerful ecclesiastics and politicians to ordinary men and women in middle- and lower middle-class England and throughout the Empire, whose perceptions of what they were doing in their leisure time were often rather different from those of, say, the Prince of Wales or Cosmo Gordon Lang. And this is still to neglect the children and young people themselves, who leave few impressions of what they saw as being done to or for them as a result of their membership. It should not surprise historians, therefore, if the views of commissioners and patrons and the policy emanating from the Imperial Headquarters were not always understood, or indeed accepted as relevant, by those far from the centre of things. Voluntary organisations have long and often flawed lines of communications and little power to coerce so that variety often has to be accepted rather controlled, divergence contained rather than condemned, with an at times resigned recognition that Batley is not the same as Bloemfontein, Manchester not comparable with Madras.

This chapter will explore some of the themes and variations of popular imperialism as revealed by the history and development of the Scout and Guide movements within the Empire. Much of what follows will be necessarily impressionistic, as little research has been done previously. For instance, hardly any work has been undertaken on the history of the Girl Guide movement, either officially or by social historians. The history of Scouting and Guiding within British dominions and colonies has been little examined and the resources for so doing are expensively scattered. The study of children's and young people's impressions and attitudes is also a peculiarly difficult form of social history which even the techniques of the oral historian only partially overcome. What follows therefore inevitably reflects a British and 'Imperial Headquarters' bias because that mirrors the materials at this author's disposal but there is no obvious reason for believing that the headquarters' view was always out of touch with the grass-roots or that policy was never effective. Although each may be operating in different spheres the evidence suggests that both headquarters and the grass-roots knew at least in part what the other was up to and responded accordingly.

The chapter will be divided into four sections. In the first there will be an examination of the imperial elements within Baden-Powell's thinking and how they were developed after the initial reception of his book, *Scouting for Boys*. Then will follow an analysis of the views and policies of the headquarters of the Boy Scouts and Girl Guides as they expanded and extended their activities and responsibilities after 1910 and also how they formulated a 'Scouting and Guiding philosophy' in the light of these developments. There will then be a treatment of how the Scout movement was actually taken up within the Empire and the implications for those in London trying to respond to those initiatives. The essay will conclude with some suggestions as to the impact of those imperial concerns upon the individual adult and child involved in the movements. In an essay of this length this final section can really only hint at the springs of what enabled Scouts and Guides to expand, adapt and survive throughout the three-quarters of a century which has followed their founding and which has seen the rise and fall of imperial sentiment both in Britain and the Empire. That both these organisations have outgrown their apparently imperial origins suggests that the cultural sources of their foundation and development are more complex than some historians have assumed.

Baden-Powell's imperial thinking

In many ways Baden-Powell is an excellent case study of the popular impact of the various strands which made up the imperial enthusiasm in the years which followed the Boer War. Unlike the other men quoted at the head of this essay, Baden-Powell was neither a politician nor a systematic commentator upon contemporary affairs. Following a fairly routine military career from the late 1870s, largely in colonial or Indian postings, he was suddenly projected into the public eye by the siege of Mafeking between 1899 and 1900, an experience which made him an almost exemplary imperial hero, a worthy successor of Havelock and Gordon. As a career soldier he had not reflected much upon either domestic or colonial affairs before his return home from South Africa in 1902 to take up the position of Inspector-General of Cavalry. In this post he was a prominent public and popular figure and the years from 1902 until 1908 mark his effective apprenticeship in the domestic concerns of Edwardian England, an involvement which led him to launch his experimental scheme of *Scouting for Boys* early in 1908. The particular qualities which Baden-Powell possessed in large measure were those of the populariser and the journalist, and his writings, of which there was an enormous quantity in the years following 1908, tends to reflect immediate contemporary concerns both domestically and imperially. It is not surprising that they can often be intellectually inconsistent, given their sheer quantity and that they were composed over a period of thirty years and for a range of potential listeners which extended from a weekly column for boys in the *Scout* to carefully constructed 'political' documents for the benefit of governments both in Britain and in the dominions.[4]

Having said this, amidst the mass of Baden-Powell's carbon copies, strands of continuing concern can be found which clearly informed his thoughts and attitudes in a whole variety of circumstances. First, there is a consistent corporatism about politics both national and imperial and a constant reiteration of the need for social and political unity against dangers both external and subversive. 'We are all bricks in the wall', is a constantly reiterated metaphor, and each citizen was urged to see him or herself as part of the national team playing the great game. This combination of social corporatism and public school language could extend from fears about German spies between 1906–8 (the 2nd edition of Baden-Powell's military manual *Aids to Scouting* repeated the old chestnut of German governesses being undercover agents) to the dangers from Bolshevism in the early 1920s. Similarly, it could be expressed at times of domestic political or social difficulty, fuelling Baden-Powell's dislike of faddist and socialist politics, and exposing elements of hysteria in his personality, as in the crisis over munitions production in early 1915.[5]

Secondly, throughout Baden-Powell's writings there is an enthusiasm for social and personal health with warnings about decadence and unhealthy living. For instance, he seized eagerly in 1907 on Elliot Mills' anonymously published *The Decline and Fall of the British Empire* as the basis for much of what he wrote on patriotic instruction in *Scouting for Boys* with all its simple-minded concentration on healthy attitudes as the basis of national strength. Similarly the idea of efficiency, so widely canvassed in all sections of political and social opinion in the years after 1902, is also much employed. Again, ideas of a healthy population with all their eugenic undertones inform much of Baden-Powell's writings for girls and their future responsibilities as the wives and mothers of the race. Finally, it would come as no surprise that Baden-Powell from the late 1920s was an enthusiastic supporter of the Fitness Campaign in Britain. This in its turn led him to have a rather ambivalent attitude towards the well-presented propaganda of the totalitarian youth movements in Germany, Italy and Czechoslovakia. On the one hand it seemed to show that there were standards of national fitness beyond anything that had been achieved in

1930s Britain. On the other, closer acquaintance with organisations like the Ballila highlighted their essentially gimcrack methods, quite alien to British voluntary tradition and to Baden-Powell's own individualistic educational philosophy.[6]

Thirdly, Baden-Powell consistently preached in favour of social and racial harmony and inveighed against both class and colour prejudice. Although frequently using the language of public school teamsmanship Baden-Powell was not uncritical of English upper middle-class education with its excessive concentration on irrelevant classical knowledge, team sports and good form, all of which he saw as excluding useful knowledge and pastimes, individual instruction and a dedication to personal service. As a result Baden-Powell remained a constant critic of the absurdities and snobbism of the English class system and unrepentently philistine in matters of good taste and high art. Possibly as a reaction to his own socially and economically insecure career in the Army, as a cavalry officer with no private means, Baden-Powell was always enthusiastic about what he saw as the natural equality and uncluttered nature of colonial life. As the Scout movement extended throughout the Empire he found no difficulty, therefore, in enlarging his fourth law for Scouts from 'A Scout is a friend to all and a brother to every other Scout, no matter to what class the other may belong' to 'A Scout is a brother . . . no matter to what country, class or creed the other may belong'. At a more personal level this unease with the English class system and its conventions was expressed through Baden-Powell's own highly idiosyncratic attitude to dress and occasion which showed both a military fussiness about detail and an extravagance and theatricality in which he could invest considerable emotional capital. Above all, in the cult of the camp was to be found his educational ideal of a free community of equal brothers, symbolic of a social and racial harmony and exemplified in the great international jamboree camps which were a feature of Scouting between the wars.[7]

The fourth theme which emerges from this mass of occasional writings is a highly personal approach to the character training of the young. I have argued elsewhere that it was from his military experience of reconnaissance and scouting that Baden-Powell developed his hostility to uniform drill-based instruction and mass methods of education, on to which he grafted an essentially popularised idea of character training for boys. Despite his belief in social corporatism Baden-Powell always remained hostile to rote learning whether in the schoolroom, army class or youth brigade. In his scheme of things, instruction took place in small groups or patrols with individual personal attention being given to each Scout either by his patrol leader or his scout master who had to have a natural sympathy with the young if they were to be effective in bringing out each child's talents. Individual character had to be developed to encourage initiative and self-reliance, eschewing charity or state support. Baden-Powell had little use for social explanations of personal inadequacy or for political remedies for social ills, relying on more familiar mid-Victorian ideals of self-help and personal independence. Despite this latter traditionalism, the fundamental individualism of Baden-Powell's methods gave his approach a highly progressive and innovatory gloss in the years which followed 1910.[8]

The final element which constantly appears in Baden-Powell's writings is a continuing suspicion of the debilitating effects of urban society and an enthusiasm for the open-air life, whether on the frontiers of the Empire or in the countryside of Britain. Baden-Powell feared that urban life was fundamentally undermining the willingness and ability of the young to pursue active, healthy and purposive lives. Thus he always railed against spectator as against participatory sports and presented the fag-smoking, slouching loafer as the object of his comic ridicule. Similarly female cosmetics and impractical if fashionable women's clothes were a butt for his humour. On the other hand, life on the frontier (often no doubt idealised) was held up as exemplary, as a place where individual freedom and talent could be best cultivated, and where an active and healthy (if philistine) citizenry developed. Complementing this enthusiasm for the frontier life, Baden-Powell also possessed a considerable responsiveness to the natural world as both a painter and sportsman. The study of natural history and the value of the direct contact with the out-of-doors were strongly etched features not only in *Scouting for Boys* but in all Baden-Powell's writings, and this enabled him to respond fully to the cult of nature and the enthusiasm for the open air which marked so much of the thinking of the Scouts and Guides and other educational movements for the young after 1916.[9]

These different and at times conflicting concerns within Baden-Powell's thinking, with their balance of domestic anxiety and colonial enthusiasm, gave Baden-Powell a flexible armoury whereby his thinking about Scouting and Guiding could readily and with apparent consistency respond as the nature and the extent of the two movements changed, and of which the many editions (with amendments) of *Scouting for Boys* give evidence. For instance, the stridently defensive tones of the first edition about the dangers to the Empire at home are already being toned down a year later in the second edition. Now juvenile unemployment, not slackness, is taken as the evidence of social and political decadence in the home country and the colonial world is presented as the place of real opportunity for the boy of character. Two years later, in the 1911 edition, the heading 'National deterioration' is deleted altogether. In the same year Baden-Powell had to prepare a Canadian edition of his manual as his ideas were taken up in the dominions. Given his views on the virtues of frontier life certain sections of the original were hardly appropriate and so the passages on social decadence and the decline in citizenship were omitted, as were those dealing with the debilitating effects of spectator sports, the fears concerning a divided society and the query 'Is our disease fatal?' Instead, colonial life is recommended for its youthful and vigorous qualities, uncluttered by social class or convention, drawing as it does upon the traditional virtues of the trapper, pioneer and frontiersman, a theme also taken up in Baden-Powell's speeches in Britain and on his North American tour in 1912. Already therefore by 1911, Baden-Powell had shifted the balance of his imperial concern from a defensive domesticity to a positive imperialism presented in terms of individual and social opportunity with a reiterated emphasis on the need to think imperially and not parochially.[10]

This elasticity of thinking enabled Baden-Powell to escape from the cul-de-sacs which trapped the more doctrinaire elements within the cadet and patriotic training lobbies before 1914. In the middle of the Great War Baden-Powell declined to be associated with a pressure group led by the Dean of Lincoln and Lord Sydenham (the latter a keen supporter of military training for the young) in their attempts to encourage the teaching of patriotic values. After the war Baden-Powell (perhaps not surprisingly having been declared Chief Scout of the World at Olympia in 1920) also resisted the blandishments of the Society of St George, arguing that true patriotic teaching could only come through conduct and action rather than through formal instruction or a reformed syllabus. Therefore even before 1914, Scouting and Guiding could be presented in a dual guise as they spread across the Empire. On the one hand, through their emphasis on personal service and brotherhood, they were an ideal vehicle of socio-political consolidation in divided and multi-racial societies, whether that society be all white like Canada with its French dimension, multi-racial and dependent like India or effectively independent like South Africa. On the other, Scouting and Guiding could also be presented as genuinely imperial, an effective creative cement for the emerging commonwealth of nations, itself presented as a living embodiment of Scouting's multi-racial ideals.[11]

Baden-Powell's own personal imperial commitment was expressed through Scouting and Guiding and remained largely free standing, and he rarely committed himself to other imperial organisations (although his support for the Empire Marketing Board and the Tudor Rose League in 1931 and 1932 is an exception). In the main his activities were conducted at a more symbolic level. In particular he was always keen to associate the royal family with the Scout and Guide movement. Each Scout and Guide in their Promise committed themselves to serve the King who was presented as the exemplar of the imperial ideal. In its turn the royal family willingly accepted this association. Almost all of the children of George V were connected in one way or another with the Scouting and Guiding movements, most notably the Prince of Wales and Princess Mary. On the return from his imperial tour of 1922, the Prince of Wales was greeted by a

Posse of Welcome of 60,000 Scouts and the occasion was used for the Prince (as Chief Scout of Wales) to appear in Scout uniform for the first time. At the Imperial Jamboree associated with the 1924 Imperial Exhibition, the Prince spent a much publicised night in camp joining in the communal fraternity of the camp fire. In the same way, Princess Mary visibly identified herself with the Guide movement in the 1920s, frequently attending Guide rallies and meetings as the Association's President. It is no coincidence that at least part of the monies donated as a wedding present to the Princess by all the Maries of the Empire should be given to the Girl Guide Association to purchase their international training centre at Foxlease. The quasi-royal and symbolically imperial associations were also made in the personal lives of Baden-Powell and his wife, Olave. Throughout the interwar period until their retirement to Kenya in 1938 the Baden-Powells were almost constantly on the move through their international tours, which predominantly took them to the dominions and colonies. Their lives and personages, weighed down with imperial honours, became those of honorary imperial citizens, received almost like heads of state, entertained at Government House, addressing great gatherings of the influential as well as rallies of Scouts and Guides, and acknowledging the crowds as they progressed. Furthermore these visits usually served an additional political purpose. As the head and founder of the two organisations, 'state visits' from the Baden-Powells were often utilised as an occasion to try and reconcile the inherent tensions within Scouting and Guiding which were thrown up in less racially harmonious societies like India and South Africa. By the mid-1930s Baden-Powell both preached and represented an ideal of a multi-racial Commonwealth which was very different from the essentially defensive imperialism which can be found in the first edition of *Scouting for Boys*. That he was able to fulfil that role was in part due to his great skills as a public figure and actor but it also resulted from the flexibility of opinions expressed in his voluminous writings.[12]

The view from imperial headquarters

The imperial role lived out by Baden-Powell in his latter years was continued by his successors as Chief Scout. Lords Somers, Rowallan and Sir Charles Maclean were all Chief Scouts of the Commonwealth and in the case of Lord Rowallan in particular the bulk of his time as Chief Scout between 1945 and 1959 was spent in these world tours. Similarly the Headquarters of the Scout Association remained 'Imperial' until 1966 and the Headquarters of the Girl Guide Association is still that of the Commonwealth while the Scout Association retains a Commonwealth Commissioner in London responsible for the few remaining dependent branches. These appointments make the point that from almost the beginning of both organisations there was an important imperial dimension to their work which profoundly conditioned their imperial thinking. As early as its Annual Report for 1912 Scouting was already being presented as a way to consolidate the Empire and proof of its success was seen by the early 1930s in its a million and a half members within Britain and the Empire.

Given this, it is perhaps rather surprising how little imperial enthusiasm is evident in the actions of the governing committee of the Scout Association (the Girl Guides are a slight exception to this until 1916). Contrary to the impression given in some of the historical writing about the Scouts, the governing committee, constituted after the Crystal Palace Rally in 1909, was not made up of militant imperialists and supporters of the National Service League. In fact, the 'working' members of the committee were cautious, pragmatic and unideological men. For instance, although the Scouts had taken a full part in the Empire Day parade in 1909 before the committee was constituted, in 1910 no formal arrangement was made and the Scouts took no official part in the Empire Festival later in the same year, participation being left as matter for local decision. In 1911 the Committee again declined an offer to organise the Empire Day parade in London and two years later also refused an invitation to participate in the Imperial Services Exhibition, preferring to hold its own exhibition at Birmingham, which included little that suggested an imperialistic purpose. It was not until 1915 that the Association agreed to celebrate Empire Day in association with the League of Empire in London, an unpopular decision as it came in the middle of the camping season and was organised on very military lines. In 1912 the Committee of the Council decided not to adopt Elgar's 'Land of Hope and Glory' as the Boy Scout March and after the war it refused a closer association with the British Empire Union. Imperial enthusiasts on the governing committee, like Lord Meath, had relatively little influence on the policy of the Association despite his being prominently placed as the Commissioner for Ireland, and even Maj.-Gen. Sir Edmund Elles, who was an active National Service League supporter and very much a working member of the Committee of the Council was not able either to push his colleagues in a more committed direction or bend Baden-Powell to his way of thinking.[13]

The reasons for this are complex. In the first place, many of Baden-Powell's close collaborators at headquarters were men for whom the Scouting scheme was not understood primarily as a means of consolidating the Empire or creating an imperial citizenry. It was also a result of the rapid spread of Scouting through the dominions themselves and an awareness on the part of the headquarters that the social context in which Scouting was developing varied immensely from one country to the next and that the capacity of Imperial Headquarters to lay down detailed and effective policy was strictly limited.

In Great Britain, for instance, the most persistent worry for the governing

Committee before 1920 was the accusation that the Scouts were the stalking horse for the cadet movements and constituted a dangerous and militaristic innovation. On the other hand, in Australia, New Zealand and South Africa the problem was the opposite, in trying to find a place for Scouting in societies which had already embraced the military through the introduction of compulsory cadet training. In the same way, the problem of securing the support of the churches and denominations in Britain was not paralleled to anything like the same extent in the dominions where racial and national issues were more pressing.

Finally, this undoctrinaire approach to Empire was linked to the fact that its principal policy makers did not see it serving other purposes through the imperial connection. There is almost none of the Christian evangelism which characterised much of the writing of churchmen and public school headmasters about the Empire in the first decade of the century and although a considerable amount of the religious and spiritual writing about the purposes of Scouting is expressed in the language of Christian knight errantry this is rarely put within an imperial context. It is an interesting fact that many of its sympathisers were more keen on Scouting's imperial possibilities than were its active workers – a point perhaps best made through a comparison of language and tone of Cosmo Gordon Lang's sermon and Baden-Powell's text prepared for the Prince of Wales' address to the Scouts at the Imperial Jamboree in London in 1924.[14]

The early history of the Girl Guides, however, presents a slightly different picture. Baden-Powell had not given any thought while writing *Scouting for Boys* to the question of whether such a scheme would be similarly attractive to girls, although his early reactions to the idea were positive, as it became clear that a programme which combined games and an outdoor training with a gloss of nursing and ambulance work could have such an appeal. A number of Girl Scouts appeared at the Crystal Palace Rally in September 1909 and as a result Baden-Powell agreed to provide some guidelines for those wishing to work with girls. As he had little interest or expertise in the field, the result was a rather thin pamphlet of suggestions put together with his sister in late 1909. What was clear was that the boy and girl Scouts had to be separated as soon as possible, and that Scouts and Girl Guides should not train or camp together. At a time when the Scout Committee was desperately trying to establish their own public credibility and respectability *vis-à-vis* the churches, a reputation for coeducational experimentation would have quickly identified the Scouts as a quirky, progressive off-shoot from the mainstream of those concerned with the 'boy problem'. Baden-Powell was also clearly worried that his Girl Guides would be similarly regarded, at a time when the women's issue was at the forefront of public attention. He therefore had to inveigh against girls behaving like 'tomboys' and emphasised in his early writings for girls the separate and distinctive responsibilities of women as wives and mothers, for which a different training was appropriate.[15]

It was not a very satisfactory compromise. Many of those who had wanted to be Girl Scouts did not like being transformed into Girl Guides and Baden-Powell's own lack of interest and assurance in the sphere of girl training meant that as an organisation it did not experience anything like the early rapid growth of the Scouts. Until the middle years of the First World War the Girl Guides remained a small patriotic and imperial organisation with strong links with the Primrose League and the Girls' Patriotic League. The early covers of the *Girl Guide Gazette* bore the motto 'King, God, and Empire' and the annual celebration of Empire Day gave the Guides more in common with the Junior Associates of the Victoria League than with the Scouts. Estimates of its membership numbers vary but it is unlikely that there were more than 40,000 Girl Guides by 1916.[16]

With the coming of the First World War, public perception about the value of girl training changed. In the first place, it established the place of non-military civilian service at home for both boys and girls as part of the total mobilisation of people and resources for war and it also identified a specific role for women as back-up support through nursing, ambulance and orderly work behind the front lines. The war also altered opinions as to the kind of work that women, particularly middle-class women, could do and even if it was not followed by a permanent shift in attitudes to paid work, it certainly enabled women to engage in a wider variety of voluntary effort. In addition, from early 1916 there developed a considerable public interest in the need to train the young for the postwar world and a strong belief emerged, affecting both Scouts and Guides, that this training should be more 'natural', that urbanisation had been responsible for many of the prewar militaristic attitudes, and that civilisation needed healing through a change in the balance of educational forces. Baden-Powell himself was sensitive to these changes in public mood and decided upon a major reorganisation and alteration in Girl Guide philosophy from 1916. His sister, Agnes, was gradually moved to one side and replaced by his young and energetic wife; a county pattern of organisation like that of the Scouts was introduced; the imperial gloss to Guiding was toned down and Baden-Powell wrote his own handbook for girls. This volume, while still acknowledging a separate sphere for women and the need of training for the unique responsibility of motherhood, also incorporated many of the 'male' activities which had been included in *Scouting for Boys* and in its emphasis on the frontier life pointed up the basic equality of status and importance of men and women as comrades and collaborators through life. These changes were combined with a philosophy of training in and through nature and the out of doors (the equivalent of the woodcraft enthusiasm for boys), and resulted in a dramatic expansion in the numbers of girls joining and women volunteering to run and organise their activities. By 1918 home numbers had almost trebled to 80,000 and the expansion continued for the next decade, reaching 494,000 by 1932 with an additional 152,000 within the dominions.[17] Therefore from the 1920s onwards the two organisations could run in parallel, representing the ideals of liberal imperialism expressed through a multi-racial harmony and an active citizenry, symbolised by the constant activity of the two Chiefs as World Chief Scout (until his death in 1941) and World Chief Guide (until her death in 1977).

In each case the Imperial Headquarters was the central policy-making body, exercising a necessarily loose-reined control as the two movements strove to accommodate the variety of local circumstances throughout the Empire. In fact tensions between the home association and abroad were relatively infrequent. In part this was due to a common fraternity and also because the dominions at least were largely left to get on with their own affairs, facing as they often did more urgent local problems of race, creed or colour. In any case, there was considerable respect for the founder country, something which was increased by the establishing of a common pattern of training for scout masters throughout the Empire – the Wood Badge. From the woodcraft training centre at Gilwell Park in Essex, successive camp chiefs saw it as their responsibility to tour the developing world, encouraging this common training, thereby complementing the more quasi-regal progresses of the Baden-Powells. At a time of woodcraft enthusiasm during the 1920s and '30s, Gilwell Park also came to represent a kind of arcadian shrine for some leaders, something reinforced by Baden-Powell's own personal identification with the place, in his title of Lord Baden-Powell of Gilwell and through his frequent presence there at the annual reunion of Wood Badge holders.

During the 1920s this sense of imperial consolidation was reinforced by the most visible sign of confraternity, emigration. Even before 1914 the Boy Scout Association had run for a few years a farm training school on Scout lines at Buckhurst Place in Kent, designed to equip city boys for future agricultural work at home (if the anticipated return to the land materialised) and within the Empire. As an experimental community it had fallen victim to the dislocating effects of war. After 1922, however, the direct personal links with the Empire were more formalised through the establishing of a Migration Department at Imperial Scout Headquarters. Under the terms of the Empire Settlement Act, 1922, the Association became one of the voluntary managing agencies for imperial settlement and during the next seven or eight years some 5,000 Scouts emigrated to the dominions under the scheme's auspices. The overwhelming majority (3,400) were settled in Australia, and in the case of Victoria a distinctively

Scouting scheme of reception and employment was set up – attempting to give the brotherhood of Scouting an imperial reality. These latter arrangements were not really a success, requiring much greater supervision and control than a voluntary organisation could supply. Scouts settled with co-operative farmers left for the city and gave no forwarding address, Scouting volunteers were not necessarily near the settlement farms, and there was no effective machinery for solving the day to day problems of settling young men into a new environment. It was with some relief that this particular scheme was wound up as economic conditions worsened in the early 1930s and as domestic Australian resistance to emigration increased. In fact the work of the Scout migration department under the Empire Settlement Act had almost totally dried up by 1931, as individual dominions looked to their own interests at a time of high unemployment. Baden-Powell attempted to encourage the Dominions Office to take a new initiative, but little had changed by the outbreak of war. It was a cause of regret to Baden-Powell and his associates that economic circumstances had frustrated this element within their imperial idealism, given that it not only highlighted the increasing autonomy of individual dominions, but also removed the element in Baden-Powell's thinking which had seen the possibility of a healthy and open-air frontier life as an antidote to over-urbanised and over-populated Britain.[18]

The links between Scouting and emigration did not entirely cease with World War II. The Victorian emigration scheme was revived in 1956, once conditions for Australian settlement had become favourable again, but only some dozen Scouts took advantage of the provisions and after 1959 any Scout enquiries were dealt with by the Big Brother Movement (another settlement organisation established in 1925 to assist the emigration of British boys to Australia). The Association also had links with the Fairbridge Society, whose object was to encourage the filling of the open spaces of the Empire with British stock. Starting in 1912 the Society (which was a memorial to one of the earliest Rhodes Scholars – Kingsley Fairbridge) established a number of farm schools in Canada, New Zealand and Southern Rhodesia for the training and settling of children in the imperial territories. In 1946 the Boy Scout Association (which had donated £10,000 from monies received in a bequest to the Rhodesia Fairbridge Memorial College) entered into partnership with the College and between 1946 and 1952 some thirty-seven Scouts and twenty-nine Cubs were placed in the school. However, the demand for the settlement of children (as distinct from families) had largely dried up postwar, and the scheme was concluded in 1956. The whole period of Scout involvement with migration had shown how fragile were fraternal imperial links when faced with adverse economic circumstances and a growing national self-consciousness amongst the dominions themselves.[19]

The influence of the Empire

So far, this essay has been concerned largely with a British-centred view of how Scouting and Guiding fitted into and contributed to a developing imperial mentality from 1910 until the early 1950s. Now it is proposed to see how that ideology actually fared within some of the very different conditions which obtained throughout the Empire. The expansion of Scouting and Guiding within the Empire was largely an interwar phenomenon and was concentrated in the dominions and Indian Empire and, not surprisingly, its social corporatism and ideals of a shared brotherhood between all races and religions quickly became enmeshed in the domestic socio-political concerns of the territories in which it had taken root. On the whole that development was reasonably smooth in Australia and New Zealand. In both dominions the principal barrier to the growth of Scouting and Guiding had come before 1914 with the introduction of compulsory cadet training. This had seriously reduced Scout numbers in New Zealand, effectively confining boy member-ship to those below the age of fourteen and also reducing the numbers of adult volunteers to lead the movement. Once these barriers were removed numbers were able to expand rapidly after 1918. In Canada it was much the same story, although the picture was complicated by the increasingly articulate French presence which saw Scouting as an essentially alien and imperial import. Baden-Powell toured Canada four times between 1912 and 1935, and particularly in 1919 emphasised the role that Scouting and Guiding could play 'in Canadianising the many foreign elements within its population'. Only through playing Scout games, outside the school walls, could 'the rising generation . . . rapidly lose the national prejudices that separate their elders'.[20] But it was, above all, in India and South Africa that the Scout movement became entangled in the politics of racial and national development. In India as in other parts of the Empire, Scouting had been rapidly adopted by the British and Eurasian communities and the question of forming native patrols arose quickly. Elsewhere in the Empire the government had far less official interest in the development of Scouting but in India the Viceroy (Lord Hardinge) was quite clear that native Scout patrols should not be encouraged. The question arose again in 1916 and the Viceroy (Lord Chelmsford) in refusing to sanction native Scouts expressed the view that it would expose them to dangerous influences. The result of the Indian government trying to ban native Scouts meant that the movement developed plurally and outside the control of Imperial Headquarters. By the end of the First World War there were four or five separate Scouting organisations within India, including both that founded by Annie Besant (the Indian Boy Scout Association) and those in fact enrolling native boys (e.g., the Seva Samiti). Nor did the question of official approval disappear. Lord Chelmsford's refusal had been provoked by the threat that Lord Pentland was about to start Scouting amongst native boys and Baden-Powell also asked Sir Michael Sadler (a long-standing Scout sympathiser) to consider the question while conducting his official enquiry into Indian education. In August 1917 the Commander in Chief in India, attempting to hold the situation, forbade all army officers to hold appointments within the Boy Scout Association, but this had little effect in damping down the demand for native Scouting, which both Sadler and Baden-Powell now supported. By the end of 1918 it had become clear that, regardless of the government's attitude, the YMCA, which had always been an enthusiastic supporter of Baden-Powell's ideas, was going to start native troops, and that unless some attempt was made to rationalise the position, the development of Scouting in the subcontinent would get out of control. As a result the Indian government changed tack and paid for Baden-Powell to come out to India in order to effect a reconciliation between the various associations. The result was the formation of the All India Council for Scouts in 1921 with the Viceroy as the Chief Scout of India, to which Mrs Besant brought her own organisation of 20,000 members.

The emergence of the All-India Council was the occasion for an almost complete turn about in the attitude of the government of India towards native Scouting. Previously regarding it as potentially subversive, it now saw the Scouting philosophy as a potential ally in the continuing battle between imperial control and the rising tide of nationalism, represented in Scouting terms by the Seva Samiti, who had not affiliated to the All India Council. As a result Scouting became officially encouraged and funded so that by 1937 there were 326,000 Scouts throughout the sub-continent, largely linked to the schools. However there had been little progress in the reconciliation of Scouting and the nationalists and Imperial Headquarters saw the movement in India as propped up by government funding, which would cease once the Congress achieved a political majority. There was an urgent need, if Scouting was to survive in India, for it to Indianise fully so that the continuing challenge of Seva Samiti with its advantages of Congress and Hindu support could be contained. However attempts to incorporate the Seva Samiti into an all-India organisation again failed at the second Scouters Round Table Conference in 1938; the oath to the King-Emperor remaining an insuperable stumbling block. In the case of India, therefore, the Scout movement paid the price of government interference before 1921, and thereafter a too close association with the imperial power for its own good.

In South Africa the Scout movement faced many of the same difficulties over nationality and colour that it did in India but in a slightly different configuration. At first Scouts in certain states of the Union, like Natal, had cadet rivals, but they did not have to cope with government opposition on the question of native Scouts. Less fearful of the political threat posed by the black population, the Governor-General established a separate Pathfinder Movement for native boys in 1918. This initiative was opposed by some whites and Baden-Powell had some difficulty in persuading them that the movement would have been founded by the natives themselves, if an official initiative had not been taken. In the early 1920s, in his discussions with Leo Amery and the Dominions Office Baden-Powell optimistically presented Scouting and Guiding as a medium of social and racial harmony and reconciliation between Dutch and English speakers, native and settler. However from the early 1930s the South African Scout Council found itself increasingly tested by the rising tide of Afrikaner nationalism with Afrikaans-speaking Scouts (the Voortrekkers) resisting any imperial symbolism expressed through flags or loyalty to the Crown. Even so, Baden-Powell remained confident that the South African Council could meet the challenge of the Voortrekkers. In 1931 he was hopeful that racial prejudice was dying out amongst the younger generation of Dutch speakers and that the Voortrekkers, who had refused to affiliate to the national council, would wither on the vine, particularly as they were receiving no direct encouragement from the Hertzog government. By 1936, when Baden-Powell toured Africa again, such hopes were clearly unrealistic, as the Voortrekkers became more and more politicised and the colour question began to assume greater significance. Federation of the various Scouting organisations was achieved (although excluding the Voortrekkers) but only after it was made clear that this did not mean amalgamation and that each section would pursue its own development along its own racial lines. As in other spheres, the 1930s was marked by the understanding that the multi-racial hopes of the 1920s were not to be immediately realised, broken as they were by the more powerful and historic forces of racial, religious and coloured hostility.[21]

Conclusion

What conclusions therefore can be drawn from this range of imperial thinking, attitudes and activity covering as it does a large part of the world's surface and over a period of six decades? At the beginning of this paper I quoted Eric Stokes' comment that 'Imperialism was above all an unformulated philosophy of life and politics' and I have tried to show how that imperial theme in its many variations was worked out in the philosophy and action of the two youth movements which seem to spring most obviously out of an imperial frame of mind.

By the time of Baden-Powell's death in 1941 the imperial element within Scouting and later Guiding had been almost totally transformed. Even before 1914 the defensive and domestic tone of Baden-Powell's earliest writings on Scouting had been adapted and made more international and multi-racial as the two movements were taken up widely within the Empire. As a consequence the rapid expansion of Scouting and Guiding during the

1920s could be seen as part of a process whereby the ideal of a genuine union of peoples of different races, colours and creeds might be realised. Through a shared British inheritance and a common Scouting and Guiding philosophy the two movements saw themselves as helping the individual nations of the Commonwealth to achieve a domestic multi-racial coherence and as aiding the development of the Commonwealth as a unique experiment in international cooperation. The following decade saw this over-sanguine optimism dissolve in the face of economic adversity, increasing dominion autonomy and the pressures arising from racial and national self-consciousness. By 1945 it was reasonably clear that the future development of Scouting and Guiding within the Commonwealth would be determined, not by Imperial Headquarters in London, but in response to local circumstances throughout the world. Imperial symbolism was retained, Chief Scouts and the World Chief Guide rallied enthusiasm throughout the Commonwealth in the years preceding and during the new Elizabethan age but no real attempt was made to reinforce the increasingly unreal bonds of an exclusively imperial brotherhood. The dominion associations quickly became entirely independent of London and, as in the political sphere, the emancipation of Britain's colonial dependencies, was marked by the accession of newly independent Scout Associations to the World Bureau. In 1975 on the retirement of Lord Maclean as Commonwealth Chief Scout, the member associations decided not to refill the post.[22]

At first sight it is surprising that this loosening of imperial bonds was not marked by any decline in national or international membership and it seemed that as multi-racial movements Scouting and Guiding could survive on the basis of their own ideals of equality and brotherhood, despite a changing imperial climate. This adaptability and change makes the point that what has been analysed and described in this essay had always been essentially a gloss to the activities of adults and children throughout the Empire, and far from the centres of policy-making and control of Imperial Headquarters in London. This is not to say that such imperial externals were unimportant for, as John Springhall has shown in his study of the Boys Brigade, the lack of an imperial philosophy and a charismatic leader certainly held back the international expansion of the Brigade and it is clear that Scouting and Guiding's imperial sheen between the wars did help it create a sense of optimism, unity and expansiveness. But it is also the case that the reasons which underlay child or adult involvement locally were not primarily imperial ones.[23]

Individual children, of course, leave few records of what they did as Scouts or Guides and even less on what they thought about it at the time. Even so, there is around the country in local record offices and in private homes (and no doubt this is paralleled throughout the Commonwealth) ample material from which to reconstruct the weekly pattern of activity from 1910 onwards. This range of scrapbooks, logs, journals and day-to-day ephemera makes it plain that imperial thinking played only a very small part in the activities undertaken and the programme followed. At the level of imperial symbolism for instance, Empire Day seems to have been little celebrated after 1918 amongst Scouts and was unpopular because it came in the middle of the camping season. From the mid-1920s also the Guides ceased to associate their Thinking Day (during which they reaffirmed the Guide promise) with Empire Day and relocated it to 22 February – the joint birthday of the Baden-Powells. Popular patriotism in troop and company meetings seems to have been confined to the breaking and saluting of the flag at the beginning of each meeting or camp-day and to participation in the annual Armistice Day commemoration. Within the training programme for Scouts there is no point at which the Scout between the ages of eleven and eighteen was specifically required to undergo any patriotic or imperial education, and the pages of the *Headquarters Gazettes* of both movements contain a great deal more on nature study than imperial enthusiasms. Popular patriotism, initially stridently defensive in 1908 and 1909, had been tempered by civilian war-service between 1914 and 1918 and rarely surfaces after 1920, unless it be through the annual civic service.

There is not the scope in this essay to explore fully the reasons why Scouting and Guiding, superficially so much the creatures of the years prior to 1914, should continue to attract significant numbers of children and adults but clearly the answer is not to be found in any imperial ideology. Rather it is likely to be located in the texture of local and family life in reasonably settled communities. Scouting and Guiding found it difficult as a rule to put down roots in strongly working-class districts and in areas of recent settlement and was usually strongest amongst lower middle-class and skilled artisan groups where there was already a pattern of church and institutional life which could draw upon the dedicated enthusiasm of a relatively small number of local volunteers. The evidence from surviving group records testifies to the fact that continuity in a particular group was the result of the work of a few individuals who often gave decades of service to a particular group or company.[24]

However, this local basis for support and activity would have had little effect if there had not been some sustaining strand which helps to explain how in very different circumstances Scouting and Guiding was able to adapt, survive and expand both in Britain and throughout the colonial world. In so far as this local material provides a clue then it is to be found in the cult of the out-of-doors, the centrality of the activity and symbolism of the camp and the reaction against the pressures and alienation of the urban environment. In fact, this should cause the reader of *Scouting for Boys* no surprise since the bulk of its contents are devoted, not to imperial symbolism or patriotic instruction, but to the world of the wild and how it might be enjoyed and used. It was therefore the camp, not the Empire, which remained for both Scouts and Guides the most enduring symbol and metaphor of their ideals in the sphere of the training of the young.

Acknowledgements

The author would like to thank the Social Science Research Council (now the Economic and Social Research Council) for its financial support, which enabled the initial research for this essay to be undertaken. He would also like to thank the Scout Association and Girl Guide Association for allowing him to consult material in their keeping, and their archivists, Mr Graham Coombe and Miss Cynthia Forbes for answering his queries, and the Committee of the Council of the Scout Association for permission to consult their minutes. Also Mr W. Lucas for permission to use 5th Bromley (St Lukes) material.

Notes

1 Richard Koebner and Helmut Dan Schmidt, *Imperialism: The Story and Significance of a Political Word, 1840–1960*, London 1964; Eric Stokes, *The Political Ideas of Imperialism*, Oxford 1960; A. P. Thornton, *The Imperial Idea and its Enemies: A Study in British Power*, London 1959; Nicholas Mansergh, *The Commonwealth Experience*, 2 vols., 2nd edn., 1982; Thomas J. Dunne, 'Ireland, England and Empire, 1868–1886, the ideology of British leadership', Cambridge PhD, 1975. For a clear contemporary statement on the association of nationality and Empire see John Ellison, 'The Church and national life' in John Ellison and G. H. S. Walpole (eds), *Church and Empire: a Series of Essays on the Responsibilities of Empire*, London 1907.

2 B. Semmel, *Imperialism and Social Reform: English Social-Imperial Thought, 1895–1914*, London 1960; H. C. G. Matthew, *The Liberal Imperialists: The Ideas and Politics of a Post Gladstonian Elite*, Oxford 1973; John Springhall, *Youth, Empire and Society: British Youth Movements, 1883–1940*, London 1977; John Springhall, 'The Boy Scouts, class and militarism in relation to British Youth Movements, 1908–1930', *International Review of Social History*, XVI, 1971; John Springhall, 'Lord Meath, youth and Empire', *Journal of Contemporary History*, V, 1970; M. D. Blanch, Nation, Empire and the Birmingham working class, 1899–1914', University of Birmingham PhD, 1975; M. D. Blanch, 'Imperialism, nationalism and organized youth' in John Clarke, Chas Critcher and Richard Johnson (eds), *Working Class Culture: Studies in history and theory*, London 1979; Valerie Chancellor, *History for their Masters: Opinion in the English History Textbook, 1800–1914*, London 1970; Henry Erskine Cowper, 'British education, public and private and the British Empire, 1880–1939', University of Edinburgh PhD, 1979; Patrick Dunae, 'British juvenile literature in the age of Empire, 1880–1914', Manchester University PhD, 1975; Patrick Dunae 'Boy's literature and the idea of Empire, 1870–1914', *Victorian Studies*, XXIV, 1980; Louis James, 'Tom Brown's imperial sons', *Victorian Studies*, XVII, 1973; Richard Price, *An*

Imperial War and the British Working Class: Working Class Attitudes and Reactions to the Boer War, 1899–1902, London 1972.

3   R. S. S. Baden-Powell, *Scouting for Boys: a handbook for instruction in good citizenship*, London 1908; Agnes Baden-Powell in collaboration with R. S. S. Baden-Powell, *The Handbook for Girl Guides or How Girls can help build the Empire*, London 1912; Samuel Hynes, *The Edwardian Turn of Mind*, London 1968, 27; John Springhall, *Youth, Empire and Society*, 15; Carol Dyhouse, *Girls Growing up in late Victorian and Edwardian England*, London 1981.

4   E. E. Reynolds, *Baden-Powell: A Biography of Lord Baden-Powell of Gilwell, OM, GCMG, GCVO, KCB*, 2nd edn., London 1957; William Hillcourt with Olave, Lady Baden-Powell, *Baden-Powell, Two Lives of a Hero*, London 1964. The bulk of the material used in this essay forms part of the Scout Association Archives, held at Baden-Powell House, Queensgate, London.

5   Baden-Powell: *Scouting for Boys*, a facsimile edition of the original parts, London 1957, 335–9; *Aids to Scouting*, 2nd edn., London 1906; 'Pessimism', 1911, SAA/TC/21; 'The Chief Scout's Outlook', *The Headquarters Gazette*, June 1915, August 1915, March 1919, November 1927 (*The Headquarters Gazette* was the official publication of the Boy Scout Association – it was subsequently renamed *The Scouter*).

6   Anon. (Elliot E. Mills), *The Decline and Fall of the British Empire*, London 1905; Baden-Powell: *Scouting for Boys*, facsimile edn., 207–38; 'The Chief Scout's Outlook', *The Scouter*, May 1930, January 1931, April 1933, October 1934, November 1934, November 1935, December 1935, September 1936, October 1937. Baden-Powell's technique of presenting issues differently according to his audience is well evidenced by his response to meeting Mussolini in March 1933. See Reynolds, 231–2, Hillcourt, 391, and article for *Sunday Despatch*, 27 March 1933, entitled 'The young man in the Making', SAA/TC/21. Also 'The Chief Scout's Outlook', *The Scouter*, April 1933.

7   Baden-Powell, *Rovering to Success, A Book of Life Sport for Young Men*; also his speech in Oxford, 14 February 1910, *Oxford Times*, 18 February 1910, and *The Canadian Boy Scout*, London 1911 (a Canadian edition of *Scouting for Boys*). The governing body of the Boy Scouts Association wished to amend the 4th Scout Law in 1928. It was not fully accepted until 1938, owing to the objections of the Roman Catholic hierarchy who could not recognise an equality of creed (minutes of the Committee of the Council, July 1928 and February 1938, SAA). For a bizarre example of Baden-Powell's taste for ceremonial see the details of his Ipise Ceremony, *Headquarters Gazette*, October 1921. It was not adopted widely. For Baden-Powell's camping enthusiasm see *Headquarters Gazette*, June 1919.

8   Allen Warren, 'Baden-Powell, militarism and citizen training in Britain, 1900–1920', forthcoming.

9   Baden-Powell: *Scouting for Boys*, facsimile edn, 71–206; *Rovering to Success*, 205–17; *Girl Guiding: A Handbook for Guidelets, Guides, Senior Guides and Guiders*, London 1918; 'Chief Scout's outlook', *Headquarters Gazette*, April 1918, January 1919, November 1919; *The Scouter*, September 1931, January 1932, January 1934.

10 *Scouting for Boys* was repeatedly reprinted and amended; see: 1st edition (1908), 2nd edition (1909), 4th edition (1911), 9th edition (1918), 10th edition (1922) and *The Canadian Boy Scout* (1911). For Baden-Powell's North American tour see SAA/TC/9. Also Baden-Powell on 'Pessimism', and 'Chief Scout's Outlook', *Headquarters Gazette*, September 1917, on the need to think imperially and not parochially.

11   For Baden-Powell's reaction to patriotic pressure groups see SAA/TC/37; 'Chief Scout's Outlook', *The Scouter*, November 1927. For Scouting as an aid to imperial harmony and domestic reconciliation, see Baden-Powell's reports on his imperial tour, 1912, SAA/TC/9, his South Africa tour, 1927, SAA/TC/53, his article for the *Empire Mail*, 1921, SAA/TC/21 and 'Chief Scout's Outlook', *The Scouter*, August 1926.

12   For the Posse of Welcome and the Imperial Jamboree see *Headquarters Gazette* October 1922, August and September 1924. For the acquisition of Foxlease see Rose Kerr, *The Story of the Girl Guides*, 1932.

13   For these policy decisions see Minutes of the Committe of the Council for January 1910, April 1910, October 1910, January 1911, December 1912, February 1913, March 1915, March 1916, September 1921, SAA.

14   For examples of ecclesiastical and public school imperialism see John Ellison and G. H. S. Walpole (eds) *Church and Empire*; J. A. Craigie, *Sermons for Empire Day*, 1910; Herbert Branston Gray, *The Public Schools and the Empire*, 1913. For the speeches of Prince of Wales and Cosmo Gordon Lang see *Headquarters Gazette*, August 1924.

15   Rose Kerr, *The Story of the Girl Guides*; Baden-Powell and Agnes Baden-Powell, *Girl Guides: A Suggestion for Character Training for Girls*, 1909; Baden-Powell and Baden-Powell, *The Handbook for Girl Guides*; Baden-Powell: 'Can Girls be Scouts?', *The Scout*, 16 May 1908; 'Girl Scouts', 25 May 1908. On the Girl Guide scheme and the need to separate boys and girls see *Headquarters Gazette*, November 1909 and February 1912, and also Minutes of the Committee of the Council, February 1910, SAA.

16   For early Girl Guide policy decisions see Committee Minute Book 1910–11, and Press Cuttings Volume 1910–22, Girl Guide Association Archive (The Girl Guide Association, Commonwealth Headquarters, Buckingham Palace Road, London). Also the *Girl Guide Gazette*, January 1914, April 1914, January 1915. The Victoria League was an organisation established by Lady Edward Cecil in 1901 to promote imperial knowledge and harmony through lectures, arranging hospitality, making imperial visitors welcome and distributing imperial literature. It had a junior branch which mounted Imperial tableaux on Empire Day, had imperial competitions and organised imperial pen-pal schemes, see *Victoria League Notes*.

17   Rose Kerr, *The Story of the Girl Guides*; Baden-Powell, *Girl Guiding*; *Annual Reports of the Girl Guide Association* 1916–1921 and 1932, Girl Guide Association Archive; *Girl Guide Gazette*, April 1916, September 1916, January 1917, April 1920, October 1920, January 1921, October 1921.

18   For the details of the Boy Scout migration scheme see *The Boy Scout Association Annual Reports* 1922–1939 and File in SAA/TC/27. For the Buckhurst Farm experiment see SAA/TC/146.

19   See Boy Scout Migration File, SAA/TC/27.

20   For the development of Scouting in Australia, New Zealand and Canada see the files relating to Baden-Powell's imperial tours in SAA/TC/9. Also S. G. Culliford, *New Zealand Scouting: The first fifty years, 1908–1958*, Wellington, NZ 1958.

21   For the problems in India and South Africa, see reports from Baden-Powell's tours in SAA/TC/9, 10, 51, 53.

22   South Africa became separately represented in 1937, India in 1938 and Canada in 1946.

23   John Springhall (ed.), Brian Fraser, and Michael Hoare *Sure and Stedfast: A History of the Boys Brigade, 1883–1983*, Glasgow 1983.

24 The general suggestions in this concluding section are taken from a variety of
    local collections, principally those relating to the history of 23rd Cambridge (St
    Matthew's) Scout Group (Cambridge City Library), 5th Bromley (St Lukes)
    Scout Group (in private hands), 5th Enfield Scout Group (P. B. Nevill Papers,
    SAA) and from the collection of local District and Group histories held at the
    Scout Association Archives. For the unpopularity of the Empire Day Parade in
    London see SAA/TC/29.

INDEX